322.10982 Ive
Ivereigh.
Catholicism and politics in
 Argentina, 1810-1960.

DATE	ISSUED TO

322.10982 Ive
Ivereigh.
Catholicism and politics in
 Argentina, 1810-1960.

The Lorette Wilmot Library
Nazareth College of Rochester

CATHOLICISM AND POLITICS IN ARGENTINA, 1810-1960

Catholicism and Politics in Argentina 1810–1960

Austen Ivereigh

M
St. Martin's Press
in association with
ST ANTONY'S COLLEGE, OXFORD

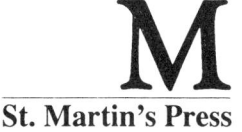

© Austen Ivereigh 1995

All rights reserved. No reproduction, copy or transmission of this publication may be made without written permission.

No paragraph of this publication may be reproduced, copied or transmitted save with written permission or in accordance with the provisions of the Copyright, Designs and Patents Act 1988, or under the terms of any licence permitting limited copying issued by the Copyright Licensing Agency, 90 Tottenham Court Road, London W1P 9HE.

Any person who does any unauthorised act in relation to this publication may be liable to criminal prosecution and civil claims for damages.

First published in Great Britain 1995 by
MACMILLAN PRESS LTD
Houndmills, Basingstoke, Hampshire RG21 2XS
and London
Companies and representatives
throughout the world

This book is published in the *St Antony's/Macmillan Series*
General Editor: Alex Pravda

A catalogue record for this book is available
from the British Library.

ISBN 0–333–62670–2

10 9 8 7 6 5 4 3 2 1
04 03 02 01 00 99 98 97 96 95

Printed in Great Britain by
Ipswich Book Co Ltd, Ipswich, Suffolk

First published in the United States of America 1995 by
Scholarly and Reference Division,
ST. MARTIN'S PRESS, INC.,
175 Fifth Avenue,
New York, N.Y. 10010

ISBN 0–312–12454–6

Library of Congress Cataloging-in-Publication Data
Ivereigh, Austen.
Catholicism and politics in Argentina, 1810–1960 / Austen Ivereigh.
p. cm.
Includes bibliographical references and index.
ISBN 0–312–12454–6
1. Catholic Church—Argentina—History. 2. Church and state-
-Argentina—History. 3. Christianity and politics—Argentina-
-History. 4. Argentina—Church history. I. Title.
BX1462.2.I93 1995
322'.1'0982—dc20   94–31880
                                                              CIP

To my parents

Contents

List of Tables	ix
Acknowledgements	x
Abbreviations	xi
Glossary	xiii
Introduction	**1**

PART I   CHURCH, STATE AND SOCIETY IN ARGENTINA, 1810–1960

1	**Scholasticism and Secularism, 1810–1920**	**39**
	1.1 From independence to the fall of Rosas, 1810–1852	39
	1.2 Catholicism and Liberalism, 1860–1890	49
	1.3 Social Catholicism and the Triangular Conflict, 1890–1920	63
2	**The Catholic Revival, 1920s–1950s**	**73**
	2.1 Neoscholasticism	73
	2.2 Ecclesiastical expansion	76
	2.3 Argentine Catholicity	82
	2.4 The discourse of integral Catholicism	84
	2.5 Social Catholicism before Perón	91

PART II   THE CATHOLIC MOVEMENT IN ARGENTINE POLITICS, 1930–1960

3	**Catholicism and Nationalism, 1930–1939**	**103**
	3.1 The coup of 1930	103
	3.2 The liberal–conservative restoration	106
	3.3 Catholic political alienation	112
	3.4 The Spanish Civil War and the refutation of Maritain	119

4 War, Crisis and Military Intervention, 1939–1944 — 123

4.1 The question of neutrality — 123
4.2 The liberal decline — 129
4.3 Integral Catholicism on the eve of the coup — 132
4.4 Catholics and the June Revolution — 136

5 Catholicism and Peronism, 1945–1954 — 143

5.1 Scholasticism in Peronist discourse — 143
5.2 The secular–theocratic impulse — 153
5.3 The bifurcation of Catholicism and Peronism — 162
5.4 Prelude to conflict: the Church campaign — 168

6 *Ecclesia contra Peronum*, 1954–1955 — 175

7 Secularism Revisited, 1955–1960 — 183

7.1 The 'Catholic' *Libertadora*, September–November 1955 — 183
7.2 The 'Liberal' *Libertadora*, 1955–1958 — 189
7.3 The University Autonomy Issue — 192
7.4 Catholicism and Frondizi — 194
7.5 Epilogue — 200

Conclusion — 203

Appendix I   Argentine Catholicity in Figures — 213

Appendix II Text of Catholic Action's first flyer of leaflet campaign, 1936 — 219

Notes and References — 221

Bibliography — 251

Index — 269

List of Tables

2.1	Unionised workers in 1941: non-Catholic/Catholic	95
3.1	Showing composition of Chamber of Deputies, 1930–1942	107
5.1	Results of the presidential election of 1946 in Buenos Aires province: percentages by party/coalition	146
I.1	Number and size of dioceses in relation to population growth, 1859–1934	213
I.2	Population in 1910 classified by religious belief and nationality	213
I.3	Showing growth in membership of Catholic Action, 1933–1950	214
I.4	Showing relation of population to no. of dioceses, 1933–1961	215
I.5	Showing religious self-identification of Argentines, 1895–1947	215
I.6	Comparison of the number of pupils in postprimary and secondary education whose parents opted in 1944 for non-Catholic morality classes; by province, in order of state school population	216
I.7	Numbers opting for sacramental marriage subsequent to obligatory civil ceremony, Buenos Aires, 1926–1946	217

Acknowledgements

I am grateful to the Economic and Social Research Council for the funding on which this research is based, and to the Interfaculty Committee for Latin–American Studies at Oxford for contributions to research expenses. Malcolm Deas supervised me with wit and geniality; the staff of St. Antony's College and the Latin–American Centre provided a friendly environment for study. Richard Mason at the Bodleian was unfailing.

In Buenos Aires, the board and staff of the periodical *Criterio*, and especially Elena Kiyamu, were endlessly accommodating, and I was also assisted by librarians at the Instituto de Cultura Religiosa Superior Femenina, the Biblioteca Nacional, the Jesuit Seminary at San Miguel, as well as the Federación de Asociaciones Católicas de Empleadas. There were many kind people at the offices of Argentine Catholic Action, where Claudia Avila furnished me with insights into the contemporary organization as well as transcripts of interviews. Sra. Magdalena dell'Oro Maini de Ayerza trustingly permitted access to her father's papers. Dr. Marcelo Montserrat allowed me to inspect Monsignor Franceschi's personal dossier. Zachary Karabell of Harvard University located important documents from State Department archives. I was also privileged to receive the assistance of a number of colleagues, some of whom were protagonists in the history that follows, some students of related issues, some both. Among many generous and patient people, Drs. Floreal Forni, José Luis de Imaz, Ricardo G. Parera, Emilio Mignone and Abelardo Soneira, were gracious providers of documents, advice and introductions, while Dr. Fortunato Mallimaci deserves a special mention for his hospitality, generosity and endless encouragement, and for sharing insights, documents, contacts, and interview transcripts from the Proyecto de Historia Oral del Catolicismo Argentino. Roberto Bonamino, Francisco Guido, Juan Gatti and Francisco Valsecchi were patient interviewees. Martin Eayrs and Pedro Towers were as ever hospitable. My brother furnished me with the technology indispensable to modern writing. Parents were, as ever, supportive.

AUSTEN IVEREIGH

Abbreviations

AASF	Asociación Argentina del Sufragio Femenino (Argentine Association for Female Suffrage)
ACA	Acción Católica Argentina (Argentine Catholic Action)
AJAC	Asociación de las Jóvenes de la Acción Católica (Catholic Action Young Women's Association)
ALN	Alianza Libertadora Nacionalista
AMAC	Asociación de Mujeres de la Acción Católica (Catholic Action Women's Association)
CCC	Cursos de Cultura Católica (Courses in Catholic Culture)
CCO	Círculos Católicos de Obreros (Catholic Workers' Circles)
CFCCP	Centro Femenino de Cultura Cívica y Política (Female Political and Civic Culture Centre)
CGT	Confederación General de Trabajo (Trades Union Confederation)
DNT	Departamento Nacional de Trabajo (National Labour Department)
FACE	Federación de Asociaciones Católicas de Empleadas (Federation of Catholic Female Employees Associations)
FORJA	Fuerza de Orientación Radical de la Juventud Argentina (Radical Party Argentine Youth Force)
GOU	Grupo de Oficiales Unidos (United Army Officers' Group)
HAC	Hombres de la Acción Católica (Catholic Action Men's Branch)
JAC	Jóvenes de la Acción Católica (Catholic Action Young Men's Branch)
JOC	Juventud Católica Obrera (Catholic Worker Youth)
LDC	Liga Demócrata Cristiana (Christian Democrat League)
LNR	*La Nueva República* ('New Republic' periodical)
PAN	Partido Autonomista Nacional (Liberal alliance)
PC	Partido Comunista (Communist)
PDC	Partido Demócrata Cristiano (Christian Democrat)
PDN	Partido Demócrata Nacional (Conservative)
PDP	Partido Demócrata Progresista (Conservative)
PL	Partido Laborista (Labour)
PS	Partido Socialista (Socialist)
SJ	Sociedad de Jesús (Jesuits)

Abbreviations

STP	Secretaría de Trabajo y Previsión (Secretariat for Labour and Social Provision)
UAM	Unión Argentina de Mujeres (Argentine Women's Union)
UC	Unión Católica (Catholic Union)
UCJ	Unión Cívica de la Juventud (Youth Civic Union)
UCR	Unión Cívica Radical (Radical Civic Union, or Radical Party)
UCR-JR	Unión Cívica Radical – Junta Renovadora (Radical Party 'Renewalist' Faction)
UCRI	Unión Cívica Radical Intransigente (Radical Party 'Intransigent' Faction)
UCRP	Unión Cívica Radical del Pueblo (Radical Party 'Popular' Faction)
UD	Unión Democrática (Democratic Union)
UDA	Unión Demócrata (Cristiana) Argentina (Argentine [Christian] Democrat Union)
UES	Unión de Estudiantes Secundarios (Union of Secondary Students)
UF	Unión Federal (Federal Union)
UPCA	Unión Popular Católica Argentina (Argentine Popular Catholic Union)
VOC	Vanguardia de los Obreros Católicos (Vanguard of Catholic Workers)

Glossary

andreísmo: Gallican conception of the Church, associated with Mgr. De Andrea

argentinidad: 'Argentina-ness'

arrendatario: renter–farmer

barrio: city *quartier* or borough

cabildo: town council

caudillo: leader-strongman, associated in nineteenth-century Argentina with direct, local leadership on horseback, subsequently with political 'bosses'.

Concordancia: ruling coalition, 1932–43

corpus mysticum: scholastic notion of spiritual community (Sp. *cuerpo místico*)

cura: priest: can be used derogatorily

desarrollismo: 'developmentalism': technocratic-industrial ideology associated with Frondizi *desengaño*: stripping away of illusions; revelation of reality.

diezmo: automatic deduction of dues to Church

distinguidos: class of urban professionals and landowners

escuela neutra: education principle by which religious instruction during class hours is banned by law.

escuela normal: state school instituted in the late nineteenth century

fuero: traditional legal autonomy claimed by e.g. Church and Army

fuerzas vivas: 'vital forces' of national life: e.g. industry, schools, family etc.

gorilismo: hardline liberal anti-Peronism

Hispanidad: 'Spanish-ness'

Hispanismo: cultural, spiritual, racial and possibly political identification with Spain.

Iglesia Nacional: liberal–conservative Gallican-Anglican conception of Church

Jocista: JOC (Catholic Worker Youth) activist

justicialismo: 'Justicialism': Peronist state doctrine

laborista: member of Labour Party

libertad de enseñanza: pluralistic education system, allowing private universities alongside state universities, religious alongside secular.

mazorca: Rosas' secret police

método propio: particular method of operation and organisation

obrerista: labour activist

oligarquía vacuna: Beneficiaries of agro-export economy; class of owners of large estates.

ordóñista: Christian Democrat faction, associated with Manuel Ordóñez

panfletismo: 'pamphleteering': method by which Catholics countered press restrictions during Church-state conflict of 1954–55

patronato: spiritual privilege granted by the Pope to the Catholic Kings in the fifteenth century, which included administrative rights over the Church in Granada and the Indies. Claimed unilaterally by subsequent Spanish kings and independent Latin-American states, allowing them to control communications with the Vatican.

peninsular: South American born in Spain (vs. *criollo*, Spaniard born in South America)

peón: Spanish-American farm labourer

porteño: inhabitant of the City of Buenos Aires

sábado inglés: non-working Saturday

sindicato único: system of union monopoly, associated with Italian fascism, in which the state recognises only one union per profession

superación: overcoming and transcending political and social divide.

yrigoyenista: Radical supporter of Yrigoyen (vs. *antipersonalista*)

Introduction

In standard readings of Argentine political history, the frailty of Argentine democracy is often explained in terms of a conflict between a liberal, progressive strain and an opposing, authoritarian tradition. The assumption of such a reading is that 'liberalism' has represented a positive and tolerant framework of Argentine politics, one that has been contested by a marginal but successfully subversive element. The dark forces of this scheme, the 'authoritarians', include 'clerical', 'scholastic' or even 'archaic' personalities who, in a recent version, 'continually challenged and resisted the mainstream liberal conceptions of state and society.'[1] In all such studies, liberalism is equated with respect for political liberties and consensus democracy; its opponents implicitly or explicitly oppose such values.

In challenging the paradigm on which these standard readings of Argentine history rest, this work examines the theology of politics in general, and the role of religion in Argentine political history prior to Vatican II in particular. Although it too identifies a centralist, authoritarian and absolutist strain in Argentine political history, absolutism and authoritarianism are identified here not with the scholastic, medieval and Catholic tradition, but are traced to political conceptions rooted in the Enlightenment: in late-colonial enlightened absolutism, and in nineteenth and twentieth century liberalism, of both right and left. The liberal tradition in Argentina, far from representing mainstream conceptions of state and society, is here seen as largely the preserve of intellectual and political minorities whose ideological precepts have defied the broader social framework. This framework, it is argued, is informed by a pluralistic and humanistic cultural tradition with its roots in scholastic thinking; indeed, much of the tension in Argentine political history is related to the divorce between the liberal-enlightened politics of statesmen on the one hand, and that 'scholastic framework' on the other.

The poverty of the 'standard' reading of Argentine history derives from a crude equation of liberalism with democracy, and of popular government with liberalism. Ignoring the theological underpinnings of politics diminishes its capacity to recognise the democratic qualities of a number of political and social movements, while simultaneously glossing over the unpopularity and authoritarian nature of others.

1

The work concentrates on two distinct areas. First, it examines the basic tenets of Catholic political thought and its traditional differences with political secularism. An analysis is offered of a number of notions and definitions prone to violent misunderstanding. Periods of mainly European history are reviewed briefly, for no understanding of the development of Argentine politics can be divorced from Europe, as both the origin and continuing reference point of its civilization, and as the background to the period (c.1920–c.1960) to which most of the study is dedicated. The line of interpretation afforded by a scholasticism vs. secularism dichotomy, as set out here, offers a fresh and often startling means of understanding the development of Argentine politics in particular and Latin–American politics in general. Second, the work concentrates on a variety of issues concerned with religion and politics generally, and Catholicism and modern society in particular. Differing strains within the Church are examined: Gallicanism against scholasticism, 'nationalist' versus 'democratic' Catholicism, various models of social Catholicism and issues arising from sociology of religion. In its analysis of the preconciliar Church in Argentina, the study undermines the coherence of what is often seen as a 'progressive' Church in Latin America after Medellín in 1968, for the continuity is much greater than is commonly assumed.

The approach offered here should not however be confused with 'Church and State', which theme (juridico-ecclesiastical relations) has been considered elsewhere in works of the traditional sort, which are referred to here only in passing. Bishops and encyclicals and pastoral letters are always in the background, for they represent the institutional Church's attempts to delimit the boundaries between the temporal and the spiritual, and to define orthodoxy; the foreground nevertheless remains the world of Argentine politics. The approach also differs from 'sociology of religion'. While theories of political secularization are deployed, together with a variety of Argentine sociological studies of religion, the focus remains that of the Catholic conception of politics in competition with its secular rivals, in Argentine political history, in both the nineteenth and twentieth centuries. What follows, then, is both a study of Catholics in politics, as well as an interpretation of patterns in Argentine political history.

Behind this interpretation lurks a paradigm which assumes that politics is at root theological or philosophical. The conception of politics inherent in Catholic theology (other Christian traditions are ignored) stands in historical opposition to Enlightenment conceptions with their roots in Roman law. The conflict may be described as one between scholasticism and secularism: the former resting on a host of distinctions between differing realms, the latter tending to abolish such distinctions. These pages consider this conflict in detail, noting that the dichotomy between the two conceptions of politics has manifested itself, in the modern world, in a variety of ways. The conflict is not one of democracy versus monarchy, popular sovereignty versus dictatorship, or left versus right but between differing philosophical conceptions of political society, aside from political forms.

The case of Argentina presents an opportunity to examine a host of issues related to the role of the Church and Catholic preconceptions in political history. Until 1810 a colony, founded by Counter-Reformation Spain; subsequently, an American nation, continuing to be dominated in all senses by Europe; and as a late-developing society, Argentina experienced the fallout of late eighteenth-century enlightened absolutism, British nonconformist liberalism as well as the French Revolution. In the late nineteenth century the country grew fast, enriched by cascades of European immigrants and British capital, with a nation-building project which borrowed from secularist strains in French politics and culture. Yet its population, when not *criollo*, was largely Italian and Spanish, and hailing from those parts of Italy and Spain bypassed by the Enlightenment. Part One sketchs Argentine development in the nineteenth and early twentieth centuries, examining the differing strains and conflicts in this tapestry of influences, and the relation of religion to society. Part Two, and the body of the study, follows the course of politics in a period of rapid change and turbulent politics in Argentina from 1930 to 1960, offering a broad and revised interpretation of both its nature and its causes.

The purpose of this Introduction is to sketch the principal faultlines of the modern clash between Catholicism and secularism in Europe – the backdrop against which Argentine politics developed. It begins in the medieval period, for without an understanding of scholastic political thought the subsequent clash is incomprehensible. The growth of modern, secularist doctrines is traced and the basis of the Church's opposition to them examined. The study concludes in the 1960s, when the pattern of the relationship of Catholicism and modernity was fundamentally altered by Vatican II.

THE CHRISTIAN ORDER AND ITS DISINTEGRATION

The life of Jesus was a Rubicon between two fundamentally opposed political notions. As against the pre-Christian conception, in which political and spiritual allegiances were coterminous, Christians upheld a powerful distinction between the temporal and spiritual realms. The state did not accept the distinction, argued Christianity to be political, and put its leader to death.

The idea of the early Church was that of a society bound not by race or nation but of a spiritual community, *a corpus mysticum*, with its own laws and principles and its own administrative authority. Yet the Church did not replace civil society, but was deemed to act in it; *of* temporal society, but not circumscribed by it. The Church stood apart, but maintained a positive view of civil society as one of God's remedies for man's corruption. Government was natural, antedating Christianity, and was seen as necessary to secure and enforce justice; for without justice no political authority could be legitimate. The State and its laws were necessary to regulate the conditions and limitations of ownership, and to secure an environment in which citizens could come to own what was theirs by natural right.

The distinction between the religious and the temporal spheres was manifest in the early Church's rejection of both emperor-worship and caesaro-papism: the first ran counter to the distinction between divinity and ruler; the second conceived of religious authority as the ecclesiastical arm of the state. As state and society became Christian, Catholic political and social theory embraced the notion of two powers: of spiritual authority expressed in the Church, and of temporal authority expressed in the State. The two spheres were considered distinct yet interdependent. As expressed by St. Augustine in the conception that was to remain dominant throughout the early Middle Ages (*Civitas Dei*), the Christian citizen is split two ways. The faithful, inhabiting a Christian community, under its own spiritual authority, transferred sovereignty to the state, and subjected themselves to temporal authority, in order that it rule in line with the moral ends demanded by the Christian people. The ruler's right to rule derived from his deference to those moral ends. Sovereignty implicitly therefore derived from the community, and was lost when the ruler violated justice and ceased to rule for the common good. In this way, the medieval conception of politics carried a strong distinction between the person of the ruler and his office. The *office* was sacred, in as much as ordained by God; the *ruler* was however subject to the law, and the law was both inherent in the community and above rulers.

Even when medieval commentaries attributed to the ruler the power of *legibus solutus*, second only to God, this idea differs fundamentally from the later divine right heresies of the seventeenth century. The medieval ruler was absolute in the sense that monarchy was not limited; but he was not absolute in the modern sense. The sphere in which he was absolute was drastically narrowed by the functions, duties and rights of kings, and their subjection to the law both above and outside them. Right rule, in the words of St. Augustine, consisted 'not in judging *of* the law' but in 'judging *according to* the law'.[2] Kings were seen as concerned with the public realm, not private law; with administrative order rather than law itself. Rulers who were tyrannical (ruling for the benefit of a few) or despotic (putting themselves above the law) caused sovereignty automatically to revert back to the community. Implicitly (for it would not have needed stating), the Church was the guardian of the moral law which marked the boundary between right rule and tyranny.

These fundamental notions formed the basis of political thought throughout the Middle Ages. The presupposition of a division of spheres was not threatened even in the eighth to tenth centuries, when the papacy underwent rapid centralization and assumed greater powers. Spiritual authority extended over all laymen, even kings, and secular authority over clergy as well as laymen, in the matters in which each were considered competent. No division between the two powers was or could be complete, and in practice medieval society increasingly fused the two, leading to considerable friction as well as fruitful political treatises. In the later Middle Ages (eleventh to fourteenth centuries), these tensions erupted into bitter polemics. At the root of the issue between the two societies, Church and State, lay the growing wealth and power of the secular realm, and the beginnings of a sense of nationhood. Intellectually, the conflict was fuelled by the revival of Roman jurisprudence and the rediscovery of Aristotle; yet the dispute (which was inevitable in dual-realm theory, at a time of rapid growth and development) continued to take certain fundamental presuppositions for granted. The contest was not between Church and State in a modern sense, for neither clericalists nor regalists could conceive of a society that was not simultaneously both Church *and* State; but rather concerned the boundaries between the two, and the degree to which the spiritual overrode the temporal law. Neither claimed an unlimited authority to make and unmake laws. Papalists argued that the Church was the interpreter of (but never maker of) the law in the highest sense, and that to the temporal sphere belonged the subsidiary provisions which law required for its enforcement. Regalists sought to confine the Church to a narrower, ecclesiastical sphere, of teaching and safeguarding the moral law; while the State, and not the Church, acted as interpreter of that law.[3]

To the Investiture Controversies can be traced the emergence of the regalist theory of Gallicanism as well as the papalist supremacy theory of ultramontanism – two differing conceptions of the Church's relation to secular politics which would persist into the modern period. Yet however extreme papalist pretensions would seem to later eyes, the theorists of papal monarchy were also those of popular sovereignty. In opposition to the regalist view, which held that the political sphere was independent of the spiritual realm in temporal matters, papalists maintained that temporal rule was introduced by men under the providence of God for their own improvement and hence should be under their control. This notion of a compact between ruler and ruled would later be taken up by the scholastic writers of the sixteenth century. They were papalists, who would continue to defend the notion of the consensual origin of power against the regalist–Gallican tendencies in the clerisy.

The scholastics of the sixteenth century, and subsequently the liberal Catholics and Christian Democrats of the nineteenth and twentieth centuries, would constantly refer back to Thomas Aquinas; his *opus* forms the single most durable synthesis of the Catholic conception of politics prior to the end of the medieval period. St. Thomas expresses the anti-theocratic or anti-clericalist tendencies of late medieval thought; implicitly against Renaissance humanism and Reformation nationalism, however, he diminishes yet further the State's right to harness religious authority to itself. Contrary to later *laissez-faire* notions of the State as mere policeman, St. Thomas regarded the State as possessing a positive, moral function: the promotion of wellbeing and the securing of justice as well as the safeguarding of order, all of which elements were necessary for a framework in which each individual could strive for personal salvation in individual freedom. St. Thomas therefore sees the State in a nuanced, carefully-balanced way: as at once pragmatic (not concerned with the fundamental ends of man's existence), moral (subject to the higher law of justice and the common good), positive (with a duty to secure justice and order) and curtailed (bound to its sphere). In acknowledging that supernatural authority is safeguarded by the Church, external to the state, 'civil society ceases to be uniquely responsible for the totality of moral virtue and is itself judged by a higher standard to which human actions must conform'.[4]

The key to Thomism is its distinction between various degrees of law. *Eternal law* is the divine reason which exists in God as the rationale of the universe; the source of all true law on earth; and prior to all other laws. *Natural law* is the participation of a rational creature in the eternal law; that part of the eternal law knowable to the human mind. *Human laws* are derived by a process of reasoning from natural law. They are fallible and contingent, and require promulgation. Yet they must meet the prior requirements of natural and eternal law. They must be for the common good, and can only be promulgated by he who has care of the whole community. A tyrannical law is one which violates natural law, and is no law at all but an act of violence which must be resisted.[5]

Who has care of the community? Much has been written on St. Thomas' preference for particular political forms. While it is true that monarchists, republicans and democrats can find in Thomism much that favours each of these forms, it is also true that not all monarchies, democracies and republics would be compatible with Thomism. Aquinas envisages a true *res publica*, one in which the people (*multitudo*) entrusts the government of the state to a ruler who has care (*sollicitudo*) of it. Whether elected or hereditary, unitary or conciliar, a valid government for St. Thomas is one which is founded on natural law and endowed by the community with the right and duty to govern for the common good. The ruler's duty is firstly to eternal law, and simultaneously to the community which raised him to the throne, and which might conceivably sweep that ruler away should he descend into tyranny. Hence, a ruler's authority was not from God if his seizure of power was illegitimate, or if he ruled unjustly. Sin and law belonged to distinct realms (not all sins were crimes and vice-versa) but if the ruler compelled citizens to sin, he must be disobeyed; if he demanded obedience in matters outside his authority, he need not be obeyed. Such limits on state sovereignty were therefore a crucial element of the medieval view of politics, and the explicit doctrine of resistance to despotism entrusted the community with the active responsibility of ensuring that it act to resist tyranny. Rooted in this doctrine is the concept of consensus government. Thomism – and in the ensuing centuries the Catholic Church – was concerned less with the mechanistic implications of such a doctrine (electoral systems, constitutional monarchies etc.) than with upholding its central tenets.[6]

Another central theme in Thomism is the notion of the common good. It is a circular notion, in which the right of political society lies in the individual freedom it guarantees; individual freedom in turn lies in order and justice. Just as the common good is less absolute than the imprescriptible rights of the person, so those personal rights encounter their limitation in the common good, which is turn working for the assurance of those personal liberties and rights. The difficulty of this idea lies in the question of primacy: does the common good have primacy over individual goods and liberties? Is Thomism therefore collectivist or individualist? Aquinas to some extent resolves this quandary by distinguishing between degrees of 'commonness': the ultimate common good lies beyond society (God), but is mediated through life in the community, and is individual in its realization. Although engaged in political society of which he forms a part, the person is engaged in political society only in a part of himself. Hence, while the common good is *per se* an individual object, legal compulsion may be required to enforce the primacy of the common good in order to assist individuals to overcome their private interests. If the state failed to do this, individualism would eventually undermine the common good; for the state to do it too much (collectivism) would be to undermine the purpose for which it has the duty to intervene: the defence and procurement of individual rights and liberties.[7] Hence, while Thomism falls short of placing an explicit boundary between justice and individual liberty, order and freedom, the principle of a balance between two good ends is upheld in a state of tension; each positive end depends on the other in order to remain good. The fundamental implication of the common good doctrine is a dual obligation on government: to care for all while simultaneously deferring to a law outside itself.

From the fourteenth century, the medieval order was gradually eroded. The revival of Roman law, which appealed especially to a new breed of secular jurists and clerks, anticlerical in spirit, coincided with the disintegration of papal authority. By the time the unity of the Church had been restored by the Great Councils, a weakened papacy faced powerful new national states. With the exception of France, the new powerful monarchies offered no serious objections to the restoration of the papacy but demanded a tacit recognition of national sovereignty, and an acknowledgement of regalian rights set forth in concordats. The concordats were the only real alternative to the Gallican view of the Church as 'purely' spiritual, and implied that the Church would in practice have only an indirect right to intervene in secular affairs. Although Catholic monarchs by definition were unable either to suffuse (as occurred in Protestant states) temporal and spiritual spheres, or to promote national absolutism at the expense of Catholic universalism, in practice, however, even in Catholic countries temporal and spiritual were blurred in favour of the Crown. Indeed, the threat of Protestantism enabled political and Catholic orthodoxy (as defined increasingly by the state) to be equated. The paradigmatic example of this trend is the Spain of Ferdinand and Isabella. There were two institutional expressions of the antischolastic doctrine of regalism which they upheld. The first was the absorption of much of the Church into the state, leading to an identification of religious orthodoxy with Spanish nationality and political obedience, so that the Inquisition, in a dramatic illustration of this confusion, was under the direct control of the Crown, yet responsible for the maintenance of religious orthodoxy. The second was the *patronato*, a privilege conceded by irresistible pressure on a weakened papacy, which granted the Spanish state spiritual jurisdiction over the reconquered Kingdom of Granada, and then over the New World. Although the Catholic Kings were conscious of the spiritual authority with which they were entrusted, care was taken to avoid basing Spain's rights in the Indies exclusively on a papal grant: 'By donation of the Holy See,' began the law of 1519, '*and other just and legitimate titles*, we are Lord of the West Indies, the isles and the mainland of the Ocean Sea'.[8] In detail, the *patronato* meant the right of the Crown to present candidates for ecclesiastical vacancies, to levy ecclesiastical tithes, to impose a royal *placet* on papal bulls, to grant permission for the foundation or extension of monasteries and religious orders, and to finance the Church's works. Even if the Catholic Kings were sincere in their adherence to this missionary aspect of colonization, subsequent Spanish monarchs of secular disposition, and, succeeding them, the revolutionary governments of nineteenth-century Latin America, unilaterally insisted on the same privilege and deployed it as the mechanism by which the Church could be harnessed to political authority.[9]

If the 'truly' absolutist Roman doctrine of monarchy nourished the new national states, so with it came the restoration of the Roman conception of property and society. Medieval society had been pluralist, in the sense that over the centuries the power of the state had remained checked by a hierarchy of intermediate societies: baronies, local jurisdictions, autonomonies and guilds. This sociological characteristic of the Middle Ages, which reflected the scholastic emphasis on civil authority as delegated by lesser 'natural societies', was eroded in the sixteenth and seventeenth centuries by doctrines which, to their critics, were not merely absolute in the traditional medieval sense but despotic, in a manner akin to the control of a *paterfamilias* over his household.

THE REVIVAL OF POPULAR SOVEREIGNTY DOCTRINES: SCHOLASTIC VS. SECULARIST NOTIONS

The trend towards autocracy and despotism in the sixteenth, seventeenth and eighteenth centuries incubated a tension that would erupt, eventually, in the French Revolution. In the second half of the eighteenth century, the drive towards modernisation promoted by 'enlightened absolutism' led to the assertion of state control over ecclesiastical minutiae, the expropriation of lands and charitable concerns, the drain of Church revenues to finance state bureaucracies, the reform of seminaries and the imposition of regalist doctrines. Throughout Catholic countries in the eighteenth century states sought the establishment of royal national churches. An undercurrent of opposition, especially among the lower clergy, nevertheless acted to counteract these pretensions; the religious orders and the Society of Jesus especially remained outspoken defenders of dual-realm theory and the universality and autonomy of the Church. The Jesuits, as the most forceful and conspicuous opponents of the attempt to create national churches subordinate to the state, were suppressed and expelled, first in Portugal, then throughout Europe and Latin America. What absolutist kings most feared was not the assertion of papal authority – the papacy was weak, and its voice within national borders suffocated by a multitude of controls – but the writings of scholastic thinkers such as Suárez and Hooker, who, in their restatement of the Thomist synthesis, upheld a contractual view of sovereignty and a powerfully social conception of the common good.[10]

Catholic anti-absolutism, otherwise known as the 'moderate' Enlightenment, was paralleled in nascent Enlightenment anti-absolutist doctrines with secularist roots. Although informed by a Christian idealism, freemasonry, rationalism, deism and scepticism sought an alternative framework of political allegiance, based on the rationalist assumption that the Church was dead and religion merely a matter of superstition. The *philosophes* sought to recover the popular origin of sovereignty, but on a new, anti-religious basis. On the eve of 1789, therefore, there appeared the first of the 'triangular conflicts': enlightened absolutism, revolutionary secularism and scholasticism. The latter two were united against the first, in their common search for the recovery of the popular origin of sovereignty. But the first two were both products of the Enlightenment, and brooked no spiritual authority above and external to the state. It was this characteristic, and not the Enlightenment advocacy of a theory of popular consensus and contract between ruler and ruled, that incubated the Catholic–secularist divide and the triangular conflict of the nineteenth century. A comparison of the differences between the contractual theories of Suárez and Rousseau will serve to clarify this fundamental divergence. Suárez' restatement of the scholastic conception of political society remains squarely in the medieval tradition. The community, or *corpus mysticum*, precedes the existence of political institutions. The purpose of the compact between governors and governed is not to *create* a society, for people are already social, but rather to enable them to pass from one social or political arrangement to another. Authority itself, not the ruler, is instituted by God. Obedience is due to leaders in so far as they are just (ruling in accordance with pre-established law). By nature, no person has dominion over another; the sovereign is therefore *delegated* by man, in order to rule in accordance with law. Against the heretical notion of the divine right of Kings, as well as against the Hobbesian notion of authority as deriving from force, Suárez viewed authority as rooted in the the desire for a common good. Sovereignty is therefore not so much a legal pact drawn up between autonomous individual wills in nature irreconcilable (as in Rousseau or Hobbes) but a consensual arrangement ensuing from the agreement of wills. Force is the instrument by which authority is made effective, but force is not the *source* of authority. The Suarezian understanding of democracy was a further elaboration of Thomist 'indirect democracy': authority derives simultaneously from God *and* from consensus; that consensus is shaped by the knowledge of eternal and natural law immanent in society. It followed that authority was simultaneously limited both by its origin in consensus and in divine and natural law, and in its extent. The state was not the arbiter and judge of eternal law, nor able to impose it; rather, it deferred to that pre-established law. Authority was directed towards providing the condition for moral development and could therefore proscribe liberties endangering the common good. But the moment that the state proclaimed its own law, attempting to usurp the source of authority itself (the Divine Right of Kings heresy), the ruler became tyrannical, authority reverted to the community, and citizens were released from obedience.

A further consequence of the indirect origin of authority was its order of precedence. The state was the *expression* of society, rather than the obverse. 'Lesser' societies – guilds, municipalities and families – were not administrative units defined by the state but pre-existent natural societies which delegated certain authority to the state for the common good. Last, Suárez like St. Thomas before him looked to the Church as the moral conscience of the community, with the right and duty to speak out against tyranny and release citizens from obedience to unjust authority.[11]

In the secularist contract theory of Rousseau, by contrast, the state defers to neither the pre-existing eternal law immanent in the community, nor the moral conscience of that community as expressed in the Church. The dispute over whether Rousseau was a liberal or totalitarian is to posit a false dichotomy: the Social Contract was *simultaneously* individualist *and* totalitarian. Confusion arises over the term 'totalitarianism', which is often deployed erroneously as coterminous with dictatorship or tyranny.[12] Tyranny refers to the domination of political institutions, rather than society as a whole, whereas totalitarianism abolishes all distinction between public and private spheres, governors and governed, and between authority and law. Authoritarianism, of which, say, dictatorship is a manifestation, does not stand in historical relation to totalitarianism, for it presupposes such distinctions, as well as a relationship based on a hierarchy of authority, which logically acknowledges a pre-existing order and therefore a curtailment on state power.[13]

Having abolished, at least theoretically, the spiritual sphere, yet retaining the moral objective of justice, the *philosophes* were faced with the logical conundrum of whether the source and justification for justice existed prior to mankind's discovery of it, or whether, as the utilitarians maintained, it was worked out on the basis of individual perception. Flinching from the individualistic implications of the latter, Rousseau resolved the dilemma of the source of right in the concept of the General Will. The General Will was not God's will (for having abolished all religious authority, nobody could know), nor the aggregate expression of individual wills (for the people could err), but rather, the unified will of the totally-associated society, revealed by the ballot. Unlike Suarezian 'indirect' popular sovereignty, Rousseaunian sovereignty derives solely and exclusively from the General Will. Rousseau's *Social Contract* was therefore a secular metaphysical notion which abolished the numerous distinctions which in medieval theory meant that the citizen was only engaged in political society in part. In Rousseau's theory, deviation from the moral ends of society is a deviation from the will of man, the *Volonté Une*, which is simultaneously the will of all, expressed in the State. There is no longer any distinction. Political society is simultaneously temporal and spiritual; it is all-absorbing: *politique d'abord*.

Hence, where for Suárez sovereignty is the attribute of the agreement of wills, in Rousseau sovereignty arises from the mathematical addition of individual wills expressed in the *Volonté Une*. Where for Suárez, the social compact which precedes the *polis* derives from the metaphysical unity of the community (that is, man is both naturally social and orientated to the common good), for Rousseau political society is an entirely artificial notion which comes into being only as result of a contract. Rousseau's society is therefore the conjunct of wills taken materially, where Suarezian society comes into being automatically in the shared conception of the common good.

The spiritual authority previously acknowledged in natural law, the Church (medieval order) and scripture (Protestant utopias), the *philosophes* located in *a priori* 'universal reason', as interpreted by political classes. On the one hand, religion was reduced to supplying the need for ritual; on the other, it was the means by which society could be bound together, according to the postulates of the state. This 'religion civile' was a naturalist creed, as in pagan times, serving the state's political ends, and was obviously incompatible with the Catholic Church's view of itself as distinct from civil society. It is easy to gloss over this fundamental departure from Catholic doctrine, for in all moral respects the Social Contract sought the realisation of Christian social ideals. In its rejection of all distinction between state and citizen, temporal and spiritual, and between temporal allegiance and spiritual citizenship of the Church, however, the state is placed above the Church, absorbing it, and creating a secular theocracy. In Rousseau's conception, the nation becomes the ultimate framework of allegiance, the will of Man expressed in the state becomes the ultimate sovereign above which there is no higher authority. The State therefore becomes the source and sanction of morality, with no rights existing anterior to, outside or above the state. Political society – in the Suarezian conception, only a *part* of society – was in Rousseaunian theory society itself.

These revolutionary notions have been famously termed 'secular messianism' or 'totalitarian democracy'.[14] The term 'secular messianism' alludes to the similarities between the Social Contract and the Old Testament eschatological revolutionary current, manifest throughout the centuries in rebellion against the Church. Religious messianism proclaims a new moral order realisable on earth where the will of God is operative;[15] secular messianism, a 'new order', where the will of Man is substituted for that of God. The essential difference resulting from this last distinction is that, in the religious case, Protestant utopians looked to God as Sovereign, holding obedience to the Bible as the basis of social authority; and so with some exceptions (Anabaptists and Calvinists) retreated from coercing society and broke away from Christendom to found sects and theocracies. Secular messianism, on the other hand, developed an internal logic of coercion: the supreme authority lay not in eternal spiritual laws outside Man, defended by the Church, but in the Reason and Will inherent in Man; hence the pre-ordained, perfect scheme was universally applicable, and conformed to the commandments of no external final authority, while being simultaneously demanded by the indivisible will immanent in all men. Rather than breaking away from society, the revolutionary vanguard demanded the complete implementation of secular-messianic precepts. Society was not an expression of a 'common conception of a single thing' outside political society, as in St. Thomas, but 'a single self-consciousness' forged by politics.[16] Not only could the state logically tolerate no spiritual allegiance which surpassed it (as in enlightened absolutism), but the secular religion (the moral ends defined by the state) must be instilled from the state into all men. The Jacobins therefore attempted to create a civil religion, by sealing the Church from Rome and attempting to subordinate it to the state. The resistance of the Church marked the beginning of the long cycle of opposition between Church and Revolution which was to mark nineteenth and early twentieth century French politics.[17]

The totalitarian element in nineteenth-century secularism was carried forward into the French Revolution by the left: initially by Jacobinism and later by its historical variant, Marxism. As a political form, totalitarianism was not fully realised until the twentieth century, in both its 'left-wing' and 'right-wing' manifestations. In the nineteenth century, totalitarianism was checked by counter-revolutions and monarchic restorations. The individualistic element of Enlightenment secularism nevertheless took root in the Industrial Revolution, as expressed by English liberalism. Society was seen as an aggregation of individuals, rather than a *corpus mysticum*; the Church an autonomous entity, independent both of state and of the public sphere, devoid of spiritual authority, a voluntary association of like-minded individuals. The 'rational' spheres of public activity – the economy, law, politics, culture – were resolutely secular and autonomous. The state was defined in terms of order but without a positive role. The State had no social purpose other than that of the defence of order and individual freedom.

The Church was opposed to the democracy advocated by nineteenth-century liberalism in so far as democracy betrayed either these collectivist or individualist tendencies. The alienation of the Church from Enlightenment doctrines was threefold. Drawing on the scholastic tradition, the Church could approve neither the Ancien Régime monarchists (Enlightened Absolutism), who sought to use the Church as a means to a political end, nor the endeavours by the left-wing state to replace religion by politics, nor individualism, which banned the Church from the public sphere and defended the autonomy of the economy from moral law. Upholders of the Christian Order opposed: firstly, the abolition of the mediating power of Church and community, as manifest in the absolutist conception of state; secondly, the Jacobin transference of the unfettered will of the secular despot onto the electoral majority; and thirdly, the Kantian autonomy underlying economic individualism.[18]

CATHOLICISM AND LIBERALISM

Political liberalism is multifaceted and open to a variety of definitions. This ambiguity reflects its genesis: on the one hand, liberalism was born out of the early resistance movements of religious minorities (in England, Catholics and Calvinists), who looked to a doctrine of pre-social, individual rights in the absence of a united *corpus mysticum*. This 'ecumenical liberalism' drew heavily on medieval tenets, conceiving of Church–state separation in terms of the incompetence of the state in religious matters, while upholding religious freedoms and recognising the religious culture of democratic society. On the other hand, liberalism attached to itself the secularist tenets of the Enlightenment: in France, the 'totalitarian democracy' of Rousseau; in England, utilitarian ethics and individualism. This 'sectarian' liberalism was either ambiguous towards popular government and natural rights, drawing as it did on enlightened absolutism, or, like the Rousseaunian notion of popular sovereignty, was intolerant of any sphere beyond that defined by the state.[19]

The early American Republic drew on ecumenical liberalism in its formulation of constitutional democratic federalism. A constitution which deferred to eternal religious laws, combined with a state circumscribed in its functions, was congenial to Catholics, who conceived Church–state separation as resting on two fundamental assumptions. The first was that the state recognized the existence of a spiritual realm (if not a unitary religious authority) into which political authority did not extend. The second assumption was that society was *essentially* religious, indeed Christian, and that the separation of realms did not imply the divorce of religion from society. In as much as democratic institutions would reflect society, the culture that they breathed would be Christian. In as much as society was composed of various religious traditions, no one religious tradition would be favoured by the state and its institutions.

Because the early American Republic was formed from transplanted, pre-existent communities with differing religious traditions, it was naturally favourable to the Suarezian conception of government as delegated by ready-constituted societies. But there were also examples in Europe of collaboration between Catholics and ecumenical liberalism. In opposing confessional colonial monarchies, Catholic minorities in Ireland, Belgium and England made common cause with liberal forces. Equally, in the initial revolutionary period in France (1789–92), Jesuits, ultramontanes and lower clergy combined with freemasons, deists, rationalists, and encyclopaedists in a common front against regal absolutism and Gallican bishops. It would be the subsequent contention of Lammenais and Montalembert in the 1820s that the Revolution had been subverted from within, by substituting the despotism of the monarchy for the despotism of the 'General Will'. They were leading figures in a movement known as liberal Catholicism, which also embraced Lord Acton and John Henry Newman in England. Liberal Catholicism developed from an ultramontane concern for the liberty of the Church, and advocated Church–state separation in circumstances unimagined by Aquinas: that both monarchy and Revolution denied the sovereignty of the spiritual realm. The French liberal–Catholic organ, *L'Avenir*, demanded a gamut of freedoms: full religious liberty; an end to state support for the Church; freedom of education, press and association; decentralization; and consensus government based on elections and universal suffrage. Politically, liberal Catholics neither fully condemned nor defended the Revolution. They sympathised with its anti-absolutist ideals but refuted the collectivist implications of its doctrines. They advocated an 'authentic' popular sovereignty based on the dual-realm theory, but which was pluralistic. In many ways, French liberal Catholicism was the ideological precursor of twentieth-century Christian Democracy.[20]

These examples of the fusion of scholasticism with religious pluralism and political liberties were nevertheless drowned by the tide

Introduction 17

of defensiveness sweeping over the papacy in the mid-nineteenth century. The entrenched Church opposition to the secularist trends of post-Enlightenment society placed liberal Catholicism in a fragile position. One way of understanding this 'fortress' Catholicism is to identify it as part of a swing, implicit in theology, between the 'Augustinian' and the 'Thomist' conceptions of Church relations with the secular world. St. Augustine, writing in the Patristic period, in a largely pagan environment of political and cultural decay, drew sharp distinctions between sin and redemption, natural reason and faith, Church and world, God and self. Freedom and intelligence were regarded in a similarly dualistic manner: as means of attaining knowledge of God, worthless if untouched by grace and faith; and as sinful if leading to Self. The dualistic Augustinian conception posited a battle between Church and world – one that, historically, led to the creation of Christian civilization; yet which began with a sharp withdrawal from the world.

St. Thomas, in contrast, wrote in the full flowering of late medieval Catholic civilization and met, confidently and discriminatingly, the intellectual and theological challenges of the revival of philosophy and science of the pre-Christian world. The Thomist conception is both optimistic and nuanced; it rejects the dualism of Augustinianism, seeking to understand both freedom and intelligence in themselves, as part of the natural order which should be turned towards God to achieve fulfilment. As models of engagement, therefore, Augustinianism and Thomism offer sharp alternatives: the one tending towards positive engagement and nuanced discrimination, the other towards categoric acceptance or refutation.[21]

The Augustinian model was one that predominated in the mid-nineteenth century, and which prevailed, in greater or lesser intensity, until Vatican II, although it was broken by a re-adjustment during the papacy of Leo XIII (1878–1903). It meant there could be little truck with doctrines of secularist or even secular origin, and the papacy was constantly concerned to demarcate the boundaries of Catholic action. By making it clear that a Catholic could not also be a a free-market liberal, or a socialist, or an individualist, the *Syllabus* of 1862 forced Catholics to swear allegiance or apostasize. But while, viewed from without, the Church appeared to 'withdraw' from the public realm, antimodernism in reality was an alternative form of engagement, based on a model of combat, and one which was to prove highly effective in the twentieth century in opposing liberalism, Marxism and fascism. This model of Catholic engagement is here termed 'integral Catholicism'.[22] In its structure and culture, integral Catholicism mirrored modern political movements. A centralized, hierarchical structure provided discipline and leadership. Clerical guidance was strong, urging votes for particular, confessional parties (if these existed) or expressly against doctrines and parties which violated Catholic doctrine. A panoply of confessional organizations, from trade unions to newspapers to youth cadres, offered alternative structures for militancy and activism. Above all a coherent worldview, complete with its historical reference points, its ideals and martyrs, presented itself as a compelling alternative to the modern dichotomies of left and right, individualism and collectivism, capitalism and communism.

The demarcation of Catholicism in politics began around 1870, parallel to the hardening of the tendencies in sectarian liberalism. The Church refuted the free-market ideology of Manchester liberalism, on the grounds that only a submission of society to higher social ends could elevate humanity above greed, egotism and the enslavement of the worker. Industrial capitalism was condemned for its alienation of capital and labour, and contrasted with the medieval conception of the economy as an aggregation of intermediate corporations – guilds and associations – defending co-operation and widespread ownership. This Catholic critique was evident in the 1848 uprising, in the 'religious socialism' of Buchez and the utopian exponents of the *ecclesia paupera*.[23] Yet the possibility of making common cause with socialism, as Lammenais had sought to do with liberalism, ran up against the inadmissible Hegelian tenets of Marxism. In refuting the left, Catholics posed an alternative in 'social Catholicism'. Against the *catholiques bourgeois* (who conceived of social action as a charitable palliative in a liberal-capitalist economy) stood *intransigeants* such as Bishop Ketteler of Mainz. Shorn of its conservative–liberal charitable elements, social Catholicism came to reflect a search for 'the right ordering of production', nostalgic for the medieval co-operative order, as expressed in the thought of Keller, from which developed the modern corporativist thought of Vogelsgang and De Mun in the 1880s.[24] Politically, independence from left and right was evoked in a series of late nineteenth-century writings, which sought to demonstrate the essential philosophical unity of the individualist–collectivist dialectic unleashed by the Enlightenment, and the Church's detachment from it.[25]

The forms which this 'political disengagement' or 'closed Catholicism' assumed, differed according to context. There were two main patterns in Europe. First, in states where large Catholic and Protestant populations co-existed, and where constitutional régimes combined with a secularist state (Germany, Belgium and Holland), denominational parties were founded, backed by multiclass Catholic electorates, rooted in networks of guilds and associations. The most successful of these was the German Centre Party, which represented 'the interests of the Catholic population, whether these interests were religious, social or political'.[26] Secondly, in states where Catholicism remained the faith of the vast majority (the Iberian Peninsula, the Italian States, France and Austria), the pattern was one of entrenched opposition between secularist states intolerant of traditional Church autonomies on the one hand, and Catholic support for the right, which offered to defend them, on the other. In France, Spain and Italy, where the model of the 'denominational party' was made impossible both by the existence of Catholic majorities and the monopoly of democracy by the revolutionary left, Catholic politics took two principal forms. The first was that of lobbies, such as the Italian *Opera dei Congressi* or the Spanish *Unión Católica*, closely tied to bishops, which brought the weight of Catholic opinion to bear on constitutional governments in order to defend Church liberties in education and marriage. The second was represented in the 'intransigent' wing which refuted engagement in the political sphere. In Spain, Integrists rejected both the regalism of the Alphonsine monarchy as well as participation in the various conservative and right-wing movements which opposed state centralism.[27]

The contention between the Church and sectarian liberalism was most dramatically illustrated in the battles over education. The French Revolution had failed to replace religion with politics; as a result of the state's attempt to take over and secularise the Church, religion had become the flagship of the Right. The second stage of the Revolution, unleashed by the events of 1848, sought to instil democracy once and for all through a generalisation of what had been previously the preserve of intellectuals. The complete autonomy of revolution was proclaimed by Quinet: 'the French Revolution', he declared, 'is its own origin, its own rule, its own limit'.[28] The Catholic faith was increasingly interpreted not as distinct from philosophy, but as subversive of it. This was the old pagan charge, resurrected by Rousseau, that Christianity, by positing a higher authority, was subversive of revolutionary objectives, whether social unity, equality, the triumph of reason or national sovereignty. The late-nineteenth century cult of empiricism and science held that morality should be disengaged from metaphysics and be rather derived from observation and analysis. Under the influence of the Comtian law of stages, and assisted by Darwinian evolutionism, philosophers came to view religion as a primitive stage in the development of man's reason, now superseded. Mankind would come to realise – 'discover' – the universal moral laws without the instruments and authority of mystical faith, religious dogma and churches. This enterprise was advocated especially by sociology, which started from the assumption that society came into being as an expression of shared moral assumptions and that these assumptions were elements and not attributes. Both philosophically and politically, the search was for a synthesis of moral belief, objective because common, to be taught by the state, that could replace definitively the religion taught by the Church.

Secular morality was upheld as a religious ideal by liberal protestants such as Gambetta and Ferry; their mentor, Quinet, placed himself with Rousseau and Kant on the side of 'freedom of religion' against Catholicism. Yet *freedom of religion* was not coterminous with religious pluralism. All were visionaries who advocated banning religious education from schools altogether, and to replace it with an official irreligion. This 'monopoly of irreligion' was inculcated, confusingly, alongside the claim that 'you could have morality without Christianity while the morality that you must have was Christian morality'.[29] Behind the secularist project of the left lay an implicit recognition of one of the tenets of scholasticism: that democracy depended on a shared moral vision: moral because of the implicit limitations of law in instilling virtue and improving society; universal because as long as France remained divided (between Catholic Royalists and revolutionary democrats) there could be no democracy. Unlike the medieval order, however, which came into being following the gradual spread of Catholic Christianity and the appearance of governments deferring to that allegiance, the secularist project sought to collapse both spiritual and temporal allegiance and to instil morality and political unity from the state. The Church could no longer be permitted to exist alongside this project, because its presence in education and society negated the objective value of *morale laïque*. The state therefore demanded a monopoly of irreligion, to be taught by a secular priesthood of dedicated *instituteurs*, instilling respect of God as revealed by conscience and reason (i.e. liberal Protestantism), according to the selective definitions of the state.[30] Similar patterns could be observed in Germany under Bismarck or Italy under Mazzini. Pluralist education – in which both lay and Catholic schools co-existed – was rejected by secularists as a threat to the moral unity of the nation, as creating *deux jeunesses*. Mazzini was categoric that the nation was not merely a temporal construct but a unit sanctioned by Divine Providence (i.e. moral absolute); from which it followed that Catholic spiritual universalism defied national citizenship.[31]

It would be therefore simplistic to equate nineteenth-century Catholicism *per se* with opposition to democracy. A more careful appraisal would have to consider the particular democracies involved. In those states where religious differences had given rise to pluralistic democracies, at least in given periods (the US, Holland, Belgium etc.), constitutional pluralism could accommodate the Catholic conception of politics in as much as the state respected autonomies and liberties outside its own sphere. In Ireland, Britain and the United States, Catholic support was for democratic parties, and frequently for the left. In countries where, by contrast, the 'Catholic' monopoly of royal absolutism (opposed by the Church, although it was implicated in liberal eyes) had been replaced by a 'secularist' monopoly, accommodation was problematic and the identification with the 'clerical' monarchists inevitable. And yet even here, the picture is more nuanced, for there were various Catholic movements, like that of Lammenais, that were simultaneously opposed both to absolute monarchy as well as the secularist strains in democracy; or thinkers like De Maistre, who advocated monarchy but, unlike the Gallican monarchy overthrown by Revolution, one which was ultramontane. The political sympathy of Catholics tended therefore to vary with the context. They supported ecumenical liberal democracies, and opposed other democratic strains emanating from sectarian liberalism.

The danger presented by the Catholic reaction against sectarian liberalism was that the Church would become *de facto* harnessed to a heterodox right, as Lammenais had foreseen and warned against. Observing this, Leo XIII issued a series of declarations acknowledging developments since 1789 as *faits accomplis*, distinguishing between those elements of modernity which genuinely refuted the Christian Order and those that did not. In the *Ralliement* of 1889–92, Leo called upon French Catholics to accept republican democracy, all forms of government being in principle acceptable 'so long as they preserve order, respect morals, and allow the Church reasonable liberty to fulfil its mission'. He then summoned Catholics to participate in and 'Christianise' public life much as the early Christians had done in states that had formally rejected Christian principles.[32] Making clear what was erroneous in modern state theories (that Church liberties were concessions of state law, that religion was a private matter, and that unfettered sovereignty resided in the numerical majority) and what was not (electoral and parliamentary regimes, freedom for all religions, modernity in general), he emphasised the compatibility between Catholicism and citizenship (obedience was always due to legally-constituted authority), and called upon Catholics to act in the public forum, without confusing the authority of the Church with party interests.[33]

These guidelines were followed shortly afterwards by the first definitive response of the Church to capitalism, in the encyclical *Rerum Novarum* (1891). The two lines of development originating in this twin formulation (political and social) were the basis of integral Catholicism in the twentieth century: a doctrinal restatement of the political and social basis of the Christian Order in modern terms. Not coincidentally, Leo XIII also encouraged a revival of Thomism, which bore fruit in early twentieth-century neoscholasticism.

Rerum Novarum identified both liberal capitalism and socialism as prone to two abuses: the absorption of the state by sectors of the economy, and the absorption of the economy by the state. Labour was affirmed to be both personal and social, hence inseparable from morality and justice; and therefore not subject exclusively to the law of the market. If a just wage could not be determined through 'free' bargaining, it was unjust. Against socialist calls for the abolition of private property, and the liberal–capitalist defence of property as an absolute right, Leo drew on the Thomist dual characterisation of property as both personal and social. Hence both individualism – where the social and public end of property is ignored, property is the privilege of the few – and collectivism – where the private and individual nature of property is not respected, the state owns all property – were evils to be refuted. The encyclical instead insisted on the gradual spread of private property to all, through just wages, labour legislation and a more active state role in safeguarding the right ordering of production. A 'just wage' would be sufficient to cover the worker's 'primordial needs' and those of his family – food, clothing, housing, education and health – while enabling him to save towards the purchase of property. Contrary to collectivist doctrines, however, the encyclical stressed that above these, man had the liberty to prioritise individually his needs; without them, he was automatically deprived of that liberty. Other 'inalienable rights' demanded by the encyclical were those of association, rest, and religious duties, which implied worker-based trade unions, limitations on working hours and Sunday rest.[34]

Rerum Novarum sought to recover the positive but pragmatic role attributed to the state by the scholastic tradition. The state was charged with defending the defenceless, and with intervening in order to bring about a more just distribution of wealth. Intervention was however curtailed by the instrumental character of the state, as a means and not an end. Unlike the secularist premiss of socialism, that the state was itself a moral agent of justice, and therefore should itself own capital, *Rerum Novarum* implied that the state's intervention deferred to a justice external to the state's definitions of it. State intervention was further curtailed by its respect for the autonomy of institutions, according to the fundamental Catholic principle of *subsidiarity*, which conceives of the state as invigilating and coordinating rather than managing and owning.[35]

Although *Rerum Novarum* was an affirmation of social morality with implications for the economy, rather than an economic theory *per se*, its assertion that the eradication of underprivilege demanded organised action and state intervention provoked the rapid expansion of groups and organisations. Social Catholicism both promoted an active role for the state in legislating the free market, and sought the organisation of workers into guilds and unions to defend justice. Yet just as the *Ralliement* did not succeed in persuading French Integrists to work with an anticlerical republic, so social Catholicism was weakened by an internal struggle over the response to a social order which had grown up in opposition to the Church, characterised by the division of classes, the divorce of capital and labour, and the self-declared moral autonomy of the market. On the one hand, the Augustinian 'Integrists' insisted on confessional guilds, arguing that worker-based interconfessional unions implicitly accepted both the Reformation and the division of classes caused by liberalism. 'Thomist' Christian–Democrats, on the other, who appeared in the wake of Leo's formulations, advocated worker-based, a-confessional trade unions, on the grounds that the struggle for social justice demanded unity of action. There were examples therefore of Catholic unions collaborating with socialist unions, and others where cooperation was all but unknown. Equally, while some Catholic unions were genuinely working-class organisations resorting to strikes and boycotts, others were confessional, mutual-aid societies abjuring strikes. There were also differences in size: while Catholic or Catholic-inspired unions would remain numerically behind socialist unions, they saw substantial growth before the First World War and in some areas were in direct competition with the Left.

Catholic unions were most successful where they were linked to a lobby or party. In Italy, a loose federation of unions under Vatican control, the UCES, expanded rural credit unions and Catholic activism at parish level, taking an increasing share of the workers' movement until 1910–11. In Germany, the Centre Party sponsorship of the *Volksverein*, nearly a million strong by 1914, strengthened unions even after they had become interconfessional. Social Catholicism, especially in France, was also a movement of opinion and ideas, based around study circles in offices and factories discussing wages, arbitration, strikes and legislation, and sponsoring trade unions.[36] As these examples illustrate, Catholic political action prior to 1914 was rooted largely in social activism, built around the parish network; the extent to which it participated in politics proper depended principally on the exclusivity of the democratic systems concerned.

CATHOLICISM AND THE MODERN STATE

Despite the triumph of parliamentary regimes throughout Europe, the loss of the papal states, and the intellectual isolation of the Church in the late nineteenth century, liberalism was in retreat. The class basis of liberal democracy, and its philosophical resistance to state intervention in the economy, provoked the backlash of socialism, while its antimilitarist, free-trade principles encountered new forces of nationalism, militarism and imperialism. Scientific Materialism, Social Darwinianism and Positivism superseded liberal humanitarianism, which proved unable to command the loyalty of industrial masses. Early Christian–Democratic movements in Italy and France, inspired by the Thomist exhortations of Leo XIII, experienced early successes, but soon ran up against the political effects of the liberal crisis. The threat from communism initially prolonged the relationship between Catholicism and the anti-centralist right, but this relationship was increasingly threatened by the right's absorption of Positivist and secularist elements in the aftermath of the First World War. Between the wars, the Church would again retreat, demanding total loyalty from Catholics and refuting all contrary ideologies. Catholic thinking became closely identified with Neoscholasticism which, fuelled by the Thomist revival, moved from a detached, idealized picture of medieval Christendom to a modernizing theology of engagement, which would shape Vatican II.

The rise of the 'new state' in the early twentieth century carried with it a spiritual reaction against the bourgeois individualism of the nineteenth century. The state began to assume elements formerly associated with the medieval Church. There were two main features of this process. First, in reaction to the disorder and *anomie* of industrial capitalism, the state became larger and more centralized; no longer entrusted merely with the preservation of order, it was called upon to deal with questions of a sociological character: the destruction of poverty, the safeguarding of health, and the regulation of capital and labour. This process, which had already begun in the nineteenth century with universal compulsory education as a means of instilling national character and values, was fuelled by the pressure of socialism, which demanded that the lack of a social conscience in the free market impelled the 'moral' state to take over economic functions. As the state came to own larger sections of the economy, society and culture became more politicised. Although pressure came firstly from socialists, statism took on many forms: the anti-socialist legislation of Bismarck or the state corporatism of Mussolini, for example, represented the application of socialist tenets to the state in the name of anti-communism. The state capitalism of Italian fascism no more protected the freedom of 'lesser associations' than did socialism: both sought to compensate for the social consequences of economic individualism by resort to state capitalism. In this 'third phase' of the secularist dialectic (the first two of which were expressed in the absolutism of revolutionary politics and the individualism of liberal economics) the modern state movements came to rest their claims on the need to put government and the State above party interest. The demand for this came about often as a result of a deadlock between parties without roots in the wider population, in a system which resorted increasingly to extra-parliamentary means to gain sectoral benefits (general strikes, militias, ballot-rigging or corruption) which placed the state increasingly at the mercy of party or class interests.[37]

Christian democracy, as a Thomist movement seeking to work within constitutional parliamentary democracy, had its first flowering in the years prior to World War I. The most successful electorally was the Partito Popolare in Italy, established in 1919. The theoretical basis of the PPI (Partito Popolare Italiano) was provided by its leader, Luigi Sturzo, who restated the Christian Order in terms which took account of modern changes. Now the party, acting in the temporal sphere, deduced the practical implications for society of the faith it professed, which was safeguarded by the Church. But unlike the late nineteenth-century lobbies, the PPI was not a party articulating Church interests (to emphasise this point Sturzo even refused to place the solution of the Roman Question, which he regarded as an ecclesiastical matter, high in the party's programme), but a 'party of Christian inspiration' which avoided even a religious referent in its name, and which upheld religious liberties. The terms 'Catholic' and 'party', Sturzo argued, were antithetical; Catholicism was a universal religion, where a party was temporal, geographically confined, and operating in the realm of human laws. To harness a religion to a party would be to harness the universal Church to sectoral interests; to distinguish the two spheres in which they operated was to allow each greater freedom, for a party should govern for the public good and not for the adherents of a particular religion, as in the confessional model. By the same token, the authority and universality of the Church were safeguarded by its independence from sectoral interests.

The party was *popolare* in as much as it was mass-based, committed to radical reform, and had roots in a network of peasant leagues and trade unions. This made it a direct competitor of the Socialist Party: both were committed to the dispossessed (while the Socialist Party's electorate consisted largely of industrial proletariat, most *popolari* were agrarian) and both achieved around 20 per cent of the vote in 1919. But while the PPI supported worker grievances, it disapproved of the political objective of class struggle and the Soviet. Not to support specific strikes, on the other hand, would reinforce capitalist and conservative forces – a quandary which illustrates the dilemma of Catholic politics emerging from its ghetto into a polity divided by the left-right secularist dialectic. The PPI was more successful in retaining its independence from both left and right than the parties it inspired in France (PDP) and Spain (PSP). In spite of these differences, the 'popular' parties shared basic orientations: they were 'of Christian inspiration' rather than Catholic; had no formal ties with the Church hierarchy; were political expressions of the social-Catholic movement and hence strongly reformist; had multi-class support; were committed to proportional representation and female suffrage; defended regional autonomies; called for greater devolution of powers on the principle of subsidiarity; favoured syndical freedom and agrarian reform, and limits on state power; looked to greater European integration and a 'sane internationalism'; and rejected both liberal–conservatism and the class struggle. Of all the *popular* parties, only the PPI was successful at the polls, and could therefore maintain its independence until 1926, when it was destroyed by fascism; both the PSP and PDP were small and had limited existence.[38]

The emergence of a contest between communism and fascism posed Catholics with an age-old dilemma between withdrawal and engagement. Because modern collectivism appeared under mutually antagonistic guises, there was a danger that in attacking one 'extreme' of the secularist dialectic (communism or fascism) the victory of the other would be assisted; while not attacking or supporting either would be tantamount to upholding the individualism and social injustice of the bourgeois order. Because the age of liberalism and individualism was disapproved by the Church, there was no reason for Catholics to oppose its passing. It was at least theoretically possible that the limitation of political and economic liberty by dictatorship should actually be more favourable to the Christian Order: a government ruling in virtue of the common good, which respected the sovereignty of the spiritual sphere, which sought to curtail economic individualism and the growing division of classes, and which was deemed capable of arresting the secularist slide towards totalitarianism, might therefore attract Catholic support. In Portugal, for example, Catholics were inclined to support for Salazar: a Christian–Democrat in his youth, Salazar was opposed equally to regalist monarchism and modern statism, sought to defend regional and corporate autonomies, and upheld a patriotism which expressed 'lesser autonomies' of family, village and Church.[39] The dictatorship of Salazar was therefore (at least in its early stages) *pluralistic*, in as much as the state itself defended those feudal autonomies which acted as a brake on central power.

The break with the right was eventually caused by its absorption of many of the liberal strands of the nineteenth century, expressed in the French Revolution. This did not happen either cleanly, or suddenly; and the European right in the inter-war period varied enormously between the unambiguous totalitarianism of Nazism at one extreme and the corporatist, pseudo-monarchism of Primo de Rivera at the other. The right often contained both pre-modern and modern elements vying for supremacy. The doctrinal boundary marking the apostasy of the right can be located by examining the early example of Action Française, a movement which defended the Church and offered a vision of France deceptively close to Catholic antimodernism, but which eventually revealed its positivist and secularist underpinnings. The religious-political doctrine espoused by Maurras, which might be termed 'clerical positivism', presaged that of Mussolini. It exerted particularly strong appeal in the wake of disamortization and Church–state separation forced through by Combes in 1904–5, which, backed by radicals and socialists, represented a last all-out effort by the Left to achieve national revolutionary moral unity. Maurras' staunch defence of the Church won him the support of large sectors of the Church; yet he would be deplored by integral Catholics – *abbés*, youth organisations, worker circles, social–reformists, Christian–Democrats and some bishops – and was condemned by the Pope in 1914 and publicly in 1926.[40]

Maurras conceived the history of the Church in the West as having curtailed the messianic, individualistic spirit of Protestantism through discipline, dogma, and unity in authority. The Positivist admired by Maurras, Auguste Comte, had effectively no need of a new 'social' religion, for the function of the 'Great Being' had been performed in history by the Church. This might be expressed in a logical equation. Human society required an overriding authority in order to suppress individualism and achieve unity and coherence; the Church provided that authority in history; *ergo*, the Church was true. Examined closely, Maurrasianism was essentially enlightened-absolutist; its appeal to supernatural law was based on the need for an order over and above individual will, and differed only from republican secular theocracy in that it sought to deploy Catholicism, rather than a secular religion, as the creed of state. This reversed the Thomist conception. In Thomism, man's temporal well-being in political society is subordinate to his ultimate purpose (personal salvation), safeguarded by his voluntary obedience to the spiritual sphere, to which the temporal sphere must conform. In Maurrasianism, by contrast, although political society outwardly conformed to the purpose postulated by the Church, it did so only in as much as the Church appeared to serve the *a priori* ends of the temporal sphere. As would be demonstrated by Mussolini, the doctrine of Maurras contained a totalitarian impulse which would logically conflict with scholasticism.[41] In the short term, however, not just bourgeois Catholics – the *catholiques sans foi* as Bernanos would later portray them – but Catholics blinded by anti-republicanism and angered by the state's treatment of the Church, would lend their support.[42]

The symbiosis of Catholicism and the right was also assisted by the outlook of the left. The left was anticlerical in theory because of its origins in Enlightenment secularism; it was anticlerical in practice because liberal capitalism had appeared (in the eyes of many workers and their leaders) to deploy the Church as a charitable palliative. The case of Spain is illustrative. Eighteenth-century enlightened absolutism had eroded ecclesiastical autonomies, causing an ever greater dependence on the state and wealthy classes; while the sweeping disamortization of the nineteenth century had thrown the Church into the arms of wealthy protectors and monarchists. In the years up to 1931, the Church lost ever more influence over the urban workingclass. A dechristianised proletariat was vulnerable to the appeal of the leftwing association of Church and privilege. By the early 1930s, it is only a slight exaggeration to talk of 'two Spains': one, monarchic, regalist, Catholic, and supportive of the discredited dictatorship of Primo de Rivera (1923–30); the other, republican, anticlerical, reformist and humanist, but carrying in its rear carriages the secular-messianic doctrines of anarchism, anarcho-syndicalism, socialism and communism.[43] There were exceptions: the Catholic Basque nationalist group PNV, which welcomed the Republic's decentralizing policy and whose outlook was Christian–Democratic; the conservative–democratic Catholics of the Propagandists and the rump of the PSP, who were caught between the reactionary politics of Catholic monarchists and the anticlericalism of the reformist Republic; and even Catholic Republicans who sought to justify the massacres as the work of uncontrolled groups. But for most Catholics, Insurgents had to be supported even if this meant the irritation of a regalist state at the war's end.[44]

Internationally, the Republican persecution of the Church, rapidly following on from that of the Soviet Union and Mexico, was to prove decisive in placing a gulf between liberals and Catholics. To liberals, the Spanish conflict was a contest between fascism and democracy, and they blamed the Church for rallying to the fascists. Catholics, on the other hand, shocked by the massacre of clergy and desecration of churches, saw the struggle as one between Christian civilization and atheistic, totalitarian communism. The liberal diagnosis, informed by both Protestant anti-medievalism and Enlightenment secularism, identified the Church as the handmaiden of authoritarianism and the effective 'cause' of its rise in Europe. Because 'fascism' was the principal enemy, liberals tended to romanticise the left, both in Spain and in Russia. Catholics, on the other hand, identified totalitarianism as the offspring of liberal secularism, individualism and capitalism, with their roots in the Reformation and the Enlightenment. Communism was the latest, apocalyptic stage in this process of dialectical degeneration, and the principal enemy of Christianity. This sometimes made Catholics blind to the heterodox, Positivist elements in Falangism, and led them to romanticise the right, whether in Spain or Italy, as defenders of a Christian civilization under threat, and the only brake on what many saw as an inevitable totalitarian backlash against individualism.

If, however, the modern dictatorships declared their own religion – whether the pantheistic creed of the Pan-Germans, the racial and naturalist idealism of Nazis, the atheistic materialism of communists, or the *romanitá* fascism of Mussolini – it would follow that a conflict with Catholics and the Church would ensue. The reason would not be that of ethics, for all these movements – as with liberals, before them – would purport to uphold Christian values; but their Enlightenment premiss would lead them to seek to install a secular theocracy. Rather than deferring to external law and the anterior societies which composed a nation, they made lesser communities relatives of the state, and state doctrine universally applicable.

Catholic opposition to the 'new right' was led by the papacy, which saw in both Mussolini and Hitler a threat equal to communism, and indeed coterminous with it. Pius XI reined in the Church from the political sphere in three ways. He severed Church ties with Catholic political parties, which were too closely linked to fragile constitutional régimes on the verge of collapse, and likely to give excuses for attacks on the Church; he attempted to unite and fortify lay Catholic organisations in an umbrella group, Catholic Action, intended to be rigorously apolitical, subordinate to the hierarchy, and sufficiently disciplined to command a loyalty that could compete with the absolute demands of the state; lastly, he sought concordats with the new strongmen in an attempt to guarantee the autonomies of Church organisations.[45]

In Italy a number of Church liberties were enshrined in the Lateran Pacts of 1929. Catholic Action membership and activities were allowed to multiply, leading to an intense rivalry between fascists and Catholics within youth organisations and brigades. When it came, the conflict exposed the Catholic repudiation of the practical implications of Maurrasianism. The Vatican in 1930–31 protested against the state monopoly of youth, the inculcation of fascist doctrine in schools, the deification of the state as well as vertical state corporatism and trade union monopolies. The conflict was latent and continual; it meant that Italian fascism, at least until the late 1930s, was prevented from outright totalitarianism by the persistence of organisations which owed ultimate loyalty to God and bishops rather than the state. A vertical hierarchy with its expression in the state furthermore abolished the distinction between law and will implicit in totalitarianism. In Nazi Germany, on the other hand, which along with Stalinist Russia represented the 'ideal' totalitarian type, the spiritual sphere was wholly eradicated. The outright abolition of Catholic unions, the absorption of Catholic Action youths into the Hitler Youth, and the persecution of Jews were all condemned in one of the Church's most ringing denunciations ever issued.[46]

The Church's position, in the 1930s–1940s, as equidistant from communism and fascism, socialism and capitalism, liberalism and totalitarianism, was encouraged theologically by the Catholic revival generally and the Thomist revival in particular. The inter-war years were auspicious for cultural receptivity to the Catholic thesis. The cataclysm of 1914–1918 had shattered prevailing optimism about human perfectibility; had thrown into relief the demonic potentiality of science and technology; and had shaken European society into a profound self-questioning. This cultural crisis – a crisis, fundamentally, of faith in modernity – appeared to many of those who did not lapse into nihilism, to confirm the papal diagnosis of modern errors. This was fertile ground for the scholastic critique of secularism. Reviews and newspapers, institutes and popular courses, radio programmes and parish organizations – all grew dramatically, propounding a revived and invigorated scholasticism, and summoning western culture to return to its battered spiritual roots. With its coherent denunciation of the secular canon, and its compelling political, cultural and social models, Neoscholasticism would continue to underlie the thinking of Catholics, both lay and clerical, until at least the 1950s.

In its early period, Neoscholasticism tended to share the nostalgic thesis of post-Reformation historical degeneration. Its positive revision of the Middle Ages verged often on triumphalism, and in its cruder expressions tended to reject modernity *toto caelo*. As it progressed, however, Neoscholasticism began to point the way to a Catholic reinsertion into the public realm, one which was more nuanced in its appraisal of modernity. The figurehead of this evolving Neoscholasticism was Jacques Maritain, already by the 1930s the leading Thomist scholar and author of classic antimodern works, who had been linked in the early 1920s to Action Française. The papal condemnation of Maurras coincided with his own reassessment of Thomism, which was announced in the midst of controversy. In 1936, Maritain called for Catholics to remain independent from both sides of the Spanish Civil War, on the grounds that, because the conflict was the fruit of Christian *embourgeoisement*, it was as wrong to massacre workers as it was to massacre priests. Neither side could therefore claim spiritual justification for its acts. Maritain justified this stance by a revised view of history. While denouncing the individualism of modernity and celebrating the 'true humanism' of pre-Cartesian Europe, Maritain saw in the spirit of the modern age not the dialectical degeneracy abhorred by antimodernists, but an impulse, however undermined by error, towards a recovery of the Christian Order suppressed by absolutism. This 'Christian idealism' – which he saw latent in the Enlightenment trajectory – had nevertheless been accompanied by an aggressive insulation from (and rejection of) the spiritual and theological basis of society and politics, the fruit of which was the 'theocratic atheism' of communism and the pagan order of fascism. The modern pluralist state – if realizable – was therefore a positive development in all that it offered for the exercise of human freedom; but democracy – a fundamentally Christian idea – had developed according to bourgeois notions of individualism and self-interest, fruit of the Cartesian dualism of the age, which had generated the collectivist reactions. Faced with this secular dialectic, however, Catholics in Maritain's view had failed to distinguish between the Christian roots and idealism of secular and anticlerical forces on the one hand, and their individualist-collectivist implications on the other. Just as anticlerical reformers (Jacobins, liberals, socialists, Republicans) had observed Church subjugation to the state and concluded there to be an alliance (an error derived from their empiricism), so Catholics (guilty of the same error) had reacted to anticlerical reformism by allowing themselves to be attached to political movements (Action Française, Spanish nationalism), which used religion for temporal political purposes, subordinating Catholicism to the state's purpose, and so compounding the error. Because Catholicism lay outside the secular dialectic, rather than fuel it, Catholic politics had to begin with a detachment from contemporary doctrines, from the 'practical atheism' of nineteenth-century bourgeois individualism and from the statisms which it had engendered. Catholicism could never be asked to specify a political or national ideal, nor to be harnessed to temporal order, because it was by nature transcendent. Rather, Christians were called upon to 'vivify and animate from within . . . to act on political realities' while remaining *au dessus de la mêlée* from the secularist dialectic.[47]

Maritain's restatements of the Christian Order in the 1940s and 1950s mark a point in the development of Catholic ideas that would profoundly influence Catholics both in Europe and Latin America, and which would sow the seeds of postwar Christian Democracy. With his formulations, Maritain recovered the Thomist model of engagement which would come to the fore at Vatican II; in politics, this meant making nuanced distinctions between those elements of the Enlightenment that had (consciously or otherwise) sought to recover elements of the Christian Order, and those which genuinely refuted Catholic doctrine. Beginning with a denunciation of Maurras, the philosopher proceeded to famous distinctions between types of Catholic political involvement in the modern secular state, which would enable Catholics to win back politics to Christianity and pursue the historical ideal cut short by the Reformation. The Christian acting on the temporal sphere would be simultaneously independent and *engagé*. His politics would be shaped by fundamental conceptions of the human person rather than an ideology. These conceptions would derive from postulates which avoided extremes engendered by metaphysical errors. The first postulate was that of a *person* according to the Catholic tradition, the individual conceived as having roots in a transcendent nature from which his dignity derives, at once free and social. This *personalistic* conception of citizenship resolved the unnatural conflict between the individual and society, and implied a series of indwelling personal rights. Secondly, liberal–bourgeois democracy, as it developed in ignorance of the social aspect of man, ignored social inequality (or believed it to be a temporary stage in the development of capitalism); this led to the reaction of collectivist democracy, which proclaimed the equality of uniformity. Between these two errors lay the *communitarian* tradition, which recognised individual inequalities as natural but sought a degree of material equality as flowing from the shared dignity of mankind. Thirdly, Christian democracy was *pluralistic*, in three main ways. Politically, it had 'organic heterogeneity': this implied decentralization, separation of public functions and of state and parties, and social organisation based on principles of federal organisation and subsidiarity. It also implied syndical pluralism: the union was an organisation freely constituted by its workers, beyond the competence of the state, which must *protect* it and never *create* it. The 'single union' – one per profession – was only tolerable as a lesser evil. Economically, its pluralism was manifest in joint ownerships and mixed societies. And juridically, the relationship between Church and State was seen as the moral authority of the Church freely moving human consciences, in a society where *authentic* freedom of religion was respected by pluralistic structures enabling different denominations to possess their own schools and parties.[48]

Maritain's tenets received effective endorsement from the Vatican at the war's end, in the papal allocution of 1946 calling for democracy: notably, a democracy rooted in the Christian conception of the state, which would bring about the social and economic incorporation of the masses. In the ten years prior to that allocution, however, Maritain would be strongly criticised for appearing to surrender to liberalism and secularism. As the Argentine case illustrates, the context in which Catholics were struggling was crucial to the reception of his thesis. The postwar Christian-democratic movement, which grew out of both the *popolare* antecedents and Maritain's 'Catholic-roots-of-democracy' theory, took root in countries where Catholics and liberals had been thrown together against fascism (Italy, Germany and France) and in other countries (Chile and Venezuela) with a pluralist, constitutional tradition. In other countries where democracy had gone hand in hand with monistic secularism, Christian Democracy continued to be caught in the crossfire between Catholicism and the Enlightenment.

THE ARGENTINE CASE

As this summary shows, the Catholic conception of the state and politics is an outgrowth of medieval notions of law, distinction of realms, the common good, and indirect sovereignty. The politics of the post-Enlightenment presented a variety of political philosophies and forms and were judged in light of scholastic conceptions of politics. Liberal democracy, as a political form, was congenial to Catholics where it was animated by ecumenical liberalism, and was expressly opposed where it drew on monistic, theocratic and totalitarian roots. Catholic political behaviour between 1820 and 1960 varied correspondingly. In Anglo-American countries, where ecumenical liberalism offered a constitutional framework congenial to the Catholic conception, Catholics tended to operate on an open model of engagement, and were supportive of a variety of political positions, tending to the left. In the continental European model, by contrast, a monistic liberalism, emanating either from enlightened absolutism or from Rousseanian theories of popular sovereignty, caused Catholics either to retreat into a closed model of engagement or to enter into a conditional relationship with the right. Later, between the world wars, the 'closed' model, or integral Catholicism, came to predominate. After the Second World War, democracies animated by ecumenical liberal principles allowed for the establishment of Christian Democratic parties.[49] The Argentine case dramatically illustrates the model of conflict between Catholicism and sectarian liberalism. The conflict was latent, if not continual, and provides a key to understanding the particularities of its political development.

Part I
Church, State and Society in Argentina, 1810–1960

1 Scholasticism and Secularism, 1810–1920

1.1 FROM INDEPENDENCE TO THE FALL OF ROSAS, 1810–1852

Until the late eighteenth century the Plate region was one of the most barren and isolated edges of Spain's empire in South America. The presence of the late-colonial Church appears therefore slight when compared with the colonial heartlands of Mexico or Peru. Yet religion was uniform, for Hispanic settlement did not compete, as in Mexico and Peru, with substantial indigenous belief-systems. Outside the settled areas, it is appropriate to think of the late-colonial River Plate as mission territory: only three dioceses, of an average of a million square kilometres, administered a population of around half a million scattered over an ocean of land. The Jesuit missions were settlements as large as the largest lay communities, extending from the city of Córdoba to the northern border area of Misiones. The expulsion of the Order in 1767 on the orders of Carlos III was therefore a severe blow, felt especially in the faculties of Córdoba University and schools everywhere. The remaining orders – Franciscans and Dominicans – replaced the Jesuits as the principal educators.[1]

The shortage of secular clergy and the dominance of the religious orders are crucial in understanding the importance of scholasticism to the culture and intellectual life of late-colonial River Plate. The colony's distance from Spain, together with its relative isolation and underdevelopment, are also significant. If Spain in the seventeenth and eighteenth centuries was sealed from both Reformation and rationalism – not least because of the absence of religious nonconformism and denominational conflict which underlay the 'secular' Enlightenment – Spanish America was yet further from these influences, both spiritually and geographically. Indeed, there were many ways in which the River Plate was thoroughly medieval in outlook. The council, or *cabildo*, survived long after it had been suffocated in Spain, and was the means by which local people screened colonial policies. And although the Church was sealed from Rome by the *patronato*, Spanish decline prior to the Bourbon Reforms meant that the colony was relatively untouched by regalism and Gallicanism. These were, after all, politico-ecclesiastical doctrines held by the higher secular clerisy in Spain, and opposed by the very religious orders which dominated Platine society.

The pervasiveness of scholasticism, and the particular influence of Suárez, began to be recognised as result of research conducted by Argentine historians under Guillermo Furlong in the 1950s. These scholars demonstrated the importance of the Scholastic revival in schools and universities in the River Plate in the eighteenth century. Even the urban merchant classes were with few exceptions both scholastic and anti-Jacobin: whatever the appeal of English economic liberalism, the merchants of Buenos Aires considered the English and their ideas religiously heterodox. Since Furlong's research it has been harder to lend credence to the traditional liberal claim that Argentine independence was a reverberation of the French Revolution. The evidence rather points to seeing it, in Stoetzer's words, as 'a typically Hispanic family affair'.[2] The birth of the Argentine nation expressed not the rationalist constructs of Rousseau, but the old scholastic theories of St. Thomas Aquinas and Francisco Suárez, persistent in the colonies in the face of Spanish regalism.[3]

This is borne out by a survey of the thinking of the independence leaders. There is no evidence that Rousseau's *Social Contract* was read in Buenos Aires before 1810, and its principles were admired only in so far as they superficially appealed to scholastic principles.[4] It is true that General Manuel Belgrano was 'widely read in the Enlightenment' but also that he remained entirely within the scholastic tradition.[5] His influential chaplain, Juan Ignacio Gorriti, was a renowned exponent of Catholic anti-absolutism. For Gorriti, independence signified the defeat of centralism; he proposed the restoration of autonomies against the power of central government, and public and private spheres so infused with Christianity that a broad range of freedoms would become available.[6] The intellectual father of revolution, Manuel Moreno, was typical in his condemnation of the determination of French rationalists 'to make God the author and accomplice of despotism'.[7] Recognising that Rousseau's proposal for a *religion civile* amounted to a secular theocracy, so subverting the Christian and democratic elements in the *Social Contract*, his 1810 translation suppressed the relevant chapter.[8]

The impulse to independence lies in local reaction to the centralising Bourbon Reforms of Carlos III. The *vicariato regio* theory, which the Reform expressed, conceived papal spiritual authority as merely symbolic, and temporal power as virtually unfettered. The practical political expression of this theory was the subordination of a range of autonomies, and its harsh implementation provoked resentment in a colony still accustomed to degrees of social and political pluralism. Ecclesiastical policy was of particular resonance: the appointment of regalist clergy at the expense of the religious orders dealt a blow to the traditional upholders of brakes on state power. The exclusion of creoles from bishoprics and high civil posts and their occupation by a crowd of newly-arrived *peninsulares*, allowed both clerical and lay creole to relate resentment at the centralising and absolutist claims of Madrid to national prejudice. The establishment of intendancies – administrative units which undermined local autonomies, notably those of the Church – provoked disputes over jurisdiction between secular-minded bureaucrats and local bishops. In 1781, a Jesuit born in Mendoza attempted to persuade the British parliament to support a self-governing South-American state; and the *Carta a los Españoles Americanos*, by the Peruvian Jesuit Juan Pablo Viscardo, was well known in Buenos Aires from 1801.[9]

The Bourbon Reforms were therefore 'a major cause of disaffection among the lower ranks of the clergy' and the religious orders.[10] Priests not only stood with rebels in defence of national pride and in opposition to absolutism, but were active intermediaries between the fathers of independence and the wider population.[11] Large sectors of the population identified with clerical grievances, and both secular rebel and priest appealed to scholastic theories in their refutation of Madrid. It is no accident that Carlos III, while asserting the state over traditional autonomies, also 'waged a relentless campaign against the "subversive" theories of Suárez'.[12] The most dramatic element of this campaign – the expulsion in 1767 of the scholastics *par excellence*, the Jesuits – only hardened the opposition to enlightened absolutism. The vacancies left by the Jesuits were filled by their students, or by Franciscans. According to Madariaga, the expulsion was proof to creoles that the monarchy was in the grip of the detested ideas of Voltaire, and so cut the link between the Crown and its overseas subjects.[13]

The severance of such a link did not automatically imply republicanism; rather, according to scholastic theory, tyrannical rule automatically reverted authority to the political community. It was significant that during the British 'invasions' of 1806–7, the defence of Buenos Aires against which awoke a nascent Argentine nationalism, the *cabildo* acted much as had the *cabildos* of the sixteenth century. The Viceroy was deposed for incompetence, and a *caudillo* was appointed who had shown himself worthy of peoples' trust. The proximate cause of independence was nevertheless the occupation of the Spanish throne by Napoleon; in line with scholastic theory, the deposition of the lawful king revoked the duty of obedience. This 'purely Spanish and medieval act' was a rebellion not against monarchy but a religious revolt against Enlightenment doctrines.[14] When Saavedra, Moreno and other prominent creoles gathered in the junta of the 25th May 1810, they swore with their hands on the Bible, before a crucifix, to be loyal to the deposed King Ferdinand VII. The pact to which they referred was not that of Rousseau but Suárez' *pactum translationis*; their profession of obedience was not to the throne but to a lawful ruler. The Cabildo debate abounded in scholastic notions: Castelli argued that the absence of legitimate government caused 'a reversion of the sovereignty to the people of Buenos Aires', and Saavedra that 'it is the people who confer authority or power'.[15] Indeed, Argentine independence had the support of lower clergy and religious orders not because it was a revolution expressing rationalist and deist notions of the sovereign will of the majority, but because it was an act, entirely within the continuum of scholastic thinking, which reflected their adherence to a longer and deeper tradition.[16]

The Junta's disorientation faced with the restoration of the lawful king (who then proceeded to declare war on the rebellious nations) was nonetheless taken advantage of by a small radical wing professing rationalist constructs. If the movement in favour of independence was shaped by scholastic thinking, its development was influenced strongly by both enlightened-absolutist ideas as well as the liberalism of this small but able revolutionary clique. The control released by Madrid was seized by local governing classes; the centuries-old bureaucratic establishments, shaped by post-Reformation absolutism and regalism, passed into the hands of the independent government. Symptomatic of this emulation of the *ancien régime* was a reluctance to let go of regalist ecclesiastical policy. As the Curial Archives in Buenos Aires show, for over three centuries there had been no communication between the Church in the River Plate and the Holy See. The mentality of much of the secular clergy had been shaped by the 'latitudinarian religious centralism' of the Spanish colony.[17] Priests forever associated with independence, such as Gregorio Funes, were also therefore advocates of the *patronato*. Equally, military leaders, anxious to counteract Madrid's charge of heresy, and conscious of the sensibilities of their soldiers, incorporated acts of piety in army life, to the extent where the national Church of Spanish regalists was counterposed to another national Church of the River Plate. This identification was encouraged by the Wars of Independence themselves, which, as one of Belgrano's officers recalled, were as much religious as they were political.[18] The *regio vicariato* remained in place as part of the sovereignty package the Juntas claimed to have inherited from the Spanish Crown. The declaration of 1813 proclaimed the independence of the Church from Madrid (whence orders had previously come) but also from Rome (whence they should now have come).[19]

The argument used by regalists that national objectives conflicted with the international character of the Church, was reinforced by Rome's initial reluctance to recognise Argentine independence. By the time such recognition had been granted in the 1830s, government was wedded to a centralist course. The Platine Church therefore remained a captive of nationalism and *raison d'état*, lacking the independence of both means and mind to challenge, as in France, the government's anxiety to harness the Church to the priority of reestablishing order. The liberal secularization programme of 1822 effectively continued the Bourbon policy by removing the remaining ecclesiastical autonomies. It was demanded that priests place patriotism above all other loyalties, that they instruct parishioners in government doctrines, and that, by ensuring religious unity and conformity, they serve the national purpose. In part due to the regalist tradition, in part to the ambiguous position of the Holy See, in part due to the fact that severing links with Madrid left the Church in Buenos Aires acephalous, therefore, the revolutionary government seeking to establish its authority emulated the enlightened despotism of Carlos III, thereby provoking further reactions, within the River Plate, against central authority.[20]

The view of the provinces was that separation from Spain had left each province master of its own destiny; the basis of association could therefore be forged only through negotiation and agreement. The radical liberal triumvirate led by Benardino Rivadavia opposed this view, rejecting any curbs on its sovereignty. The junta was suppressed, and its attempted comeback brutally quelled. The provincial delegates, who had been invited by the junta to agree on a basis of unity, were now ordered by the liberals back to their provinces, and the *juntas provinciales* were dissolved. Rivadavia's 'oligarchy of intellectuals' raised the spectre of Jacobinism; in the provincial view, his resistance to negotiation and agreement disentitled them to dominion over the other provinces.[21] In a mirror reflection of 1810, therefore, following the overthrow of the triumvirate, and the collapse of the 1819 Constitution, the River Plate disintegrated into petty states under *caudillo* rule.

In Buenos Aires Province from 1820, the Unitarian liberal government restored under Rivadavia sought a strong, central executive with enlarged powers capable of carrying through a programme of education reform and economic development. Rivadavia's constitutional thinking was shaped by Bentham, yet was interlaced with Spanish enlightened despotism and went much further in the power attributed to the executive. In other respects, the programme was Jacobin in orientation: the abolition of the autonomies of 'lesser societies' – the old Spanish *fueros* – was accompanied by severe legislation controlling labour. Rivadavia's enlargement of the state created an intense competition for patronage, a phenomenon which lies behind much of the instability of the 1820s.

If Rivadavia's authoritarian, centralist and absolutist enlightenment doctrines clashed with broadly medieval and scholastic notions of local autonomies and consensual politics, the resistance he provoked by his secularization programme gave the tension a specifically religious character. The combination of English liberalism, born of religious nonconformism, and Spanish absolutism, which sought to subordinate and control the Church, lies behind the 1822 reforms. There were four elements. First, both the legal immunity (*fuero*) and financial independence (*diezmo*) of the Church were abolished, thus further undermining ecclesiastical autonomy, and making Church dependent on the state. Second, the control of marriages, births and deaths, as well as that of schools and a multitude of charitable institutions was absorbed by the state. Third, monasteries were abolished, their occupants expelled or laicised, and a host of properties taken over or sold off. Fourth, freedom of religion legislation was promulgated, granting 'perfect liberty of conscience' to the British, full rights of worship, and (although they preferred to occupy a vacant Jesuit chapel) the freedom to construct Protestant churches.[22]

That these measures should have been seen as an attack on the Catholic faith was unsurprising given the presence in Rivadavia's entourage of Anglicans, Protestants and regalists, among whom was an apostate priest – referred to by the future Puis IX as a 'dogmatic materialist' – who propagated at Rivadavia's behest the theories of Destutt de Tracy.[23] The application of liberal tenets, designed to counter Church privileges in nations where denominational divisions made such privileges anathema, to a religiously-united society steeped in scholastic tenets, was the first of many acts of marginalised intellectuals in defiance of wider values.

The view of British and American representatives in Buenos Aires, which remains that of much liberal historiography, to the effect that the inclusion of religion defence in the federalist uprising was little more than a political method of exciting the masses, fails to take into account the provocative and unpopular character of liberal reform. The Buenos Aires *cabildo* was outraged; provincial governments refused to allow their children to be instructed in secular doctrines, even at the state's expense; and anticlericalism displeased *estancieros* already concerned about apparent favouritism towards merchants. The doctrinaire governor of San Juan, who injudiciously declared freedom of religion in an outlying province where there were no other cults, was publicly ousted. An uprising in Córdoba under General Bustos had clerical and popular support, especially from the University; and the legendary leader of Santa Fe, Facundo Quiroga, rebelled under the cry of ¡*Religión o Muerte!* The Unitarian General José María Paz, leading troops to recapture Córdoba from Bustos, found himself up against a barrage of popular allegations that he had forbidden baptisms and converted churches into barracks.[24] In Buenos Aires, where clerical indignation at Unitarian anticlericalism had been aroused at Rivadavia's removal of the Bishop of Buenos Aires *in sede vacante*, the government and official press further fuelled indignation by ignoring the papal delegate. The lack of political wisdom this showed was proved by the delegate's tour of the Confederation in 1824. He was received everywhere by large crowds and took away the firm impression that the government's attitude had provoked popular hostility.[25]

Such evidence helps explain why, in the two years of civil war which separated the end of Rivadavia's short-lived presidency in 1827 and Rosas' rise to power in late 1829, as the American Consul observed, the 'lower classes [were] much exercised by religious passions'.[26] The argument of *Federal* propaganda, that Unitarian irreligiosity was the cause of its brutality, was lent credence by the pointless execution of the moderate *Federal* Dorrego, whose deathbed piety much moved the populace. In 1830 the papal nuncio in Rio de Janeiro reported that in the furious battle between Unitarians and *Federales*, 'the pious people stand with the Federation'.[27]

Rosas' self-justification, which social instability and political violence made increasingly cogent, was that liberty resided in the return of rule of law and protection of the Church. In 1835 the Provincial Assembly granted Rosas dictatorial powers for two ends: to defend the Argentine Confederation, and to save the Apostolic and

Catholic religion. The character of 'religious federalism' was negatively shaped both by the Protestant zeal of the British, and by the doctrinaire liberalism of reformers. In this French battle, seen by liberals as the promotion of liberality and rational progress against fanaticism and intolerance, and more broadly as a defence of religion and the rights of the Church against an intellectual clique of reason–worshippers allied to Protestant bankers, there was little question of which had popular support.[28] The political wisdom of Rosas lay in his adjustment both to the rough religiosity of the common man and his sense of nationhood. Yet Rosas also increased trade with Britain and granted land for the construction of an Anglican Church, a move which shows that defence of the Church was not antithetical to religious pluralism.[29]

For all his identification with the Church, however, Rosas was a child of Spanish absolutism. He restored neither the monasteries nor the Church's autonomies and deployed the clergy – in the tradition of Spanish eighteenth-century absolutism – as a clerical arm of government. Throughout the twenty one years of his dictatorship, Rosas sought to use the Church to muster popular passions and instil discipline. The Church was in no position to resist: it was weak, isolated, impoverished and acephalous, and barely capable of a vigorous, independent existence, as the re-expulsion of the Society of Jesus showed. The dictator's invitation to the Jesuits to return was not a sincere attempt to restore the Church's authority, for he was attracted by a vision of a more rigorous state clerical service. Faced with their obdurate refusal to propagate state propaganda and participate in the dictator-cult, Rosas began to interfere with the Society, first by cajoling and threats, and finally through *mazorca* intimidation. Unable to harness the Jesuits to the political objectives of the state, he eventually expelled them again in 1843.

Rosas also acted in the manner of late eighteenth-century absolutism in his policy towards the papacy. As part of his attempt to woo the ultramontanes in Buenos Aires, Rosas had initially endorsed the restoration of relations with Rome. Once in power, however, he was given to furious anti-papal tirades in which the Vatican was accused of 'interfering with the sovereign authority of a foreign power and moreover a nation of a different religion [sic]'.[30] Papal bulls issued since 1810 which had not been approved by the Executive were declared null and void, and discussion of the *patronato* with the Holy See was refused. Concomitantly, Rosas extended political control over ecclesiastical *minutiae*, from the colour of vestments to the appointment of clergy. The *mazorca* issued whippings to clergy suspected of lack of enthusiasm for the Holy Federation; and both priests and police were answerable to the dictator's wife. The growing despotism of the régime inevitably reinforced the servility and mediocrity of the clergy. Some of the 'federal priests' were recruited from among the same groups as the army, and would be remembered for their alcoholic verbosity and ignorance as well as their tirades against government enemies from the pulpit. As Jesuits had observed with disapproval, government workers regularly organized ceremonies of popular devotion to the administration, during which garlanded portraits of the dictator would be placed on altars next to a crucifix. There was no period in Argentine history when the Church would be more thoroughly absorbed by the state.[31]

How religious was Buenos Aires under Rosas? We rely for our knowledge largely on the reports of the Jesuits during their brief return, as well as the testimonies of foreign travellers. The Jesuits were shocked by the innocence and ignorance of inhabitants, but impressed by their 'early-Christian' piety. Few failed their Easter obligations but weekly mass was rare. Popular song was both orthodox and pious. Away from the towns, visitors to houses would salute their hosts with an *Ave María*, and a foreign visitor who did not kneel before a street procession of the eucharist might receive blows from a stick. The faith of the River Plate, interwoven into country life, mostly superstititious and untutored, co-existed with overt displays of indifference, especially to marriage. Nor could popular ignorance be wholly attributed to the paucity of clergy and the problems posed by the enormity of the landscape, for the illiteracy and superstition of creole priests differed little from those of their charges.

This impression suffices for the period from independence until the beginnings of national organization, following Rosas' fall in the 1850s. Both Church and society stagnated. The average surface area of the four dioceses was a staggering 716,000 square kilometres, and the average population per diocese – higher than in 1810 – remained a paltry 168,750. The combination of an acephalous Church, shortages of secular priests, vast distances and low population, had petrified under Rosas. Despite encouraging popular religious adherence and building churches, the dictator's political subordination of the Church further undermined the creation of a proficient and independent clergy. Both anecdotal evidence and the testimony of the Jesuits point to the marriage of popular piety and a dictator-cult, in the context of a mostly uneducated, subordinate clergy and the continued lack of bishops. This picture flies in the face of the notion of a Church revival, popular in later nationalist historiography.[32] The façade of state-sponsored religiosity having been lifted after the dictator's fall in 1853, the severity of the Church's position was exposed. There had been no ordinations for years before Rosas' fall, and only thirty five secular priests catered for the whole of Buenos Aires Province. The small number of solid clergy of the colonial period had all but disappeared. The religious orders were depleted. Seminaries lay idle, and state funding – on which, following Rivadavia's 1820s secularising laws, the Church was wholly dependent – was lacking. There was no independent hierarchy. In 1863, the Minister of Justice described the Church in Argentina as 'deserted', and mourned that the only candidates for vacant parishes were imported clergy with no knowledge of Spanish. Evangelization of the Indians – to which the Constitution was committed – remained theoretical. Only two priests could be found to accompany Roca's mighty Conquest of the Desert in 1879.[33]

The Church therefore lagged behind the process of national organization. The major problems remained the lack of leadership and shortage of clergy. Although the population per dioceses doubled between 1859 and 1895 (1895: 240,000), the number of diocese, of an average half a million square kilometres each, never exceeded five, an administrative void matched in Latin America only by Bolivia. Domestic religious organisations, mostly female, and generally confined to pious interior provinces such as Córdoba, could not make up the shortfall. The gap between widespread belief and low participation in sacramental and parochial life was partly filled by European missions. Irish Dominicans and Sisters of Mercy, led by the indomitable Fr. Fahy, paved the way for German Redemptorists and French Lacordairists, who established a presence in Patagonia and among immigrant communities.[34] The Jesuits returned, and founded the Colegio del Salvador in 1868; French Dominicans were present in secondary schools. Sixty per cent of the clergy of the period were European, and tended to congregate in urban areas. The largest and most influential of the incoming Orders were the Italian Salesians, who later provided half of the Church's bishops.[35] But neither the influx of foreign clergy nor the growth in the number of churches could keep pace with immigration; in 1895, just over a thousand priests – both secular and regular – catered to a population of around four million: a ratio of one priest per 3,390 inhabitants.[36] The poverty of organisation can be seen in the severe lag between diocesan expansion and population growth [Table I.1, Appendix I].

1.2 CATHOLICISM AND LIBERALISM, 1860–1890

The overthrow of Rosas in 1852 initiated the process of pacification and unification that would lead, in fits and starts, to the foundation by the 1880s of a modern nation–state with its federal capital in Buenos Aires. Economy and society began to be transformed: by (principally British) foreign capital; the construction of railways and telegraph, docks and customs houses; an expanding land area and burgeoning exports of wool and beef; as well as a working population swelled by waves of immigration – much of it seasonal Spanish and Italian labour. The first president of an Argentine Republic was chosen by an electoral college of provincial delegates in 1862. Institutions were founded: a school network and a national army, paid from new national taxes, as well as a judiciary and civil bureaucracy. A federal army – which did not however possess a military monopoly until the 1880s – was created to counter provincial militias.

The overriding ambition of this project was modernisation, of which Britain was the economic, and France the cultural, model. The architects of national development were men of the Generation of 1837: liberals exiled under Rosas and inheritors of the mantle of Rivadavia. Politics was the preserve of a small group of urban merchants, lawyers and landowners in Buenos Aires, and remained so after the institution of elections in 1863. Tiny numbers participated and the elections themselves were 'ritualistic parodies'.[37] Yet elections reflected their desire for constitutional government and an administration founded in law, in contrast to the arbitrary despotism (or tyranny) of Rosas. Where the deposed dictator saw himself as leader of a loose confederation of semi-autonomous provinces, the liberals were concerned above all with creating a strong sense of united nationhood. They detested the provincial, patrician world of the interior, and undertook to weed out both its militias and its autonomies, waging war almost continuously until the 1880s on local *caudillos* until they were definitively suffocated. Yet it was not merely a question of imposing the hegemony of Buenos Aires on other provinces, for the presidency was occupied mainly by *provincianos*. Rather, the Period of National

Unification (1852–1880) was the result of a *project*, with its political roots in the enlightened absolutism of Carlos III. A strong, almost Hobbesian central executive, perceiving the paths to modernity, declared war on obscurantism and barbarism, sought to populate the empty spaces with 'laborious' immigrants from Protestant lands, and to inaugurate a federal structure with the city of Buenos Aires as a national capital.[38]

The liberal classes were initially accompanied in this project by prominent Catholics who shared their desire for stable institutions and economic development in a framework of civil liberty. Men such as José Manuel Estrada and Félix Frías had been exiled, along with liberals, from Buenos Aires Province under Rosas, and they shared both a disgust for tyranny, and a determination to forge a unity that would prevent its recurrence. Both liberals and Catholics saw the project as one that would transcend the dichotomy of *Unitario* vs. *Federal*. Both abhorred the tyranny of Rosas, but both saw the proximate cause of his rise to power in the doctrinaire excesses of Rivadavia. This unity of purpose, sustained by the challenge of establishing Argentina's legal and institutional framework, nevertheless concealed fundamental divergences in conception which were revealed once the ideas of the Men of 1837 were able fully to be implemented after 1880. By this time Catholics, strengthened by the Church's Romanisation, would resist the state's attempt to impose a state monopoly of secular education. As in France, however, the Church-state clash of the 1880s was much more than a dispute over temporal-spiritual jurisdictions, exposing the gulf between the Catholic and liberal views of state and society.

The political differences between Catholics and liberals could be seen in their contrasting analyses of the causes of the Rosas dictatorship. They agreed that Rosas had been popular. They also agreed that this fact alone did not legitimise his rule. Both argued that popular sovereignty must be curtailed in a higher law, in an authority beyond mere popular will, but here Catholics and liberals differed on where to locate that law. For Catholics, the tyranny of Rosas lay in his subordination of the spiritual sphere. The combination of the unfettered will of the sovereign on the one hand, and the abolition of the distance between ruler and ruled on the other, had given rise to an abominable combination of powers. Right rule instead consisted of government which respected the final system of values out of reach of both caprice and tyranny. In Argentina, the Church safeguarded that final system of values; respect for the Church and deference to it as the moral conscience of the people would both curtail the sovereignty of the state and place a brake on the caprice of popular will. In respecting the freedom of the Church, the state was necessarily curtailing its own sovereignty. The Catholics who expressed this view were 'liberals' in the tradition of Lammenais and Montalembert. They acknowledged the definitively republican character of South America, and its right to self-rule according to scholastic theories. Government should therefore reflect the moral community; Frías argued that peace and order would come about by governors and governed sharing and deferring to the same spiritual authority, above both, enabling decisive authority while restricting it to its proper sphere. Pointing to Chile – which had been more loyal to its faith than Argentina, and was therefore more united and more stable – Frías argued that, 'my compatriots . . . will only save the *patria* . . . by declaring themselves partisans of order under the shadow of the cross'. Estrada advocated democracy in its 'true' sense of consensual government in law, buttressed by an independent judiciary and separation of realms.[39]

In the liberal analysis, law was located in 'right reason'. Argentina's backwardness lay in its having bypassed the Reformation and the Enlightenment. The Church was a Hispanic relic, which acted as a brake on the free exercise of reason. In its subordination to the dictator, the Church had showed itself yet again the handmaiden of despotism. Expressing deist assumptions, liberals advocated the limitation on sovereignty not in the Church, which should be excluded from political society autonomously defined, but in the secular authority of 'universal' law, revealed by reason. Because reason – as Rosas' popularity demonstrated – did not reside in the people, it followed that the country should be led and instructed by an enlightened clique capable of defending itself against those irrational beliefs which undermined order and instinctively sought dictatorship. Liberals therefore located the restriction of state sovereignty in their own reading of universal laws. As conceived philosophically, liberal rule was self-justifying, autonomous, instrumental and limitless. The Alberdian formula underlying the Constitution of 1853 expressed these assumptions institutionally in a form of constitutional monarchism, tempered by reason narrowly defined by government, on the basis of restricted suffrage, the whole shored up by a monopoly of violence. The parallels with the enlightened despotism of the eighteenth century were self-evident, yet liberal ideas were fuelled now by a second, radical enlightenment strain.[40]

Formed in the schools of Rousseau and Kant, the Men of '37 were adherents to the 'organic' ideas of the 1848 Revolution, and especially to the *nouveau christianisme* of Saint-Simon. They perceived the battle of history as one between the national and the colonial, the progressive and the backward, the dark and the light. The universal law operating in history was that of the 'Divine Will', the *principio regenerador* of the New Christianity as revealed by France. The source and sanction of this 'pure', 'social' Christianity, purified of its 'corrupt' Catholic tradition, was not merely individual conscience, for individual conception of the divine conspired against the unifying, moral necessity of a 'social religion'. Like Rousseau's civil religion, the new Christianity should transcend the individual apprehension of the divine, to be capable of acting as the inspiration and guide of collective and individual conduct under the leadership of the enlightened minority. As in France, therefore, liberals sought the role achieved by Christianity in the Middle Ages.[41] But whereas medieval Catholic Christianity assumed a division of spheres and the autonomy and the supremacy of the spiritual jurisdiction, so preventing temporal authority from arrogating to itself the source and sanction of spiritual values, Argentine secularism, like that of France, looked to a single belief system to be instilled by the state, deferring to no authority outside itself. The state was conceived therefore as *active upon* society, in instilling the virtues required for citizenship and democracy. The autonomous and authoritarian tenets of enlightened despotism combined with the urge to condition the population in the tenets of French deism.[42]

This theoretical radicalism was nevertheless tempered by a strong dose of political pragmatism and realism, at least in the pre-1880 period. It was argued that Rivadavia had failed by moving too far too fast, especially in his secularization programme. 'Religion', noted Alberdi, 'is the most powerful mechanism available for moralizing and civilizing our people. . .What authority will morality have [in their eyes] without the divine seal of religious sanction?'[43] This conservative–agnostic position assumed that society at large was not prepared for the transition to the reign of reason; church religion would therefore be tolerated for political objectives. At the same time, Alberdi sought to encourage Protestant immigration. The Protestant was seen as industrious and enterprising in contrast to the laziness and ineptitude of the Argentine; to bring Anglo-Saxon ideas and labour – which had proved their superiority over the degenerate Arab–Hispanic type – to America, was therefore to civilize it further.[44] Religion was a tool of secular belief, not the expression of conscience.[45] Freedom of religion was advocated in order to break through the 'exclusivity' of Catholicism; while the Church was seen as the state's legitimating and moralizing agent.[46]

It is only by taking into account this blend of liberal radicalism and conservative pragmatism that the ecclesiastical provisions of the 1853 Constitution are readily comprehensible. There were two main aspects: establishment on Anglican/Gallican lines, although with tighter control; and religious liberty. First, Catholicism was the established religion of state, protected and financed by government. Second, the *patronato* was upheld; the state controlled the appointment of bishops, and the Church in Argentina had no immediate right of communication with Rome, except via the state, which had right of veto over papal bulls and missives. Third, there was complete freedom of religious belief and worship, Protestant churches being equal before the law yet free from state control. The final document was therefore an amalgam of enlightened despotism, Gallicanism and religious pluralism.[47]

State religious policy between 1860 and 1880 reflected these priorities. On the one hand, relations with Rome (re-established under Urquiza in the 1850s) were revoked; on the other, President Mitre intervened to prevent the expulsion of the Apostolic Delegate and allowed the Archbishopric of Buenos Aires to be created in 1865. Under Sarmiento and Avellaneda (1868–1880), the government backed the 'civilizing mission' of the Church while retaining the controls unilaterally awarded by the *patronato*. Sarmiento, like most of the liberal classes a freemason, nevertheless deplored masonic attacks on the Church, just as Avellaneda repudiated the burning by anticlericals of the Jesuit Colegio del Salvador in 1875. Because he was persuaded that the establishment of universities should not be undertaken by the state, Sarmiento even supported the establishment of the Jesuit University in Santa Fe. Yet where Catholic sentiment interfered with his preference for Protestant education, Sarmiento was quick to quell opposition, fining and imprisoning parents who refused to have their children taught by Protestants in Baradero. At a provincial level, conflicts were numerous. In the dispute over the Oroño laws in Santa Fe, when popular outcry at the governor's introduction of obligatory civil marriage and conversion of convents into agricultural colleges led to his overthrow in 1867, the government acted harshly, imprisoning protesting Jesuits and backing the legislation. In Entre Ríos in 1868, a parish priest was killed and the bishop assaulted after disputes between masons and Catholics; and in Paraná, the first Normal School was placed under the control of bitterly anticlerical Positivists.[48]

Such events reflected the first stirrings of a conflict between a Church growing in strength and independence, and a rapidly modernizing state seeking secularization. The Church remained, in infrastructural terms, a weak institution. It had failed to expand as fast as the population, for three major reasons: firstly because, unlike the pattern of North-American immigration, most immigrants were Catholic and emigrating to a Catholic country, so there was less urgency for clergy to follow them.[49] Secondly, the centuries-old legacy of the regalist state-church undermined local initiative. 'The habit of dependence on higher authorities for such things', observed an American student of Argentine rural life in the 1940s, 'is one reason why farm families who desire church facilities fail to initiate projects to obtain them'.[50] The third factor was the isolation of the Argentine Church; because of the liberal governments' insistence on the *patronato*, the Church could only communicate with Rome via the state. This in turn meant that Argentina lacked an ultramontane higher clergy with the organizing zeal of, for example, the English Catholic bishops of the same period.

Yet relative to the Church's position at the time of the Constitution of 1853, when it was described by an eminent spokesman as 'torn apart, anarchic and oppressed',[51] expansion had been substantial. Seminaries installed in the 1860s and 1870s laid the foundations of an educated national priesthood, and the first students were sent to study at the Latin-American College in Rome. Because this was a process which only began in the late nineteenth century, its effects were not evident until the early twentieth. Most of the influential clerical figures of the period 1930–1960 were of this late nineteenth-century generation. The creation of the Archbishopric of Buenos Aires in 1865 made possible the organisation of a team of bishops, four out of five of whom attended the First Vatican Council in 1870. In Córdoba, between the end of the nineteenth century and 1915, ten confessional schools were opened and five new religious orders established in a city of only 135,000 already boasting the largest concentration of Catholic institutions.[52] This expansion also enabled the emergence of a lay Catholic élite, occupying educational posts and newspapers, and gathering in associations and clubs. Although more of the leading classes of Buenos Aires would be attracted to freemasonry and rationalism, the Catholics among them were sufficiently strong to lead a nationwide campaign against the secularising laws of the 1880s.

As in Europe, the Church in nineteenth-century Argentina was culturally on the defensive. Among professional men transfixed by European modernity, rationalist doctrines proved more attractive than an ossified Catholicism associated with the backward, Hispanic past. Freemasonry, although numerically small – 2,500 in 1906 – exerted a strong influence in politics, law and the press. Argentine masons, like their French counterparts, were strongly anti-Catholic and the principal proponents of secularism. Masonic anticlericalism frequently played on the feelings of rootless immigrants, many of whom originated in southern Europe, where low observance and hostility to clergy co-existed with ritual religiosity. In the 1860s and 1870s, masonic campaigns succeeded in transforming the environment to the point where it was no longer the casual participant in Church-organised processions who might fear the crowd, but the priest. Even in Córdoba, the clergy was advised by the diocesan government in 1902 to carry the host discreetly to avoid defamation. Because a predominantly female congregation was a poor bulwark against physical assaults on churches, violent anticlericalism, although rare, went largely unopposed. The major instance was the burning of the Colegio del Salvador in 1875, which had been encouraged by a newspaper campaign against the Jesuits over a period of weeks.[53]

The Church was sensitive to these indications of hostility, and was quick to link them with the French Terror of 1793. Yet the burning of the Salvador was the most serious of a string of isolated events over a long period, and said more about the lawlessness of immigrants than it did about popular hostility to the Church. The outward manifestations of adherence to Catholicism remained near-universal: births, deaths and marriages remained sacramental activities, and an impressive majority continued to identify itself, at least nominally, with the teachings of Jesus Christ as safeguarded by Rome, rather than with those of the Great Architect of the Universe or Comte's *grand être*. In comparison even to Brazil, Mexico and Peru, outside small professional groups Argentina remained at the margins of rationalism and illuminism. The major threat to Catholicism, it was frequently observed, came rather from Catholics themselves, who were mostly wedded to the idea that religion was a ritual matter that could safely be reconciled with varying degrees of agnosticism. It was often observed that episcopal injunctions were wholly ignored; and the decline in religious observance, fuelled by a climate of sudden fortunes, led the Bishop of Paraná to characterise Argentine Catholics as 'atheists out of convenience rather than conviction'.[54]

Although a minority cult, secularism benefited from this widespread nominalism, and exerted a creeping pressure on the civil and legal framework. The Civil Code of 1870, for example, did not conceive of inter-denominational marriage, subjected married Catholics to canon law and enshrined marriage as indissoluble; but in 1875, laws were passed depenalizing prostitution. In the 1870s, the Chief of Police earned a rebuke from the Archbishop for allowing, for the first time, traffic to circulate in Holy Week; while *El Católico Argentino* observed that on Sundays roads were being re-paved and post-office workers doing overtime, with the blessing of the municipal authorities. And while the state closely inspected the theatre for indications of anti-patriotism, it allowed priests to be made figures of fun.[55]

The main area of conflict between a still predominantly Catholic society and a secularising project of modernization, as in Europe, was that of education. In the 1860s and 1870s, state schools – often staffed with North-American Protestant teachers – were founded, secular in orientation but permitting Catholic education. As long as religious education remained within state schools, the state could compensate for an undermanned Church's lack of access to wide areas of society. In the 1880s, however, the Positivist drive towards a state monopoly of secondary education, capable of instilling secular morality, led the government to pass an education law banning religious education from state schools altogether. The state thereafter entered into competition with the Church in education, and no longer made up for deficiencies in the Church's presence in schools. The poverty of infrastructure and scattered parishes could hardly compensate for the loss of dogmatic teaching in the expanding public school system.

The Civil Marriage Law of 1888 had a similar effect. By making a church wedding optional, and marriage before the state compulsory, state and Church no longer collaborated to encourage marriage but entered into impossible competition. The law further depressed the low marriage rates, such that by the time of a comprehensive 1902 survey of illegitimacy, the rate had doubled to 211 children in a thousand born out of wedlock, which was high compared to Europe although lower than in the rest of Latin America. The statistics revealed a strong regional imbalance, from the lowest in Santa Fe and Buenos Aires, which compared favourably to Rome and Paris, to its highest in Corrientes, where there were more illegitimate births than legitimate.[56]

It was in these outlying areas that sacramental participation was lowest. This was not due to irreligion but the inaccessibility of churches. A tiny number of parishes, dispersed in an enormous territory, in dioceses that embraced various provinces, meant that *gauchos* might wait five years to hear mass.[57] The appetite of a visiting British methodist was clearly wetted when, as late as the 1920s, he described the hinterland as 'untouched', and ripe for Protestant evangelisation.[58] Little had changed by the 1940s, when an American student observed 'the sharp contrast between the splendid church structures to be found in all large cities and in even in relatively small cities, and the almost complete absence of churches in the open country'. He went on to note that, 'religious pictures and mottoes are so prevalent in rural houses as to be almost universal' and agreed that country people were 'not irreligious' but 'practically churchless'.[59] In Buenos Aires, the association of religious practice with womanhood was so strong that in the education debate of the 1880s Sarmiento called for 'the school without my wife's religion'.[60] Although women were traditionally allotted the expressive religious roles – and not just in Latin society – in Argentina the virtually total male absence from Sunday mass, which continued until the 1920s, astonished foreigners.[61]

The clash in the 1880s between liberals and Catholics had its roots, therefore, in larger trends. The emergence of an ambitious modernizing, nationalist, secularizing project, unfettered by the pragmatic restraints of the 1860–1880 period, was made possible by the weakness of the ecclesiastical infrastructure, and secularizing trends generally. The 'liberal project' sought to provide a new framework of social allegiance; invigorated by the arrival of new political classes imbued with Positivism, the aims became more ambitious. Positivism satisfied a spiritual as well as logical void left by the decline in scholasticism. For this generation, the technical accomplishments of Scandinavians and Anglo-Saxons acquired an almost mystical value. Religion – and the baggage of the Hispanic and colonial legacy – were not merely to be superseded, but to be actively suppressed by a new creed. It was necessary to 'exclude the ideas, sentiments, superstitions and customs of our Hispanic and colonial past', and to 'renovate the ethical environment' by 'substituting faith in miracles for faith in industry, faith in theological mendacity for faith in scientific truth'.[62] Roca's slogan 'Peace and Administration' was a positive policy, designed to impose unity and order on an unruly people without national allegiance.[63] In economic terms, Positivism endorsed the immutable and irresistible laws ascribed to the free market. It was a thesis apparently proved by inflows of British capital, the inrush of immigrants, a sudden export boom and the seemingly miraculous expansion of the economy.[64] Indeed, the modernization project could now be implemented without needing to defer to wider support. The federalization of Buenos Aires, the convincing dominance of the federal army, the benefits of a network of provincial alliances, and the eradication of rival provincial powers, had all brought about the sovereign autonomy of the modern state. Electoral fraud was frequent, but widespread indifference (around 10–15% of the population regularly voted) and heavily-restricted suffrage made it unnecessary. A party was created which claimed to absorb and represent all vital national interests; Juárez Celman gave voice to this mystical notion in his assertion that the PAN incarnated absolute popular will. The party's domination was self-perpetuating, although factionalised.[65]

The ascendancy of Roca in 1880 coincided with that of the Gambetta–Ferry cabinet in Paris; the French secularization programme would form the model for Argentina, to the point where a law passed in Paris would shortly after be emulated in Buenos Aires.[66] It was to protest the imminent secularization programme in Argentina that the Catholic Movement first emerged as a distinct force within the leading classes, identifying itself as Catholic *qua* Catholic. It consisted of a small but influential group of jurists, statesmen and journalists, led by José Manuel de Estrada and Pedro Goyena in associations and a string of periodicals. They were republican democrats seeking an 'ecumenical liberalism' on the North–American model, who had broken with the Generation of 1837 over its laicism, warning in the 1870s of the eclipse between civil and religious spheres to the detriment of the latter. Increasingly critical of 'positivist fanaticism and materialism', and of the growing tendency of society to ignore the condition of the wage-worker in favour of the 'free' contract, Estrada warned that political liberty – defined increasingly as unlimited sovereignty of the executive power – was growing at the expense of civil liberty. Argentina's major weakness, in the view of the Catholic lobby, was its lack of 'organic' social organization. Hispanic centralism had been accentuated after independence at the expense of lesser, natural societies; the competence of the state – vastly enlarged in the 1880s – grew at the expense of the person and his natural affiliations. Catholics counterposed a balance between social needs and private activity, defended by a state 'both moderate and moderating' whose sphere of activity was confined to strictly necessary functions. This vision would necessarily clash with the instrumental and autonomous character of the Alberdian-positivist state.[67]

The education debate of 1884 for the first time saw the division of congress into two blocks, dubbed inaccurately (given the lay character of the Catholic block and the illiberality of secularists) by the press, *el partido clerical* and *el partido liberal*. The secularist proposal for education based itself on the proposition that, first, religious education violated the freedom of religion prescribed by the constitution and, second, undermined the need for a 'universal morality' which only secular education could offer. Law 1420 has frequently been misinterpreted by historians as a pluralist measure designed to accommodate non-Catholic immigrants. But as in France, secularists did not seek pluralism; they would not permit the teaching of a number of religions to reflect the variety of beliefs of immigrants (who were anyway overwhelmingly Catholic), nor to make agnosticism an option. The Law instead prohibited the teaching of religion in school altogether (the so-called *escuela neutra*), while making all pupils obliged to receive compulsory morality lessons from the state. The influence of French revolutionary thinking was paramount in the political justification for the state monopoly of irreligion. The state recognised no higher principles, and therefore had sovereignty over the Church; while Catholicism, by positing a dual loyalty, encouraged disobedience to the state.[68]

Catholic objections to the secular education law were expressed in a variety of fulminations against liberalism and modernism. Yet their speeches in Congress do not bear out the contention that the Catholic demand was for 'control of education by the Church'.[69] Catholic deputies submitted a counter-proposal for subsidising all schools of a minimum standard irrespective of religious denomination. In support of this counter-proposal, the arguments they advanced were essentially scholastic. An 'irreligious state' was an impossibility in a democratic Christian country. The state was delegated by society and not the other way round. The educational and legal framework should therefore reflect religious consensus and, according to the postulates of that Catholic consensus, should respect the division of spheres. For the state to declare itself the sole source of morality was in violation of freedom of religion, for it amounted to compulsory inculcation of a religious morality that was not that of the Argentine majority, nor of any denominational minority. To argue that God was above religion, meanwhile, was to arrogate a minority sectarian deist view to the state, and to impose it on a people whose understanding of God was predominantly Catholic. Liberals sought the allegiance of the citizen's conscience. In the Catholic conception, the proposal was thus both absolutist and anti-democratic.[70] True democratic republicanism, they argued, was irreconcilable with the state despotism of the absolutist Kings of Spain reflected in this law.[71]

The justification of Roca's Minister of Education and Worship, Eduardo Wilde, for both laws drew on the need for religious plurality in order to encourage Protestant settlement. Yet Protestants had full rights and liberties under the Constitution, and had not called for secular marriage or education. The largest Protestant settlements were in Santa Fe, and there had been no general call for civil marriage there in the 1860s. The only recorded civil wedding following Oroño's unpopular law was that of an Austrian blacksmith.[72] Indeed, although the greater proportion of non-Catholics were foreign, the overwhelming majority of foreigners were Catholic. Religion did not therefore follow native immigration patterns, and inter-denominational tension was rare. Protestant and Catholic clergymen frequently co-operated, as when a Scottish pastor demanded Sunday Rest laws with the approval of Catholics.[73] Tensions over land in outlying areas rarely had a religious or national character. The immigration tides which washed over Argentina in 1870–1920 left a religious makeup only marginally different from the one which preceded them. The hopes of Alberdi and Sarmiento, that the empty spaces would be filled with industrious Protestants, were frustrated by the overwhelmingly Catholic composition of immigrants. In 1910 – a high water-mark of foreign presence in the country – Catholics still made up 92 per cent of the population [Appendix I, table I.2].

The government's victory revealed the imbalance of organized forces. Although in the interior the two camps were more evenly supported, in Buenos Aires the government's domination of the media was manifest in the twenty newspapers campaigning for laicism against two that opposed it. Fortified by the victory, the central priority of the government's religious policy under Eduardo Wilde was the suppression of ultramontane and Romanizing tendencies. A number of bishops were suspended following a pastoral in Córdoba forbidding Catholic parents from sending their daughters to a school run by North–American Protestant teachers. The attempts of the Apostolic Delegate to mediate led to his expulsion. In the course of the subsequent uproar, the Holy See broke off diplomatic relations; Wilde praised science for having superseded 'thousands of years of mystical hysteria',[74] and three professors from the University of Córdoba were sacked. Contributors to *La Unión* were suppressed: Estrada was relieved of his Chair of Constitutional Law in Buenos Aires following his defence of the bishops; and Emilio Lamarca was sacked from his Chair of Political Economy after publishing criticisms of the high rate of government borrowing, which he correctly predicted to be unsustainable. In the absence of empirical research, it is difficult to gauge the popular response to these measures, although one indication may lie in the absence of support for the government from the American Protestant teachers Wilde had imported. One publicly agreed with the Bishop of Córdoba that the religion taught in schools should be that of the majority; while another brought to Jujuy, Miss Stevens, was converted by her class to Catholicism and retired to a convent.[75] When religious instruction was subsequently restored, in 1943, it proved overwhelmingly popular [Table I.6, Appendix I].

Popular outcry was certainly sufficient to provoke the foundation of a Catholic Party, the Unión Católica, in 1884. Estrada made clear that the political organization of Catholics *qua* Catholics was neither inevitable nor irreversible. 'Respect the Christian Order', he significantly remarked, 'and religious questions will not become political banners, and Catholic parties will have no *raison d'être*'.[76] The party's programme bears numerous similarities to that of *L'Avenir* in France in the 1830s, from which the UC took its inspiration. The party called for: respect for provincial autonomies, universal suffrage, freedom of press and education, an end to protectionism and the government banking monopoly, the legalization of trade unions, and open, honest government.[77] It was never true of the Catholic campaigns of the 1880s that they were concerned merely or even principally with anticlerical legislation.[78] The Catholic Union was a political-Catholic hybrid, located between the Italian lobby and the German Centre Party, although smaller than both. The party scored some successes (among which were Estrada and Goyena as deputies for Buenos Aires Province, and the proposal of a number of candidacies) against a virtually impenetrable government electoral monopoly. In spite of an alliance with a number of opposition groups, the most important of which was the Mitre faction, in the *Partidos Unidos*, the opposition failed to prevent the election of Juárez Celman. During his administration (1886–90), the Catholic Union kept up a criticism of the banking monopoly, excessive speculation and corruption, and of the massive spending that finally ended in the financial crash of 1889. But it failed to prevent the Civil Marriage Bill of 1888, following which to marry in church prior to marrying before the state became a prisonable offence.[79]

The Catholic critique of corruption and irresponsible borrowing and inflation received support in 1889 from the Unión Cívica de la Juventud, whose own repudiation of despotism, and calls for clean elections and broad suffrage, bears similarities to that of the Catholic Union.[80] An alliance of Catholics, *civistas* and *mitristas* lay behind preparations for the Revolution of 1890. There were tensions within the coalition, however, firstly over the use of violence in the uprising, and secondly over the education and civil marriage laws. *Civistas* such as Barroataveña were radical secularists; Alem was masonic and liberal; and Mitre's *La Nación* had been a strong exponent of secular education. In the parties' meetings, therefore, reference to the secularist laws was avoided.[81] It was an alliance arising not from a common conception of politics, but a shared repudiation of the government. Estrada's justification for revolution was eminently scholastic in its view that government had violated natural law and hence forfeited its authority.

Following the Roca-Mitre pact, by which Juárez Celman was ousted and the predominance of Roca's candidates ensured, the Unión Cívica split between the UCN (Mitre) and the continuation of the UCJ in the UCR (Alem). A number of Catholics remained with the UCR, while Estrada continued to lead a reduced Catholic Union. Roca, seeking to curry favour with the Church in the face of popular indignation, supported the candidacy of 'the Catholic doctor', Luis Sáenz Peña, so bringing about an end to the Church–state conflict. Roca's maneouvre, together with the deaths of the UC's most prominent figures, led to the party's demise in the 1890s. It had been the major opposition force of the 1880s, but, devoid of a social base and party organisation, was too dependent on a reduced group of intellectuals – 'a General Staff without battalions' as Groussac described it – to survive the political monopoly of power.[82]

Roca's *rapprochement* with the Church was facilitated by the abandonment of dogmatic secularism by liberals generally, and a recovery of the pragmatic (if agnostic) clericalism of the previous two decades. The transition from French-type radicalism to English-type conservatism reflected concern in the governing classes at the emergent working-class threat. Although a multitude of Catholic congresses were critical of the growing materialism and class polarisation, the Church was cultivated by the leading classes as a force of social order. Carlos Olivera's civil divorce (1901) and Church–state separation (1903) bills – the last secularist initiatives from the liberal camp – failed. *La Nación*, which had strongly favoured the secularising laws of the 1880s, significantly noted in 1903 that whatever the bills' virtues, 'political factors, and considerations of social order and timing should be uppermost'.[83] After the turn of the century, the secularist torch was passed to the socialists. As liberalism divided between conservatism and socialism, the Catholic movement became channelled into social Catholicism, which attempted to stand outside outside both liberal-conservatism and the left.

1.3 SOCIAL CATHOLICISM AND THE TRIANGULAR CONFLICT, 1890-1920

Breakneck expansion had produced sharp imbalances in the economy and placed severe strains on the social order. Between a quarter and a fifth of Buenos Aires' 1,600,000 population in 1910 lived in squalid *conventillos* – nurseries of disease, crime, political agitation, and home to one of the world's highest concentrations of prostitution. An expanding economy had produced an inevitable rise in property ownership, but the pace was too slow to prevent spiralling rents, overcrowding, and a homelessness which after 1900 was in many ways worse than in the nineteenth century. As a pastoral economy, Argentina had avoided the European pattern of slums accumulating around smokestack industries; yet landholding patterns had precluded a homestead population, so further fuelling urban populations and instability in the labour market. Social agitation at the turn of the century, fuelled by Anarchist and Socialist movements, shocked the PAN administration into tighter public order legislation and crack-downs on militants. These measures served only to exacerbate class agitation and hostility. Despite the conclusions of an exhaustive report by a Spanish doctor who had been connected with the Catholic movement in the 1880s, liberal–positivist faith in the science of the market precluded a concerted attack on the roots of poverty, and Congress blocked attempts by Catholic and reformist Socialist minorities in Congress to introduce even moderate housing initiatives.[84]

Argentina's ruling classes did not face, as in Europe, a cohesive labour movement capable of widespread disruption. The cultural heterogeneity of immigrant labour made working-class unity on single issues or general ideologies problematic.[85] The most important group were the Anarchists, who nevertheless embraced a mere five per cent of the capital's working class. Nor did militancy extend into political action, for most Anarchists were unnaturalized citizens and apolitical. Conversely, labour reformists with representations in Congress for the most part lacked roots in the working class. The Socialist Party minority in Congress from the 1890s was composed of a group of doctors and lawyers committed to the amelioration of working-class conditions through parliamentary reforms. As liberal–positivists driven by Second International determinism, they discouraged the naturalisation and political registration of workers until they had displayed the requisite consciousness, so restricting membership to a relatively exclusive, and almost wholly Buenos Aires-based group of intellectuals.[86] A further limitation on its appeal was its militant secularism. According to the tenets of socialist orthodoxy, religion was a form of mental suggestion, and divorce laws and Church–State separation were demanded by its leaders. This discourse, which was eminently that of the radical liberals, was nevertheless at odds with the majority of immigrants, whose roots lay in areas of Spain and Italy bypassed by Enlightenment rationalism.

Social Catholicism was an outgrowth of the Catholic movement of the 1880s, and specifically of *Rerum Novarum* in 1891. The social-Catholic critique of liberal capitalism was inseparable from the Church's indictment of secularism. The loss of the notion of the common good implicit in economic liberalism was blamed for the moral crisis which underlay capital–labour exploitation and social injustice. As a movement, therefore, social Catholicism refuted both liberal-positivist laissez-faire economics on the one hand, and socialist collectivism on the other, and looked to working-class organisation, labour legislation, trade union laws, and a mediating role for the state according to the doctrine of subsidiarity. From its beginnings in the Workers' Circles, the movement came to embrace a number of different groups and models. Membership of the Workers' Circles (CCO) grew steadily before 1930, reaching 20–30,000; the Social League's rural unions embraced around 6,000 and the Christian–Democratic League around 5,000; added to which were the female unions established in 1917–1921 of over 2,000 members. A conservative estimate of around 40–45,000 Catholic union membership in the period 1915–1930 is at odds with the almost total lack of mention in labour histories. By comparison, Anarchists and Syndicalists succeeded in mobilising around 100,000 workers at the high point of labour militancy in 1917–1921, but the figure dropped sharply outside these years.

As in Europe, Argentine social Catholicism betrayed the influences of both 'closed' and 'open' models. The CCO bear similarities to the French bourgeois *Cercles* established by De Mun, and were a mixture of mutual-aid society, research organisation and promoter of social doctrine. They underwent a substantial if gradual expansion. Street campaigns and lobbying supported bills in Congress, a number of which were successful, presented by the three social-Catholic deputies. The Workers' Circles were essentially guilds, on the paternalistic model, which sought to insulate workers from the harsh effects of liberal capitalism with legal advice, subsidies, hardship funds and cheap credit. The Social League was modelled on the German *Volksvereine* although influenced by Italian rural-Catholic activism. Its major achievements were the rural guilds formed by small farmers – the *Cajas Rurales* – from 1911, which pooled resources, enabled cheap credit and the defence of prices, and allowed for collective bargaining with large buyers. The Social League was a major social institute in national life, ran a large library, and branched out into a network of publications and centres.

At the 'open' end was the Christian–Democratic League (LDC) founded in 1902. Well versed in the thought of Toniolo and other Italian Thomists, the Christian–Democrats carried a white flag to emphasise 'purity of doctrine', and rejected both liberal individualism and socialist collectivism as 'two forms of the same tyranny'. Like early Christian Democracy in Europe, its model was open and modern, looking to a 'social reconstruction on the basis of guilds and unions *adapted to the demands of progress and modern civilization*'. The LDC instructed workers in their rights, and encouraged their self-organisation into unions, as against what the LDC regarded as the paternalistic statism of socialists or the seclusion of the CCO. It scored particular success in organising dockworkers, who struck massively in 1903. But Christian Democracy was too densely ideological and activist for an increasingly Gallican Church. The LDC's relations with the hierarchy were poor, and they were forced increasingly to concentrate on women. This shift in Catholic focus also reflected the difficulties in penetrating industrial labour at a time of anarcho-syndicalist militancy. Women were more natural adherents to Catholic social doctrine, numerically closer to the Church and less vulnerable to left-wing or Anarchist militancy of the then robustly male archetype. The first, successful weavers' union, established by the Christian Democrats in 1904, was supplemented by that of the matchmakers in 1917. To these were added the Nueva Pompeya syndicates in 1917–18, in turn inspired by the 'Blanca de Castilla' study and union centre for women.[87]

Relations between socialists and Catholics were a mixture of cooperation and friction. Social-Catholics and socialists shared similar agendas: the Unión Demócrata Cristiana, for example, advocated universal and female suffrage, minimum wage, a gamut of labour laws, state protection of trade unions and worker councils in factories – a programme not dissimilar to that of the socialists. The path taken by Alfredo Palacios, from CCO activist to socialist deputy, may indicate a greater crossover than might at first be apparent; even as a socialist, he continued to campaign with Catholics to introduce social reform and anti-prostitution legislation, and later attributed the source of his socialism more to Christianity than scientific nineteenth-century doctrines. On the other hand, there were many indications of a competitive hostility, especially during the LDC's campaign of street debates and addresses in working-class areas, the *Conferencias Populares*, which often led to clashes.[88]

There were two major reasons for the failure of social Catholicism to develop, as in Italy, into a major political movement and constitutional party. The major factor was the Gallicanism of the Curia. Ultramontanism having being suffocated by the clampdown of the 1880s, the Church had been 'made safe' sufficiently for liberal–conservatives to begin to value it as a means of social cohesion. The 'pragmatic' or 'clerical-agnostic' strain in Argentine liberalism had come to the fore, faced with the threat from the left; and the upper clergy – selected and controlled by the *patronato* – did not resist their role as guardians of 'national' values, especially when they shared liberal–conservative anxiety about the left.[89]

The second reason must be located in the architecture of Argentine politics. Until the electoral reform law of 1912, the monopoly of government by the PAN was unshakeable. The UCR, which had expanded into a modern party with a substantial middle-class clientele, maintained an intransigent refusal to participate in fraudulent elections in which few were eligible to vote. In this context, a reformist, democratic option was untenable. On the one hand, the intransigent opposition to social reform of liberal–conservatives fuelled the legitimacy of labour militants. Conversely, the resort to terrorism and violence by Anarchists in 1910 legitimised the government's call for suppression of labour activism. With Congress monopolised by anti-reformists, reformists had little chance of effectiveness through legislation; without reformist legislation, Anarchist militancy was legitimated.

The outbreak of social unrest in 1910 nevertheless marked the beginning of the liberal–conservative political decline. The electoral reform law of 1912, which broadened electoral suffrage to all males, irrespective of property and literacy qualifications, grew out of the recognition that social peace depended on broadening the basis of legitimacy of the liberal project. Electoral participation leaped from twenty to sixty-five per cent of males, although the total male population eligible to vote was restricted to the forty-five per cent of the population made up of naturalised citizens.

The almost exclusive beneficiary of electoral reform was Argentina's only modern, popular party, the UCR, and its compelling leader, Hipólito Yrigoyen. During its twenty-six years of electoral abstention, in protest at the refusal of Conservatives to broaden suffrage and hold legitimate elections, the party had established a tentacular nationwide network of committees. Its diffuse ideological tenets – expressed in a mystical nationalism and a teleological claim to represent the 'essence' of Argentina – was based on a single, overriding idea, that of popular sovereignty. The autonomous, enlightened-absolutist domination of the liberal classes gave way to a popular government which would carry forward the liberal project on a new basis of popular legitimacy. Although the Conservatives formed the opposition, the expansion of the electorate after 1916 – doubling in size between that year and 1930 – rapidly reduced their presence in Congress. Like the Conservatives before them, the Radicals took advantage of the prodigious powers invested in the executive to intervene in provinces to suffocate opposition. The spoils awarded the governing party discouraged coalitions and reinforced the monopoly of power.[90] Like the PAN before it, therefore, the UCR became the sole governing party, unfettered by the need for compromise with the opposition, embracing a series of factions like a royal court.

Because the Radicals remained within the confines of the liberal project – differing from it only in its belief in electoral majorities – the socio-economic framework remained intact. The social tensions incubated by Conservative intransigence were therefore transferred onto Yrigoyen's administration, with the single difference that he could no longer ignore either the interests of large sectors of the middle class, who were the beneficiaries of state patronage, or the demands of labour. The first Radical administration (1916–1922) succeeded therefore only in fuelling the social question, impossibly attempting to court the support of the Syndicalist unions through state arbitration while retaining middle-class support for the state as the guarantor of social order. Workers vented their pent-up claims in unprecedented strike activity. The government at first attempted to patronise the Syndicalists, but then resorted to army repression, leading to the massacres of workers of 1919–1921 in Buenos Aires and Patagonia.

Yrigoyen's undoubted popularity was the major factor in maintaining Radical legitimacy. He was supported by Basque, Irish and Italian immigrants in the *barrios* of Buenos Aires, and deferred to the Church sufficiently for socialists to accuse him of clericalism.[91] The origins of the UCR in the 1890 Revolution, when Catholics and *civistas* had fought alongside in common opposition to the PAN, meant that there was always a Catholic element in Radicalism in spite of its liberal origins. As president, Yrigoyen opposed divorce legislation and refused to ratify the laicist constitution of Santa Fe in 1921. Because the Church was weak, and Argentine society largely secularised, Radicals could speak of themselves as *laico, pero no anticatólico* (secular, but not antiCatholic) without too great a fear of contradiction. This self-definition betrays the influence of Krausism, a nineteenth-century liberal Spanish movement which allowed its adherents to reject the institutional Church while retaining its spiritual and moral values. The influence of Krause also permitted Radicalism to appeal to mass support in a society that was Catholic, and to imbue its discourse with a pseudo-religious imagery and lofty moralism that stood in favourable contrast to the materialism of the *régimen*.[92]

A Krausist, Christian spirituality was nevertheless no substitute for the dual-realm theory of scholasticism, and the Rousseaunian underpinnings of Radical Party philosophy were unmistakable. Yrigoyen's conception of the Radical movement – as the agent of the final spiritual values incarnate in the personality of the nation – was a circular notion, similar to that of the PAN, in which the state was beholden to a law which was possessed by no authority other than itself. He spoke of the *concepto irreductible* of the national spirit, similar to that of Rousseau's *Volonté Genérale*. 'The supreme teachings of the Argentine nation' were incarnated in government, such that, from 1916, 'the Republic has ceased to be governed in order to govern itself'.[93] The true colours of the UCR were shown in Yrigoyen's support of the illuminism of the University Reform Movement in Córdoba in 1919.[94]

The labour conflicts of 1917–1922, which like the University Reform were reverberations of European revolutionary ideas, threw the leading classes onto the defensive. Faced with social breakdown, the upper-middle classes both in Buenos Aires and Córdoba took to militancy of their own, in strikebreaking organisations and leagues. Both the Asociación Nacional de Trabajo (ANT) and the Patriotic League employed Catholic nativism and a Maurrasian discourse, and attracted prominent Catholic establishment figures and priests. The use of the Church as a force of social order, as prescribed by liberal–conservatives, was permitted by important ecclesiastical figures who effectively acknowledged the failure of reform in the face of left-wing militancy. The most notable was Mgr. De Andrea, whose growing dominance of the social-Catholic movement alienated its more dynamic wings. His public sermons addressed to the Great and Good in fund-raising banquets were typical of liberal-regalist *catolicismo de conciliación*, largely bereft of doctrine and instead replete with sentimental, patriotic references. Religion was seen as a cement; but it was a Christianity made safe by patriotism, with a common reference point in tradition, favourably contrasted with the new, dissolute, immigrant Argentina. In this discourse, which stood at opposite poles from the *Syllabus*, the Church was re-cast in a neo-Anglican mould. The Church, like the army, was an institution *within* the liberal state, indeed a department of it. The army defended the liberal project against its enemies; the Church performed a unifying, palliative role as an agent of social cohesion within market capitalism. The Gran Colecta Nacional of 1919, which De Andrea organized, was symptomatic; the Collection paid for an extensive cheap housing project and training centres, but the distinction between social justice and the necessity for counterrevolution were intermixed.[95]

The Unión Popular Católica Argentina created by De Andrea was an attempt to unify the various social-Catholic initiatives in an umbrella organisation closely tied to the hierarchy. In so doing, however, it destroyed the vitality of social Catholicism. Firstly, the subordination of the most dynamic social-Catholic organisations to a rigid, *dirigiste* framework undermined the need for flexible, pragmatic, grass roots organisation. Secondly, by asserting ecclesiastical control of the Catholic movement, each organisation could no longer adopt platforms that were merely *not contrary* to Church doctrines, but were now representative of the hierarchy. This particularly affected the LDC and the Social League, which ran the risk of confusing particular policies (such as proportional representation, upheld by the Christian Democrats) with the Catholic doctrines on which they were based, so threatening to compromise the Church as a whole with these particularities. Thirdly, De Andrea's own social-Catholic conception, which was opposed by the CCO founder, Fr. Grote, as well as the Jesuits, the Christian Democrats and other *integral* groups as complementary to liberalism, implied the victory of the conservative model over the radically-reformist. Lastly, it confounded attempts at forming a Catholic political party. Christian democracy struggled on in the face of episcopal disapproval, in study centres and electoral lobbies, but would suffer in the investiture controversy of 1923–24.[96]

The Church hierarchy in the 1910s–1920s had come to reflect liberal ambitions for it. In Europe, the restoration of Catholic universalism and the detachment of the Church from the regalist state – often brought about, ironically, by liberals – had occurred in the late nineteenth century, so allowing for the growth of a potent social-Catholic movement in France, Italy and Germany. In Argentina, on the other hand, Romanisation was only beginning to occur. It was reflected in the activities of the Jesuits and social-Catholic activists, and in the organisation of social congresses. This nascent movement implicitly refuted the liberal-Gallican *Iglesia Nacional* model. Because the path of Argentine liberalism had stopped short of Church–State separation and the expulsion of the Church from the public sphere – as occurred in France – Church and State had retained a link not dissimilar to that of the Church of England. With its capacity to select 'safe' bishops, the state was able to safeguard the Church both as a bulwark of social order and a charitable organization, so giving validity to the left's ideological assumption of religion as an opiate. The establishment of the UPCA and De Andrea's identification with the conservative reaction of 1917–1922, represented the temporary victory of the *Iglesia Nacional* over integral and ultramontane tendencies.

From the undoctrinal, emasculated Christianity of the *Iglesia Nacional* on the one hand, and the increasing clericalization of liberalism on the other, emerged the political outlook which, for all its heterogeneity, is termed 'nationalism'. Theologically, nationalism in this early period remained within the absolutist–Positivist continuum; culturally, it ranged from clericalist (in the Gallican sense) to pantheistic. Most early nationalist writers were ex-Positivists who turned on the liberal project for its materialism, cosmopolitanism, avarice, utilitarianism, individualism, cult of science and progress, and neglect of 'traditional spiritual values'. Religion was proclaimed as a foundation of nationality; Spain as the nation's *alma mater*. Manuel Gálvez rejected the doctrinal, dogmatic Catholicism of the Jesuits in favour of a 'Hispanic spirituality' he saw as latent in the pre-liberal patrician world of the provinces. Federico Ibarguren admired the Church as an element of continuity and stability, and Rojas regretted that the Church in Argentina did so little for 'nationality' compared to the Anglican Church in England. He called for the suppression of

private schools, whether religious or ethnic, in favour of a cultural homogeneity, or *argentinidad*.[97]
Such ambitions remained firmly within the Positivist framework, and were not markedly different from the *culto de la patria* advocated by *El Monitor de la Educación Común*. 'With the supression of religious morality', it typically intoned, 'only a morality based on patriotism can replace it . . . Let us make every child of school age a fanatical idolater of the Argentine Republic'.[98] The 'suppression' to which the *Monitor* referred was that of religious education: the Church having been relegated to a voluntary, private sphere, there was no longer a contradiction between secular Christianity as upheld by the state, and a Christian dogma safeguarded by the Church. Catholics were no longer portrayed by liberals as having foreign allegiances. Instead, Jews were singled out by the apostles of secular patriotism as immigrants with alien loyalties and ideologies.[99] Another strain in early nationalism was that of Leopoldo Lugones, who was militantly anti-Catholic, not because philosophically he differed substantially from the other nationalists but because he better understood the nature and implications of Catholicism in its doctrinal integrity. He was also able to carry nationalist arguments to their logical conclusion, arguing – more honestly than did the other Traditionalists, who merely implied it – for the subordination of spirit to force, of piety to power, and of conscience to order. *Argentinidad* expressed an immutable set of moral values which force was necessary to defend; it was both a pantheistic neo-Hellenic creed and a Nietzchian adulation of heroism.[100]
A similarly ambiguous blend of clericalism and liberalism was apparent in the Argentine Patriotic League, established in 1919 to fight the perceived threat of communism. The League borrowed from both Traditionalism and social Catholicism of the *andreísta* mould; it was both moralistic and philanthropic, refuting the 'economic' argument of class for a 'patriotic' thesis that borrowed heavily from liberal-conservative arguments around the turn of the century: that labour unrest was the product of foreign influences, alien to the edenic and harmonious nature of Argentine society. Equally, the LPA's language of vilification – excoriating its enemies as *turba* and *montoneros* – was typical of the liberal project.[101] These liberal leftovers aside, the League was nevertheless hardened by a militaristic and atavistic element, which owed much to Maurrasian influences.
In the first two decades of twentieth-century Argentina can be found the germ of all the strains that would subsequently be present in nationalism. All were philosophically of Enlightenment origin, and can

be located in the nineteenth-century liberal project itself. All have in common the absolute sovereignty of the state and its autonomy from external law, as well as the assumption that all other institutions – Church, army, rights, law – have their origin in the state, and are subordinate to it. This common thread aside, there were differing strains. The liberal–conservative, clerical tendency in nationalism was typified in the agnostic Alberdian view, derived in turn from Spanish absolutism, of the Church as an agent of state moralization and unification. Although this view would be superseded by the secularist and Positivist outlook of the 1880s, it would return to liberal–conservatism at the turn of the century once the Church had been 'Anglicanised'. The Positivist view of the state as an active agent upon society, conditioning society according to the precepts of the state, would pass into the thinking of Traditionalists such as Rojas and more extremely, into the neo-pagan pantheism of Lugones. The Rousseaunian strain in Argentine nationalism, meanwhile, would be expressed in Yrigoyenist radicalism, subsequently by FORJA in the 1930s, and later by Perón.

The growth of nationalism in the 1920s–1930s was concurrent with the Catholic revival and its recovery of the Roman, integral and neoscholastic core of Catholicism. With it came an attack within the Church on De Andrea not only for his implicit endorsement of liberal capitalism, but also for his acceptance of a liberal democracy which had come into being in defiance of scholastic tenets. The 'new ultramontanism' of the 1920s was echoed in a doctrinal, integral Catholicism which offered its own explanation for the crisis of democratic legitimacy which culminated in the 1930 coup. As in Europe after the First World War, these changes were assisted by the retreat of philosophical liberalism, the broad search for new (or possibly old) cultural and philosophical categories, and an incipient tension between Catholicism and both nationalism and liberalism that will mark the period as a whole.

2 The Catholic Revival, 1920s–1950s

2.1 NEOSCHOLASTICISM

Two factors were instrumental in wresting Catholicism from the complementary assumptions of clerical nationalism and the emasculated religious conceptions of the *Iglesia Nacional*. The first was the defeat of De Andrea in the archiepiscopal controversy of 1923–24. For the first time since the restoration of relations with the Vatican in the 1860s, Rome refused the government's nomination of an Archbishop, so provoking a constitutional crisis. Faithful to the regalist model, Alvear's government insisted on the state's supremacy, rejected the Vatican's nomination of the Bishop of Santa Fe, and stood by their choice of De Andrea. The see remained vacant for two years before a compromise candidate was found, during which time the opposition of those who had resisted *andreísmo* came to the fore.[1] De Andrea and his supporters later imputed Rome's opposition to the campaigns of Christian Democrats and Jesuits; but they underestimated the importance to the Vatican of restoring the doctrinal basis of Catholicism in Argentina. The rejection of De Andrea was a decisive act by the Vatican to put an end to the Gallican tendencies of the Church hierarchy. Hereafter, the way was open for integral Catholicism.

The second factor was the reflection in Argentina of the trend throughout the western world of a Catholic revival. The 1920s began to show evidence of this, but not until the 1930s did it begin to make a mark. It was accompanied by a reassertion of the scholastic conception of society and politics, in opposition to the liberal project. The two institutions most to be marked by this reassertion were the Church and the Army. If *andreísmo* had reflected the assumptions of regalism, the prevailing military view prior to the 1920s expressed the origins of the army in the 1880s. Both conceptions defended the liberal view of the state as the source of the social and political framework of the nation, relative to which Army and Church were subordinate entities. In the course of the 1920s, this conception was challenged by a revival of the notion of community, expressed in a moral, spiritual and legal framework, outside and above the state, which Army and Church existed to defend, and to which the state must conform. As this new conception began to prevail, the liberal order was increasingly seen as standing in violation of this framework; in scholastic terms, absolutism and tyranny – ruling for the benefit of the few, undelegated by the community, autonomous from a wider framework of values, and overreaching the limits of government to claim the totality of political society – automatically reverted authority to the community. The Army was the agent of this reversion, in as much as a president could only rule with military backing. The 'scholastic' military conception was therefore not that the army should intervene more, or rule in lieu of civil authority; any more than the Church, in marking the boundaries of the moral and legal framework, wished to install a theocracy. Rather, the Church released citizens from obedience to an absolutist government; the army was the agent of the reversion of sovereignty to the community.

It is important to note, however, that this 'new' conception within both Church and Army was not universal and continued to be challenged by liberal and regalist strains in both institutions. It would not be until the 1930s–1940s that the Church had come to be dominated by the Roman, integral tendencies; while the 'professional' view within the army co-existed, and would continue to co-exist, with another, equally strong, that upheld the liberal model.

The emergence of scholasticism within the Church was marked by the foundation in 1922 of the Cursos de Cultura Católica, by a teacher, Atilio Dell'Oro Maini. The CCC had their roots in the 1915 Catholic Youth Congress, which expressed frustration at the bourgeois, undoctrinal Catholicism of the leading classes. The Catholic University experiment of 1910–1920 having failed, its degrees unrecognised by the liberal state, the CCC attempted to fill the vacuum with a nationwide movement of study circles debating theology, philosophy, social doctrine and the humanities, and would be the nursery of the intellectual Catholic élite of the 1930s–1940s. Refuting the clerical and confessional social and political conceptions of De Andrea, they envisaged the training of leaders who would occupy influential functions in the public life of the nation independently of the Church. The emphasis was therefore on the training of leaders at a time when knowledge of encyclicals and doctrine was meagre. With the possession of the Lamarca library, and drawing on the latest fruits of the European *renouveau catholique*, the CCC were heavily Thomist and dogmatic, studying the origins of modern errors in the writings of the early Maritain, and the historical theses of Hilaire Belloc and Christopher Dawson.[2]

The CCC were born in the midst of the investiture controversy, and spoke out strongly against the *patronato*. In violating canon law while demanding that the Church respect state law, it was argued, the Supreme Court obliged the president legally to betray the faith which constitutionally he was obliged to profess. Throughout the history of independent Argentina, the state had sought to make the Church serve its interests. Catholics had less liberty than Jews, Protestants and Masons. Having captivated the Church, the state had violated Catholic precepts in civil marriage and education laws, while continuing to uphold the colonial and despotic *patronato* laws. Catholics must fight for union between Church and state, a union which would restore the independence and sovereignty of the Church in the spiritual sphere. If the state were to remain obstinately secularist, the Church must free itself through Church–State separation and a concordat. 'Either liberty or a concordat', the CCC concluded, 'never subservience'.[3]

Underlying the archiepiscopal investiture controversy Dell'Oro Maini saw 'the decomposition of our militant Catholicism'.[4] The task of Catholics was to reverse the decades of nominalism and ritualism, in which public life had become divorced from the precepts the country popularly proclaimed. The scholastic values at the heart of Argentine nationality had been suffocated virtually since 1810 by a minority, dogmatic liberalism. Catholics had grown accustomed to expect concessions from the state rather than lead a movement of ideas and people which the state would come to reflect. Argentina was to be 'Catholicised' in all areas of public life – social, economic, political and cultural – not by parallel or confessional unions and parties, but by laymen operating in the temporal sphere, with a sound background in doctrine.

The vehicle of this transformation was the magazine *Criterio*, which a leading group of CCC intellectuals established in 1928 to 'prepare the Catholic conscience'. Its first editorial was a manifesto of the integral–Catholic movement of the 1930s. *Criterio* was to be both popular and doctrinaire, agile and combative, 'an organ of definition' dedicated to propagating Catholic doctrine in its integrity by returning to sources. Refuting the role liberalism sought for religion, as a private matter to be conducted discreetly and ritually behind temple walls, *Criterio* declared no field of public life to be independent from the Catholic criterion.[5] The magazine's radicalism was not, however, to the taste of a number of Gallican bishops, while its resistance to official ties ran up against the attempts of shareholders to reach a broad Catholic readership.[6] After years of disputes, and in a state of bankruptcy, the magazine passed in 1932 under the control of Mgr. Franceschi, from which time it became the dominant voice of Argentine Catholicism and reflective of the new *integral* spirit of the 1930s.[7]

2.2 ECCLESIASTICAL EXPANSION

The history of Argentine Catholicism is broken by the International Eucharistic Congress of 1934. The Congress not only demonstrated the existence of 'Catholic Argentina' – in a massive expression of popular piety, which shocked and delighted onlookers – but marked the beginnings of the Church's rapid expansion in society. By the end of the decade, commentators both Catholic and non-Catholic were commenting on the religious revival, which was most marked among men, because men had been conspicuous for their nominalism.

Despite the Church's official message to delegates, that Buenos Aires was the second largest Catholic city in the world (after Paris), fecund in charitable and apostolic works, the Committee admitted that right up to the event there was little certainty of the popular response; as an organiser recalled, 'never had the people been put to such a test'.[8] The sight of the main square, flanked on both sides by the Argentine and pontifical colours, and the installation of a network of loudspeakers throughout the city centre carrying the voice of bishops, would have been unthinkable only forty years before. In the event, the week-long Congress not only passed off without disturbances, but was massively attended. Around 1,200,000 people – over a third of the city's population – received communion; seven hundred thousand women and 100,000 children communicated in the city churches on one night alone; on the same night, 400,000 men lined the immense Avenida de Mayo to receive hosts brought by underground train from the Cathedral, and to confess to hundreds of overwhelmed priests under streetlamps.[9] A priest typically recalled,

> We had calculated badly. We did not believe many men would come. The idea was that they would meet, and attend a homily by Monsignor Franceschi in the Plaza de Mayo. As it turned out, it was impossible. Nobody could move a step in any direction. Buenos Aires had never seen anything like it. The nuns made hosts the whole

afternoon, and continued the whole night. In the Cathedral, mass was said continually, without interruptions, until past dawn. The priests brought the chalices on the Avenida de Mayo underground train. I heard confessions the whole night through, on the steps of Loria station. You can't imagine it. People who hadn't confessed for over twenty, thirty years . . . people who had never confessed in their lives came to confess. I had one who, while he was confessing, I realised he wasn't baptised. And the man cried and cried because he wanted his confession to be valid. The whole night I spent resolving all sorts of cases, things I had never imagined, and to sharpen my abilities to deal with situations that not even all the casuistics of the courses in Rome had prepared me for. And right there we heard confessions, and gave communion too, because nobody could move one step. . .[10]

The Eucharistic Congress came to symbolise what was later described as a revolution, rolling back the tide of laicism and indifference, and beginning an era of 'reCatholicization'. The formerly exclusive identification of mass attendance with womanhood began to be broken. Throughout the 1930s, priests reported men confessing and communicating after long years of absence, and evidence points to a rapid and sustained increase in mass attendance. The growth of outward religious expression was most marked among the young, tens of thousands of whom in the course of the decade enrolled in Catholic Action [Table I.3, Appendix I] and related organisations following its foundation in 1931. Where in the rationalist university climate of the turn of the century, youth had been 'privately' religious, if at all, by the 1940s a substantial proportion of middle-class youth was made up of Catholic activists. 'No young person is today ashamed to proclaim he is Catholic', *Criterio* noted in 1942. '[Our young] are ready to . . . take communion as readily in the street as in church, [and] to raise their heads without pride . . . but fearlessly'.[11] Catholic Action Youth Rallies often brought together 5–10,000 delegates in various provincial cities, and marches of five times that number.[12] As elsewhere in Latin America, ACA was unmatched for sheer numbers and capacity of organisation. The figures do not take into account the varying commitment of members, some of whom might be active members in dynamic parishes, others less so. The training and preparation of members was however both long and comprehensive, and therefore precluded nominal adherence. At the same time, the figures underestimate the 'various hundreds of thousands of adherents in their respective affiliated organizations', who did not undergo the rigorous preparation of a militant, but who belonged to any number of Church groups and societies.[13]

Catholic Action was the 'long arm of the episcopate', the extension of the formal Church into the secular world. Its objective was to 'Christianise' society in factory, office and home by galvanising apathetic Catholics into loyalty to the Church and its doctrines.[14] ACA's creation and rapid growth was a major factor in the reversal of the secularizing spiral of the nineteenth and early twentieth centuries, in which the Church was increasingly unable to satisfy the sacramental and spiritual needs of an expanding population, and was 'pushed back' by the secularist outlook of the state. The result of the secularizing spiral was that early twentieth-century society claimed to be religious, and to be a believer was after 1930 a respectable matter; yet while organized atheism was a restricted, intellectual affair, indifference was widespread. Behind the systematic atheism of the Left and positivist nationalism lay the persistence of nineteenth-century scientism; but for most Argentines atheism was 'practical', by default. Because most Argentines were *fronterizos* – unconsciously Catholic and potentially secularist – the example and values of institutions and work environments were crucial. Catholic Action's task was to achieve a presence for the Church in wider society by 'spiritualising' the climate, to bring down the barriers to *fronterizos* returning to the Church. The work of Catholic Action and an increase in priests and churches therefore contributed mutually to the increase in Catholicity.

The Church's institutional expansion also dates from the year of the Eucharistic Congress. The creation of ten dioceses in 1934 doubled their number and halved their surface area. Diocesan expansion for the first time ran ahead of population, which grew by a third in the period 1930–1960, despite an interregnum in the Peronist period [Table I.4, Appendix I]. At the parish level, however, the increase in vocations managed only to keep pace with population expansion, such that the ratio of inhabitants per priest in 1960, including both secular and regular clergy, showed little improvement over that of 1947 (1947: 4,512/1; 1960: 4,231/1). Spain in this period had one priest per thousand inhabitants, and France around one in two thousand. Chile had twice as many as Argentina, while Ecuador, Colombia and Uruguay all had more. Discounting the monastic population, in the city of Buenos Aires at the end of the 1930s 270 priests catered to a population of 2,360,000: around one secular priest per 8,400 inhabitants. Despite similarities in size, Buenos Aires did not reach the number of parishes in Paris in 1802 until 1955. In the interior, the size of the parishes remained the worst on the continent. Argentina's physiognomy remained an obstacle; the average does not take into account the immense difference between the barren, scrubland parishes of Patagonia, where a parish could stretch over 20–30,000 square kilometres, and those of prosperous and populated areas – Buenos Aires, Santa Fe and La Plata – where it rarely exceeded 1,000 square kilometres. Hence, while parishes were enormous, their populations were around the Latin-American average of 15,000, showing considerable improvement in the first half of the twentieth century. The ecclesiastical expansion nevertheless remained an urban phenomenon: although its population tripled in the years 1911–54, the population per parish in Buenos Aires was halved.[15]

To a large extent, however, technology assisted the Church in overcoming the obstacles of geography. At the Eucharistic Congress, a chain of transmitters enabled mass to be heard through nineteen radio stations nationwide. Thereafter, radio regularly brought the Church to audiences in the open spaces. The fundamental problems of infrastructure however remained. Protestant missionaries – often supported by wealthy North American Bible organisations – continued to take advantage of constitutional liberties to fill the gaps left by the Church. The activities of Rural Catholic Action were perforce restricted to those of basic instruction, or to providing radios for distant villages to enable them to hear mass. Low levels of literacy conspired against autonomous organisations, and farmers were rarely near enough priests to receive guidance. Rural activists nevertheless praised 'apostolic impulses verging on heroism', which they found in the interior, which contrasted with the cynicism and individualism of *porteños*. It was this simple country piety which in the 1930s–1940s arrived with the flow of migrants to the industrial belt of Buenos Aires.[16]

This internal migration – which had begun by 1930, and increased steadily throughout the decade – was one of the major factors behind the prodigious expansion of the Church in towns and cities. The expansion can be measured not just in terms of buildings. Among the first regular broadcasting stations was the Church-owned Radio Ultra, which began transmissions in 1936; and Mgr. Franceschi's weekly allocution on Radio Splendid in the 1930s was the single most popular radio programme of the era. Street meetings and demonstrations, megaphones and loudspeaker vans were all symptomatic of a claim on public space. Publications grew prodigiously in both number and circulation; the nationwide Catholic daily *El Pueblo* and the intellectual weekly, *Criterio*, were the major 'semi-official' national publications at the head of a gamut of local publications and newspapers (notably in Córdoba) in Catholic hands. To the established presses owned mostly by the religious orders were added new, lay publishing companies, of which the largest, Editorial Difusión, between 1936 and 1942, sold six million books from a catalogue of 622 titles, and would continue expanding until closed by Perón.[17]

Advances into academe however ran up against both the anticlerical legacy of the University Reform Movement and state secularism. The Catholic University established in 1910 closed again ten years later, its degrees unrecognised by the state. This shortfall was to some extent countered by the printing press, by study circles and 'Universidades Populares' in working-class areas, and by the presence of Catholic intellectuals in Academies. The Courses of Catholic Culture in 1922 were designed to compensate for the lack of a university, and much of Argentina's Catholic élite was to emerge from its ranks. The Junta de Historia Eclesiástica Argentina from 1942 sought to rescue the role of the Church in Argentine history, and to counter the 'black legends' of liberal historiography. Permission to found Catholic universities was not granted until 1958. The first of these was the Jesuit-controlled University of Córdoba, followed by the Universidad del Salvador, and the Universidad Católica of Buenos Aires. A number of others were founded in the following years in provincial towns.

The links between Church and nation encouraged by the Junta de Historia Eclesiástica were reinforced by the nationalist revision of Argentine history, one of the effects of which was to rescue the scholastic assumptions of independence. The links were also increasingly strong with the Army, where the increased presence of the Church was evident in field masses, army chaplains, the blessing of swords issued to graduates of military academies, and the frequent proclamations of loyalty to patron saints. Equally, the presence of the Army in major Church events (most especially the Eucharistic Congress of 1934, when seven thousand soldiers received communion on their knees) became common. The Catholic revival, coterminous with the coming of age of the 'new classes', coincided with the increased involvement of the military in public life. Although the 1930 coup was devoid of references to the Church, the 1943 *pronunciamiento* made explicit Catholic references in the regalist tradition; while the Lonardi administration was placed under the Virgin's protection. A graph representing the inclusion of key Catholic words in military pronouncements would show a sharp upward trend throughout the period 1930–1960.[18]

The social proximity of the Church to the 'new classes' – children of immigrants, seeking integration, and the internal migrants – was strongly to mark the Catholic revival. In comparison with the rest of Latin America, Argentina had a high proportion of native-born clergy: around half in 1947. Because foreign priests generally came from Spain and Italy, and because the majority of the native-born clergy were children of immigrants, the Church in Argentina reflected wider integration patterns. Although we lack detailed research on the social and national origins of priests, the study by De Imaz of the social profile of Argentine bishops in this period is a useful indication of the clergy as a whole. The average bishop in the 1960 episcopate was born between 1890 and 1910, in a rural small town, the son of an immigrant farmer (*colono*, aspiring to be *arrendatario*), probably Piedmontese or Basque. Only eight per cent of bishops were foreign-born, fifteen per cent were sons of 'native' (creole) Argentines, and an overwhelming seventy-seven per cent were sons of immigrants. The traditional Argentine families produced few bishops (five, all from Córdoba). Eighteen were from 'middle-class' families, and another eighteen from worker families.[19] This picture is at odds with even specialised studies, which often assume a close correlation between the higher clergy and large landowning families.[20]

The Church in fact recruited from humble families long before other national institutions (administration, law, medicine, industry), and even the Army – that other avenue of social mobility for the immigrant's son – was more exclusive. Only a third of the officer corps of the late 1920s were first-generation Argentines, and over half came from traditional families; officers of worker origin were all but unknown.[21] Because the Argentine landed classes surrendered few of its sons to either Church or Army (preferring law, business, banking, estate management and politics) it was easier for the Catholic revival expressly to refute the ideological identification of Church with privilege made by the left. This sociological characteristic of the Catholic revival also underlies many of the social and political cleavages which would emerge in the 1930s, between the 'Catholic and national' lower and middle classes of the 1930s–1940s, and the 'liberal and cosmopolitan' landowning (but predominantly urban) bourgeoisie.

For the urban middle classes, the connection with the Church was principally that of education. Because the 1884 secular education law had excluded the Church from state schools, Catholic education was perforce private. Around three-quarters of the private schools in 1943 were run by the Church; the remaining quarter was made up of Protestant, Jewish and 'ethnic' schools. In 1918, one out of five secondary students were privately educated; by 1943, the year religious education was restored to state schools, the figure had risen to two out of five. By 1958, 52 per cent of pupils were privately-educated; from 45 per cent in 1955, the student body in Catholic *escuelas normales* had risen by 1958 to nearly 70 per cent of the national total.[22] In the 1930s–1940s, however, Catholic private schools stood in contrast to the social identification of the Church with Argentina's new groups. Traditionally agnostic creole leading classes (with the exception of a number of leading families in 'old' provinces such as Córdoba) contrasted not only with the faith of the immigrant classes, but also with that of creole families in the interior. Anthologies compiled in the 1930s of popular song demonstrated the persistence of popular piety, even in areas of low institutional Church presence.[23] By contrast, the twentieth-century offshoots of nineteenth-century secularism – liberalism and socialism – were associated with small sectors of the urban middle classes.

2.3 ARGENTINE CATHOLICITY

The question, how Catholic was Argentina in 1930–1960? raises a host of difficulties of definition and methodology. It can be answered by applying three tests, beginning with the weakest (self-identification, entailing no active belief), progressing to an option in favour of religious education for children (suggesting a degree of identification with dogmatic Catholic teaching), and concluding with sacramental participation (involving an active expression of belief) of various kinds.

A comparison of the comprehensive surveys of religious affiliation conducted by the national censuses between 1895 and 1947 [Table I.5, Appendix I] allows us to assess shifts in Catholic self-identification. The apparent decline of six per cent is made problematic by the method of the 1895 census, which asked, 'if you are not Catholic, what is your religion?' – thereby excluding agnostics. It is therefore probable that the 1895 figure is inflated, although the reduction in the number of self-declared Catholics in 1947 also reflects the growth of immigration from northern Europe since 1895. There were some variations between provinces in 1947. Catamarca and La Rioja, for example, showed the greatest proportion of Catholics (over 99 per cent) in contrast to areas of concentrated Protestant settlement in the south where Chubut, for example, showed 83 per cent. In the Federal Capital, where agnosticism and Jewish and Protestant presences were higher than anywhere else in the country, the figure still stood at just under 90 per cent of respondents declaring themselves Catholic.

The restoration of religious education to primary and secondary state schools in 1943 is a better indication of Catholicity than self-identification, for it allowed any parents who did not wish their children to be given a Catholic moral education to opt for a non-dogmatic morality class of the sort imposed by the state in the late nineteenth century. The figures demonstrate at least that the vast majority of Argentines preferred Catholic education to non-dogmatic alternatives. The overall take-up rate is one or two percentage points lower than self-identification, which is comprehensible given the exclusion of private schools from the statistics. The tables [Table I.6, Appendix I] demonstrate three characteristics of the relation of religion to province: first, the most densely populated provinces were overwhelmingly Catholic, and with the exception of the Federal Capital, never went below ninety per cent. Second, the highest proportion of non-Catholics were found in sparsely-populated southern areas where the concentration of Protestants was high. Thirdly, the figure for the Federal Capital (85.5 per cent) reflects the higher level of positive agnosticism as well as the presence of non-Catholic immigrant communities.

Sacramental participation was far lower than either nominal adherence or preference for religious education. Regular mass attendance in the 'agnostic city' of Buenos Aires was estimated in 1945 at around 25 to 30 per cent.[24] Also lower was the marriage sacrament, but this statistic is complicated by the civil marriage law of 1888, which made marriage in church without first marrying before the state a crime. By stipulating a medical certificate (which demanded travel and expense), the civil marriage law discouraged country people from a civil marriage, thereby precluding a sacramental wedding. Alejandro Bunge's important study in 1940 concluded that if legal recognition were restored to canonical marriage, missionaries and priests could halve the illegitimacy rate within a few years (although he also showed a strong link between illegitimacy and poverty, and similarly between illegitimacy and infant mortality).[25] Taking into account the singularity of obligatory civil marriage, which undermines the eloquence of church wedding figures, the statistics [Table I.7,

Appendix I] nevertheless register a substantial increase. Under half of those calling themselves Catholic in the 1920s chose to have a sacramental wedding after a civil ceremony. By the 1940s, that figure stood at over 70 per cent. This increase may be interpreted either as evidence of the potency of the Catholic revival, or as testimony to the greater accessibility of churches, or both. Birth rates remained low, and were declining in the course of the period: down from 40 per 1000 inhabitants at the turn of the century to 23 in 1944, expressing in part the socioeconomic ambitions of immigrants, yet evincing an unmistakable relation between declining birth rate and poverty. Nearly 40 per cent of worker families had one child only and 30 per cent two children. These figures pointed to insecurity and instability in both marriage and employment, and would be the focus of Catholic social concern.[26]

2.4 THE DISCOURSE OF INTEGRAL CATHOLICISM

Respectful of the Catholic revival, the liberal–conservative government, restored in 1932, was quick to identify with the Church. General Justo closed the Eucharistic Congress with a public expression of piety, and thereafter sought to include prelates at state banquets and ceremonies. Although the government did nothing to abolish the main clauses of the *patronato*, in the large diocesan expansion of 1934 which he sponsored, Justo nevertheless acknowledged the exclusive jurisdiction of Rome in ecclesiastical appointments and the delineation of diocesan boundaries – an acknowledgement which solicited a respectful Bull from the Vatican. These apertures encouraged the nascent Catholic movement. Moves were initiated throughout Argentina to restore religious education in primary schools; social encyclicals were discussed in provincial legislatures; and bishops and priests began to be consulted and pastoral letters commented.[27]

But while the left – which kept up the secularist discourse of the late nineteenth century, after its abandonment by liberal–conservatives – was anxious to see in this renewed public presence indications of 'clericalism', Church–state cordiality obscured the essentially antiestablishment character of the Catholic revival. Integral Catholicism was nourished by two traditional protests: on the one hand that of the Catholic Union's political critique in the 1880s, the legacy of which was revived in the 1920s by the CCC; and on the other, by the denunciation of the social consequences of economic liberalism by the social-

Catholic movement of the 1890–1920 period. Yet it was above all the model of 'fortress Catholicism', characteristic of the preconciliar Church in Europe from the mid-nineteenth to the mid-twentieth century, which was to nourish Argentine Catholicism after 1930.

The arrival of this model has to be placed in the context of the decline of the liberal–regalist *Iglesia Nacional*, upheld by Mgr. De Andrea and Archbishop Espinoza in the 1910s–1920s. The Gallican conception complemented the liberal–regalist view of the Church as a voluntary association, supported by the state, with its functions clearly defined and demarcated by the powerful groups within society. It was a conception fundamentally challenged by integral Catholicism. Where *andreísmo* had been culturally agnostic, blending Church and tradition, integral Catholicism looked to a 'new', 'authentic' culture, which it saw as lying in the scholastic framework suppressed by generations of liberalism. Rather than seeking to blend Church with society, integral Catholicism sought to reform society in line with Catholic doctrines. Instead of accepting that the Church's social function was to alleviate the harsh consequences of the free market, integral Catholicism demanded that the economic structures must themselves be transformed in the light of Church social doctrine. Where *andreísmo* accepted a subordinate role within the spiritual–temporal hierarchy, integral Catholicism sought to recover the spiritual supremacy and autonomy of the Church. Where, in the 1910s–1920s, the hierarchy saw itself as an autonomous organisation within a liberal and pluralistic society, sponsoring its own organisations (hospitals, unions) of a confessional character, the bishops of the 1930s, by contrast, sought to 'Catholicize' pre-existing organisations, so that the basis of society itself was Catholic, thus dispensing with the need for confessional groups.

The legacy of *andreísmo* in the 1930s were the confessional union federations, the Workers' Circles and the female employees' FACE. Both continued to be important Church organisations, but the model on which they were based was not *integral*. De Andrea would remain the central, unifying figure of the minority 'liberal' wing of Catholicism, associated with the Buenos Aires upper-middle classes, favouring class reconciliation within liberal democracy by means of socio-economic legislation and mutualism. Since the late 1920s, De Andrea had conceded preeminence to other bishops whose social origins and ultramontanism reflected the transformation of the Church in Argentina in this period. The new bishops – there were twice as many in the mid-1930s as ten years before – were now closely associated with Catholic Action and the new spirit of *Criterio*, from both of which De Andrea would remain marginalised.[28]

Integral Catholicism was associated with the new Argentine social classes: the children of immigrants, and the internal migrants who arrived from the interior, alien to the bourgeois agnosticism of Buenos Aires. For these arrivals, previously marginalised by nationality and geography, the Church furnished the means of social integration and articulation otherwise denied them. Political exclusion heightened loyalty to the Church, and provided a means of contesting that exclusion; while the restoration of fraudulent democracy and the growing significance of the social question appeared to vindicate the late nineteenth-century Catholic critique of liberalism. These classes had never been 'liberal' in as much as they were always outside the liberal project. But they were not the only groups who would fuel the Catholic revival. Much of the urban middle class (especially in Buenos Aires) would also turn to the faith of their youth faced with the perceived failure of Positivism.[29] For these groups, the collapse of the liberal order was a *desengaño*, which no longer permitted the 'sensual dreams' of an expanding economy to disguise 'the slavery of the social majority'.[30] Looking back on the nineteenth and early twentieth centuries at the Eucharistic Congress, Mons. Franceschi recalled that 'we preached, if not in the desert, then among enemies'; now, War and economic depression had put paid to 'a materialist optimism which prevented people from seeing the deep realities'.[31]

Integral Catholicism was defined by Pope Pius XI in his instructions to Argentine Catholic Action to 'concentrate all efforts into ensuring that the integral life of the Republic be regulated by Christian principles'.[32] These principles were not only those of the state and law, but of workplace, office and school. 'Integral' firstly therefore meant 'whole', in contrast to the 'partial', or 'diluted' religious conception espoused by liberals, both secular and Catholic. The attachment of the adjective 'integral' did not imply to its users an alternative form of Catholicism, but the *authentic* religion, safeguarded by Rome. Indeed, the term 'liberal Catholic' was one of opprobrium, loosely applied to those who sought through bad faith or religious superficiality to reconcile Church doctrine with liberal individualism, laissez-faire capitalism and the subordination of morality to individual will. It was deemed necessary constantly to demonstrate to the everyday agnostic or liberal that what he saw as compatible with the Church was not. Nominal religiosity was scorned as the 'rose-water faith' of the *santurrones* (sanctimonious) and *beatones* (showily pious); Argentines who restricted their faith to the duration of Sunday mass, were *pitucos* (toffs) or *católicos de domingo* (Sunday Catholics). These *católicos liberales* were considered synonymous with the bourgeois order of individualism and social disintegration, with pious bosses who underpaid workers.[33]

Against the tradition of *andreísmo*, associated strongly with charitably-minded *damas* and *beatas*, integral Catholicism asserted a revised notion of womanhood. Catholic women now scorned the bourgeois 'tradition of superficiality, in which the decorative and frivolous predominate, of ignorance of the great moral and social problems of the day and very often a lamentable lack of broad, universal ideas'. This tradition was associated with women's surrender to the liberal–bourgeois male; but equally the women's branch of Catholic Action rejected feminism – the 'false rigours' and 'erroneous spirit of emulation' – in favour of 'the path indicated for her by God: that of maternity; material, spiritual and supernatural'. This conception of womanhood appealed not to an allegedly novel type but rather to 'the strong and just ideas' of pre-modern female civic participation. The powerful medieval female archetype was counterposed to the modern liberal view of woman as sentimental and decorative among the middle classes, and slave without rights in the lower.[34]

Integral Catholicism also refuted the liberal–Gallican notions of 'tradition' and 'patriotism' by speaking instead of 'nationality'. The reference point of nationality was the scholastic framework of society – widespread, submerged, omnipresent, violated, and now resuscitated in the hands of newly-articulate classes contesting the liberal hegemony. Reflecting the 'integrating spirit' of Catholic immigrants was therefore a 'counter-nation', one which refuted the technocratic values of the liberal project. 'We believe in a new youth,' proclaimed Catholic Action, 'that is profoundly Argentine because it responds to the purest Christian tradition of the fatherland'.[35] To be Catholic was to be close to the underlying spirit of Argentina; to be truly Argentine was to recover the Christian heritage suppressed by liberalism and rationalism; religious unity was synonymous with national unity. The nation was a spiritual community, a *corpus mysticum*.[36]

At the International Eucharistic Congress, the visiting Archbishop of Toledo lent historical weight to this idea by depicting Latin American independence as a Catholic protest against the encyclopaedic deism of the French rationalists then usurping the Spanish throne. Catholicism was therefore at the heart of Argentine nationality, as part of an older spiritual unity with Spain.[37] It followed that the task for Catholics, as Mgr. Franceschi argued at the Congress, was not therefore one of *converting* Argentina like latter-day missionaries, but rather of calling upon society to accept the undiluted, all-embracing implications of the faith it nominally professed and which lay at the heart of its nationality. The country was already 'incorporated into Christ', in three ways: in its 'authority', or leaders collectively considered; in its laws; and in its customs and social values. That in Argentine history civil and ecclesiastical powers had clashed, that governments had acted in an unChristian fashion, did not negate the reality of this incorporation. Secularists, he argued, had often exaggerated Catholic arguments; governments had retained a Catholic element sufficient to produce reactions against the dechristianised state; above all, the state had retained an overt identification with the Church.[38] By implication – and this would be stated with ever greater force in the course of the decade – it was the political classes who had resisted this reality, bobbing on the surface of a society they barely recognised.

The focal point of Church organisation, and the nursery of many future political leaders, was Catholic Action, which replaced the UPCA and became the new model of integral Catholicism. With the support of a rapidly-expanding network of parishes through which it spread with astonishing speed, ACA was more widely present nationwide than the political parties. No organisation of the time could match its vitality nor youthful composition; few rivalled its publishing output; and none was capable of mobilising such large numbers. Only the diminutive Communist movement could match it for loyalty, discipline and youthful vitality, yet was incapable of ACA's huge federal assemblies. ACA also resembled a communist movement in its possession of a coherent, 'total' ideology, its *método propio* of penetration, and its sense of mission. But rather than ushering its members into rigid structures regimented from above, the emphasis was on making each militant a leader. Hence, although in matters of doctrine and discipline, obedience to episcopal and especially papal authority was stressed to what would later appear a remarkable extent, organisation was highly decentralised. Militants belonged to small, semi-autonomous, parish 'centres' responsible for their own organisation and expansion. ACA's tangential expansion linked together interlocking circles, which collectively reinforced the sensation of the 'Mystical Body' as a tangible reality. It was made visible in vast federal assemblies, when provincial cities would be occupied for days at a time amidst speeches and outdoor masses celebrated in main squares.[39]

The effectiveness of Catholic Action lay not only in its structure but in the rigour of its training. Regular prayer, communion, confession, spiritual exercises and readings, a thorough knowledge of Church social doctrine, liturgy and encyclicals and a five-month pre-membership trial, all formed part of a militant's preparation. There were then three stages: *discussion* of strategy, in which doctrine would be matched to specific tasks; *penetration* of the militant's environment (whether school, office or factory); and *formation* of a circle, of as broad a social composition as possible. Although Argentine Catholic Action reflected the Italian model, based on parishes and cadres (rather than specialised branches, as in France), there were particular groups in schools and universities, notably the combative and apologetic *Propagandista* group inspired by that of Herrera in Spain. ACA also offered the largest summer camp network of the time, as well as 'tent missions' taken to poor suburbs of Buenos Aires, to prepare them for the reception of churches. All the branches – youth and adult, men and women – ran a chain of reviews and articles, and published their own books and guides. Women were especially active. In a period when women were barred from university, and still without the vote, ACA's study centres, academies, and teaching institutes were vigorous centres promoting an expressive civic role for women and campaigning for female suffrage and just wages. The Men's Branch (HAC), in contrast to that of Young Men, was the smallest and least productive, reflecting the traditional male reluctance to manifestations of piety and Catholic militancy. But it was in many ways the most influential, embracing professional consortia of doctors, lawyers, architects and economists, many of whom occupied posts in local administration. Its influence was especially strong in Córdoba, where it operated a string of middle-class clubs and associations.[40]

Argentine Catholic Action also reflected the intransigence and self-discipline of its counterpart in Italy, where loyalty to the hierarchy – *Nile Sine Episcopo* – and a unity of action and method were necessary to resist the total claims of fascism. ACA promoted spiritual loyalties incompatible with any other.[41] In this way, the organisation and structure of Catholic Action reflected and reinforced the discourse of integral Catholicism, the major enemy of which was the dilution of Christianity through laicism. At the root of social injustice, fraudulent democracy, individualism and the disintegration of society was the divorce of Church and society. The solution to these problems lay in neither palliative reforms nor philosophical innovations nor an autocratic state, but in breaching the divorce between ostensible faith and practical belief. It was an objective that had to begin by uprooting the pervasive naturalism and individualism that had followed on from the disintegration of the Christian Order, as a result of which the Church had been rendered compatible with secular beliefs, doctrines and interests. Integral Catholicism therefore looked back to an ill-defined point prior to secularisation, at which Catholic values permeated matters held in the modern world to be independent of religion.

The radical, minority wing of integral Catholicism was informed by antimodernism: a philosophy of regret which posited the three 'R's (Reformation, Renaissance and Revolution) as tending ultimately towards totalitarianism and the destruction of western civilization. The expositions of Argentina's most influential antimodernist, Fr. Julio Meinvielle, offered a compelling, and equally historicist, counter-dialectic to that of Marxism. But for most Catholics of the time, Meinvielle was too dualistic and Augustinian, prone to facile explanations of modern ills, especially (influenced by Belloc) in relation to Jews.[42] The mainstream Catholic movement looked to a future spiritual rather than a temporal–historical era. In the youthful, triumphalist, popular spirit of Catholic Action, there was little evidence of antimodern romanticism, and Hispanism was harder to grasp for an Italian immigrant or provincial creole than it was for a second-generation *gallego*, especially at a time when those of Spanish origin sought to demonstrate their patriotic Argentine loyalties. The Catholic movement was seen by most militants as a revolution, a modern struggle, to *instaurar todo en Cristo*, to found a nation from its scholastic ingredients. It held itself to be neither an innovation nor a restoration, but a combination of both: a return to sources, to the essence of faith and mystical truth, in order to transform modernity from within.[43]

Integral Catholicism was therefore a model of engagement with modern society which sought to transform it without in the process compromising the Church or watering down the substance of Catholic belief. Throughout the 1930s and 1940s, there are continual reminders from bishops and leaders to militants that a Catholic could not be a liberal, nor a conservative, nor a socialist, nor a communist, nor an adherent to 'extreme' nationalism (the nation conceived in terms of absolute authority and unlimited sovereignty). Insofar as any of these doctrines possessed elements of truth, they demonstrated the persistence of Christian elements in secular philosophies. But as ideologies, as cosmovisions, they were founded on anthropocentric philosophical conceptions ultimately incompatible with Catholic dogma:

> The true solution of the modern crisis lies in *integral Catholicism*, and not in adaptation of conceptions of heterodox origin. Let it be us [who advance this solution]; let us not ask of others what is ours. Above all, let us have the patience to *prepare* the way.[44]

This ambition carried profound implications for the political, social and economic order, but could not be identified with any particular political movement. The directives of the hierarchy, as well as the lengthy and influential weekly editorials of *Criterio*'s editor, Mgr Franceschi, simultaneously stressed both Catholicism's independence from secular forces and its relevance to every field of national life. The Church could not be harnessed to politics, and even less to a political party. Rather, political parties should recognize the scholastic framework of society. This framework was recognized by the new classes demanding political and economic participation and an end to liberal hegemony. The political parties could only ignore that framework at the expense of upheaval.[45]

2.5 SOCIAL CATHOLICISM BEFORE PERÓN

Liberals had for decades proclaimed the purpose of the Church to be exclusively that of leading souls to heaven; Christianity therefore had no relevance to 'pragmatic' socioeconomic issues. The 'rational' sphere of society – politics, law, the economy, society itself – was held to be separate from spiritual values. The consequence of this laicism, in the Catholic view, was the divorce of the economy from morality, so that considerations of wage and employment conditions were guided not by human and moral ends but by those of the allegedly scientific (autonomous) laws of the market. The exclusion of the Church from society led to the suppression of the human purpose of the economy; this in turn led to class hostility. The first step towards the Christianization of the economy was therefore the loss of that blind faith in deterministic market laws. Neither free competition nor the market would by themselves produce either greater overall wealth or more equitable distribution. The underlying strength of any economy lay in the spread of private property through just wages. For this to come about, the state needed to intervene with a view not to absorb but actively to correct social and economic imbalances.[46]

Catholics were especially concerned to confront the liberal-bourgeois notion of charity as a substitute for justice. Where liberals saw charity as a valid method of compensating for distortions in the market, integral Catholics saw the problem of unjust distribution as primarily one of the right ordering of production. Used as a palliative for injustice, such 'false love of the poor' as *Criterio* termed it, was the sweetener used to disguise the bitter pill of an unjust order. A sandalmaker who in spite of hard labour was unable to feed herself and her family was in need not of alms but of a just wage. Charity should *supplement* justice, not claim to be a substitute for it; charity, in the papal definition, was the spirit of justice in particular, 'abnormal' circumstances. If charity was needed to bring men's standards of living up to 'normal', it was not charity:

> *Normally* a man should not need charity, he should be able to look after his home and his family without sending them to shelters or receiving milk and meat tokens; he should be able to dress himself and them without needing to receive hand-outs; he should be able to cultivate his intelligence; what is more, he should be able by means of modest savings to satisfy the desire of all one day to own their own home.[47]

In the place of unfettered free-market capitalism supplemented by charity, Catholics promoted an alternative socioeconomic model drawn from *Rerum Novarum* and *Quadragesimo Anno*. A balanced economy was sought, based on 'institutions in which the individual escapes on the one hand the inorganic dispersion of anarchy, and on the other absorption by the state'.[48] Capital and labour, divorced by the 'libertarian' economic revolution, must be re-united. Work could not be separated from the worker, for labour was destined to satisfy in the first place his material needs and security, and in the second to enhance his human development. Capital should ideally therefore be in the same hands as labour; falling short of that, the state must be able to restrict the freedom of capital to prevent it working against these human objectives.[49]

A strong and active state was considered necessary to resist the pressure of trust capitalism on government; but any possibility of the state absorbing the means of production was rejected. The solution lay in an economy of smallholdings and small businesses, which the state should actively encourage without itself actually creating, through minimum wage legislation and credit facilities. Subdivision of land was a matter of urgency, to be effected with a view to productivity and the principle of owner-occupation. These measures would stimulate the 'natural', 'organic' growth of businesses, guilds and owner-occupied farms, as encouraged by *Quadragesimo Anno*, without incurring the dangers of the Italian fascist 'vertical state corporatism' which the encyclical condemned. In the second, fascist, case, the state itself established, owned and administered the corporations, erroneously transferring, like communism, the ownership of capital to the state. In the first case, the state encouraged the emergence of a smallholder economy through state checks on monopoly capital and the introduction of judicious legislation. The right ordering of production would then emerge, encouraged but not engineered by the state.[50]

Underlying the refutation of both liberalism and socialism was the Thomist conception of the person: the individual conceived in relation to 'lesser societies'. Man was both free and social, and hence should be neither regimented by the state nor divorced from his natural associations by trust capital. The means of production should remain independent of the state to ensure economic flexibility and to encourage creativity, and should ideally be concentrated in the hands of workers. Salary levels could not be exclusively determined by market laws, but should conform to a higher standard of justice, expressed in the family wage, sufficient for the worker to save towards owning his own property, as well as to meet the 'primordial needs' of his entourage. There were times when companies needed to reduce wages in order to survive economic slowdowns; the retention of this flexibility was vital, and pointed to the need for workers to be included in the management structure.

Although Catholic social thought remained strongly influenced by the guild idea, in the 1930s worker trade unions capable of bargaining effectively with management were advocated, and the government much criticised for refusing to endorse and encourage unions through legislation. Alongside worker associations with capital, Catholic Action with the blessing of bishops promoted unions created for the sole purpose of bargaining with employers, thus reviving the LDC priorities. Unions (*sindicatos*) were seen as the major instrument for achieving just wages in modern capitalist societies, and should be encouraged and protected by the state, while avoiding state control. The ideal was for a central union body, sufficiently united to confront capital, but which would safeguard internal pluralism, and which was independent of both political parties and the state. It was a concept better defined in practical terms in the mid-1940s, but would remain frustrated, initially by liberal resistance to the very notion of trade unions, and later by Perón, who sought to tie them to the state.[51]

Social Catholicism was promoted by the Socio-Economic Secretariat of Catholic Action, founded in 1934 under the directorship of the economist Francisco Valsecchi, with advice and guidance from Jesuits in the Catholic Institute in Paris and from the International Labour Office in Geneva. The Secretariat was well financed, and included a number of influential priests, among whom were the ubiquitous Mgr. Franceschi and the Spanish Jesuit Gabriel Palau, founder in Spain in 1907 of Popular Social Action, and *persona non grata* there.[52] The Secretariat was a combination of research institute, propaganda office and lobby, with access to a team of specialists, advisers, lawyers and researchers. Its effectiveness lay in its recourse to the Catholic Action and parish network, and it would concentrate heavily on lobbying government. Socio-economic instructors were established throughout the ACA network. Study centres were opened. An information office made available existing but often scarcely-known social legislation to employers and workers. A family wage scheme, in which salaries were geared towards the number of children, was implemented by some conglomerations (among which were CADE and SIAM Di Tella) as well as a host of smaller firms. Texts, encyclicals and summaries of European social thought were published, and courses and conferences — most notably the large and influential *Semanas Sociales* — were organised. Leaflets in simple and direct language [Appendix II], directed especially at workers, were distributed via ACA's socio-economic delegates nationwide outside factories, stations and social clubs. The leaflets reached towns and cities in the interior via the parish network, where they were reproduced by delegates in newspapers, read over local radios, and discussed in churches and in street conferences. The blame for social conditions was placed squarely at the feet of liberal capitalism, while workers were urged to refute the efforts of communists.[53]

The second sphere of the Secretariat's activity was the promotion of social laws. Surveys were carried out and blueprints for legislation drawn up by means of the Catholic Action parish network.[54] In 1936, ACA supported Senator Sánchez Sorondo's bill granting enlarged police powers for the suppression of communism, but was critical of the government's lack of positive action in attacking the underlying causes of 'social unrest, widespread injustice and abuse, and the sufferings of the working classes'. ACA urged ten immediate measures:

a law granting state protection to trade unions; arbitration tribunals; extension of the minimum wage to embrace the family wage; extra wage protection for large families; improvements in housing, and cheap housing initiatives; subsidies on essential foodstuffs and clothing; obligatory social security legislation; unemployment assistance; and subdivision of large farm estates.[55] None were taken up by Congress.

The third area of the Secretariat's activities was the promotion of unions and worker associations. Success in this field remained slight compared with the gains of the left in this period: in 1941, shortly before the foundation of the Catholic Worker Youth, only a sixth of all unions were explicitly Catholic [Table 2.1]. The Bishop of Rosario exaggerated only slightly when he lamented, at the end of the 1930s, that 'unions have escaped a Christian direction'.[56] The major successes remained female unions. Of these, the most important was the Seamstresses' Union founded by Catholic Action in the mid-1930s, which came to embrace seventeen thousand women nationwide. The SAOC joined forces with the existing Catholic womens' union federation, the FACE (Federación de Asociaciones Católicas de Empleadas), and the socialist FOV (Federación Obrera del Vestido), to form *comisiones paritarias* which established prices and work conditions for all members. For fourteen years, until the clash with Peronism, the three syndicates made joint representations to the labour authorities. The result of this collaboration was the joint socialist-Catholic *Ley de Trabajo a Domicilio* of 1941, which established eight-hour days, Sunday rest, paid vacations and accident insurance. It was the second major example of socialist-Catholic co-operation in the passage of legislation of the century, and the only major example of Catholic success before 1943 in persuading an obdurate Congress to pass social laws.[57]

Table 2.1   Unionised workers in 1941

Non-Catholic		Catholic	
Communist (CGT)	271,510	CCO/FACE	61,500
Autonomous	118,980	Independent *sindicatos*	8,709
Syndicalist (USA)	26,980		
Total	417,470		70,209

Source: IIIa Semana Social de Estudios Sociales Organizada por la Acción Católica, Buenos Aires, 1945, p. 208.

The history of the foundation of the Seamstresses' Union illustrates the strengths of the Catholic unionisation strategy and obversely its weakness in attracting male industrial workers. After studying the principles and methods of syndical formation, the 'El Centavo' group (staffed by AJAC members) established a seamstresses guild, with forty collectively-purchased sewing machines. The guild grew to four hundred women, enabling them to cut costs and take on large orders, as well as receive just wages for strictly-limited working days, and attracted a deluge of requests from poorly-paid seamstresses:

> The seamstresses would go to the textile stores, and the stores would cut and prepare the cloth, and give it to the seamstresses to sew at home. They would be paid, say, twenty cents for sewing a man's shirt . . . The payment was horribly low. It was the worst-paid job in the country. And they would come to us and say, 'señoritas, you in El Centavo pay well and the *rusos*' – as they called them – 'pay badly.' What could we do? We had learned in the Escuela de Servicio Social that the workers must defend themselves, that is, we had to promote a union. So our four hundred seamstresses began to visit their neighbours in the outlying suburbs where they lived – Nueva Pompeya, Flores, Belgrano and Caballito – and invited them to form a syndicate. Then the Socio-Economic Secretariat . . . asked the parish priests in those zones also to invite them to unionise.
>
> So at Sunday mass, the parish priests would say, 'all you women who sew at home and are badly paid, and who want to be paid more, pass through the sacristy'. And in the sacristy there would be Social Catholic instructors, trained by Mgr. Franceschi, who told them what a union was and invited them to 850 Montevideo Street. The union was called Sindicato Argentino de Obreras de Confección, and we came to have seventeen thousand associates. We later founded branches in La Plata, Rosario, Tucumán and Córdoba.[58]

Women could be unionised because they were already part of the parish network. Conversely, because male workers stayed away from church, ACA's promotion of unions depended on 'numerous teams of true workers, previously won over to our cause and prepared to go among their companions to sustain Catholic principles, ideas and initiatives'.[59] This presented a problem of class. Because workers made up only around eleven per cent of male Catholic Action membership, in the male-dominated industrial areas of Greater Buenos Aires, the Catholic movement failed, in the late 1930s, seriously to compete with communism. Both the FACE and the autonomous Catholic unions were female; only the CCO was made up principally of male workers. Although the Youth Wing of the CCO, the VOC, was more dynamic, campaigning for laws, organising demonstrations and running a chain of 'Popular Universities' in impoverished areas, these pre-1930 unions retained the mutualist character of *andreísta* social Catholicism.[60]

The possibility of making substantial inroads into industrial labour was dramatically increased in 1941, when the Catholic Worker Youth (JOC) was founded. The contrast with early twentieth-century worker organisations was enormous. Where the Workers' Circles had been mutualist, paternalistic and confessional, the JOC was grass roots, exclusively working class, aconfessional, and identified with industrial labour. Active members were 'militants' from the ranks of labour, and with a *método propio* quite distinct from that of the predominantly middle-class Catholic Action. JOC operated on the *see–judge–act* principle. First a group studied an issue (wages, conditions, health, lack of representation); then considered possible solutions through questionnaires, which were centrally archived; and then acted through a campaign or group to remedy the deficiency. Not a trades union but a 'workers' movement' that would encourage unions, JOC saw itself at the vanguard of the 'social revolution' advocated by integral Catholicism. It grew rapidly in Buenos Aires and La Plata, and was well established in Rosario and Tucumán and other interior cities by the mid-1940s. Its cell-based and autonomous characteristics make its precise expansion hard to quantify. Assemblies were however impressive. In the diocese of La Plata alone, demonstrations of 2,000 were recorded in 1942 despite the state of siege, and 10,000 in 1944. JOC was present in most of the major industrial sectors, organising joint strikes and boycotts with communists and socialists, and setting up factory discussion groups and weekly study circles in which self-education, preparation, training and pragmatic action were all. The adherence to JOC's exclusively working-class composition was strict; its members held that 'a workers' section will be in better condition if it is badly managed by workers than well managed by non-workers'. There was a particular JOC pride in being *obreros de masa*, part of the culture of Gran Buenos Aires, in contrast to those of the VOC, who, while workers, 'being from the Capital, had a bourgeois culture'.[61] Like the communists, the JOC task was one of penetration; unlike communists, however, this was carried out not by an élite but by workers themselves. The process was one of gradual assimilation, beginning with study of social doctrine and gradually incorporating the spiritual life.[62] In addition, as with all Catholic activism of the period, the JOC had a vigorous female section, demanding a specific social emphasis on women workers:

> I spend eight hours every day of the week in a factory. Nevertheless I tell you: *women should not have to work!* Factory labour breaks the unity of her life and the meaning of her mission. Her place is in the home. God did not create her to supplement her husband's meagre salary, but to be a companion, a girlfriend, a wife and a mother. That's why we women are in the JOC. Because the JOC understands our vocation and our destiny, and will always struggle, unto death, to restore to women their lost Christian dignity.[63]

Although Congress remained obstinately resistant to a thorough legislative reform of the type proposed by Catholic Action, the growing influence of social Catholicism was perceptible among the governing classes. A discernible shift in government attitudes was heralded by the ascension of Dr Ortiz in 1938, who was accompanied in his brief tenure by a group of Catholics in Acción Cívica Social. Ortiz' presidential message included social-Catholic language and assumptions; he called upon Argentines not to emulate foreign political doctrines but rather to 'spiritualise' (*darle contenido espiritual a*) the parties.[64] His Interior Minister instructed the Commission responsible for the new Labour Code to study *Rerum Novarum* in detail. The newly-appointed Labour Department President, José Figuerola, a decisive figure in the following years, and close to Catholic Action, placed himself in the 'social-Christian School', and embarked upon a strategy of state mediation in labour disputes. From the late 1930s to the mid-1940s, references were increasingly made to encyclicals by deputies and in both national and provincial legislatures. The Province of Santa Fe, which was the first to pass family wage legislation in 1942, voted in 1938 to include *Quadragesimo Anno* on the statute book. The popular authoritarian governor of Buenos Aires, Manuel Fresco, who hounded the left and restored religion to schools, had an approach to public housing, school construction, and public works based explicitly on social Catholicism, one which 'was far in advance of anything else in Argentina, indeed in all South America'.[65] There was also evidence of social Catholicism penetrating army circles, many of whose members had connections with Catholic Action. The chief military plotter of the 1930s, Diego Luís Molinari, a Radical supporter, included the family wage scheme among his proposals.[66]

These were all indications of the changing climate from which Perón was to emerge in 1945. The Catholic movement was instrumental in bringing about this climate, and was beginning to make concrete advances in influencing both the state and the worker movement. The liberal project however proved resistant to substantial reform.

Part II
The Catholic Movement in Argentine Politics, 1930–1960

3 Catholicism and Nationalism, 1930–1939

3.1 THE COUP OF 1930

Although it was a nationalist group that lay behind the the thinking of the 1930 coup, it was not necessary to be a nationalist to favour Yrigoyen's overthrow. Most of the parties, including the Conservatives and the Independent Socialists, were among the loudest voices calling for the army to intervene. The coup met with no resistance and, in spite of Yrigoyen's landslide electoral victory in 1928, had broad support. The causes of the 1930 coup ran deeper than the 1929 economic crisis, and had at their root the lack of legitimacy at the heart of Argentine democracy.

The first element of this illegitimacy was unfettered authority. On the one hand, the Radical Party (UCR) was Argentina's only party capable of mass support, and had remained in government continually since 1916; on the other, the enormous powers attributed to the executive by the 1853 Constitution endowed the president with virtually unrestricted authority. By the late 1920s, the role of Congress had been reduced to little more than a rubber-stamp; intra-party factional differences (between 'Yrigoyenist' and 'Anti-personalist') had come to replace divisions over policy. Taking advantage of the power of federal intervention in the provinces (which enabled a determined president virtually to refashion the political composition of provincial government), Yrigoyen intervened fourteen times in less than two years to unseat Conservative provincial leaders. The second element was the increasing resort to extra-constitutional and even violent means of suborning opponents: the assassination of the political *caudillo* of Mendoza, the shoot-outs at Lincoln, and the increasing activities of government paramilitaries (the Klan Radical) were all examples. The third element was the expansion of state patronage. The Alvear interregnum (1922–1928) had reimposed tight fiscal controls; but Yrigoyen's second term oversaw the resumption of Radical *largesse*. The bureaucracy became 'a vast employment agency serving the government's ends' and with increased state spending came the growing domination of state over society.[1]

The army's move in 1930, which was led by General Uriburu in the context of the president's rapid deterioration and a Congress frozen by infighting, had been planned by two main groups. The first were Uriburu's men, the Professionalists. Yrigoyen had continued the liberal policy of harnessing the army to the state by including officers in the patronage network, and by distributing promotions on the basis of party loyalty, in order to safeguard the army as a department of state. These policies were now challenged by military groups upholding a 'professional' view of the army as independent of party and state, and existing to uphold legal, constitutional government. It was not so much that the army sought now to intervene in politics; rather, officers could no longer endure the state intervening in military affairs.[2] The 1930 coup was therefore the first expression since the 1890 Revolution of the scholastic view of state and politics. Abuses of power and unfettered authority amounted to tyranny; and tyranny causes a reversion of sovereignty to the community. But if General Uriburu and his followers could agree on the legitimacy of intervention – indeed on its moral necessity – they had no clear idea of what would ensue from intervention, short of restoring institutions and again calling elections. The second military faction of the 1930 coup, led by General Justo, identified with the fortunes of the Conservatives and were defenders of the liberal project of the 1880s. They sought the restoration of the Conservative Party, which had been making rapid recent gains; and were determined to preclude the Radicals, and especially Yrigoyen, from again assuming the presidency.

The *uriburistas* were nationalists, but nationalism was a heterogeneous creed. Uriburu had been a junior officer in the Revolution of 1890, where he stood with Estrada against the 'despotic' Juárez Celman. His political ideas were influenced by a young, nationalist periodical, *La Nueva República*, which was more Maurassian than Catholic, its ambiguities springing from the process of realignment within nationalism following the papal condemnation of Maurras in 1927. *La Nueva República* was nevertheless close to the Cursos de Cultura Católica and *Criterio*, and their contributors were of similar social backgrounds. There was considerable crossover between the two periodicals, but it was a relationship marked by tensions and disputes. Many nationalists had backgrounds in liberal–Positivism, socialism or even anarchism, and had turned bitterly against the Enlightenment. Some, like Lugones, had lapsed into nihilism or a cult of violence. Others had been awakened to the Catholic tradition via neo-Positivism. In the view of one Catholic intellectual, the Republican nationalists were 'heterodox all, who arrive at Catholic conclusions by an empirical route, and in a frequently intemperate fashion.'[3] Following the papal condemnation of Maurras, the *La Nueva República* writers were forced to declare their position. Some formally rejected Maurras, while continuing to adhere to his abhorrence of democracy. Others, like Julio Irazusta, saw the contradiction between Thomism and Maurrasianism, and declared themselves Thomist. This process of reassessment was frequently lengthy and problematic. In his memoirs, Juan Carulla described how his admiration for Maurras was gradually superseded by a recognition that the answers he had been seeking in Maurras were in fact answered by the Church.[4]

To the pages of *La Nueva República* and the pronouncements of Uriburu can be traced the subsequent threads of Argentine nationalism: some leaning towards Thomism, others towards Maurras; and the debates between that magazine and *Criterio* show the beginnings of the impact of the Catholic awakening within this sector of the Argentine intelligentsia. Antimodernist Catholics and clerical nationalists shared common enemies: they reviled the political school of Hobbes and Rousseau, spurned rationalism and secularism, and stood against the democratic strains arising from the French Revolution. But hereafter they might differ. All could agree, for example, on Mussolini's strengths, but *Criterio* saw in the latent Church–state conflict indications of the dictator's impulse to totalitarianism. A number of articles placed fascism under the spotlight of Catholic theology, and found it to contain heterodox Maurrasian elements. Against the *LNR* vision of the Middle Ages as an aggregate of hierarchies and corporations under a strong state, of which the Church, stripped largely of its spirituality and autonomy, served as a social buttress, *Criterio* counterposed a pluralist medievalism in which the state was circumscribed to its temporal functions. These were the beginnings of debates that would last throughout the 1930s over 'acceptable' and 'unacceptable' nationalism.[5]

The ambiguities were present in Uriburu's speeches following the coup. He spoke favourably of democracy and the need for its defence against tyranny. He denounced fascism and spoke of a temporary dictatorship in order to restore the nation's constitution and institutions. Committing both himself and members of his provisional government not to take part in any future electoral contest, Uriburu promised to lift emergency measures and to restore elections as soon as possible. Yet a number of his supporters spoke of a revised political system which placed more emphasis on corporative than individual representation.[6] Such speeches, and the presence of the Argentine Civic Legion, suggested fascism to liberal critics. But there was no popular mobilisation nor any attempt to go beyond a 'clean-up' of institutions and a campaign on graft. In April 1931, municipal elections were held in Buenos Aires Province, which were won by the Yrigoyenist Radicals, and presidential elections were scheduled for November 1931. The results of the April elections had been worrying for Uriburu and unacceptable to Conservatives. The return of the government that had been ousted only a year before for tyranny was inadmissible, and the elections were promptly annulled. The liberal–conservative faction in the army, led by General Justo, took advantage of the confusion to lead a palace takeover. Like General Roca in 1890, Justo restored liberal hegemony, spurning, like his predecessor, his military uniform in order to occupy the presidency at the head of a coalition government made up of parties without popular support, and based once more on controlled elections.

3.2 THE LIBERAL–CONSERVATIVE RESTORATION

It has become a commonplace of Argentine political history that the Conservative Restoration put an end to popular government and returned the architects of the liberal project to power. Yet given Radical abuses of power, and the untenability of a nationalist alternative, there were no new political groups capable of occupying the vacuum. The liberal–conservative order restored by Justo was not popular but it was moderate. He had the support of other small parties and factions similarly committed to the liberal project: the Conservatives (PDN), the Antipersonalist Radicals (a faction opposed to Yrigoyen's domination of the party) as well as the 'Independent' Socialists (who upheld the original reformist ideas of Juan B. Justo against the communist tendencies in the party). Together, these parties formed the Concordancia. None had much electoral support, but were conspicuous for the quality of their leaders.[7] The coalition was opposed in Congress by a smaller alliance of the conservative Santa Fe-based PDP and the 'orthodox' Socialist Party, whose support came almost exclusively from the Federal Capital. Both parties had deplored the coup, and in the 1930s made lofty criticisms of corruption and electoral fraud; their voter support was nevertheless threadbare and declined in the course of the decade [Table 3.1].

Table 3.1 Showing composition of the Chamber of Deputies, 1930–1942

Party	1932	1934	1936	1938	1940	1942
PDN [1]	56	60	55	59	49	48
PSI [2]	43	43	25	25	5	17
UCR-AP [3]	17	16	11	5	7	19
PDP [4]	14	12	6	–	–	–
PS [5]	11	6	2	–	–	–
UCR [6]	–	2	40	64	49	48

[1] Conservative
[2] Independent Socialist Party | Concordancia
[3] Antipersonalist Radicals

[4] Progressive Democratic Party (Santa Fe) | Opposition, 1932–1937
[5] 'Orthodox' Socialists (Federal Capital)

[6] Mainstream Radicals | Opposition, 1937–1942

Source: D. Cantón, *Los partidos políticos argentinos entre 1912 y 1955* (Documento de Trabajo n. 31, Instituto Torcuato Di Tella), Buenos Aires, 1967, pp. 26–7.

The only majority party remained the UCR. Its electoral abstention in the early 1930s was both enforced and self-imposed. On the one hand, the party's participation in attempted military uprisings in the early 1930s gave Justo the justification for its proscription; on the other, the UCR voluntarily returned to its pre-1912 policy of non-participation in rigged elections. Once the party returned to an electoral strategy in 1935, it did well in Entre Ríos and Córdoba, but was defeated in Buenos Aires Province by ballot-rigging. In 1936, the UCR allied with the PS–PDP block, and came close to a majority. But as the 1937 presidential election approached, the rising Radical tide alarmed the Conservatives, who 'simply stole the election by fraud and by force'.[8] Justo's handpicked successor, the Anti-Personalist Radical Roberto Ortiz, attempted to counter this repudiation in 1939 by a thorough clean-up of elections, enabling the UCR to achieve a larger presence in Congress in 1938. The reform was however cut short by Ortiz' illness and the assumption of the presidency by the conservative Ramón Castillo, who quickly blocked the reform strategy, permitted scandalously fraudulent elections in Buenos Aires Province under the disapproving eye of army observers, and so again reduced Radical representation in Congress. The Radicals reacted bitterly, voting down Conservative legislation and economic reforms, and forcing Castillo to rule by decree until the army removed him in 1943.[9]

The disrepute into which liberal government in the 1930s fell did not derive solely, or even mainly, from its proscription of the UCR, or even from its manipulation of elections. In comparison with previous governments since 1880 the Concordancia exploited the presidential powers of veto and provincial intervention with circumspection. Government did not depend on coercion. Fiscal aptitude replaced the Radical benefactor-state. Ministries were occupied by able managers, who designed innovative state mechanisms to guide the economy out of recession.[10] More significant were the financial scandals, and especially those related to Argentina's openness to foreign capital. Nationalists pointed to the country's weakness in the international division of labour, trapped between the United States and Great Britain: the first refusing steadfastly to import Argentine foodstuffs, yet providing her with most manufactured goods; the second remaining her most important meat market, generating currency she used to buy American industrial *matériel*. Vulnerability to the economic priorities of these countries was demonstrated in the absence of domestic investment capital, which a 1935 census revealed to be no more than half of the total. The other half was popularly considered to be venal: the average Argentine, Britain's Ambassador recalled, was convinced that London shareholders in Argentine enterprises were wallowing in rich profits.[11] The Chaco War was cited as evidence of capital at the service of American imperial ambitions, and the oligopsonist practices of the great foreign firms did nothing to lessen these suspicions.

The traditional agro-exporting sector's anxiety to maintain the foreign connections was in this way linked increasingly to self-interest. The old liberal argument that what was good for foreign markets was good for Argentina, in the 1930s began to seem a rationalisation of privilege at a time when new sectors of society sought housing, jobs and investment in infrastructure. When, finally, strong and decisive action was required to meet a new economic crisis, this time brought on by the Second World War, petty party rivalries, such as that which prevented the passage of the Pinedo Plan in 1940, brought to a head the frustration felt by many Argentines at the inability of Congress to govern. Congressional stupor exacerbated popular scepticism, and threw the apparent moral decline of the leading classes into sharp relief.

Scandals involving foreign companies and public figures, political violence, the clientelistic nature of the party machine, and the frivolous consumption of the landowning classes, were all features of the decade subject to public inspection and repudiation.[12]

Underlying this repudiation, therefore, was a tension between state and society. Government was not tyrannical, or even despotic; but it lacked roots in a wider consensus at a time of social and economic changes. The basis of the economy was land, but the success of the agro-export economy had been accompanied by imbalances and tensions. In the 1920s, over 60 per cent of the population lived in small towns as renter–farmers (*arrendatarios*). Of a total rural population of 1.5 million in 1937, twenty thousand urban-based landlords owned seventy per cent of the land. Only a third of farm occupants were owners (compared with 90 per cent in Canada). The Depression brought to a breaking-point the many traditional inadequacies of the rural sector: scarcity of credit, debt bondage, and low prices forced on farmers by both the lack of storage facilities and the dominant purchasing cartels. These conditions, combined with itinerancy and reliance on seasonal labour, further undermined the stability of the family, depressing marriage and birth rates and encouraging illegitimacy. In the course of the decade, land was further concentrated and mechanization undertaken, squeezing out seasonal labourers and *arrendatarios*. The rural proletariat began to move towards the cities. The trend was strongest in the late 1930s, when 70,000 entered Buenos Aires each year.

The Depression also threw into sharp relief the weaknesses of the liberal agro-export strategy. The traditional trading relationship with Britain, already under pressure from the growing importance of the United States as supplier of capital and industrial goods, was delivered a sharp blow by the sudden drop in export prices and withdrawal of British investment. Although the 1933 Anglo-Argentine treaty allowed Argentina to defer radical changes in economic strategy until the 1940s, the decline in the agrarian sector, the establishment of state mechanisms of intervention, and the expansion of industry pointed to the inevitable emergence of a new kind of economy. These changes, and especially the growth of new industries, were partly the consequences of a changing demography: the population of Buenos Aires was swelled (1914: 1.5 million; 1947: 4.7 million) by both immigrants, and, after 1930, when immigration all but dried up, by internal migrants from the decaying rural sector. Foreign-born men made up 40 per cent of the male population in 1930, but only 26 per cent in 1946. The nationalisation and urbanisation of immigrants and their children generated social and political tensions, opening up a cleavage between the urban landowning classes – the architects of the liberal project – and the new classes desirous of greater social, economic and political participation.[13]

In the industrial belt of Buenos Aires where, attracted by the nascent industries, the migrants settled, and in the ghettoes of older working-class suburbs, conditions testified to the imbalances produced by fifty years of breakneck expansion. Since 1880 liberal administrations with varying degrees of fiscal responsibility had proved themselves capable of maintaining business confidence and a steadily expanding economy. But they had dogmatically adhered to the belief that the workings of the market would lead in time to a just and equitable distribution. The social legislation forced through Congress by socialists and Catholics had been piecemeal and poorly enforced; notwithstanding the introductions of indemnities and the *sábado inglés*, in the 1930s it remained so. Rapid economic recovery kept unemployment (at a time when it was high the world over) exceptionally low, but salaries lagged behind inflation and real wages declined as a whole. Women and children – who made up a quarter of meatpacking workers in 1935 – worked for substantially less than men, in frequently appalling conditions. The housing shortage – a 1937 survey revealed that 60 per cent of working-class families in Buenos Aires lived in one room – was especially acute. Most workers' salaries were insufficient to maintain a family. It was the combination of these conditions which produced a low birth-rate among worker families, seventy per cent of whom had less than two children.[14]

The labour movement, which remained weak and divided, was dominated in the 1930s by communists. Although socialists remained significant, the communist CGT–1 was responsible for nearly all the increase in union membership and virtually every large strike between 1936 and 1943. The strength of communism was due in part to its operation outside the liberal–political system. In contrast, the socialists opted for an alliance with Justo, in order to secure the passage of labour laws. This meant that not only were they compromised with the liberal establishment from which most workers were excluded, but also that they embarked on a strategy to wean workers from the Radicals. A third socialist schism in 1936 however coincided with the UCR participating once again, which left socialists with only a skeletal presence in Congress and a divided union movement. In so far as they were an offshoot of Argentina's liberal political classes, therefore, the non-communist unions had as little wide appeal as the parties themselves.

In a deeper sense, however, communism was of limited appeal to the new classes who arrived in the urban areas in the course of the 1930s. The Spanish Civil War, which caused the temporary unification of the left, following orders from the Comintern to form a common 'democratic' anti-fascist front, was replete with contradictions for the communists, who had formerly seen the Radicals and Socialists as 'imperialist'. The ideological tension between a worker nationalism which the communists saw as fascism, and their own commitment to class struggle and anti-imperialism, was never fully resolved. Comintern policy was directed largely at industrialised countries, in ignorance of semi-pastoral export economies like Argentina's. This in turn exposed the problem of the PC's ideological density and lack of national credentials at a time when the vast majority of workers sought to throw off foreign loyalties. The success of communist labour militancy therefore resided almost wholly in its capacity to deliver pragmatic gains for workers; but it could speak only for workers in heavy plants and had no broader working-class appeal. The new classes started from assumptions which were outside the Enlightenment tradition.[15]

The liberal–conservative restoration did not resolve the crisis of legitimacy in Argentina's democracy. Politics was dominated by leading landowning families, wedded to the liberal project at a time when the agro-export model, even if it could deliver a steady economic growth, was unable to deliver standards of living to a growing urban population. The two major parties, the Radicals and Conservatives, were democratic; but just as the Radicals had claimed that their majority base legitimised their use of undemocratic methods and fiscal *largesse*, the Concordancia claimed that fiscal responsibility and moderate government depended on ensuring – even through illegitimate means – that the 'right' people continued to govern. Political society remained exclusively defined at a time when political exclusivity was denounced as a cover for social and economic privilege. Liberal obstinancy to thorough reform meanwhile accelerated class division and fuelled the appeal of communism. Yet because outright dictatorship was contrary to common values, an emasculated, unaccountable democratic system in which all the parties were implicated enabled the liberal classes to cling to power.

3.3 CATHOLIC POLITICAL ALIENATION

The Christendom model – which Catholics insisted to be the popular ambition – was self-contained and without loose ends. But it rested on a careful distinction of spiritual and temporal spheres. What was true for Catholic Action was true for Catholics in general: none could belong to a political organisation *qua* Catholics; if they did so, as citizens, the organization could not sustain a political philosophy that contravened Catholic tenets. The distinction was made between the technicalities of politics *in sensu stricto*, which were irrelevant to religion *per se*, and, to employ a papal phrase, 'the politics which touches the altar', which trespassed on the religious sphere. The first was a matter of party politics, of policies and means rather than ends, while the second touched on the spiritual ends of society. Hence matters such as Church–state relations, marriage, the family, the right of worker association, social justice, private property, education, and the human ends of the economy, were matters in which the Church was considered competent and in defence of which Catholics should publicly act. Particular political and electoral systems, on the other hand, were matters on which Catholics held private views. The Church did not therefore prescribe a particular political option for Catholics, but defined the boundaries within which that option could freely be exercised.[16] Participation in elections was encouraged, but Catholics could not vote for any party which sustained platforms incompatible with Church doctrine. These included unilateral Church–state separation (rather than a concordat), the expulsion of religious education from schools, and divorce. A political party wishing to attract the Catholic vote would ensure that its platforms placed no contradiction between a voter and his conscience, but could not deploy the authority of the Church in its favour. In this way, the Church sought to uphold the basic scholastic framework of society, within which any number of electoral systems and parties could compete.[17]

In the 1930s, however, all the political parties upheld platforms and doctrines contrary to the Christendom model. The careful distinction of temporal and spiritual authorities was irrelevant in a system where the parties considered themselves autonomous. The exclusion of the UCR was condemned in the Catholic press. But in the course of the decade the intractable demands of integral Catholicism exposed the insufficiency of the UCR as the repository of Catholic votes, in two ways. First, even the vague social reforms advocated by the 1936 Pastoral Letter were absent from the party's programme, let alone the more thorough social transformation called for by ACA's Socio-Economic Secretariat.[18] Second, the arrival of the University Reform generation in the party's ranks caused the Radicals to revert to their secularist origins. In 1937 Alvear signed a manifesto describing Religious Education in schools as dogmatic, unscientific and undemocratic, in spite of a survey conducted in Buenos Aires Province showing 98 per cent support for its restoration.[19] Similarly, the Conservatives, in spite of their formal abandonment of secularism, were reviled by integral Catholicism for their vision of the Alberdian *Iglesia Nacional*, upheld by *La Prensa*, which defended *la buena, la vieja moral familiar*, and a Church subordinate to the state and confined to a voluntary charitable association.[20] Ballot-rigging, corruption, the absorption of the state by sectors of the economy, and above all the government's resistance to thorough social reform made Conservatism repugnant to Catholic activists.[21] A brief interlude from this alienation was afforded by the assumption of the Anti-Personalist Radical Roberto Ortiz, when a group of Catholics entered government in support of his social and electoral reforms, to which *Criterio* and ACA also lent their support; but the reforms were short-lived, and he was replaced by a Conservative. In spite of shared social concerns, the Socialist Party's dogmatic anticlericalism, which hardened in the course of the decade to the point where no member was admitted who had married in church, was an insuperable obstacle to Catholic support; while the PDP, which had an admirable record in protesting fraud and corruption, forfeited Catholic sympathy by a similar dogmatism.[22]

It was significant that the 1931 Pastoral letter was not a factor in the elections of that year, or at any time in the decade, whereas the same Pastoral issued in 1945 was considered decisive in Perón's 1946 victory.[23] This demonstrated both the importance of the Catholic revival in shaping attitudes between the two elections, as well as the insularity of all parties from Catholic tenets in the 1930s. In the 1934 elections, the major parties, according to *Criterio*, 'were fundamentally homogeneous: liberal–individualist, Rousseaunian–democratic, and silent on the deep problems of the moment'. The review noted the widespread alienation from the party system, and saw in the growth of 'a violent and aggressive nationalism' a 'logical reaction against political introspection'.[24] In 1937, *Criterio* repeated this criticism, noting the pervasiveness of electoral *caudillos* garnering votes through 'jobbery, local tax exemptions, small loans and similar favours', while the government's failure even to pass a trade union law made worker organisations illegal. 'If we continue along this path', Franceschi warned, 'the discredit into which our institutions are falling will favour ... regimes ... in which all popular participation will perish'.[25] An autonomous and autocratic democracy lent justification to the exponents of its violent overthrow. The choice was stark: 'reform of democracy, or dictatorship'.[26]

The political ambiguity of Argentine Catholicism in the 1930s derived from its simultaneous repudiation of both liberal democracy and dictatorship. Catholics attributed the illegitimacy of Argentine democracy to its philosophical underpinnings; a Christian–Democratic party on the Italian *Popolare* lines was therefore seen as at best a contradiction, at worst an endorsement of liberalism.[27] Argentine democracy was liberal; liberalism, of the monistic, secularist, variety (as opposed to ecumenical liberalism) excluded the Catholic conception of politics. The principle of the popular origin of sovereignty was upheld as a genuine democratic principle in contrast to the unpopular, pseudo-democracy of Argentine liberalism. Dictatorship, as a form of government resting on force, was contrary to scholastic thinking. The prevailing view of Church leaders was therefore that Argentina did not need superficial changes in régime, but instead required a profound renewal at the base of society. Neither 'an army gathered round a cross' nor a Christian–Democratic party would achieve the profound reform which social doctrine made imperative.[28]

Nationalism was seen as an alternative to both dictatorship and liberal democracy. Throughout the 1930s, the Catholic press in Argentina discussed European nationalism and its possible application to the Argentine context. Mussolini was admired for his vigour and recognition of the moral purpose of society, which made him politically superior to nineteenth-century *laissez-faire* administrations.[29] But the papal condemnation of fascist state corporatism in 1931 and the *Duce*'s run-ins with the Church generally, confirmed the disquiet expressed in the late 1920s. ACA received reports from its Italian counterpart of the anti-statist campaign, and *Criterio* in the early 1930s engaged in a dispute with the *Giornale d'Italia* over fascist differences with Catholic social doctrine. The condemnations hardened in the course of the 1930s, and similarities with Nazism (which was condemned outright in the Argentine Catholic press) were increasingly identified. *Criterio* saw in fascism a restoration of heretical divine-right theory, attributing the same infallibility to the leader as had Rousseau to the majority will, so that 'by different paths, both [liberalism and fascism] end up at the same crossroads: absolute state sovereignty'.[30] In neither case did the state defer to a spiritual sovereignty external to the state, from which flowed natural and personal rights. Totalitarianism was therefore a transposition of individual autonomy onto the state, and was equally heterodox.[31]

A similar process of sifting was evident in Argentine nationalism itself. There were numerous elements of Argentine nationalism which pointed to heterodoxy. Historical revisionism, for example, sought to reverse liberal cultural canons by favourably reviewing the dictatorship of Rosas, who was praised not only for being close to popular values, and a true defender of Argentina from foreign predators, for which there was strong evidence, but also for his 'support' of the Church, for which there was rather less.[32] This was the clericalism of enlightened absolutism, and not the orthodoxy of scholasticism, and betrayed the origins of nationalism in *fin de siècle* liberal clericalism. Heterodoxy was evident in numerous nationalist assertions, reminiscent of the Divine Right of Kings heresy, that the power of the chief of the state came from God alone.[33] The 1936 Nationalist Programme was strongly reminiscent of the Juárez Celman administration in its assertion that, 'The interests of the nation constitute the supreme Argentine public order . . . [against which] none can evoke rights'.[34] From the pages of *Criterio*, Franceschi engaged the major nationalist writers of the period, sympathising with their repudiation of liberalism, but identifying areas in which doctrinally they were closer to Maurras than the Church. This was nevertheless a *dialogue* between Catholicism and nationalism, tied by their common repudiation of liberalism, one which recognised the power and popularity of the nationalist critique. The task was one of promoting a 'sane nationalism' over 'groups of merely electoral interests' in solving the antagonism between state and society, and in order to prevent the totalitarianism of right or left.[35] This recognition formed the basis of the Catholic attitude to nationalism in the 1930s. It was expressed as far back as 1932 when, noting nationalism's rapid growth and vitality, *Criterio* promised 'our support, and a collaboration which, steering the movement along the right paths, will ensure its triumph'.[36]

'The right paths' were those that avoided secularist premises, permanent dictatorship and state corporatism; and which led instead to a respect for federal traditions and the freedom and rights of the Church, and which could reconcile political liberty with social justice through an energetic encouragement of 'lesser institutions'. It would be a specifically Argentine nationalism, which drew on Latin and Catholic roots, and which rejected servile imitations of foreign models that were irrelevant, as with ethnic and separatist movements, or those which, like the Maurras–Mussolini doctrines of statism and materialism, were predicated on nineteenth-century errors. Nationalism could descend into totalitarianism if it adopted the Jacobin premise; i.e. if it conceived of the individual in isolation from the community, as morally autonomous, which, when aggregated, composed the infallible will of the majority and the surrender of all rights to the state. Modern totalitarianism drew upon these same nineteenth-century Comtian–positivist conceptions. Even if the state was not actually totalitarian, the Fascist theory that if the state is to represent the nation then the people composing the nation (and all its subsidiary communities) are to be made part of the state, was the exact opposite of Catholic doctrine, which held that the state was delegated by the nation for defined and limited purposes. Whereas 'the totalitarian state is of unlimited finality and universal sovereignty', noted *Criterio* in 1933, 'the state according to Catholic doctrine is of subordinated finality and restricted sovereignty'.[37] In a circular to its members in 1935, Catholic Action defined four areas of nationalist apostasy. First, dictatorship *as a permanent form* of government (rather than as a temporary emergency measure carried out in virtue of the common good) was the inadmissible consequence of the state's self-justification. The second was the conception of the nation as final authority, and not as a member of a family of nations respecting the higher value of universal fraternity. Thirdly, violence serving particular political ends, or carried out against the state (even if the state were atheist) was inadmissible. Fourth, the Fascist conception of the corporation was unacceptable in that it sought to tie corporations to the state.[38]

Ultimately, therefore, the crucial difference between an acceptable and unacceptable nationalism depended on its religious conception. This was not the same as 'anticlerical' and 'pro-clerical'. An overt identification with the Church, as Argentine liberalism showed, was not evidence that the state deferred to the Church's spiritual authority, or indeed any spiritual authority outside itself. Mere identification, typical of liberal–conservative governments seeking the support of the Church against the Left, was also a feature of Italian fascism. The right religious conception of nationalism went deeper than either clericalism or respect for canon law. At the heart of the state's attitude to spiritual sovereignty lay its wider political character. Although a government had to have authority (i.e. strength) in order legitimately to govern, it could not be its own justification, but rule in accordance with a value both anterior to and superior to the state itself. From this anterior and higher value, safeguarded by the Church, flowed the inviolable rights of the human person. These were rights both outside and independent of the state, which the state must recognise. The Kantian autonomy underlying monistic liberalism formed the basis of totalitarianism. As Europe in the 1930s appeared to demonstrate, totalitarianism succeeded the breakdown in the liberal state, transferring that same Kantian autonomy from the individual to the mass. Such a path could only be prevented by a Christianised nationalism: one that would mend the breach of state and society without collapsing into nineteenth-century errors. But of what sort? *Criterio* frequently quoted Salazar, and discussed various kinds of corporativism, rejecting any which were engineered by the state.[39] Corporativism was seen as the means of breaking the link between the state and the capitalist classes by means of a socioeconomic representation, rather than an individualist system which favoured the powerful. The Argentine constitution refuted the notion of a popular democracy by defining government as the rule of reason. Yet the right of enlightened rule in Argentina's case stood in contradiction to popular consensus. The task was to reform Argentina's democracy such that it could rule for the common good, without falling into the trap of statism and dictatorship. The reform required was 'moderate in its terms, but profound in its spirit'.[40]

Into this debate erupted Maritain's changing ideas. The philosopher's prestige was unquestioned in Argentine Catholic intellectual circles, where his early books – especially *Trois Réformateurs* and *Antimoderne* – were standard reading. His expositions during his two-month visit to Buenos Aires in 1934 made him a focal point of unity for Catholics of a variety of persuasions, as well as exciting the admiration of traditionally liberal groups, and opened up an avenue for a minority Catholicism of liberal–democratic orientation for Catholic contributors to *Sur*. Maritain caused immediate controversy among the antimodernists, who accused him of downgrading the cohesive medieval ideal, and for attempting, like Lammenais and Sangnier before him, to 'theologize' democracy. The apparently radical shift from the antimodern pessimism of *Trois Réformateurs* to a more optimistic view of the French and Russian Revolutions as a misplaced Christian idealism, proved too relativist for a 1920s generation familiar with the theory of the dialectical degeneration of history. But this was an area of largely academic debate, which was freely conducted in *Criterio* and confined to CCC circles.[41]

The major difficulty posed by Maritain's evolving theology of politics was its refutation of all nationalism as coterminous with fascism. *Criterio* approved the philosopher's condemnation of fascism in 'Pour le bien commun', but objected that Maritain had failed to distinguish between the 'modern' statist nationalism of Mussolini and the 'antimodern' nationalism of Salazar.[42] In the view of a number of leading Catholic intellectuals, Maritain's contention that *all* modern secular doctrines were tainted by the empiricism and materialism of the nineteenth century led logically to an inadmissible position of disengagement.[43] The philosopher noted prophetically (because it was these sociological characteristics which underlay the rise of Peronism ten years later) the dangers and opportunities of 'a great mass of people without roots or internal structure nor geographical stability', placing pressures on the traditional structures in a desire for articulation and a greater share in production. The social and economic integration of this mass was pressing, but it could not be cut short by a strong government, however well-intentioned. 'If it is a question of *taking power* by means of a coup d'état in the fascist mould, civil war will ensue; and if such a coup is Catholic, it runs the risk of blaspheming the name of Christ among men.' The task called, rather, for the formation of intellectual and political cadres, capable of integrating this mass within a democratic, pluralist structure, organised in 'a party which does not claim to bring together a few Catholics, or even Christians, but all those who wish to commit themselves to this historic enterprise'.[44]

Maritain's 'passionate defence of non-involvement'[45] was hard to swallow for a nascent Catholic movement which saw in a Christianised nationalism the opportunity to overcome the breach between state and society. To Maritain's critics, detachment would amount to restoring the Church's former *complementary* role, which integral Catholicism had refuted so strongly. Fr. Castellani, who approved entirely of Maritain's call for transcending the individualist-collectivist modern dialectic, expressed a typical view in his disagreement with the philosopher that the Church could only stand back in Puritan disgust. Nationalism was the raw material at the Church's disposal. Argentina was not France, where the co-existence of Church and Revolution made necessary an accommodation. Nor was it a nation having to choose between fascism and communism. Argentina had bypassed the Reformation and the Enlightenment and the secularist dialectic; it had no need to accommodate it. Enlightenment secularism and deism were minority views on the surface of society, upheld by those for whom it suited their privileged position. But they were out of step with the Catholic nation. The task was to restore the scholastic framework, not to step back from history.[46]

Castellani's argument implied that Argentine nationalism, despite certain heterodox elements, was in the main free of them. There was justification for this view in that the majority of Argentine nationalists had been 'Catholicised' in the course of the 1930s. The confidence of integral Catholics in the capacity of nationalism to overcome the individualist-collectivist dialectic therefore overrode Maritain's cautions. A small number of Catholic intellectuals took up Maritain's call, but as the 1939 Catholic Action booklist demonstrates, Maritain's long-term commitment to a democratic Catholic movement was overwhelmingly outweighed in the ranks of integral Catholicism by the 'collaboration with nationalism' line of thinking.[47] The Spanish Civil War, which forced Maritain to defend his position of non-engagement, would confirm in Catholic eyes that the showdown between communism and Christian civilization was imminent. Maritain's position would be widely portrayed in Buenos Aires as not only puritanical but immoral.

3.4 THE SPANISH CIVIL WAR AND THE REFUTATION OF MARITAIN

Because the connections between Spain and Argentina were so close, the Spanish conflict was to mark a whole generation. The issues were passionately debated; Argentines of all parties and persuasions threw themselves into actively supporting either the Loyalists or the Insurgents, raising funds, campaigning or even volunteering. No independence was considered possible. The communist-led CGT joined forces with liberals on the left (the PS) and the centre (the PDP and the UCR) and a section of the Spanish community, in favour of the Republic. Liberal conservatives, following the lead of Britain and France, maintained official relations with the Republican government, while in private hoping for a Nationalist victory. The establishment press, *La Prensa* and *La Nación*, were also pro-Insurgent. The liberal literary review *Sur* toyed with Maritain's disengagement but subsequently declared itself Loyalist.[48]

Apart from the Basque community in Buenos Aires, much of which identified with Euskadi motives for preferring the Republic, the choice for Catholics was fundamentally between supporting the Nationalists or following Maritain's independent stance. But faced with the horrors of Republican massacres, independence was barely more feasible than it was in Spain itself. Only a clutch of Maritain's devotees writing in

Sur found his argument in favour of Christian detachment acceptable.[49] For Catholics generally, Maritain's stance appeared to advocate opting out of a struggle in which the Church faced extinction from one of the parties involved. Whatever the Church's implication in the bourgeois order, to allow the forces responsible for the violent destruction of the Church to govern Spain was unthinkable. This view was reinforced by *Criterio*'s editor, Mgr Franceschi, whose dispatches from the war concentrated heavily on the churches burned and gutted by the Republicans.[50]

The differences between Maritain and those Argentine Catholics of the dominant 'collaboration with nationalism' school were not diagnostic in character. Maritain's explanation of the conflict, that the secular-messianism of the Republicans had been engendered by an unjust liberal–capitalist order, was shared by integral Catholics. Hence, although Catholics and liberal–conservatives in Argentina were thrown together in the pro-nationalist camp, the character of their support for Franco strongly differed.

The Spanish tragedy was held up by integral Catholics as a mirror to the liberal order in Argentina. The violence was the tragic consequence, Franceschi wrote from Spain, of bourgeois complacency and frivolity, of a small, self-indulgent class which had ignored wider society in favour of immoderate gains. They had undermined the moral basis of society by rejecting the common spiritual ends of the community; now, Spanish society was collapsing in the anarchy and terror of left-wing messianism, which threatened not only their lifestyles (for which Franceschi had little sympathy) but western civilization at its (spiritual) roots. Those who believed for so long that they could relax behind the defensive walls of fascism had brought about the revolution; they were the Marie Antoinettes, the 'mundane assassins' who tomorrow would be the victims of the 'revolutionary assassins'.[51] As Falcoff observes, there was little comfort in the Catholic thesis for Argentina's landowning classes. The analysis of the Left, which presupposed an identification of the Church with the defence of capitalism and the capitalist order was therefore (at least in Argentina) wide of the mark.[52]

Their differences instead arose over the character of Spanish nationalism and the notion of engagement. Both agreed that Right and Left were in Maritain's words 'two symptoms of the same evil'.[53] But where Maritain saw nationalism as an (implicitly fascist) defence of the liberal–conservative order, *Criterio* saw Franco as transcending the left–right dichotomy.[54] Catholics in *Sur* attacked this view, arguing that the predominance of conservative and capitalist interests again seeking an alliance with the Church validated Maritain's premonitions. Independence was called for, because the alliance with nationalism to forestall communism would perpetuate the collusion which was responsible for the workers' initial receptivity to the left-wing thesis.[55] *Criterio* responded with a contention that Spanish nationalism was not merely a reaction of force nor a defence of capital; if it were, *partisan* support for Franco would be unjustified. Defence of the Church against the persecutors of the Church, dominated by Stalinists in the Republican ranks, was a valid minimum justification for support; this made the war just. But *partisan* support for Franco was also justified because at stake in Spain was not a conflict between capital and labour, nor freedom and despotism, as the liberal–left maintained. Rather, the Spanish nationalists, in the opinion of *Criterio*, sought to transcend the liberal–bourgeois order. The Catholic element would win out against heterodox tendencies evident in Falangism. Franco was not a statist, nor centralist; he was free from secularist errors, looked to the devolution of power, a social programme and the extension of property. Catholic support was therefore justified and necessary.[56]

This was not a conflict in which sound empirical judgements flourished. Argentine Catholics, eager to believe that in their spiritual *alma mater* was a movement which they could hold up as desirable for Argentina, placed too much faith in the scholastic character of the Insurgents. *Criterio* demonstrated its intemperance in lauding the 'national' character of Spanish nationalism and refusing to admit Italian and German intervention in the war. The review also fumbled over Guernica (which alienated much of the Basque community in Buenos Aires) and ingenuously accepted nationalist explanations for the assassination of García Lorca (which offended the intelligentsia).[57]

Yet the weakness of Maritain's claim to independence had been shown by his links with *Sur*, the liberal–Gallican review *par excellence*. In the wider battle in Buenos Aires to roll back the frontiers of laicism, Maritain's preference for detachment, publicly stated in a pro-Republican review which stood for the patrician, secularist mould of the 1880s, placed him, in the Argentine context, on the side of liberalism. This placed *Criterio* in the awkward position of refuting the world's leading Thomist. Rather than this, Franceschi attempted to put distance between Maritain and *Sur* by attacking the literary review, thus forcing *Sur* to define its philosophical position. In its defence, *Sur* announced a naturalist belief in 'eternal spiritual values', and criticised the Church for 'intervening in politics'.[58] The statement neatly encapsulated liberal detachment from the wider Catholic moral consensus, defended by Victoria Ocampo as intellectual independence but attacked by integral Catholicism as an apologia for the same moral autonomy underlying the unjust distribution of wealth and the patrician pseudo-democracy of the *oligarquía vacuna*. It enabled *Criterio* to justify its classification of *Sur* as left-wing for, as Spain demonstrated, communism was incubated in an unjust system for which liberal intellectuals, in their moral detachment, were as responsible as the advocates of the moral autonomy of the market.[59]

As these disputes showed, it was increasingly difficult, in the late 1930s, to reconcile a pure scholasticism with political engagement. The refusal of integral Catholics to operate within a liberal–democratic system they considered to be insulated from the framework of society led them to collaborate with nationalism. From their reading of contemporary Europe, commentators could discern a pattern to which Argentina, some twenty years behind Europe, appeared to be conforming. There was a large and dangerous breach between state and society. Government lacked legitimacy. The political classes were coterminous with the major economic interests, and sought to retain the basis of the liberal project when that project could no longer meet the needs of a new, mass society. The electoral and constitutional paraphernalia of politics disguised the evident fact that Argentine democracy was not a contest between various parties within defined rules. It was a legitimation of the rule of reason, when the rulers had forfeited their claim to be acting for the common good. Because liberal-individualism generated collectivist reactions, as demonstrated by the rapid growth of communism, rapid and drastic reform was required. Only a Christianised nationalism could bring about such a transformation: only nationalism could bridge the breach of state and society, and only Christianity could prevent it from collapsing into totalitarianism. But was Argentine nationalism Christian?

4 War, Crisis and Military Intervention, 1939–1944

The analysis of many Catholics, that the decay of the liberal system was incubating a totalitarian reaction of left or right, had received dramatic validation in the Spanish Civil War. The outbreak in 1939 of World War II, in which Argentina, notoriously, remained neutral until shortly before its conclusion, added new ideological dimensions to the political choices they faced. The question of Argentine neutrality formed the background to a mounting political, social and economic crisis, one which appeared to confirm the decline of the literal project. Faced with hostility from the United States to Argentine neutrality, nationalism became more vociferous; yet while Catholics generally opted for neutrality, they rejected the apostasy of a number of nationalist groups favouring the Axis. The war exposed the differences between integral Catholicism and secular nationalism; both added their voices to calls for the army to intervene faced with the collapse of liberal government.

4.1 THE QUESTION OF NEUTRALITY

Contrary to the thinking of many North-American commentators (not least the State Department) that Buenos Aires' opposition to intervention indicated the fascism of its government, neutrality was nothing new. Presidents Ortiz and Castillo were the executors of a foreign policy established by 1880s liberalism and maintained faithfully by Yrigoyen in the First World War; one that refuted the claims of PanAmericanism, defended a close relationship with Britain, and which expressed a New World distrust of Old World bellicosity. When Ortiz secretly proposed to Washington, in 1939, that Argentina should side with the Allies, news leaked to the press and provoked widespread indignation. At this stage neutral, the United States rejected the offer, and Buenos Aires resumed its traditional impartiality. Argentines did not wish to go to war for a variety of reasons: ethnic links with the nations (but more rarely their régimes) in conflict with the Allies; a desire for a British victory but hostility to PanAmericanism; as well as a form of reasoning – which has been likened to that of North-Americans during the Napoleonic Wars – which concluded that there were many practical advantages to neutrality. The Nazi–Soviet and then the Allied–Soviet pacts caused considerable ideological confusion, and blurred the moral imperative. There were also strategic considerations, as well as geopolitical priorities: neither Buenos Aires nor London wished to see Argentina come under Washington's orbit. Nor were the colonels' reasons for continuing the neutrality policy after the 1943 coup substantially different from those of Castillo. As the British Ambassador to Buenos Aires recalled, their attitudes 'were fundamentally identical with those of nearly all Argentines of whatever class.'[1]

Ideological justifications for or against neutrality were thus the preserve of a minority, whether liberal or nationalist. Some army officers, weaned on the 'great dates' of Argentine history – the attempted English 'invasions' of 1806–7, and the occupation of the Falkland Islands in 1833 – expressed a fellow-travelling conviction that an Axis victory would liberate Argentina from the 'yoke' of Anglo-American domination, and this view was encouraged by nationalist groups of various complexions. Within these small groups, positive identification with the Axis was much rarer than the conviction that an Allied victory would encourage communism in the postwar period.

A number of Radicals, meanwhile, had their own reasons for advocating neutrality. The 'Renewalist' faction, the FORJA nationalists, as well as the 'intransigent' traditionalists under Sabattini in Córdoba, all sustained neutrality as an assertion of sovereignty. (In Sabattini's heady teleological thinking, the war demonstrated the decadence of Europe, the counterpart of which was the great future destiny of American civilization). On Comintern orders Communists were also at first neutralist. Seeing the war as a struggle between two 'imperialisms', British and German, their initial advocacy of non-intervention angered the socialists in the CGT, for whom, like the Americans after 1942, the battle was a struggle between democracy and fascism in which all were morally implicated. When the Russian–German pact was broken in 1941, however, socialists and communists were thrown together on the same side. After Pearl Harbour, all the left was 'democratic' and interventionist.[2]

The liberal minority who, in contrast to popular feeling, advocated intervention, considered themselves democrats. In the domestic context, however, an Argentine 'democrat' was likely to think differently from most Argentines, who favoured both neutrality *and* democracy. Interventionism did, on the other hand, correspond to certain domestic political strategies. The American (after Pearl Harbour) and communist (after the revocation of the Hitler–Stalin pact) matrix suited the opposition of displaced liberal supporters of Justo to the conservative supporters of Castillo. Castillo, who had become president following Ortiz' illness, spoke for the Conservative Right, which, unlike the moderate liberal–conservatism of Justo, had little patience with political liberties. In the context of war, Radicals and socialists could express their anger at the resumption of fraud and rule by decree from 1941 by accusing the Castillo administration of fascism, and pointing to neutralism as evidence. All the traditional liberal groups – AntiPersonalist Radicals, socialists and liberal–Conservatives – were present at the foundation in 1940 of Acción Argentina, a lobby which promoted a declaration of hostilities as proof of Argentina's commitment to liberal values. In Acción Argentina's sharply dualistic matrix, there was no such valid position as 'democratic neutralism': *all* neutralists, whatever their motives, were pseudo-Nazis. Acción Argentina was therefore identified *toto caelo* with the US State Department, and kept up a barrage of propaganda, which quickly found its way into American newspapers, portraying Argentina as a liberal nation subverted by fascism.[3]

Among the founders of Acción Argentina were also to be found the small group of Maritain devotees who had first appeared in *Sur* during the Spanish Civil War. Faced with the overwhelming support for neutrality among Argentine Catholics, towards the end of 1941 these writers established an explicitly Catholic magazine, *Orden Cristiano*, which attempted to express the Acción Argentina matrix in theological terms. *Orden Cristiano* occupied a resplendent *fin-de-siècle* edifice in the heart of the Barrio Norte and was financed by the Duhau estates. Its attitudes reflected those of the pro-British agro-export classes supportive of General Justo. (It was one of the many ironies of the time that the pro-British landowners associated with General Justo called for intervention, when Britain favoured Argentine neutrality). No greater contrast could have been offered with integral Catholicism. It was a revival of the of the old *Iglesia Nacional* model, in the tradition of Deán Funes. After decades of absence from the Catholic press, the speeches and sermons of Mgr De Andrea reappeared in its pages, alongside those of a handful of priests (no bishops, aside from De Andrea) who had been marginalised by the intransigent antiliberalism of the Catholic movement.

This reassertion of liberalism and Gallicanism, from the heart of the Barrio Norte establishment, was greeted with little favour by bishops and Catholic activists. They especially resented the review's self-appointed role as the Church's anti-fascist inquisitor, in the Acción Argentina mould; and especially when the target of its accusations was the outspoken neutralism of the venerable old Catholic daily *El Pueblo*.[4] The discourse of *Orden Cristiano* was fanatically liberal. Deploying Rousseaunian language, the review spoke of the present era as that of 'the divine right of peoples, which has succeeded the doctrinal aberration of monarchy'. The magazine defended a 'sane liberalism', which it defined as that of 'the productive revolution, the entrepeneurial spirit, the division of labour, and the benefits of technology'. To attack this sane liberalism was to 'favour pagan totalitarianism'. In the war context, support for the Soviet Union was valid in order to combat Nazism. Hence, the writers who had advocated independence in the Spanish Civil War wrote in *Orden Cristiano* that independence in the Second World War was impossible. The battle was between totalitarianism (Nazism, fascism) and liberal democracy, in which alliance with the Soviet Union was indispensable and independence amounted to appeasement. The insistence upon this moral obligation could at times be hysterical. 'It is useless to protest: "I'm Argentine" . . . "I'm a Catholic" . . . and therefore neutral!"', *Orden Cristiano* thundered. 'No! You are a Nazi, a dis-graceful Nazi!'[5]

Diametrically opposed to the 'democratic' Catholics were the Catholic nationalists, many of whom identified – as a result of the Spanish Civil War – with the vision of *Hispanidad*. This represented a cultural, political and spiritual standpoint 'above' all the parties in the War, yet supportive of the Franco régime's partisan neutrality. Hispanists refuted equally 'pagan' fascism, 'atheistic' communism and 'liberal–Protestant' PanAmericanism, defending instead a 'supra-national society' of Hispanic peoples, bound by a common spiritual tradition. Freed thereby from implication in the major doctrines at issue, they could discuss at ease the most preferable outcome of the war. Some argued that the abhorrent prospect of Nazi domination was outweighed by the (correct) prediction that an Allied victory would strengthen both Soviet domination and communism in democracies after the war.[6] *Hispanidad* was expressed most elegantly by contributors to the literary magazine *Sol y Luna* (1938–1943), edited by Mario Amadeo and Juan Carlos Goyeneche. *Sol y Luna* was to *Sur* what Hispanism was to PanAmericanism. Where Victoria Ocampo's review was liberal, cosmopolitan, illuminist, naturalistic and individualistic, *Sol y Luna* was nationalist, medievalist, spiritual and dogmatic. Both were eminently establishment reviews: *Sur* was financed by the agro-export earnings of the Ocampo estates, *Sol y Luna* by state conglomerates. Their similarities in presentation inevitably led to elegant mutual put-downs. *Sol y Luna* insisted that *Sur* brought together 'all the profiteers of Argentine alienation... flustered by the premonitions of the hour'; while in *Sur*'s eyes, *Sol y Luna* spoke for 'Castille, but the Very Old, a whiff of musty starch, the hushed sound of armed men on guard, the crackling of firewood in an *auto da fe*'.[7]

Both *Orden Cristiano* and *Sol y Luna* were secular establishment reviews. The ranks of the Church and of Catholic activism kept a cautious distance from both. For Catholic Action and *Criterio*, as for the majority of Argentines, neutrality did not signify sympathy for the Axis nations, whose régimes had been expressly condemned in authoritative papal documents published in the Argentine Catholic press. Nor was there a moral imperative in favour of intervention. They made clear that the fellow-travelling strategic priorities of both liberals and nationalists (as with the insistence by certain nationalists that to attack fascism was to assist communism, or Acción Argentina's assertion that not to support the Soviet Union amounted to pro-Nazism) were heterodox. In the integral-Catholic conception, totalitarianism possessed a shared identity. Right and Left were moral fictions, as reflected in the Nazi–Soviet gangster pact. To ally with either was to sup with the devil.

Criterio was especially anxious to counteract the liberal thesis, expressed in *Orden Cristiano*, that the battle was one between totalitarianism and democracy. To equate monarchy with totalitarianism was a gross error. Monarchy and democracy were *forms* of government; totalitarianism was a *doctrine*, that could be present in either. Totalitarianism was a political conception with its origins in the French Revolution, in which absolute power was achieved and retained through mass mobilisation, and in which all rights were surrendered to the state. Such a doctrine was implicit in the moral autonomy of individualism which, transposed onto the state, was totalitarian. The Catholic conception of politics, conversely, was compatible with a variety of political forms, in which rights devolved inherently from God and were defended, not conferred, by the state. It was therefore both historically and doctrinally false to posit the 'totalitarian democracy' of Rousseau as the only alternative to Hitler, for the two were doctrinally related.

Criterio also set about correcting nationalist heterodoxies, distinguishing between the 'spiritual' and 'patriotic' identification of Catholics with Spanish culture and tradition on the one hand and the 'political' identification of Hispanists with Franco's régime on the other. Franceschi, who had supported the Spanish Insurgents against the Republicans on various grounds, now appeared to distance himself from Franco. Observing that (as Maritain had warned) Spanish falangism had much in common both with regalism and with the statist errors of Italian fascism, he expressed disquiet about the régime's tendencies, for which he was attacked by a number of nationalists.[8]

This attempt to preserve the Church from being dragged into the ideological debates surrounding the war was also evident in Catholic Action. Militants were called to order and warned against appearing in nationalist or democratic meetings with their ACA lapels. A Catholic Action militant was ostensibly free to participate in any of these secular gatherings, but was warned constantly against supporting a doctrine condemned in authoritative papal documents. All forms of totalitarianism were expressly refuted, as was liberal individualism. Nazism and Soviet communism were the Church's sworn enemies. 'Extreme nationalism' which advocated national supremacy and violence was inadmissible. In short, a Catholic was a Catholic; he should have no truck with ideologies of heterodox origin.[9] There was a society, a *corpus mysticum*, a 'Catholic nation'; and both liberals and fascists were out of step with it, as the Catholic Action Youth review, *Sursum*, made clear:

> There are Catholics . . . who, forgetting everything that should never have been forgotten – the papal condemnations, the social agony of the *patria*, and the anguish of the poor – work in Acción Argentina, an entity which commemorates the Bastille and defends privileges and interests which are not those of the Catholic nation.
>
> There are also Catholics who sustain in publications, meetings and private conversations that the Axis is fighting for our culture, and who create confusion in the young by selective definitions of concepts such as totalitarianism, neopaganism and Macchiavellianism, which the Church has long considered and condemned. They join movements which they proclaim to be immaculate, in support of programmes of dubious orthodoxy, serving both directly and indirectly the cause of a political philosophy entirely alien to the Gospel, together with interests which are also not those of the Catholic nation.[10]

This concept of a Catholic nation became firmer in the war years, and was reinforced by isolationism. Neutrality expressed not disengagement but an assertion and vindication of the truth of the Church and her doctrines. The war was the final historical con-sequence of the refutation of the Church: the secularist apocalypse. PanAmericanism, which demanded a common American struggle against fascism, was seen as no more than a cover for American imperial ambitions. The fury of the State Department at Argentine neutrality was seen as evidence of the failure of these ambitions. The Catholic refutation of PanAmericanism was also religious in character. North-American Protestant sects proliferated in Buenos Aires in the war years. A contemporary American visitor identified one hundred and thirty evangelizing missions in the heart of the Federal Capital alone, which bore no correlation to the Protestant population there; and the same observer noted this phenomenon as one of the principal causes of anti-American resentment.[11] In contrast to Anglican and Lutheran churches, which served particular communities and had good relations with the Catholic Church, Protestant missionaries from the United States provoked hostility by classifying Latin America as for practical purposes heathen and pagan.[12] Such a situation would in any circumstance be likely to provoke inter-denominational *odium theologicum*. In the War years, however, the relationship between evangelizing Protestantism and PanAmericanism appeared almost symbiotic. In attempting to gain support from the State Department, for example, missionary organisations publicly argued that they should be seen as fostering democracy, given that the origins of democracy were Protestant. This contention, ironically, coincided with the antimodernist contention against liberal individualism: that its roots lay in the Protestant Reformation. Catholic Action issued a number of warnings to its members that Protestant missions were the Pan-American fifth column.[13]

4.2 THE LIBERAL DECLINE

The outbreak of war in Europe struck a fatal blow to the liberal project. The loss of markets in Central Europe and the inability of Britain's wartime economy to provide the *matériel* required for Argentine industrialization, meant that shipping to and from Britain had halved by late 1940, with little certainty that the old bilateral relationship would ever resume.

Argentina had lost Britain without yet gaining the United States, and required rapid industrialization to replace British imports. An imaginative plan submitted to Congress by Ortiz' finance minister Federico Pinedo, in mid 1940, had sought to curb inflation, mitigate hardship through a substantial social programme, and to encourage domestic industry to manufacture what could now not be imported. The Plan in effect acknowledged both Britain's imperial decline and the future economic dominance of the United States, by committing Argentina to a future bilateral relationship with the latter. The industrial emphasis implicit in the Plan rested on the assumption that wheat and beef could be exchanged with America for machines. Unlike the British economy, however, that of the US was not complementary to Argentina's but directly competitive. Argentina could only therefore export foodstuffs to, and receive manufactured goods and industrial *matériel* from, the United States, if protectionist barriers could be overcome through negotiation.

Yet negotiation would only be possible with congressional support, and Congress, following the resumption of electoral fraud, was in no mood to be supportive. The unedifying factional struggle within government between the pro-Ortiz Radical reformists, the Conservative Right under Castillo and the old pro-Justo liberal–conservatives, paralysed government. In protest at the resumption of fraud, which resulted in the Radicals losing their recently-restored majority in Congress, and at the Palomar Land Scandal which had been used by the Conservative Right to discredit Ortiz, the UCR voted down the Plan and virtually all important subsequent legislation, including the budget. The plan's defeat was an unsightly example of what the nationalists called 'politicking', thereby reinforcing the nationalist contention that liberal democracy was dead in the water. In reality, however, the Pinedo Plan was unlikely to have succeeded in the face of US hostility to Argentine neutrality. The refusal of Buenos Aires in 1941 to join the Pan-American block, which many Argentines saw as an umbrella for US hemispheric dominance, angered Washington, and destroyed any possibility of negotiating a trading relationship.[14]

The Pinedo Plan therefore failed on two fronts, both domestic and foreign, leaving the Castillo government rudderless, unable to legislate and unable to be removed through the ballot box. When, in early 1942, the Argentine foreign minister, Enrique Ruiz-Guiñazú (who was Hispanist rather than Anglophile but firmly pragmatic in his neutralism) resisted American attempts to secure a hemispheric alliance by attempting to form a block of neutral Latin-American countries, Washington responded angrily. Not only was there no possibility now of securing a trade agreement, but Washington imposed a devastating embargo both on arms and on the industrial *matériel* of which the US had become Argentina's sole supplier. The embargo, which lasted until 1949, was sufficiently effective and widespread – even in the face of British opposition to it – to constitute a veto on Argentine industrialisation. It was accompanied by an unrelenting public campaign, replete with references to the Fascist Menace, spearheaded by US Senators and State Department officers, with encouragement in Buenos Aires from Acción Argentina, opposition politicians, and American correspondents. The tone of these American dispatches is exemplified by the *New York Times* Buenos Aires correspondent, whose chronicle of 'the inside story of the coming of fascism', showed a black swastika engulfing a map of Argentina.[15] North-American newspapers assumed that the great majority of Argentines favoured a declaration of war and were only held back by a pro-Axis government. This myth was fuelled by liberals in Acción Argentina, *Sur* and *Orden Cristiano* to the point where they would call upon the Americans to invade, on the grounds that neutrality did not represent 'the will of the people'.[16]

Devoid of his own mandate, and ruling by decree, Castillo's authority came to rest entirely on the Conservative right. The constitution was suspended, the press muzzled, public assemblies forbidden, and preparations for a fraudulent election made. In the eighteen months prior to the coup, which were unrivalled in Argentine political history for confusion, intrigue, and legislative paralysis, the epithets of 'democratic' versus 'nationalist', charged with wartime significance, are nevertheless ambiguous. The 'democratic' Radicals, for example, who favoured the restoration of clean elections from which they stood to emerge the victors, conspired with the army to overthrow the Conservatives. Liberal–Conservative supporters of Justo were both Anglophile and interventionist; they, too, were 'democrats', supportive of the traditional Justo ballot-rigging policies, but not those of Castillo. Acción Argentina favoured PanAmericanism and the liberal cause, but included Conservatives who favoured ballot-rigging and Communists who were democrats on Comintern orders. Nationalists abhorred PanAmericanism and favoured *Hispanidad*, but a Hispanist might as well be found in the Castillo 'democratic' government (Ruiz–Guiñazú) as in the 'nationalist' opposition. There were neutralists favouring Castillo's presidency and neutralists calling for the army to intervene. Or, 'exaggerating the paradox, one could say that the *democrats* divided into ballot-riggers on the one hand and those favouring a military coup on the other'.[17]

Argentina had reached a juncture in which, as many critics indicated, politics revolved around the old factional struggle between Conservatives and Radicals. The moderate 'controlled democracy' of Justo had given way to Castillo's rule by decree; both were constitutional presidencies. The major democratic party was prevented from taking power by means of ballot rigging; yet the ruling party was unable to legislate without recourse to rule by *diktat*. The twin challenges of foreign policy and the economy could not be resolved because of political stalemate, while in wider society dissatisfaction and frustration, partly accumulated and partly due to war-related rises in inflation and unemployment, were mounting among the rapidly-expanding urban working class. The overthrow of the administration was therefore widely supported, to a far greater extent than in 1930, by nationalists, Radicals, the left, unions, the Church, and most importantly of all, the broad social strata which had grown up outside the liberal–democratic system. Few sought army rule as an alternative to civilian government, but all could agree on the need for the military to intervene. The proximate cause of intervention was Castillo's selection of his successor, a sugar baron from the north west famous for the slave-labour conditions of his plantations. The political parties (UCR, PDP and PS), convinced that the candidate would win through ballot-rigging, began conspiring with sectors of the army, and offered General Ramírez, then Castillo's Minister of War, the provisional presidency. Castillo, learning of the plan, attempted to sabotage the coup, and was defeated on the 4th June 1943.[18]

4.3 INTEGRAL CATHOLICISM ON THE EVE OF THE 1943 COUP

The early 1940s – the apogee of integral Catholicism and Catholic Action – was a period in which the new social order was most clearly delineated by Catholics. One source for this vision was the leading economist of the period and a contributor to *Criterio*: Alejandro Bunge. In the late 1930s, Bunge had been a major influence on José Figuerola, a leading figure in the Labour Department, close to ACA, the architect both of Ortiz' attempted labour reforms and, subsequently, the main author of the First Five Year Plan under Perón.[19]

Bunge's vision of 'a new Argentina' was published in 1940. Criticising the mentality of the governing classes – which assumed that Argentina was still an immigrant, exporting, pastoral economy – he presented statistical evidence of a declining birth rate, rural stagnation and widespread misery. The old liberal model, he argued, which was always morally questionable, was now no longer rational. The bilateral relationship with Britain which it assumed was defunct, while America in the postwar era could not fill the hole Britain had left. Argentina's future economic expansion therefore depended on creating an internal consumer market. Although foreign trade in the postwar period would remain vital, the priority of government should now be to invest in people, by spending on health and education and working towards the distribution of urban and agrarian property on the basis of progressive taxation, credit banks, cheap housing schemes, and a diversification of manufacturing. While avoiding both statism and autarky, the state's role in this new economy would be vigorous in providing the legal and monetary framework to permit the working classes to become both consumers and political participants.[20]

The 1941 Social Week organized by ACA to celebrate the anniversaries of *Rerum Novarum* and *Quadragesimo Anno* offered an important opportunity to contrast Argentine social reality with the moral standards of justice set forth in the encyclicals. The conclusions were grim. The state had not intervened to protect the poor, who were progressively worse-off; workers were barely-unionised, fearful of unemployment and deeply divided; the new industrial classes retained the individualist mentality of *hacer la América* criticised back in the 1880s; the individual contract was nullified by labour conditions, unemployment and the reduction in working hours; while private property, far from being extended, was increasingly concentrated; and there was a clear correlation between this trend and the increase in misery. The housing situation, which was desperate, was a major factor behind the instability of the family and social instability generally. The relation between prices and salaries had broken down. Inflation and rents were ruining working-class families, and required urgent state action. In the interior, landholdings the size of Belgium and Portugal remained in the hands of a single far-off owner, alongside rising unemployment, malnutrition and chronic debt. Farmers were being forced off the land into expanding city ghettoes, where two-thirds of the labouring classes were permanently in debt.[21]

Having gained access to the National Labour Department at the outbreak of the War, via José Figuerola, the Socio-economic Secretariat of Catholic Action had stepped up its campaigning. The assumption of Castillo dealt a blow to social-Catholic plans. The Family Subsidy Bill was accompanied by a vigorous campaign but encountered legislative paralysis. The same fate befell the Minimum Wage Bill, which ACA presented following a consultation by the Labour Legislation Commission. The Bill, which envisaged a minimum wage to cover the material and educational needs of a worker and his family, and to save towards the acquisition of property, was accompanied by calls for the sanction of three complementary laws: family subsidies, work insurance and subsidised housing.

The most interesting proposal, given subsequent developments, was a Bill granting legal status to trades unions, presented by a congressional deputy connected with Catholic Action. A law protecting and encouraging unions had long been a Catholic demand. The 1943 bill, which was presented on the eve of the coup (which sealed its fate) advocated syndical pluralism (the principle that there could be as many unions per profession or company as were desired), democratic constitutions (secret balloting on leaders and strikes), and apoliticism (a prohibition on unions being subsidised by political parties or movements), as well as a simple and rapid legal procedure that assumed *personería gremial* rather than *personería jurídica*. The former was predicated on the belief that union rights were not *granted* by the state but *recognised*, so preventing the totalitarian state-union or single-union conception.

The continued failure of these proposals to bypass the legislative paralysis of Congress reinforced the mounting sense of urgency and frustration within the Church. Studies, surveys and reports carried out by the Workers' Circles Youth Section, the VOC, provoked a series of dire warnings from bishops on the state of injustice. A Collective Pastoral Letter in 1941 condemned in the strongest terms the continued abuse of the Christian stipulations of a just wage, as well as trust capital, the witholding of land from peons in order to extract the highest rents, and the urgent problem of housing. To reverse this situation ACA called upon government to assume an energetic role in preventing capitalist and landowner absorption of small business and farmers, while avoiding state capitalism. The ambition was for a society of smallholders, to be introduced gradually by progressive taxation, adjustments in inheritance law, and the introduction of credit banks and housing associations. The individual minimum wage was seen as insufficient to meet the demands of elemental justice, and was necessarily constrained by imbalances in costs of living between provinces. A just wage was instead conceived as a 'family wage': minimum wages supplemented by family subsidies (for each child) to be built into labour contracts. In general, however, ACA foresaw the gradual transfer of property as a process to be brought about by the working classes themselves, organized into unions. This assumed legislation of the type presented in 1943, based on similar blueprints in the 1930s. The corporativist element was still prevalent in Catholic thinking: the reforms envisaged an important role for worker and employer unions in supplementing the representative functions of parliament. But ACA now warned against the dangers of substituting corporate representation for individual, and called instead for the statutory consultation of unions in the elaboration of socio-economic legislation.[22]

Politically, integral Catholicism appeared wedged between the two heterodoxies of liberalism, which it had always combated, and extreme nationalism, which increasingly threatened to drag the Church into an autocratic state. There was a growing acceptance of Maritain's view that the victory of nationalism would result only in the perpetuation of old errors. As *Criterio* noted:

> We Catholics have attacked and combated liberalism even before its first social consequences were apparent; we Catholics have fought liberalism when all were agreed that we lived in the best of all worlds and that indefinite progress would bring eternal happiness to the world; so that, in these moments when the liberal disaster is bleeding the world, we do not need [certain nationalist] mentors who claim that we should follow them in 'their' struggle against liberalism. 'Their' struggle is not our struggle; ours carries the solution and theirs aggravates the problem and brings about future disasters. Just as the liberal era seduced many Catholics, the danger today is that [nationalism] will drag with it Catholics who will be responsible for the ills of tomorrow.[23]

Because the 'collaboration with nationalism' option was made increasingly problematic by the apostasy of nationalism, a number of Catholic activists close to Mgr. Franceschi established in mid 1942 the Renovación movement. Renovación was the first attempt to establish a political movement ('party' would have been liberal–democratic) directly from the ranks of integral Catholicism. Its members were of the new generation: leading Catholic Action militants and student leaders, 'who perceived the defects of the liberal system in Argentina, but who energetically repudiated totalitarian alternatives'.[24] Faced with the wartime dichotomy, Renovación rejected the nationalist 'fellow-travelling' preference for neutrality, while simultaneously repudiating the 'semi-colonial' status assigned to Argentina by PanAmericanism and British economic interests. The movement defined itself as nationalist, in as much as it was anti-liberal and neutralist; but it was expressly democratic. The influence of the socioeconomic programmes advocated by ACA was strongly evident: Renovación demanded thorough reforms on the lines demanded by Bunge, while rejecting fascist state corporatism. The discourse of Renovación – which was attacked by nationalists for being weakly ambiguous and by liberals for being further evidence of Argentine fascism – identified with a 'true', Catholic 'third position', and was to be influential on Perón, whom Renovación vigorously opposed.[25]

Renovación's plans to become a leading postwar movement were frustrated by the June coup and Perón's rise. The movement's significance lies in its vision of a multiclass alliance that would bring about radical socioeconomic changes while adhering to democracy. This principle was widely accepted in the Catholic press in the war years, when refutations of the state corporatism of nationalism, not least as a result of European fascism, were common. *Criterio* concentrated heavily on the 'pragmatic', reformist, interventionist states of wartime Britain and New Deal America, which Franceschi argued to be no longer liberal at all. The Anglosaxon nations showed that it was possible to reform liberal democracy in order to avoid a collapse into communism and a totalitarian reaction. Yet in Argentina the failure of Ortiz' reform programme and the Pinedo Plan – both of which had been openly supported by *Criterio* – seemed to demonstrate the obstinacy of Argentine liberalism. With their failure, crisis now loomed. Thorough reform could only be resisted now at the cost of social upheaval. Conservatism in Argentina amounted to a defence of an unjust order which preserved property for the few, denied union rights and female suffrage, and conspired against popular political and economic participation. Drawing on Thomist distinctions, *Criterio* argued that temporary dictatorships were frequently the only defence against tyranny and despotism.[26]

4.4 CATHOLICS AND THE JUNE REVOLUTION

Although it would share many traits in common with the Uriburu coup of 1930, the Revolution of June 1943 expressed a number of the changes of the intervening decade. The Professionalist strain in the army had grown stronger, parallel to the rise of integral Catholicism. By the 1940s, both Church and Army had grown conscious, to a far greater extent than in 1930, of the scholastic underpinnings of their roles. Faced with social decomposition and the abuse of public institutions, the army could and should intervene, just as the Church should speak out when spiritual fundamentals were transgressed. The two were related. The life of the soldier could therefore be compared with that of the priest: one concerned with defence of institutions, the other with the defence of the moral order.[27] Neither Church nor Army were concerned with the business of government, but with the fundamentals of society. The Argentine democracy of 1930–1943 ignored the moral consensus of society and abused its institutions.[28] The army was therefore justified in its intervention, faced with evidence that the system could not or would not reform itself. The fact that the government had been elected by fair means or foul was irrelevant. 'The harsh axiom of Argentine politics', as one historian has observed, was that, 'no constitutional authority is strong enough to prevent a determined president from imposing his will, even if this involves violation of the laws and the constitution itself'.[29] Only the withdrawal of the army's support could prevent despotism.

Uriburu in 1930 had expressed a minority view within the army, one which lacked self-assurance. He had been rapidly displaced by the liberal faction, for whom the army was coterminous with the ideological project of liberalism. In 1943, there was a new determination to prevent such a recurrence. The democratic parties, in the officers' opinion, had forfeited their right to govern; to return the state to them would be to sanction the continued violation of institutions. Yet unlike the liberal faction, the Professionalists strongly adhered to the view that army rule could not replace civilian politics. The justification for intervention remained that of the defence of institutions. Hence, a clean-up of institutions and a return to elections at the war's end was largely inevitable. The constraints imposed by Professionalism on the one hand, and the army's duty to protect the nation from further abuse of its institutions on the other, inevitably created considerable confusion in the junta's ranks. All officers could agree on the need for authentic apoliticism – outside ideologies, social classes and political factions – as well as the need to remain invulnerable to pressure from economic interests. Their positions on the war were in the majority neutralist; although there were minority wings of pro-Allied and pro-Axis officers, most officers defended isolationism as a sovereign right born of lack of identification with the terms of the world struggle. There was little by way of planning for the future. With the exception of General Rawson, who was close to the pro-Allied sectors of Conservatism and AntiPersonalist Radicalism, and had little overall influence, there were two principal factions under two officers. The first was close to Catholic nationalism and identified with General Ramírez. The second, under General Farrell and later Colonel Perón, was identified with the GOU Lodge, and the strain of popular nationalism informed by FORJA.

The first months of the coup reflected these shared priorities. The junta's concern was for order, to be imposed on two fronts: against communists, who were proliferating in labour ranks, and against the politicians and speculators to whose activities the officers directly attributed the widespread social unrest. Congress was dissolved; corrupt governorships such as that of Marcelo Barceló were purged and investigated; reductions in prices of basic foodstuffs, as well as rent reductions designed to alleviate working-class poverty, were decreed; child labour was regulated, and a commission to study cheap housing established. A public morality programme was expressed in decrees prohibiting advertisements for procuring illegal divorce, closing bawdy houses, and imposing a not especially severe moral censorship of films. Acción Argentina, which had been working closely with the US State Department in encouraging the Americans to invade Argentina, was suspended; some months later – faced with accusations of partiality – the military government also decreed the suspension of nationalist groups close to Axis embassies.[30]

In its language and deployment of symbols, Ramírez' tenure was conspicuously identified both with Catholic values and with nationalist critiques. Military addresses were replete with references to 'Catholic' and 'national' values.[31] The Catholic influence was strongly evident in the officers' proclamation, which promised a clean-up of public life, the pacific resolution of the social question, and the return of institutions to moral integrity.[32] General Ramírez' letter to *Criterio* went beyond a vague deism or conservative clericalism and praised 'that Christian justice illuminated from Rome by the encyclicals'.[33] For the first time since the early nineteenth century, government was occupied by men without dogmatic or social insularity from the 'Catholic nation'. Ramírez' proclamations gave *Criterio* confidence. Editorials noted that while both justice and elections were desirable, they were for the present incompatible. The pressing need was for the state actively to intervene to control rents and prices, and to purge institutions of graft.[34] Franceschi called for Catholics to support Ramírez' efforts:

Every Argentine conscious of his duty should place his trust in the present government, supporting it with all his energies and accompanying it in its task. I refuse to think what will happen if the men of the 4th of June fail, for I see no more than two possibilities: either the return to politicking . . . or the dominion of a triumphant sergeant. Both extremes fill me with horror.[35]

On the other hand, the ruling officers reflected the heterogeneity of Argentine nationalism. Although he accurately defended Argentine neutrality as an expression of popular Catholic sentiment, Ramírez was equally prone to a 'Cross and Sword' discourse irritating to the Church. Decree No. 9471 of September 1943, promoting Our Lady of Carmen to the rank of general, was symptomatic of this indelicate promotion of military values over Catholic.[36] Ramírez' secretary would later declare that Catholicism had been a useful instrument for combating communism.[37] This ambiguity was also evident in the military government's initial social policy. Although ACA applauded – as did the unions – the curbs on prices and rents, it published the decree of July 1943 regulating unions without comment. The decree reflected none of the Catholic ambitions, compared poorly in its statism and complexity with the Casiello Bill, and – had it remained on the statute book – would have excluded Catholic unions and made all worker organizations subject to state control. The military conception of capital–labour relations was crudely geometric, and reflected anti-communist priorities.[38]

But in spite of these ambiguities, this was a government which had opened the state to wider values, and therefore offered the possibility of collaboration. A number of prominent Catholics were invited to occupy provincial and cultural posts. Leaders from Renovación, together with a number of intellectuals from the CCC – Atilio Dell'Oro Maini, Mario Amadeo and Tomás Casares – were all appointed to education ministries. In a move that showed the government's determination to restore religious education to schools, Gustavo Martínez Zuviría – a popular novelist close to ACA and Catholic circles, abhorred by the left – was designated Minister of Justice and Public Instruction. The other civil appointments – which were again mainly in the field of education – were of nationalists with a Maurrasian and Positivist background, clerical rather than Catholic, and included Bruno Jordán Genta, Ramón Doll, and Federico Ibarguren. The decision to include these civilians was related to the Storni Affair in October 1943, when a bungled attempt at arms procurement had demonstrated American intransigence and hardened the neutrality resolve within government and the public at large. The army was resolved to retain power until the war's conclusion, and to place the administration on a more secure footing. Institutions were 'depoliticized'; political parties and nationalist groups were dissolved. Liberal critics in universities, a number of whom were active in opposition to the government, were forcibly removed. Finally, religious education was restored to state schools, with special exemptions for those children whose parents asked them to be excluded.[39]

The Religious Education Decree rapidly became the symbol of opposition of the displaced liberal establishment. Faced with evidence that the army was determined not to hand back control of the state to the parties, the parties, with support from displaced teachers and bureaucrats, accused the army of an 'authoritarian project' in collaboration with the Church.[40] But while the symbolic significance of the decree was enormous, and although it was promulgated by an unelected government, it was in fact the least authoritarian of all the government's measures. The law merely confirmed a trend which had become apparent during the 1930s, when religious education had been returned to secondary school curricula by the legislatures of the most populated provinces. The Church's own strategy was for the implementation of Religious Instruction by degrees, moving towards eventual congressional ratification. The December 1943 law was not so much a bid by the army to 'win over' the Church,[41] but a unilateral initiative by Catholic nationalists to overturn the cornerstone of the liberal project. It was considered imprudent (given the government's unconstitutionality) by the bishops, who were singularly unprepared. The Catholic media were quick to point out that the decree was an insecure victory, which would require later congressional ratification, and which would feed the suspicion – which the US State Department and Argentine liberals were anxious to exploit – that the Church sought to secure by force what it could not win by persuasion. The decree, noted *Criterio* defensively, 'satisfies longheld and widespread desires, but does not in any way compromise the Church'.[42]

The terms of the Decree, furthermore, were hardly authoritarian. Unlike law and order legislation, the decree took into account objectors (children could freely opt out if their parents sent a letter); Catholic dogma was only to be taught in state schools, leaving private denominational schools unaffected; the courses, which were orthodox, doctrinal and Thomist, were undertaken by Church-approved teachers rather than the state; and non-Catholic teachers (less than two per cent) were exempted. The 'authoritarianism' of the decree lay rather in the fact of its promulgation by a military government. This in turn raised a host of problems. Were the rent freezes also an undemocratic imposition? Certainly the take-up rate of religious education was massive, an average 93.5 per cent nationwide, thus confirming what Catholic surveys had long demonstrated.[43]

Liberal opposition to the decree expressed a deep-seated anger at the violation of a central cultural canon. For integral Catholics, too, the decree was highly symbolic. The laws of 1884 had been a landmark victory of the secularist battle to fashion a new, anti-religious basis of politics and society. That project had now been overturned, not by the army, which merely reflected wider assumptions, but by changes in society at large. If the 1884 Law had been a victory for the cultural project of the liberal minority, the Religious Education Decree was a triumph of the values of the new classes. Through them, the Church had recovered its 'public space', and this was reflected in a variety of ways in wider society. Much of the army had abandoned its old Germanophile and masonic elements; and despite the communist advances, workers increasingly participated in a 'national' and 'Christian' discourse which was at odds with the rationalist paradigms of the left. Yet the military decree was not merely a reversal of Law 1420. The decree respected conscience, as secularist Christianity, taught to all pupils in spite of most being Catholic, had not. Moral education had not been entrusted to the Church by a clericalist state; rather, the power to form consciences had been taken from the state altogether.[44]

Although the June Revolution pointed to a new kind of society and politics, neither Catholics nor any other group were ready to grasp the mantle. Only months after taking power, the junta was rudderless, waiting largely on the war's outcome. The officers faced the full fury not only of the liberal establishment, but of the US State Department, which took advantage of military fumbling over arms procurement to isolate Argentina in the hemisphere. As a result of irresistible pressure from his colleagues, Ramírez in February 1944 broke off relations with Berlin, accusing the Germans of espionage. It was a major defeat for isolationism; for the Catholic nationalists, it represented a capitulation to Washington. The crisis provoked a haemorrhage of civilians, beginning with Ramírez and Martínez Zuviría, and continuing in a steady stream therafter.[45] Renovación withdrew its collaboration in 1944, and its members resigned provincial posts, although the movement's leader, Bonifacio del Carril, remained in the Ministry of the Interior to assist General Perlinger in his failed attempt to stop Perón.[46]

In the course of the following eighteen months, Colonel Perón was able to take advantage of the vacuum. He did so in the teeth of opposition from the Catholic nationalists, who were quick to recognise both his lack of integrity as well as his personal ambition. Yet the civilian collaborators of the June Revolution had been short on political pragmatism. There was a central ambiguity in nationalist Catholic ambitions which was never fully resolved: on the one hand, there was a need thoroughly to reform the state in order to prepare a new basis for popular government; on the other, they were opposed to exploiting the machinery of state to create new political alliances. Once again, the political future was wrested from them; this time, however, the coup was to lead to what they had long advocated: a new basis of popular, democratic government which placed priorities on socio-economic reform.

For Catholics generally, Peronism was strongly appealing for precisely this reason. Perón, who was long on pragmatism and short on integrity, would say of the nationalists that they pronounced erudite speeches in empty theatres. His political perspicacity led him to build up a base of support among junior officers and labour, and to accept the weakness of Argentina's position *vis à vis* the United States by taking up Washington's offer to sign the Act of Chapultepec in exchange for declaring war on Germany in March 1945. This same realism led him to recognise the importance of the Catholic revival in informing the wider strata of the population outside the liberal establishment. Scorning the lofty categories of the CCC intellectuals, he would instead make a successful appeal to the popular, social radicalism of integral Catholicism. In so doing, Perón managed to break through the cycle of twentieth century Argentine politics: of discredited liberal governments followed by disorientated military juntas.

5 Catholicism and Peronism, 1945–1954

5.1 SCHOLASTICISM IN THE DISCOURSE OF PERONISM

Aware that communism depended on a concept of class struggle which was coherent as long as capital resisted justice and the state defended capital, Perón placed the newly-autonomous state at the service of unions seeking improvements in the conditions of labour, while excluding communists. This strategy was not Perón's alone; he was assisted by José Figuerola in the National Labour Department, whose initial attempts under Ortiz had not been forgotten by unions. But by revoking the repressive union law, by supervising labour contracts, and by forcing employers to meet the demands of social legislation, Perón had the means and the will to demonstrate to labour that not only was the state independent of the major economic interests, but that it also recognised the need for coherent social reform through a transformation of the political economy. The social laws which began to stream from government departments in 1944–1945 – the Peon Statute, the maternity protection law, the creation of a cheap housing commission, the regulation of child labour – were often taken directly from union blueprints, and rapidly acquired the force of law, in stark contrast to the legislative ossification of the previous years.[1]

A sociological debate has long raged over the meaning and nature of labour support for Perón. According to early commentators, liberal and left-wing parties represented the 'rational' interests of workers; labour support for Perón necessarily therefore came from recently-arrived migrants from the interior, vulnerable to 'charisma'. The notion however of a cleavage between 'traditionally-minded' migrants and 'rational', i.e. left-wing, workers, was shown to depend on unsustainable categories of migrant and non-migrant. Indeed, most of the 'new' unions were created after 1946, before which union support for Perón came almost wholly from rank-and-file members of socialist and syndicalist unions. A later explanation therefore pointed to labour pragmatism, and the gains that workers made prior to 1946. Yet this, too, was shown to be largely spurious, given that labour made few precise material gains before Perón's first term. It seems hard not to conclude that worker support for Perón came from traditionally left-wing unions, and was born of a growing political identification.[2] Evidently, labour cooperation with a non-socialist, non-liberal–democratic state, entailed a refutation of the left-wing thesis. However, if it is accepted that the Enlightenment-based tradition of liberalism and socialism was alien to the popular sectors, support for Perón does not seem so misplaced. Argentine workers were socialist only conditionally. The 'condition' depended on the liberal–socialist divide: as long as the state defended the interests of capital, the socialist thesis was coherent; as soon as the workers perceived the state not to be defending the interests of capital, it was rendered incoherent. It follows that the deep-seated ambition of labour was for an arbitrating state overseeing labour–capital relations in deference to a higher justice. Such an interpretation would coincide with research showing the growth in the worker movement, from the late 1930s, of a 'national' and 'Christian' discourse.[3]

Hence the oft-noted cleavage between the workers' own perceptions and those of their socialist leaders. At a time when the left-wing parties repudiated the military government as fascist, supportive unions backed Perón against his detractors in the military government, thus suggesting that they did not share the left's democracy/fascism matrix. The context of war and neutrality added an extra 'national' dimension to this repudiation. Washington's especially intense pressure on Argentina produced both indignation and a sense of Latin–American solidarity in the CGT, which had begun to emphasise defence of national sovereignty at a time when the left-wing parties remained committed both to intervention and to the American–Soviet alliance. Hence, throughout 1944–1945, there were realignments within the CGT and within member unions, union schisms, disputes over union leadership, a growing independence from the left-wing parties and on the part of some a growing identification with Perón's political vision. By October 1945, Perón had established a working relationship with the majority of traditional unions; most, at this stage, were sympathetic to the state's new openness to labour, and sought to take advantage of arbitration facilities while retaining a reasonable degree of autonomy.[4]

The surrender of that autonomy and the growing identification of the fortunes of labour with Perón's political future, has to be placed in the tense, polarised context of 1945. On the one hand, labour was dependent on Perón. The British ambassador noted 'the hysterical hatred of the wealthy' towards his early, mild reforms.[5] Perón was a *de facto* worker by virtue of capitalist repudiation of him. The opposition of capital was made clear in the business Manifesto of June 1945, which condemned Perón's 'excessive interventionism' and served notice of the capitalist resolve to combat recent labour gains. Nor, at this point, could unions look to any assistance from the left, which saw the capitalist manifesto as furthering the anti-fascist cause and so supported it. On the other hand, Perón was dependent on labour. He searched for mainstream political allies and found none: Sabattini, by now the UCR's principal personality, with a strong, if provincial, popular following, spurned his overtures, while businessmen were impatient of what they saw as blackmail in Perón's *après moi le déluge* appeal to them.

As the cultural rift became increasingly identified with class, therefore, the colonel shifted towards a position that was overtly identified with labour against 'the oligarchy'. Arguing that the class struggle became a reality when capital opposed the dignity and rights of workers, he portrayed the liberal exaltation of freedom as concealing the self-interest of a minority of wealthy. Against the 'dictatorship of capital' Perón counterposed a 'true democracy' where workers would have the socioeconomic standing to enable them to take their place as political citizens.[6]

With this eminently well-adjusted discourse Perón was able to create a mass-based political alliance sufficiently fast to avoid the military government handing back power to the liberal parties. By the time Socialists and Communists combined with Radicals (although Sabattini remained aloof) and Conservatives in the March of Constitution and Liberty led by the American ambassador, Spruille Braden, they had lost most of their unions to Perón, who was now unstoppable. The breach between the liberal establishment and the 'new classes' hardened into a clear Peronism versus anti-Peronism: democracy versus fascism according to liberals; social justice for the people versus privileged oligarchy, according to Peronists. The Socialist Party continued to claim that it spoke for the 'authentic' working class, but spontaneous stoppages and strikes nationwide following Perón's arrest by fellow officers, and the mass demonstration which led to his release and announcement of elections, showed that for the majority of labour the political future of Perón was identical with its interests and aspirations.[7]

The trade union legislation of December 1945 reflected this interdependence. The decree effectively vetoed independent unions, and therefore fulfilled Perón's need for a politically-loyal labour movement. At the same time, the legislation incorporated a series of union demands, such as automatic deduction of dues and a limitation to one union per profession (*sindicato único*), thereby endorsing the CGT's desire for a unified, consolidated, protected labour organization in a privileged alliance with the state.[8] Perón was assisted not only by left-wing support of employers, but also by Braden's hastily constructed attempt to prevent Perón's victory in February 1946, by publishing documentary evidence of an alleged Nazi connection with Argentina. Although the allegations of the Blue Book were scorned both by Braden's successor in Buenos Aires and by subsequent research, at the time they were published gleefully by the liberal and left newspapers, enabling Perón to identify the establishment with national betrayal. In a clean election in 1946, Perón won with a clear majority against the Unión Democrática alliance of Radicals, Socialists, Conservatives and Communists.[9]

Who voted for him? The Peronist victory was decisive but, as a breakdown of the results in Argentina's major province demonstrates [Table 5.1], both alliances in the 1946 election had parties with broad bases of support. The division between Peronist and anti-Peronist cannot therefore be described as 'popular vs. antipopular', as in the FORJA paradigm. Nor, in spite of the rhetoric, was the class basis of the election categoric. While Perón received strong support from heavily-populated industrial areas, much of the 'marginal' population (recently-arrived migrants) retained previous political loyalties. In the interior Perón attracted votes not from a rural proletariat (which also

Table 5.1 Results of the presidential election of 1946 in Buenos Aires Province: percentages by party and coalition

Alliance	Party	% per party	% per coalition
Peronists	P. Laborista:	36.6	54.8
	UCR–JR:	15.9	
Unión Democrática	UCR	31.7	
	P. Conservador:	6.0	39.3
	P. Socialista:	3.1	
	P. Comunista:	2.9	

Source: I. Llorente, 'Alianzas políticas en el surgimiento del peronismo: el caso de la Provincia de Buenos Aires', in M. Mora y Araujo and I. Llorente, *El Voto Peronista. Ensayos de sociología electoral argentina*, Buenos Aires, 1980, p. 292.

retained its Conservative and Radical loyalties) but from small-scale agricultural entrepreneurs. In Córdoba Province, for example, the poorest provinces returned Unión Democrática candidates, while in the *pampa gringa*, the most modern and prosperous agricultural sector, home to immigrant *arrendatarios*, support for Perón was overwhelming. In towns, support was amorphously lower middle-class; yet in Buenos Aires Province, where [Table 5.1] the UCR–JR took half of the Peronist vote, the party was associated with both rural and urban bosses. Only in industrial areas where unionised labour was strong was Perón's support class-based, but the working class as a whole was far from exclusively Peronist. Yet to affirm the social complexity of Peronism is not to say that it was 'populist', for the support of marginal urban populations and dispossessed farmers tended to go in 1946 to Conservative and Radical Parties.[10]

This analysis of the Peronist vote makes any explanation of Peronism as 'charismatic' unsustainable, for those social groups most likely to be 'won over' by charisma are precisely those groups – poor migrants from the interior – which retained traditional political loyalties established in the 1930s under the influence of electoral *caudillos*. As a description of Peronism, fascism, even if defined mildly as 'reactionary dictatorship', assumes major economic interests and middle classes allying to forestall a working-class communist revolt, whereas Peronism clearly represented labour and was abhorred by the major economic interests. The few Argentines who could be called 'fascist' – authoritarians and traditionalists of the 1930s–1940s – nearly all opposed Perón. Despite his corporatist ambitions, furthermore, most *fuerzas vivas* remained outside the state, of which the unions were the only important organized element. It is true that the Labour and UCR–JR parties were dissolved in favour of a single party, but neither was much more than an electoral vehicle. The dissolution of the Labour Party was unopposed by the majority of union leaders, who renounced political autonomy in order to safeguard union autonomy and to possess a strong voice in government. Nor was this symbolic: between 1946 and 1955, some three thousand trade unionists occupied government posts; while almost half of the Peronist block in Congress and three ministers in the first cabinet were made up of men from the ranks of organised labour.[11]

Another interpretation of the Peronist/anti-Peronist divide is offered by a 'national(ist) vs. anti-national(ist)' dichotomy. This interpretation is suggestive because it alludes to a cleavage, part historical and part cultural, between the 'old' Argentina of the liberal project and the 'new'

Argentina which contested it; and further points to a division expressive of a cultural loyalty beyond strictly material or class factors. Its main weakness however is the ambiguity of the term 'nationalist'. Although Perón would draw on much of the language and values of 1930s nationalism, his constituency did not lie in the nationalist groups. Maurrasians and Catholic nationalists who had joined the June Revolution abhorred Perón for having twisted its ideals for partisan political purposes; and a number correctly foresaw in his empiricism a future collectivism. The 'Yrigoyenist' nationalists of FORJA, on the other hand, threw their support behind him, seeing in him a revival of French-Revolutionary notions of popular sovereignty. But the biggest nationalist grouping, the ALN, was suspicious of Perón's flirtation with unions, and ran its own candidates. If 'formal' nationalism is rejected in favour of a 'national sentiment', inflamed by the blatant interference of the United States, which led to a vote for Perón out of 'patriotic resentment',[12] it is hard to account for the fact that *arrendatarios* resented American interference, and not poor farmers. There *was* a cultural divide in Argentina in the 1940s, but it requires a more coherent terminology.[13]

The possibility of a Catholic sympathy playing a role in Perón's victory has often been suggested. Yet – to understate the matter – 'neither [Perón nor Evita] was known as a religious person until Perón launched his candidacy'.[14] The historian searches in vain for evidence of a Catholic background. For Perón openly to live out of wedlock, as he did until marrying Eva Perón in a civil ceremony in late 1945, was an open defiance of matrimonial sanctity about which he appeared unconcerned. Faced with this paradox, attempts have been made to account for Catholic support for Perón by suggesting 'understandings' on a number of issues vital to the Church – such as state subsidies and religious education – between Perón and bishops, which led them to influence voters in the government's favour.[15] The mechanism of this influence has traditionally been located in the Pastoral Letter issued shortly before the elections, which 'effectively' vetoed support for the opposition alliance, the UD. Reversing these arguments, but from a similar perspective, some historians deny altogether any grounds for the Church favouring Perón in 1946. Yet these studies risk portraying the Church as ideologically irrelevant, when it is hard to ignore the argument that the relationship between Catholicism and Peronism was from the start both intense and conflictual.[16]

The weakness of all these interpretations lies in their view of the Church acting in politics as a form of lobby or corporation, representing a particular constituency, and marshalling its votes to secure constituent benefits. Such a model however belongs to the United States or other countries where Catholics form minorities. In Catholic countries in this period, the model was that of 'neo-Christendom'. Whatever the state's view of the Church, the Church saw itself as the guardian of the moral and spiritual framework of the nation as a whole. The Pastoral reflected a standard, and longstanding, ecclesiastical outlook. It is not the case that 'in 1946 the Church supported Perón by reissuing a pastoral that forbade Catholics to vote for parties that upheld lay schools, divorce, and the separation of church and state'.[17] The Pastoral Letter, issued in November 1945, which repeated the stipulations of 1931, also incorporated papal pronouncements against totalitarianism, exaggerated nationalism as well as economic liberalism. It was released, as before, prior to the announcement of candidates and policies, in order to allow participating parties to adjust their electoral programmes accordingly.

The question of whether or not the Pastoral in the event influenced voting patterns is problematic. Although the UD was an amalgam of parties, from liberal–conservative to Communist, at least one of which sustained platforms contrary to the Pastoral Letter, Perón was chary of overt support for any of its tenets, and refrained during the election campaign from committing himself even to the ratification of the Religious Education Decree.[18] His circumspection derived from the ambiguity of being the candidate of two parties, one of which, the Partido Laborista, whose leaders had a socialist background, favoured the expulsion of Church education from schools; and the other of which, the UCR–JR, had a significant Catholic component.[19] The small group of 'democratic' Catholics in *Orden Cristiano*, who voted against Perón on the liberal premiss that the election presented a choice between democracy and fascism, had little difficulty in justifying their decision canonically.[20] They pointed to the Pastoral's warning against totalitarianism, argued Perón was a totalitarian, and voted accordingly. Articles in the mainstream Catholic press argued that Perón sought to 'use' the Church, and deplored the encouragement of class hostility, the use of papal encyclicals and religious imagery for electoral purposes. *Criterio* ran two long and unambiguous condemnations of the inadmissibly statist trades union law. Unsurprisingly, the issue was hotly debated among Catholics.[21]

A second, invalid assumption, is that Perón had good relations with the Church hierarchy, when he was from the first greeted with suspicion and coldness by bishops. There was even less sympathy in

Rome. The Vatican Secretary of State, the future Pope Paul VI, who had been an educator of the Italian Christian Democrats, was close to Maritain; the French philosopher was in turn in regular contact with 'democratic' Catholics in Buenos Aires. *Orden Cristiano*'s director, Alberto Duhau, even lobbied Cardinal Spellman and Spruille Braden to have Archbishop Copello recalled to Rome on the grounds that he had not expressly opposed Perón. As a result the Vatican, aware simultaneously of Perón's appeal to Catholics and of Christian–Democratic critiques, remained merely cordial in its relations with both the candidate and the president.[22]

The reasons for a widespread Catholic endorsement of Perón are to be found not in institutional nor canonical factors, nor in the alleged episcopal views and powers of persuasion, but rather in Perón's remarkable capacity to echo the priorities, shaped by the Catholic revival, of Argentina's 'new classes'. Perón's first public references were almost wholly devoid of references to the Church, and betrayed his own views, and those of FORJA, in his identification of the French Revolution as the 'source of social justice' in history. But he learned quickly from José Figuerola in the Labour Department, whose vision of class collaboration and a mediating state was in turn influenced by the Spanish Jesuit Joaquín Aspiazu, as well as by Alejandro Bunge. Perón also enjoyed the collaboration of two socially *engagé* priests, Virgilio Filippo and Hernán Benítez, who saw in the emergent movement an identification with labour demands and the social and economic incorporation of the working classes demanded in Pius XII' allocution of Christmas 1944. Absorbing this discourse, Perón by the end of 1944 was beginning to make explicit references to encyclicals, and to employ key Catholic terms and concepts. He spoke of dignifying labour and humanizing capital; of the gradual extension of ownership to those who worked land; and of the equidistance of the 'National Revolution' from all (implicitly Enlightenment) ideologies. He evoked the alienation of non-liberal Argentina in calling for democracy to be rescued from the monopoly of the liberal establishment, while articulating integral-Catholic alienation from the secular dichotomy in his 'Third Position'. Politically, this implied a refutation equally of individualism and of collectivism, and of Left and Right; economically, it expressed equidistance from both capitalism and communism; and internationally, it appealed to the Catholic justification for neutrality in Argentina's independence equally from the US and USSR. Perón also borrowed Catholic distinctions between a liberal democracy which defined freedom and equality in a purely political sense, on the one hand, and a 'true' (socioeconomic) democracy, on the other. The mediating role for the state in harmonising and reconciling capital and labour was explicitly reminiscent of *Rerum Novarum*.[23]

As in his dealings with the unions, Perón backed up his discourse with positive action. Social-Catholic activists were impressed by his determination to implement the priorities of the encyclicals, which had been already demonstrated by 1946.[24] The family wage plan presented by ACA in 1941 became law. The VOC plan for technical training in factories and regulation of child labour was adopted in its entirety in mid-1944. These and other measures led ACA's Socio-Economic Secretariat confidently to assert that legislation emanating from the newly-created Secretariat of Labour & Prevision (STP) 'signals the beginning of the Christian restoration of the economy of our country'.[25] After years of lobbying and frustrated reports on the progress of laws, the Secretariat now concentrated on publicising the STP legislation, and on organising elaborate campaigns involving all ACA branches, as well as JOC and VOC, to encourage workers to enforce the legislation. It was unquestionable that, as the Secretariat concluded in May 1944, there now prevailed, 'a new climate, more favourable to social principles of Catholic inspiration . . . in families, in all social classes, and in our cultural and public institutions'. If the June Revolution had opened the door to Catholic values, culturally and sociologically, Perón appeared to embrace not just the values but also the social and moral implications of the Catholic revival.[26]

If the hypothesis is posited that the root of the popular identification with Perón lay in his capacity to echo the tenets of integral Catholicism, a number of the anomalies of the Peronist/anti-Peronist division in 1946 are explained. In Córdoba, for example, the anticlericalism of Sabattini's UCR contrasted strongly with the medievalist discourse of the dissident Radicals in the UCR–JR. Dissident Conservative leaders who became Peronist candidates were also 'Catholic traditionalists'. Middle-class Catholic support for Perón came from ACA, which in Córdoba had a mass character, and which held large outdoor meetings campaigning for radical social reform; from the numerous Catholic consortia of lawyers, architects and doctors; and the 10,000–strong Córdoba Workers' Federation, which was Catholic until it was taken over by the CGT in 1945. JOC, in spite of the trade union legislation, threw in its lot with Perón from the start. Because those classes with an 'integral-Catholic' conception were likely to be children of immigrants from southern Spain and Italy, areas at the margin of the currents of the Reformation and Enlightenment, the support Perón received from immigrant *arrendatarios* in Córdoba, and the attraction to the UCR–JR of rural bosses in Buenos Aires Province, are both accounted for.[27] Conversely, within the urban upper and middle classes, whose outlook had been shaped by the liberal project of the 1880s, repudiation of Peronism was near universal.[28] In these social milieux, it was conspicuously Catholics who favoured collaborating with worker demands, and who openly supported Peronism, to the disgust of their neighbours.[29] The minority of Catholics in *Orden Cristiano* who stood for the liberal *Iglesia Nacional* model represented by De Andrea, deployed language identical with the liberal establishment. *Orden Cristiano* loftily declared that the 1946 elections were 'fraudulent, because the consciences of the ignorant masses have been once again corrupted'.[30] Similar patterns can be seen within the women's movement. The Asociación Argentina del Sufragio Femenino (AASF), which campaigned throughout the 1930s for labour laws and female suffrage with support from ACA, threw its support behind Perón and later provided many of the leading figures of the Partido Peronista Femenino. Left–liberal feminists – upper-class women such as Victoria Ocampo and María Rosa Oliver – in the Unión Argentina de Mujeres (UAM) abhorred Peronism to the point where they chose the UD (against female suffrage) rather than Perón (who favoured it openly) in 1946. The disparity in popularity between the two forms of female politics was reflected in the 1952 vote for Perón following the female suffrage law, a very large proportion of which came from women.[31]

The integral-Catholic/liberal dichotomy also suggests an explanation of the bewildering ferocity of liberal repudiation of Peronism. Liberal hostility, whether from right or left, was visceral, and suspended the allegedly 'rational' criteria of Enlightenment political alignments. Hence, the left joined the American 'capitalists' against the working class, feminists voted against female suffrage, and Conservatives marched alongside Communists. All were united in a common cultural struggle against the irruption of values which Perón echoed. This was, of course, the end of the war, and the repudiation of fascism, as in Europe, created strange bedfellows. But as the neutrality issue had demonstrated, Argentines outside liberal groups did not share the latter's moral fervour on this issue; nor, as worker support for Perón showed, did they consider Perón fascist (or at least attributed the same meaning to the word). The term *fascista* in Argentina in the mid-1940s, Fr. Castellani significantly observed, performed a similar function to that of *papist* in seventeenth-century England, to connotate 'something at once indeterminate and horrible'.[32]

Liberal anger and scorn were provoked by Perón's subversion of the right of the 'enlightened' to rule, and the language was one of indignation. The socialist *La Vanguardia*, for example, referred to the workers who had demonstrated on the 17th October as a 'horde' or *chusma*. Despite the workers' remarkable pacificity, Communists talked of 'barbarous' Peronists going against 'modesty and honesty, against decency, against culture'. They saw 'right reason' everywhere subverted. A socialist leader referred to 'powerful and primitive forces' which 'broke the rules of living logic and reason' and which 'altered the appraisals and values for other appreciations and value judgements'.[33] Liberal revulsion stands in uncomfortable juxtaposition to the language of Peronist workers, who talked of recovering *'an old lost language . . . a fundamental historical line*: the most appropriate for a national and popular movement'.[34] A leading socialist, Nicolás Repetto, appeared to acknowledge the possibility of such sentiments echoing a deeper (religious?) loyalty, when he blamed socialist propaganda for its absence of 'those conditions which gave human life a more elevated and spiritual tone'.[35]

5.2 PERONISM'S SECULAR–THEOCRATIC IMPULSE

The identification of the 'new' Argentina, underpinned by scholasticism and shaped by the Catholic revival, with Perón, testified to his remarkable capacity to act as a channel, or conduit, of values and priorities. Yet Perón's own outlook was shaped by secularist, Rousseaunian values, which were soon to manifest themselves once in power. In the period between 1944 and 1949, the discourse of Peronism became increasingly detached from apparently scholastic underpinnings. As the nationalists had observed, behind Perón's ear whispered the ghosts of Macchiavelli and Rousseau: the first seeking to identify with the Church for express political purposes, the second seeking to install a civil religion that would abolish all distinction between state and law. Yet the climactic nature of his election would carry forward Catholic goodwill for some years.

During his first term, Perón consolidated his identification with Catholic priorities in a number of ways. He endorsed the congressional ratification of the Religious Education Decree in 1947, oversaw substantial increases in state contributions to the ecclesiastical budget, appointed well-known Catholics at high levels of the administration, maintained an 'open door' policy with Church leaders of enormous symbolic significance, and adopted Christian social thought as the 'official' doctrine of government, prior to the creation of *justicialismo* in 1949.[36] He was careful to identify himself with Hispanic values and the spiritual community of Hispanidad. Nor was this merely symbolic, for Argentina's support of Spain in the United Nations, in defiance of post-war liberal triumphalism against Franco, gave substance to Argentina's professed equidistance from both the 'Protestant-individualist imperialism' of Britain and America and the 'atheistic totalitarianism' of the Soviet Union.[37] A Catholic influence is observable in many of the documents of the first period. The Rights of the Worker of 1947 located the origin of those rights in the *personality* of the worker, in contrast to both individualist and collectivist conceptions.[38] In Córdoba, the local constitution was changed to incorporate Catholic values as the principal objective of education; while the 1949 Peronist Constitution, influenced by that of Ireland of 1937, committed Argentina to subsidiarity, defended moral and religious education from state intervention, and upheld the Church's 'divine mission' to teach. The document also placed particular emphasis on the family, and appealed directly to Aquinas and pontifical documents in definitions of property as simultaneously social and personal.[39]

The First Five Year Plan, whose principal architect was José Figuerola, echoed a host of women's concerns from an explicitly Catholic standpoint. It instigated tax relief for large families, endorsed the family wage, protected female labour, and gave housing priorities to married couples. The Plan also approved national campaigns, led by women, aimed at reversing the declining birth rate, protecting pregnant women, repressing abortion, sustaining the indissolubility of marriage and campaigning for legal recognition of canonical marriage. The discourse of Eva Perón also borrowed in its initial stages from Catholic feminism. Women were seen as the conscience and moral force of humanity. Female altruism and sacrifice were counterposed to the egotism and materialism of men. And the Partido Peronista Femenino made much of the pre-modern 'heroic' notions of femininity.[40]

Peronism was as 'naturally' Catholic as it was 'naturally' creole. It owed more to the straightforward understanding of the *barrio* parish priest than to the detached and individualist formulas of the intelligentsia. It spoke the language of the common man; valued family, motherhood, and justice. Yet Peronism was from the start controversial in activist Catholic circles. *Criterio* had objected strongly to the trade union law, which was little more than a blueprint of the inadmissible *Carta del Lavoro*; it had criticised Perón's exploitation of class resentments for political purposes; and there were many indications in the Catholic press that the very flexibility of Perón's thinking signalled the dangers of empiricism and Machiavellianism. Ironically, the tendencies in Peronism towards statism and despotism violated the very doctrines which early documents defended. This in large part explains the subsequent view of many Catholics that Peronism was twisted and subverted by Perón. At root, the active support of integral Catholics was conditional on the state's recognition of the spiritual supremacy of the Church. A Peronism that ceased to defer to a higher spiritual law safeguarded by the Church, would cease to be the Peronism voted for in 1946. A popular parish priest, Fr. Rodolfo Carboni, made this clear in responding to the allegations of *Orden Cristiano* that in supporting Perón the clergy had compromised the dignity of the Church. If the 'democratic' Catholics, he wrote,

> mean that the majority of the clergy inclined in the last elections towards Colonel Perón, and advised that others do the same, what they affirm is correct. And if Colonel Perón were to defraud the expectations of the Catholics who voted for him – which I do not believe will happen, for one has the impression of a man who will know how to listen to the Church – even then the 'democrats' will be able to say nothing against us. We would always have done what was asked of us. We were obliged to vote according to our principles; we were not asked to be prophets.[41]

The union issue was the first major contention between Catholics and the government. The CGT leaders had favoured the Professional Associations Decree of 1945, for all it offered them in terms of political weight; it was congenial to Perón for all it permitted him by way of economic planning and political mobilisation. In 1944, the CGT leadership denounced the intromission of religion in unions, appealing to Perón's own definitions of unions as politically and religiously 'neutral.' In September of that year, an application was made for legal recognition of 23 unions, including the important Luz y Fuerza Union led by Luis Salas, and seven more in formation, which all belonged to the newly-formed Catholic Confederation of Unionised Workers. Perón's refusal effectively condemned independent Catholic unions. Only the old mutualist, CCO type of syndicate, tied to the hierarchy –

and in the 1940s languishing – could survive, for these were Church organisations rather than independent unions of social-Catholic inspiration. In order to be a legal union, it was henceforth necessary both to be part of the CGT, and ideologically and religiously 'neutral' (i.e. Peronist).

Criticism from Church quarters was immediate. *Criterio* denounced the Professional Associations Decree of December 1945 as the state corporatism condemned in *Quadragesimo Anno*. The law would henceforth grant the state inadmissible powers in *determining* rather than *recognising* the legal validity of professional associations; allowed for only one union per profession; and while preventing unions from being instruments of political parties, permitted them to mobilise in the state's favour. The legislation preventing a union from declaring itself doctrinally socialist or Catholic was totalitarian. The prohibition on gender-based unions, which the Church argued to be essential for the specific needs of women workers, would clearly harm female syndicates, the majority of which were Catholic.[42]

The union issue did not provoke a Catholic-Peronist split in 1944 for four principal reasons. First, in the context of the polarisation of the pre-election period, *jocistas* and other *obrerista* Catholics shared the concern of labour for a unified front against capital. Perón's argument that syndical pluralism would benefit the bosses was therefore more convincing than doctrinal considerations. Second, Church organisations of the *andreista* mould were not favoured by integral Catholics; a united union movement that was at least officially 'Christian' (as Peronism identified itself) was to be preferred to confessional unions excluded from a left-wing CGT. Third, syndical liberty would allow unions to continue to be instruments of left-wing political parties, and unions tied to parties further undermined the united front against capital. Fourth, integral Catholics recognised the need for Perón to secure labour support; heterodox tendencies could be tolerated if they could be amended after the election. In spite of warnings from nationalist Catholics, Perón's good faith was still assumed in mainstream Catholic ranks. The strategy of Catholic Action was to lobby government to alter the terms of the decree prior to the congressional ratification in late 1946. A counter-proposal submitted by ACA was for a combination of syndical pluralism (any amount of unions per profession) within a framework of syndical unity (delegates from each union representing the profession as a whole in a higher body); the freedom to allow unions to be founded on religious or political principles, while being independent of the Church and political parties; as well to allow for women's unions, which catered to specific needs.[43]

In the face of overt Catholic opposition, however, the decree was ratified, unaltered, and would remain so, despite ACA's efforts again in 1948.[44] The failure to overturn the union legislation showed two tendencies in Peronism which would gradually harden. The first was the retention of collectivist assumptions in the union movement in spite of their formal rejection of socialism. Alongside the overt references to Christianity were allusions to 'the social function of property' and the class struggle.[45] Union leaders would frequently emphasise the 'practical' superiority of Christianity as practised by Peronists.[46] The second factor was Perón's own statist-corporatist conception of the unions as arms of the state. The Catholic union legislation would destroy any possibilities for political mobilisation of workers.

Still in need of broad political support, Perón weaved between the anticlerical views of labour leaders and the official adoption of social Catholicism. The tension became apparent in the congressional debate preceding ratification of the Religious Education Decree. Opposition to ratification came from a number of *laboristas* with socialist backgrounds. Perón, who understood the popularity of religious education, was nevertheless careful not to put pressure on them until after the Partido Laborista had been dissolved, and made immediate moves to demonstrate that he was not 'in the hands of the Church' by implicating three priests in the trumped-up revelation, the following year, of a 'plot' by the *laborista* Cipriano Reyes. (The priests were set free; Reyes languished in gaol, where he rediscovered his Catholic faith). This pandering to worker anticlericalism was followed by other signals to labour that the state was above the Church: in 1948, for example, the government withdrew religious subsidies from the Diocese of Mercedes following the Bishop's refusal to defrock a priest who had offended a local Peronist *caudillo*; and a year later, a prohibition on public religious processions was ordered. Typically, Perón would not allow bishops' protests to develop into outright opposition, either by denying giving the orders or by making reparations. These patterns pointed to Perón's need to retain a Christian discourse while he attempted to separate it from the Church.[47]

The conflict with Catholicism became latent when the 'union model' of political organisation began gradually to extend into society at large. While continuing publicly to laud the Church and to tolerate Catholics in government, Perón moved away from a position which ostensibly deferred to Catholicism as the spiritual basis of Argentine society, and towards an elaboration of a secular doctrine, with its origin in the state, that would draw on Christian ethics and doctrine devoid of its external source. Logically, the appropriation of the higher law would collapse spiritual and temporal distinctions, harness law to will, and create a self-augmenting totalitarian impulse. It was evident in the formula of the 1947 Declaration of Workers' Rights, which, in spite of its superficial likeness to Thomist conceptions of the person, fixed the source of rights in positive law, rather than in eternal law, as did the French Revolutionary *Droits de l'Homme* on which it was clearly based.[48] Hence, the state conceded rights, rather than deferring to them. Rights were concessions of positive law, did not inhere; they could equally be withdrawn by the state.

The creation of an official state doctrine, *justicialismo*, in 1949, pointed to the government's determination to detach Christian discourse from the Church and to deploy it as an ideology capable of uniting Argentines. Similar to Rousseau's *religion civile* in that it recognised no anterior source (to the state) for the truths it proclaimed, *justicialismo* was an ideology that sought to occupy the moral and spiritual space belonging, in Argentina, to the Church. Its totalitarian implications lay in the empirical premiss on which it was predicated. Like fascism, or Nazi 'national Christianity', *justicialismo* upheld Christian and humanist values; but like those doctrines uprooted them from eternal principles of which the institutional Church in a Catholic country, guardian of the spiritual sphere, is the defence, thereby abolishing the distinction between law and will. Liberalism had endorsed the moral autonomy of the individual; Peronism endorsed the moral autonomy of the state.

The face of Peronism was now showing itself as turned towards the French Revolution. In spite of its superficial resemblances with nationalism and clericalism, and in spite of its pseudo-corporatism, Peronism was essentially modern, relying on mass mobilisation and elections and notions of nationhood and popular will that were born in 1789. The urge towards a civil religion began to be publicly evident when the state entered into competition with the Church for the appropriation of spiritual authority. In 1948, Perón chose to award an episcopal cross to Monsignor De Carlo, Bishop of Chaco and Formosa, for his work with the poor. The Church's disapproval was made clear in the absence of Archbishop Copello. That the award was intended to demonstrate that the state could choose 'its' priests was made clear in an accompanying lecture on how the Church should return to the purity of its sources. The same speech offered indications of Perón's own secularist outlook. Religions were portrayed as relative, as expressions of culture; and the history of thought was a Comtian progression through stages (Christ's Word was merely a philosophical advance on Greek thought, in turn superseded). Most obviously of all, the state was the arbiter of 'good' and 'bad' Christianity.[49] Again, in 1950, Perón presented a classically secularist contrast between the 'real' (i.e. empirical, 'practical' Peronist practice of) Christianity, identified with the 'people' as a form of *religion civile*, on the one hand, and a Church of irrelevant rites and vestments, on the other. In defining Peronist 'popular Christianity', he presented a philosophy of good works – descramentalized, demystified, and plebeian:

> I think that to be a good Christian it is not just a question of performing the externals of religious ritual. A good Christian is not one who goes to mass every Sunday . . . A bad Christian is one who, making efforts to fulfil the formal requirements of religion, underpays his workers . . . That is why, *compañeros*, Peronism, which perhaps sometimes does not respect the forms but which tries to assimilate and carry out the deeper message, is an effective, real and honourable way to realise Christianity . . . We want to be Christians in our works, not out of the clothes we put on nor the formalities we respect . . . that is our Christianity. the practical, Justicialist Christianity.[50]

There were three main phases in the state's attempt to appropriate spiritual authority. In its first phase, the state established parallel institutions to compete with those of the Church, while attempting to arrogate objective spiritual values such as 'justice' to the state. Generally, Catholic organisations remained intact, but deprived of legal benefits; and a counter Peronist organization would be established alongside it, as with the Peronist Hogar de la Empleada directly emulating the long-established Hogar de la Empleada owned by the FACE.[51] Legal recognition of Catholic unions would be withdrawn whenever they competed with a Peronist equivalent, as occurred in Córdoba in 1949 when the Catholic Public Employees' Union was disallowed.[52] Evita defined her 'work' as 'neither philanthropy, nor social solidarity, nor beneficence' but 'strictly justice'.[53] Similarly, Perón sought 'a just balance between workers and bosses, under the protection of *the justice which emanates from the state*'.[54] The work of the Peróns was portrayed as a form of *aggiornamento*, not practising what the Church preached but preaching what the Church had failed to practise. Temporal and spiritual came to be inverted altogether: thus, 'Christianity will be true when love reigns among men . . . but love will come only when men . . . are Justicialists'.[55]

The second stage of secularization was the growing use of religious symbolism and imagery. This characteristic of Peronist discourse from the late 1940s has been often misinterpreted by commentators as clericalism, or even more grievously as a symptom of a Church–state alliance in the old regalist Cross-and-Sword mould. It was the precise opposite: the use of religious imagery followed on from an attempt by the state to detach Christianity from the Church. Peronist doctrine was entirely devoid of reference to the Church, and no effort was made to appeal to it. Nor, when Peronist propaganda began to enter schools, was the ambition concealed. Schoolchildren learned from Eva Perón that Perón belonged to 'that class of people who created new religions'. Presidential speeches came to be filled with moral exhortations, backed up by Biblical citations, selectively interpreted; Peronist doctrine was to be 'preached' rather than taught, and the new Constitution was portrayed as an attempt to overcome 'egotism'.[56] State literature and propaganda associated Eva's death in 1952 with renunciation, sacrifice and martyrdom. She was the *Jefa Espiritual de la Nación*, a secular Virgin Mary, and featured on the standard school edition of her autohagiography with a halo.[57]

In attempting to harness the spiritual sphere to the state, the Peronist Third Position logically ceased to defer to a higher spiritual authority *beyond* the secularist dialectic, but attempted 'a harmony between opposites . . . flight from the instability of extremes towards the point of balance between them'.[58] As in the Rousseaunian theory of the General Will, democracy was defined in Peronist discourse as 'one where the government does what the people want'; there was no higher interest than that of the *conjunto*; while 'people should control the government' and the majority always obeyed. Having made their choice, the people handed over all rights to the state: 'the people chose us. Therefore, this problem is no more. The Republic does what we say.' And as in Jacobin notions of national sovereignty, the 'nation' was portrayed as a personality, the final moral authority, the ultimate end for which 'good' Argentines laboured. The nation was the final moral value outside the the state, but as Peronism was the incarnation of the national will, the nation was necessarily defined by the state. This self-fulfilling circularity, which is the central tenet nourishing totalitarianism, resulted in an incessant outpouring of arbitrary moral categories. A set of *chiaroscuro* dichotomies entered Peronist discourse.

Pueblo (good) was counterposed to *anti-pueblo* (bad); the *pueblo* worked for the good of the nation, while the *oligarquía* lived off others.[59] The 'Twenty Truths of Justicialism' collapsed in a welter of philosophical commonplaces and manichean absolutes.

The final stage of Peronist secularization was the annihilation of truth as an objective datum, and the objectivisation of *justicialismo*. In this stage, from around 1952–3, doctrines were seen as mobile, to be dispensed with as they became unnecessary or antiquated.[60] Loyalty tests were imposed on bureaucrats, and party membership required of all who worked for the state.[61] Laws ceased to be designed for unforeseen cases and indeterminate transgressors (in keeping with a law outside the state), to become both *personal* (aimed at particular groups) and *partisan* (directed at opponents of the régime).[62] Peronism began to seek a simultaneous temporal and spiritual fusion of individual wills in a single self-consciousness. The first article of the Peronist Party Statute in 1948 had announced the Party to be 'a spiritual and doctrinal unity' incompatible with division.[63] This principle began to be applied in schools. The purpose of education, according to the Second Five-Year Plan, was that of 'uniting all Argentines in one sole desire, one sole will'.[64] Like the proponents of *morale laïque* in late nineteenth-century France, Perón judged the intrinsic value of a doctrine by its capacity to be universally instilled.[65] The 'human mass' must become 'a harmonious being'; the Escuela Superior Peronista, established in 1953, sought to overcome all 'heterogeneity of interpretations'.[66]

Logically, therefore, those groups which had remained outside the ideological community defined by the state could not be tolerated. Their very presence subverted the state's quest for homogeneity. They were excluded from political society, and stripped of rights. Newspapers – among them the socialist *La Vanguardia* and the Catholic *Los Principios* – were closed; control of the liberal-conservative *La Prensa* was wrested from its shareholders by the CGT; Bunge's review, the *Revista de Economía Argentina*, which had contributed so much to early Catholic-Peronist thinking, was closed. The headquarters of the 'people's enemies' – the socialist and Radical parties, and the Jockey Club – were assaulted. Peronists came to exert a monopoly of the media, and posters of a recognizably socialist and fascist heritage exhibited the chiselled features of the Peronist 'New Man'. State doctrine began to be promulgated in schools.[67] Detached from all external spiritual authority, caught in a spiral of self-justification, both the discourse and political temperament of Peronism had by 1953 become, like the French Revolution or communism, limitless, all-embracing, circular, its vocabulary shorn of referents:

> Peronist doctrine upholds the truth, the naked truth, the absolute truth ... one sole doctrine: the Peronist; one sole flag: that of the fatherland; and one sole greatness: that of the flag, and that of the fatherland.[68]

5.3 THE BIFURCATION OF CATHOLICISM AND PERONISM

It is impossible to locate a point in which Catholicism and Peronism separated. Catholics had taken up a variety of positions towards Perón in 1945. 'Democratic' Catholics had been in outright opposition from the start; nationalists had opposed Perón himself, but sympathised with a number of features of Peronism; the higher clergy had kept their distance; integral Catholics in general embraced Peronism with enthusiasm, although conscious of certain worrying trends. As was evident from the debates and critiques of 1945–6, Catholic support had always been both critical and conditional. This critical stance began to harden in Perón's first term. Between 1949 and 1951, the year of the failed *coup d'état*, Catholics observed the Peronist slide into collectivism with mounting concern, and a number of nationalists became involved in anti-government conspiracies. By 1952, Catholics had turned against Peronism, although some still hoped to correct its decline. From 1953, Catholics passed into active, rather than loyal, opposition. A peaceful but effective anti-government offensive began in the winter of that year, provoking Perón's eventual response in November 1954, which marked the beginning of the overt Church–state conflict.

Catholics in government did not all break with the régime before Perón's second term, although their loyalties were at times severely tested.[69] For others who had collaborated with government but not committed themselves to party membership, the break occurred in 1950–51, when a drive was undertaken by the Party to secure oaths of loyalty from bureaucrats.[70] The Catholic press, prior to this point, had generally taken a stance of critical support. The Córdoba newspaper, *Los Principios*, and the bitterly anti-Peronist *Orden Cristiano* (which closed in 1948 after bishops insisted it removed 'Catholic magazine' from its masthead) were severe in their criticism; *Criterio* and *El Pueblo* sought rather to encourage the orthodox tendencies in government and to indicate its lapses into heterodoxy. In addition to its strong critique of the politicization of the unions, *Criterio* condemned an incipient state capitalism, which it blamed for impoverishing the middle classes and the rural sector.[71] CGT leaders who spoke of Peronism 'superseding' Christianity were reminded that Perón had publicly acknowledged the authority of encyclicals and therefore the theological basis of social justice.[72] While indicating the heterodoxy of the preamble to the 1947 Declaration of Workers' Rights, *Criterio* nevertheless argued that Peronist social reforms represented an overdue recognition of injustice, a failure to support which would amount to its preservation.[73]

This stance of 'critical collaboration' in the late 1940s was based largely on two premisses: the first, that Peronism represented a continuation – however distorted – of the ideals of the June Revolution; and second, that it could be encouraged in the right direction. Because of the influence of Catholics in the formulation of a number of crucial documents, Peronism initially possessed a doctrinal underpinning to which Catholics could point. Of Perón's own discourse, *Criterio* had no doubts as to its secularist primogeniture: the Third Position was an ideological hybrid of capitalism and communism distinct from the Christian conception, which was '*outside* the sphere of those two materialisms'.[74]

The implications of this critique were especially relevant in Argentina's foreign policy. These were the years when the Catholic parties in Europe faced an expanding Soviet bloc and large communist parties within its borders. Argentine Catholics, having maintained that neutrality in the Spanish Civil War was impossible and in the Second World War the only just position, now argued that in the Cold War detachment was again out of the question. The West was no longer allied with totalitarianism. It was a brutal choice between capitalism and communism; equidistance from both was inadmissible, for the former granted greater liberty. Perón's Third Position in foreign policy was therefore seen by critical Catholics as morally relativist. Meinvielle's influential periodical, *Presencia*, called for Argentina to align with the United States against communism, while continuing to reject Panamericanism.[75] Behind this apparent inconsistency was a coherent pattern. The postwar situation in Catholic eyes was similar to the Spanish Civil War: a struggle between Christian civilization, however imperfectly adhered to, and atheistic communism. This dichotomy had not been apparent in World War II, when the Allies were allied with the Soviets. The difference between the Catholic Third

Position and that of Perón was fundamental, and can be seen in the contrast between Perón's advocacy of neutrality in the War – which reflected the FORJA–Sabattini view of national sovereignty as a moral absolute[76] – and that of Catholics.

Catholic disillusionment with Perón was even greater when he was compared with the great leaders of postwar Christian Democracy in Europe, De Gasperi and Adenauer. In 1945, when Maritain's appointment as French Ambassador to the Holy See was widely seen as a Vatican endorsement of his thinking, *Criterio* favourably revised the philosopher's *opus*, noting that it had only ever disagreed with Maritain's practical stance over the Spanish Civil War. Christian Democracy demonstrated that democracy and liberalism were not coterminous, and many Argentine Catholics repented of their former collaboration with nationalism. There was a sense in which Peronism succeeded in highlighting the secularist errors attached to nationalism in a way that Maritain's arguments in the 1930s had not. Shortly prior to the 1946 elections, *Criterio* had defended 'the democratic doctrine of Christian inspiration', citing as its sources the papal allocution of Christmas 1944 and 'the theories of Jacques Maritain'. The review now overtly criticised nationalism as the 'internal enemy'. Nationalism, in Franceschi's opinion, had definitively apostasised.[77] He had called then for 'deputies who are Catholic *[católicos diputados]* but not Catholic deputies *[diputados católicos]*', following Maritain's famous distinctions.[78] After the elections, *Criterio* fell silent on domestic politics, concentrating on the 'Catholic-roots-of-democracy' scholasticism that lay behind Christian Democracy in Europe, as if inviting its readers to contrast it with Peronism. In the late 1940s and early 1950s, however, the review began overtly to condemn a number of the features of the Peronist state: the introduction of Peronist propaganda in schools, the government's encroaching press monopoly, the deification of state and leader, the politicisation of universities, the CGT's takeover of *La Prensa*, as well as the purge of 'disloyal' bureaucrats.[79]

The 'Catholic nationalists', CCC intellectuals and Hispanists, who were consistently better at locating heterodoxy in other movements than at organizing their own alternatives, had accurately observed the Rousseaunian-collectivist strain in Peronism. The analysis of *Presencia*, that Peronism had descended into a 'Pampean Marxism', was echoed by Virgilio Filippo in the late 1940s, who abandoned the party amid fulminations that it had been contaminated by Marxism, liberalism, and socialism.[80] Nor was this mere rhetoric, for Peronism, as a mass and worker based movement, had in many ways more in common with the French Revolution's historical variant, Marxism, than with the predominantly middle-class Revolution of 1789. The appeal of Peronism in the early 1950s to Marxist intellectuals such as Jorge Abelardo Ramos, Rodolfo Puiggrós and Isaac Lebenson, was unmistakable; they argued that Peronism was a transitional phase towards the authentic seizure of the means of production by the proletariat.

There was evidence, too, in the economy, of the Peronist slide into socialist collectivism. Rocketing inflation was evidence that social gains had been achieved through the 'fictions' of confiscation and state-engineered fiscal policies, and not, as in Catholic social doctrine, through a gradual redistribution of wealth via the interaction of social forces under the supervision of a state committed to defending unions and just wages. Absenteeism, political strikes and work-to-rule were symptoms of a profoundly demoralised working class. The combination of rising demand and decreasing productivity demonstrated heightened class tension and a loss of investor confidence, both of which sprang from the state's political manipulation of labour. The slavery of liberal capitalism was now being replaced by the tyranny of state capitalism; and the working class, far from being emancipated through the spread of property, had become further proletarianised. Peronism had been the great lost opportunity, which remained popular and valid only insofar as it continued to uphold the ideals which it was defrauding.[81]

A group of conspirators began meeting with disaffected military officers concerned, among other issues, at Perón's attempt to harness the army to the state. Most of the lay conspirators were associated with the group of civilians who had joined the military government of 1943. Among them were former Catholic Action militants and members of Renovación. Some, like Mario Amadeo, had kept a distance from Peronism; others had campaigned on nationalists tickets. Basilio Serrano, who had been active in supporting Perlinger's attempt to stop Perón in 1944, subsequently accepted Perón's offer of an appointment as Director of the newly-created Department of Federal Economy, while refusing Peronist Party membership. When his position became untenable following the loyalty drive, he resigned his post and joined the conspiracy.[82] The failed uprising of 1951 was also planned by liberals under General Menéndez, and was something of a rehearsal for the successful coup of 1955. It exposed the differences in view between the Catholic wing under General Lonardi, who favoured the retention of much of Peronist social and labour legislation, and the liberals, who demanded its eradication.[83] The disputes between them contributed to the weakness of the uprising, which was suppressed without difficulty. The coup's failure was followed by a crackdown on Catholic nationalists. *Presencia* and other periodicals were closed, and a number of activists were imprisoned or fled into exile. Others went underground, awaiting a new opportunity.

After some years languishing, following the loss of many of its leaders to Peronism, Catholic Action from the early 1950s was rejuvenated by their return to its ranks. Activists began to deliver criticisms of Peronist social policies, focusing on the family and the rapid impoverishment of the middle classes. Articles pointed to alarming statistical trends in illegitimacy and the declining birth rate, and to the threat to the family from excessive state intromission. Canonical marriage remained bereft of legality; bills to abolish legal distinctions between legitimate and illegitimate children threatened to undermine legal support of marriage, and, like the Peronist proposals to legalise prostitution and divorce, indicated the government's waning commitment to defend Catholic morality in law.[84] Another focus of Catholic Action militancy was Perón's attempt to break the Church's hold on Argentines. The most dramatic early example was in 1950, when an American Spiritist sect organized a rally in Luna Park. That Perón viewed the rally as an opportunity to compete with the National Eucharistic Congress of that year, was confirmed by the reading of a presidential telegram during the meeting. It is hard to understand the dramatic effect of this gesture without taking into account the atmosphere preceding the event. For weeks before the arrival of the papal delegate, Buenos Aires was for the first time adorned with Spiritist posters – even affixed to churches – negating the divinity of Christ. For an almost uniformly Catholic country governed by an allegedly Catholic president, this was intolerable. ACA activists attended *en masse*, disrupted the act with pamphlets and songs, were expelled, and marched through the streets chanting *Viva Cristo Rey*. The uproar in the Church's favour was such that Perón considered it judicious to make public reparation by kneeling before the Blessed Sacrament at the Eucharistic Congress. For the next three years he was careful to avoid another direct confrontation.[85]

The retreat of Catholics back into their own organizations was also evident in universities, where ACA founded a series of student societies, among them a women's university group.[86] Formerly Peronist Catholic students established their own university association, the University Humanist League. *Humanistas* were anti-ideological ('we do not propagate any complete system of life') and adhered to philosophical principles derived from a Christian vision of man. Their manifesto significantly advocated a 'true' third position; implicitly, the Peronist Third Position was a travesty. Ideologically, the Humanist League symbolised the return of the 'triangular conflict' (now between liberalism, Peronism and Catholicism) that would characterise the post-1955 period. Gathered in its ranks was a whole generation of *engagé* Catholic intellectuals, trained by Catholic Action, who would after 1955 cross between Christian Democracy and Peronism in an attempt to recover a revolution they regarded as betrayed by its leader.[87]

The bifurcation of Peronism and Catholicism was also evident in the heart of the movement itself. Labour had the most invested in Perón. The phenomenal expansion in unions – from from under a million workers in 1946, to over two million in the early 1950s – occurred mostly in the private sector, and largely as a result not of state sponsorship but of the new conditions which prevailed from the 1940s. A number of unions – notably the Catholic-inspired Luz y Fuerza and Vestido syndicates – had been able to preserve a degree of autonomy. From 1950, however, having itself absorbed autonomous unions, the CGT began to be absorbed by the state. A system of command and control was imposed, known as *verticalidad*, which led to newly-appointed CGT leaders acting as collaborators in state planning. *Verticalidad* was accompanied by a creeping 'officialism', such that union affairs were displaced in CGT periodicals by praise of Perón and his wife.[88] These tendencies were resisted by Luz y Fuerza and by the JOC, which began to forge close links with dissident unions. This was the first challenge to what had been an unalloyed *Jocista* identification with Peronist trade-unionism, yet did not imply a break. Of all the Catholic groups, the JOC was the most loyal of loyal opponents, continuing to identify itself as Peronist while struggling to counteract the absolutist and officialist tendencies within the CGT. This strategy was supported by young radical priests returning from Louvain and Paris, who congregated around the JOC on their return to Argentina. For these priests, jealously independent of the hierarchy, Peronism and the working class would become the focus of future Church energies.[89]

In Córdoba, the most conspicuously Catholic of all Argentine cities, General Auchter had been replaced in 1948 by an unreconstructed Peronist governor, who moved swiftly to impose a definition of Peronism exclusive of other loyalties. Catholic unions were refused legality in 1949, and *Los Principios* (which had been critical of the new governor's profligacy and hubris) was closed shortly thereafter. The introduction of Peronist progaganda in schools, and the demand that teachers profess loyalty to Perón, moved ACA to demonstrate its strength in congresses and campaigns. The JAC Federal Assembly of 1952, attended by ten thousand delegates nationwide, reverted to the language of the 1930s in its call for the environment to be christianised. Equally significant was the announcement of a plan to create and reinforce Catholic organisations, with the implicit objective of countering those of the state. There were gestures of overt defiance, such as ACA's organization of a parallel Labour Day, or its campaign against the government-funded film *Barbara Atómica*. But the most important loyal opposition came from the professional classes, where Catholic consortia of engineers, doctors, lawyers and architects, and a variety of associations in businesses, faculties, hospitals and the provincial legislature, condemned the Peronist slide into collectivism.[90]

5.4 PRELUDE TO CONFLICT: CHRISTIAN DEMOCRACY AND THE CHURCH CAMPAIGN

Political organisation remained problematic. Because they had invested in Peronism as part of a larger process of restoring the scholastic framework of politics, the government's growing despotism and collectivism left Catholics confused and divided. Resort to the army by Catholic nationalists had failed, and government remained officially Christian. Evita's funeral in 1952 – which provided government with a magnificent opportunity to inaugurate the state Christian cult – showed the potency of an undoctrinal Christianity harnessed to state objectives. The Church had remained silent during the mourning, refusing, on the one hand, to endorse the state-sponsored martyrology which accompanied her funeral, but, on the other, was respectful of popular feeling. Peronism had to some extent succeeded in channelling religious feeling; and this, in itself, confused the political arena. Unlike Italy, there was no clear ideological chasm between Catholicism and communism; and unlike Europe, the curtailment of civic liberties made debates and congresses difficult. In spite of these obstacles, integral Catholics subjected Maritain's formulations to a favourable revision. European Christian Democracy was evidence that socially-redistributive policies could occur within a framework of political liberty. Civil liberties had themselves become a major priority, and a number of

Catholic nationalists repented that they had insufficiently valued political pluralism in the 1930s.[91] Yet there remained a strong division between the scholastic discourse of integral Catholicism, and the liberal–Gallican background of those who had written in *Sur* and *Orden Cristiano* during the Spanish Civil and World wars. The dominant figure in these circles was Manuel Ordóñez, an experienced figure close to the liberal establishment and to the Gallican discourse of Mgr. De Andrea. Closely tied by tradition to the liberal project, the furious opposition of 'democratic' Catholics to Perón in 1946 had blinded them to an understanding of the original popularity of Peronism. The democrats had openly identified themselves with Christian Democracy in 1945, and had continued to promote it ever since.[92] A new group had emerged in the years since Perón's victory, composed of a younger generation of Catholic professionals from Córdoba and Rosario. They had organised in study circles and associations, and were closely identified with the French tradition of *Esprit*, and the writings of Maritain, Mounier and Lebret. The view outlined by a member of this 'new' generation in 1951, Salvador Busacca, was predicated on the assumption that Peronism had been a reaction to the liberal-individualist injustices of the 1930s–1940s, which could now be succeeded by a democratic and Christian party. It was a thesis that drew closely on the European experience, and especially on the experience of fascism.[93]

The problem with the analysis of both groups was its categorisation of Peronism as fascism. Whatever Perón's own conceptions, Peronism was larger than its leader; it was an eminently local product of a scholastic enviroment, which had degenerated through its leader's hubris and the collectivist assumptions of a group of ex-socialist labour leaders. But vast numbers of Argentines supported Peronism because they identified with its original language and assumptions. Peronism was, above all, the cultural and social expression of the common man, who had found new dignity and worth in its discourse. That incorporation was a reality precisely because it was *in spite of* Perón himself. Perón had merely echoed values and assumptions which were Christian and pragmatic, ones that would persist long after he disappeared. Such was the analysis of the third group in the debate of the 1950s: integral Catholics who had emerged out of the groups of the 1930s–1940s (Catholic Action, Renovación, Hispanism, social activism), some of whom had occupied posts in the June Revolution and subsequently in Perón's first administration, and who also included participants in the 1951 coup. Their group – *La Unión* –

was a meeting-house of prominent intellectuals and writers committed to an understanding of Argentine politics in its own terms and history. This placed them squarely on the side of the 'nationalists' against liberals and rationalists, but they continued to refute the strains of nationalism (such as *rosismo*) originating in Maurrasianism. In the early 1950s, the ambition of *La Unión* was to rid the country of Perón himself, and to restore Peronism to its rightful place as a Christian labour movement in line with scholastic thinking.

The meeting ground for these three groups from late 1953 was the review *Polémica*. Its purpose was to bring leaders together in a single party of mass appeal that would steal the increasingly homeless Catholic vote from Peronism. It was the beginning of a dialogue among Catholics that would last many years. At the time, however, only a year before the Church–state conflict and in an atmosphere of growing tension and political repression, it succeeded only in laying bare the tensions between those who had anathematized Perón in 1946, and those who had 'conditionally supported' him or who at least understood his popularity. Despite the two groups' common platforms – a-confessionality, federalism, subsidiarity, elections, Christian humanism, further social and economic integration of labour – the divisions between a liberal–French and a scholastic Catholicism proved insurmountable, fuelled as they were by the triumphalism of the democrats and the hostility to them of integral Catholics. The nationalists criticised what they saw as an inability on the part of the young Christian Democrats to grasp the meaning of Peronism, as well as their French formulas, which they saw as doctrinal to the point of becoming ideological, and out of step with the popular, pragmatic and national values of the majority of the Argentine electorate. For their part, the young Christian Democrats regarded the nationalist heritage as tainted by authoritarianism.[94] These disagreements were echoed on the practical level. The nationalists' scholastic assumptions led them naturally to favour a coup to rescue the country from despotism; for the democrats, this resort to the army was evidence of the nationalists' lack of democratic credentials.[95] The greatest sticking-point of all was Manuel Ordóñez. For the young Christian Democrats, however, his prestige and experience made him their natural leader, and they moved rapidly towards the formation of a party, with Ordóñez at the helm, in July 1954. This put paid to the dialogue. The nationalists formed their own party, the Unión Federal, which was not formally constituted until August 1955. Both the PDC and the UF were active in defence of the Church during the Church–state conflict of 1954–1955, but would follow quite different paths. The UF formed the major civilian element in the army conspiracy against Perón, and would be the political brains behind General Lonardi's sixty-day administration. The PDC was unconnected with the coup, and joined the liberal parties in opposition to Lonardi.

Criterio had called in February 1954 for the formation of 'professional, cultural and economic associations' that could defend the interests of the middle classes, much as it had called in the 1930s for associations to represent the working classes.[96] But the deliberations among Christian Democrats were lay initiatives, and were not part of any 'ecclesiastical' strategy.[97] The bishops, aware of divisions among Catholics, gave no support to the PDC, either in 1954 or thereafter.[98] Christian–Democrat plans were furthermore insignificant compared with the nationwide official Church campaign against Perón, and cannot be considered a proximate cause of the Church–State conflict. That such a campaign existed reduces the cogency of interpretations focusing on the influence of Perón's anticlerical advisers. It is certain that the education minister was motivated by hostility to the Church; the Vice-President was a freemason who considered Argentine devotion to Christ and the Virgin Mary to have been superseded by Perón and Eva; while the ex-socialist Minister of Justice was a renowned anticlerical.[99] But it is not clear that these advisers '[exaggerated] the importance of scattered episodes involving Catholic Action or individual members of the clergy'.[100] The information contained in Perón's speech of 10 November 1954, which marked the beginning of the Church–state conflict, was remarkably accurate.

The generalised Catholic offensive had four major elements. First, Cardinal Caggiano, who of the hierarchy had been the most conspicuously sympathetic to Perón's social programme in the 1940s, made an important address to the JOC in which he called for a strategy of penetration and Christianisation of labour. The theme was not new, and harked back to the language of the early 1940s; what was new was the implication that Peronist unions had abandoned Christianity, and that an active campaign was required to correct this trend. Second, the government's attempt to found a state corporation of secondary students in July 1954 was interpreted by Catholics as unambiguous evidence of totalitarianism, and they moved to counter it. ACA in Córdoba confronted the government-sponsored UES Students' Day with an ambitious Students' Week. The UES demonstration brought 10,000 onto the streets but ACA, mobilising a network of religious schools and Church youth organisations, produced eight times that number in a humiliating demonstration of the Church's superior power of assembly. Third, in schools throughout Argentina religious education teachers were actively campaigning against the imposition of Peronist propaganda. The content of the religious education courses (that the state was circumscribed and delegated by the community) clearly conflicted with the propaganda demands of absolute loyalty to the state. Fourth, a pastoral letter read in churches at the beginning of November protested against the activities of an American evangelist faith-healer again sponsored by the government, and contained a clear incitement to Catholics to begin a nationwide campaign of the first priority.[101] Perón's aggressive response came only a few days later, correctly identifying the locus of the rebellion (Córdoba) as well as the organisers of the various campaigns.[102] As far as 'the infiltration of unions' was concerned, a leading *Jocista* recalls:

> When Perón in 1954 denounced a Christian penetration of unions, it was true. I led it. It was called the Comisión Intersindical, based at the JOC headquarters, in Díaz Vélez Street. But our penetration wasn't *anti-Peronist*; it had the objective of encouraging as far as possible the Christian elements in Peronist unions. We manifested our discrepancy with the idolatrous cult of Perón, and with the absolutist characteristics imposed by the Peronist Party – obligatory affiliation, and so on – because we were convinced these were wrong ... In his speech from Olivos, Perón denounced the group without naming it. He was right; only we weren't anti-Peronists.[103]

As this comment shows, for *obrerista* Catholics Peronism represented something larger than Perón; it was even possible for Peronism to remain worthy of support in spite of Perón.

Another interpretation of the causes of the Church–state conflict is of a more theoretical nature, and argues that Perón turned on the Church as the last bastion of autonomy in a totalitarian state.[104] In spite of Peronism's indisputably totalitarian impulse, however, the state still had far to go in subordinating the army, the major economic interests, and the liberal opposition – all of which operated, albeit in difficult circumstances, outside the circumference of political society. The Peronist machine exerted a thorough control over the organs of state, but the loyalty Peronists demanded from Argentine society in the 1950s they were still far from commanding. Once the Church's opposition to the régime placed it outside the moral consensus, the dictator's fall was swift and unopposed. This fact alone makes Argentina under Perón in the 1950s quite different from authentically totalitarian states, which in the twentieth century have been able to crush the Church without collapsing as a result. Neither Hitler nor Stalin nor the Mexican Revolutionary state were brought down by internal stress, even after wholesale and bloody persecutions of the Church.

Perón himself understood the extent to which he continued to depend on political strategy, rather than straightforward suppression, in moving towards his domination of state and society. Aware that his popular legitimacy depended on his identification with the Catholic moral consensus, in 1948–1953 he was careful not to confront the Church while attempting to steal its thunder. His speeches made public his former distinction between an authentic 'Christianity of the people' and the 'hypocritical' Christianity of the Church, challenging Argentina to choose. Faced with mounting, and organised, Catholic opposition, he was forced to act. To have admitted that the Church *qua* mystical body (rather than specific individuals within it, for political motives) had turned against Peronism, would have amounted to an admission that Peronism was not Christian. Because he could not make such an admission, Perón sought instead to counter the Church's right to define Christianity.

This gave the anticlerical campaign of 1954–55 a number of peculiar characteristics. Although the small group of anticlericals in cabinet and the CGT adopted language typical of secular messianism in Spain or Mexico, Perón himself consistently claimed to defend the Church's own message, denouncing 'certain priests' or 'particular organisations' as unrepresentative or incongruous with the Church as a whole. It was not a mass affair. Both in language and in ambition, the Peronist assault on the Catholic Church had greater similarities with the old state–church creation of Henry VIII than with the official atheism of communists. At the height of the conflict in June 1955, this appeared to be recognised in the bishops' diagnosis:

> the intention is, then, to create an *authentic* Christianity to replace the Catholic Church which, according to statements [by government spokesmen], it is not. This means that it is necessary to begin by undermining the Church's prestige, reducing her by every means to a state of impotence, so that an authentic Christianity may be established by the state. The state, however, has neither the end nor the function, and even less the mission, to create a religion,

which even though it may be called authentic, from the mere fact of proceeding from the state and identifying with it, constitutes an attempt to dominate consciences in their most sacred aspect, that of the freedom to worship God.[105]

6 *Ecclesia contra Peronum*, 1954–1955

The year-long campaign to silence and weaken the Church was unpopular.[1] It stupefied most Peronists, who stood apart from the ranks of bishops and Church organisations and who still took at face value Perón's self-portrait as the agent of Church social doctrine. There was no mass anticlerical sentiment for government to exploit. The state campaign was masterminded by a small group close to Perón: cabinet ministers, the CGT leader Eduardo Vuletich, and the head of the Peronist Womens' Branch, Delia de Parodi, were responsible for most of the hectoring speeches. The press campaign was masterminded by Peronist communists such as Jorge Abelardo Ramos and Rodolfo Puiggrós, as well as an assortment of Spanish Republican refugees and professional Radical journalists.[2] The Peronist Party, in Congress or at large, made few contributions, dutifully echoing state propaganda, but with little enthusiasm. Peronist deputies who refused to sanction anticlerical laws were not repressed but merely invited to stay away from Congress. The enormous Catholic meetings and processions were challenged by none except the police, and by small mobs from a revamped nationalist organisation, the Alianza Libertadora Nacionalista (ALN). At street level, the methods employed to undermine the prestige of the clergy were crude and unconvincing. Thugs hired to dress as priests and enter buses with prostitutes on their arms ran up against sane popular logic that clergy choosing such company would have first removed their cassocks.[3]

With the machinery of state, media and party at Perón's disposal, however, the campaign was both extensive and brutal, although it varied in its intensity and was interspersed with periods of attempted reconciliation. Initially, between the 10th November 1954 and May 1955, the government attempted to silence the Church by removing its public presence. Catholics still remaining in the civil service were expelled and priests teaching in schools were banned. Catholic Action, following its successful demonstration in Córdoba, saw its legal status withdrawn and its leaders arrested. Denouncing both 'clericalism' and 'bad priests', the official media created criminal charges to justify arrests of clergy, amidst accusations that opposition parties were using the Church as a means of combating the government. Mgr. Franceschi and Mgr. De Andrea – the two dominant figures of the twentieth-century Church, who in no other sense were close – were incarcerated together. They were joined by outspoken priests: those who had commented on the bishops' pastoral letters at mass, as well as lower clergy (Frs. Filippo and Carboni) who had publicly abandoned Peronism.[4] Church leaders were banned from access to radio and newspapers; *El Pueblo* and Editorial Difusión were ransacked and closed; while other publications (especially those with international reputations such as *Criterio*) battled with paper shortages and disruptions in circulation.

In an echo of the Mexican persecution, public religious acts were forbidden, and hospitals and prisons declared off-limits to priests and Catholic charities. During the Christmas celebrations of 1954, traditional religious street decorations were replaced by comic caricatures. The CGT was ordered to remove crucifixes from union headquarters. Tax exemptions and state subsidies benefiting Catholic private schools were withdrawn, causing most to close within a month.[5] In order further to isolate the Church, and to achieve the veneer of religious legitimacy, Perón's patronage of rival cults became more conspicuous. Sudden favours and privileges were bestowed on Jews, Protestants and Spiritists; and it was arranged for the president to be publicly decorated by the Orthodox Patriarchs, then under Politburo control, of Jerusalem and Palestine.[6] Speeches attempted to persuade the people of Perón's Divine Right. The CGT leader even presented the interesting possibility of God being Peronist: 'if there is one man who could preach Perón's doctrine before Perón', Vuletich insisted at a rally in Luna Park, 'that man [sic] would be God himself'.[7]

A gamut of laws removing corporate privileges and autonomies were squeezed through Congress, using a variety of semi-legal and entirely unconstitutional techniques. In a significant echo of Eduardo Wilde's plans in the 1880s, priests teaching religious education in state schools were to be replaced by state-appointed 'spiritual counsellors'. Seven religious feastdays were abolished, and the Church's charitable status was withdrawn. Prostitution, which had been made illegal in 1936 following a joint socialist-Catholic campaign, was again now legalized. Licensed brothels were opened following a 'campaign on immorality', in the course of which four hundred homosexuals were arrested. Pointing to 'evidence' that eighty per cent of those arrested had been educated in Catholic schools, Perón argued that the 1936 law banning prostitution had taken away legitimate 'escape valves'. Thus far, the laws had either reversed previous legislation, or were within a late nineteenth-century anticlerical tradition. The legalisation of divorce, however, was unprecedented in Argentine history. The legislation was prepared in haste and was poorly worded. It applied solely to cases of 'presumed death', but the provisions were so ambiguous that Radical congressmen (a number of whom were sympathetic to the principle of divorce legalisation) withdrew in protest.[8]

Catholics organised rapidly. The structure and spirit of Catholic Action – an organisation created by a Pope seeking to protect the Church within fascist states in Europe – lent themselves naturally to combating persecution. The first objective of militants was to counter both the news blackout and Perón's insistence that he had no battle with the Church *per se*. By the end of December, groups of pamphleteers had appeared, circulating information, pastoral letters, foreign agency reports, news of arrested Catholics, and gestures of solidarity from around Latin America. Distributed at first by hand and through the post, over the ensuing months the pamphlets became professional broadsheets with large print-runs, extending into the interior via a network of 'cells'. The growth of the network was such that, by mid-1955, press agencies, embassies, unions, social clubs, clinics, police stations, government departments and army officers were in receipt of several a week. The government made strenuous efforts to defeat the pamphleteers with police clampdowns and emergency legislation forbidding 'the diffusion of rumours in whatever form'. But while there were a number of successful raids on houses and convents, which resulted in the confiscation of printing presses, the network grew tangentially. The cell structure of Catholic Action enabled this expansion: pamphleteering groups operated autonomously, via chains of communication which depended on ignorance of secondary contacts. A cell captured by police was therefore unlikely to lead to the capture of others. Yet the success also depended heavily on widespread collaboration from laypeople absent from confiscated Church documents. A young *panfletista* recalled,

> Around that time – the end of April [1955] – the pamphlet campaign [*el panfletismo*] had acquired impressive characteristics. We were no longer just the nucleus of Catholic militants, belonging to Catholic institutions. The Catholic at the midday Sunday mass was also involved. The Catholic who had been baptised and received his first communion, because of the persecution experienced a resurgence of his forgotten faith. The former pupils of religious schools began to

take up again their old ties with forgotten teachers and coreligionists.... Without their formidable contribution, Catholics directly tied to lay Church organisations would have been able to do very little.[9]

The second objective of Catholic militancy was the defence of churches and clergy. A series of armed groups appeared, with a manifold brief to guard churches, prevent government stooges disrupting mass, and to ensure the safety of clergy in the event of a sustained assault. These *comandos tácticos* maintained a network of transport and 'safe houses' and were able rapidly to convert a priest or nun sought by the police into a bourgeois citizen. After June 1955, a number of *comando* combatants were trained by dissident sectors of the army as a civilian wing of the impending coup. During the coup itself, they were entrusted with specific tasks such as the takeover of radio stations.[10] Research into one of these groups in Buenos Aires showed that, like *el panfletismo*, the *comandos tácticos* were a middle-class affair. Most participants were lawyers, doctors, engineers, economists and students; eighty per cent were at one time ACA militants; under half were associated with the PDC or the embryonic Unión Federal.[11]

The third objective was direct confrontation. This strategy contrasted with that of the bishops, who preferred meetings with the president and public criticisms couched in language sufficiently broad to allow Perón to retract.[12] Some activists, impatient with the episcopal strategy, called for the bishops to undertake a 'manly defence', and threw copies of an 'Open Letter to General Perón and the People' by the thousand from the top of a tall building in the centre of Buenos Aires.[13] Mostly, however, Catholic mobilisation attempted to *ganar la calle* with demonstrations of public piety sufficiently large to make legal prohibition of 'public religious acts' unenforceable. Deprived of ordinary means of communication through newspapers, its leadership decimated by arrests, ACA nevertheless elaborated a sophisticated network of communication by which the faithful could be summoned by their thousands to mass or Vespers at the central Cathedral. This was no mean feat. The normal methods by which Catholics were notified about public processions – through the media – were no longer available; indeed, the government-controlled newspapers and radio would attempt to confuse the public by announcing religious acts when there were none, or by reporting the bishops as having postponed them. There were twelve instances in the course of the year in which tens of thousands overflowed the Plaza de Mayo, kneeling to hear services over loudspeakers. The most dramatic was Corpus Christi – a eucharistic procession of deep traditional significance in Catholic countries. In spite of strenuous government efforts to ban and then postpone the event, over a quarter of a million people marched in silent procession behind papal and national flags in a definitive show of defiance. The procession culminated in the Plaza de Mayo, before the presidential palace, where the eucharistic celebrations lasted well into the night.

Corpus Christi was a turning point: proof that the attempt to separate the institutional Church from the faithful had failed. Perón panicked, ordered the police to burn the national flag and publicly imputed the act to Catholics. The Cathedral was besieged by the ALN, and hundreds of Catholics were imprisoned inside. Parishes throughout the Federal Capital were raided by police; the ACA headquarters were ransacked and destroyed. The Archbishop of Buenos Aires and the Vicar General were expelled. From Rome came news of Perón's excommunication by Pius XII. Almost simultaneously, an attempted *coup d'état* led by the naval airforce, mistimed and in poor weather, resulted in the deaths of hundreds of Peronists foregathered in the Plaza de Mayo in a Peronist counter-demonstration organised by the CGT. Perón, forewarned of the impending bombing, escaped, but, in at least one version of events, allowed the CGT demonstration to go ahead, with bloody consequences.[14]

This tragedy gave the administration an opportunity to respond with an act that would send powerful signals to a generation all too familiar with the atrocities in Spain twenty years previously. Yet Argentina in 1955 was not Republican Spain in 1932. No churches were burned in working-class areas, nor even in the middle-class suburbs. And like the Peronist burning of the Jockey Club in 1952, which was unoccupied at the time, the incineration of the churches was carried out at night and produced only a cardiac victim. The razing and gutting of the ten churches carried all the hallmarks of state organisation. The churches were in central Buenos Aires, in an area under martial law. Small groups carried out the act, under police supervision. The fire service was ordered to stay away. Catholic militants, who had been prepared for such an act, could not get past the police barricades. The churches were among the city's oldest, some of them late-colonial. They would eventually be reconstructed; the devastation of the Curia's archive and library resulted in losses that were both incalculable and irrevocable.

Perón recanted. He tried to deflect blame by sacking his cabinet. Calling for unity and reconciliation, he released hundreds of imprisoned priests and laymen, and offered to rebuild the churches at the state's expense. The bishops however spurned the offer, and the calcined aisles remained exposed to the public. Visitors began to arrive from all over the country, so fuelling disaffection and indignation. Although the hierarchy accepted Perón's offer of reconciliation, priests and laymen remained firm in their resistance.

In the course of the next two months, during which Catholic demonstrations were broken up with water cannons and the Curia denounced a renewed anticlerical campaign, a state of siege was restored in the face of growing evidence of a conspiracy combining nationalist Catholics and disaffected officers. Because Perón had effective control over much of the army, the plans changed constantly. Most Catholic activists were not party to the plots, but lobbied the army heavily with pamphlets calling upon it to act, with arguments that bear a remarkable similarity to those of 1890, 1930, 1943 and 1951: by not withdrawing their support for a régime that violated moral law, the army negated its professional, apolitical role. In their inaction, the armed forces had become the sole guardians of tyranny.[15]

As in 1951, the army conspiracy consisted of two principal wings. On the one hand was that of General Lonardi, with his base in Córdoba, with the support of the coordinator of the Cuyo conspiracy, General Lagos. Both were close to Catholic circles. The other wing was represented by the Campo de Mayo garrison in Buenos Aires, led by General Aramburu, with support from the Navy. Aramburu spoke for a tradition stretching back through General Justo to General Roca in the 1880s.[16] In the division between the two wings lay the seeds of the subsequent bifurcation of the Revolución Libertadora. In 1955, after suffering a series of setbacks, the liberal faction accepted Lonardi's authority with great reluctance, and largely because of the mutual necessity of deposing Perón.

The role of the political parties in Perón's overthrow was meagre. In comparison to *el panfletismo*, they had done little to create a climate of opinion favourable to the coup. Having opposed Perón's 'clericalism' in the 1940s, they issued a declaration of condemnation of the persecution of the Church couched in terms of a larger defence of rights and liberties.[17] The Radical Party issued a message of solidarity with the Church early in the conflict in November 1954; but as the conflict progressed, the party's ambiguous stance towards the Church was exposed. The UCR's subsequent affirmation of the party's 'longstanding tradition of respect for freedom of worship' was incongruous in the context of outright persecution.[18] Behind the absence of condemnation of anticlerical laws lay a division within the party over religious policy, stemming from an ideological tension between Krausism on the one hand and University Reform secularism on the other. Recognising the need for a united front against the régime, the leader of the UCR National Committee, Arturo Frondizi, suppressed the debate and spoke vaguely of the importance of 'spiritual values' in his famous radio broadcast of July 1955, without denouncing the religious persecution itself, for which he was severely censured in Catholic pamphlets.[19]

The protagonists of the 1955 coup were therefore military, both liberal and Catholic, with the assistance of Catholic laymen. The laymen belonged to the scholastic and nationalist tradition, rather than that of Christian Democracy. This was reflected in the political vision of the post-Peronist military government, as outlined by Catholic intellectuals in the weeks prior to the coup. On the eve of Perón's overthrow, Mario Amadeo, the principal thinker behind the Lonardi–Lagos conspiracy, published a systematic summary of its general principles. Starting from the fundamental premiss that in 1943 the country had required new forms of political coexistence and an urgent recognition of the social question, Amadeo argued that the coup had begun a revolution which Perón overtook and distorted. Peronism was therefore 'the morbid deformation of a process of transformation which the country urgently required . . .' It followed that 'the political elimination of the author of this swindle should not therefore imply a denial of the issues which brought him to power.' The question was not just that of safeguarding labour gains but also of ensuring the definitive incorporation of workers into the polity. The new civic role of the labour movement was to be defended, firstly by allowing the CGT to continue to represent workers, and secondly by liberating the labour centre from political forces and the state.

Amadeo's argument centred on the need to prevent the exclusion of Peronism from political society. In part this was political pragmatism: any attempt to persecute labour in the name of the rejection of the ideals for which Perón stood would cause him to be resurrected as the incarnation of those ideals. But the argument also rested on a principle of democracy which Argentina had ignored throughout its history: the state's duty to recognize the equal validity of all shades of public opinion. If one sector were excluded as 'unqualified' for democratic and civic participation, the transition to democracy would be cut short by its self-contradiction. The most delicate issue was therefore that of culpability: the notion that people should be punished for their loyalty to the *ancien régime* was as totalitarian as the Peronist government had itself become. All political persecutions were to be energetically repudiated, and only those guilty of embezzlement or fraud (i.e. of breaking the law) be brought to justice. Provisional government was to be as brief as possible, moving quickly to elections, encouraging in the meantime the collaboration of all political parties, including the Peronist, to form a consensus government.[20]

Unlike 1943, an immediate return to elections would not be made problematic by the insularity of the political parties. In the Catholic view, a forthcoming electoral contest would be played out between two parties, the Radical, with its broad middle-class support and heterogeneous traditions, and the Peronist, a labour-based movement which would require an internal reform following the departure of its leader. The Peronist Party was a legitimate representative of broad sectors of the population, once it rid itself of a tyrannical leader, and chose to operate within the framework of law. This confidence was not however shared by liberal participants in the 1955 coup, with whom the Catholic conspirators had little contact. It was not just that liberals were demanding acts of revenge and purges, although many of them were. More significant was the liberal view that Peronism's violation of basic rules disqualified it from future civic participation. Party, unions, press and Peronists themselves – all were tainted in ways that excluded them from political society. Within weeks of the coup, the enlightened-absolutist project would rapidly reassert itself in the hands of liberal officers, the traditional parties and left-wing competitors for working-class allegiance.

7 Secularism Revisited, 1955–1960

The initial atmosphere of conciliation that existed among the varied opponents of Peronism in 1955 was similar to that which prevailed after the defeat of Rosas at Caseros in 1852. *Criterio* congratulated its old adversaries, *La Prensa* and *Sur*, on their restoration. While they were both in prison, Mgr. Franceschi had sent *Sur*'s director, Victoria Ocampo, a Bible. Liberals and Catholics, noted *Criterio*, despite their traditional differences, shared 'an authentic love of liberty and justice'.[1] Yet there were other historical parallels between the post-Rosas decades and the years succeeding Perón's fall. Catholics and liberals would again clash over concepts of liberty and democracy, over the role of the state in education, and over definitions of a political community. The pattern was remarkable, and showed that, whatever the gains of the Catholic movement in restoring institutional liberties after Perón, the outlook of Argentina's political classes, whether liberal or nationalist, remained rooted in a secularist and absolutist conception of the state.

7.1 THE 'CATHOLIC' LIBERTADORA, SEPTEMBER–NOVEMBER 1955

The major new factor in Argentine politics after Perón's overthrow was the presence of an organised working class ostensibly loyal to Peronism if not to Perón himself. Unions and workers had expressed widespread disaffection with Perón during 1955, but they were equally anxious not to surrender either their gains or their new political presence. The position of the Church was delicate. The consequences of the Church's limited presence in labour, and the efficacy of Peronist discourse, had done much to persuade workers that social justice was coterminous with the Peronist state, and that, in so far as the Church upheld social justice, the Church was Peronist. Yet the Church had confronted the Peronist state, and Perón had been overthrown in the name of the Church: Lonardi's aeroplanes carried the slogan *Cristo vence*, and the conspirators' passphrase was *Dios es justo*. In their traditional stalking grounds in the *barrios* of Gran Buenos Aires, *Jocistas* were asked if they were with the Peronists or with the priests; doors were shut in their faces and their newspapers torn up. Three hundred priests in Córdoba signed a document attesting to a campaign in which they were being blamed for Perón's overthrow and singled out as *curas oligarcas*. The defensiveness of the bishops was made evident in a pastoral directed specifically at workers, which denied an 'alliance' between Church and capitalists, and which went on to classify the unjust distribution of wealth and property as equally reprehensible as communism.[2]

The overriding concern of the Catholic mainstream – whether *obreristas*, Christian Democrats or the nationalists close to Lonardi – was to move on from Peronism rather than returning to the *status quo ante* 1943. All warned, as Amadeo had done before the Revolution of 1955, that the original Peronist ideals needed to be respected; to attack them would alienate the working class and reinforce its loyalty to the deposed leader. Perón in 1946 had offered himself to the working class as the agent of Catholic social doctrine; in 1955, Catholics needed to demonstrate that social justice was Christian rather than Peronist. The JOC assessors called for the strengthening and consolidation of the CGT, as well as internal elections and its autonomy from the state and parties after years of political manipulation – a call echoed by the Avanzada group of the Christian Democratic movement.[3] *Criterio* warned that if the Liberating Revolution were to purge its enemies, it would contradict the very purpose of the Revolution itself.[4] Bonifacio del Carril, who had headed Renovación in the 1940s and was now close to Lonardi, noted that 'the masses who voted for Perón are a decisive reality in Argentine political life; and can in no way be ignored or minimised'. Above all, it was necessary to restore the consensual relation between capital and labour originally envisaged in Peronist discourse.[5] From the pages of *Criterio*, Franceschi shortly before his death noted that the hunger for social justice was the most positive legacy of Peronism:

> This hunger, this awareness, although exaggerated, egotistical and charged with social hatred, is, perhaps, the most positive thing the deposed dictator has bequeathed us. It is not something to be destroyed and wiped out, but to be corrected, satisfied and encouraged . . . To fall again into liberal injustice would be an unpardonable step backwards with potentially disastrous consequences.[6]

The concept of the Revolution as expressed by General Lonardi coincided strongly with the Catholic view. The coup was a moral act designed to rescue the country from tyranny, abuse of institutions, and the persecution of the Church. Its legitimacy lay in its objectives and in its pursuit of reconciliation. The purpose of the Revolution was to prepare a return to constitutional government capable of synthesising the civic liberties of democracy with the socioeconomic consequences of the incorporation of the working class into the polity. The revolution was nonpartisan, aimed at restoring freedoms of speech and press, fair judicial processes and the autonomy of the universities. The *Libertadora* was not therefore surgical but remedial; although Perón himself could not return to power, there was no reason to prevent the Peronist Party – following an internal clean-up – from participating in subsequent elections. Above all, the coup was not a political act benefiting the opponents of Peronism nor indeed any political grouping. There were, Lonardi announced, 'neither victors nor vanquished'.[7]

A number of Lonardi's collaborators had roots in Catholic nationalism or Church activism, and like him, were of eminent background. Mario Amadeo, leader of the Unión Federal, and Lonardi's Foreign Minister and principal political adviser, had edited, together with Juan Carlos Goyeneche, his press secretary, the Hispanist review *Sol y Luna* in the 1930s. The government's press spokesman, Clemente Villada Achával, was from a landed Catholic family in Córdoba, whose father had served in the Ministry of Education in 1943. Atilio Dell'Oro Maini, who had remained outside nationalism in the 1930s, was a redoubtable Catholic educationalist, and the founder of the Cursos de Cultura Católica in 1922 and *Criterio* in 1928: in 1955 he was appointed head of the education ministry. None of these appointees had been Peronist; but Lonardi was careful also to include three appointees who had broken with Perón over his persecution of the Church. Among them was Luis B. Cerruti Costa as Minister of Labour, a lawyer close to the Peronist Metalworkers' Union and a man in whom the CGT could have confidence; as well as General Bengoa as Minister of War, who had resigned from Perón's cabinet in early 1955.[8]

In order to reflect the role of liberal officers who had played a part in the coup, Lonardi counterbalanced these appointments with liberals: three Navy officers, including Admiral Isaac Rojas as Vice-President; as well as a number of civilians, including Eduardo Busso as Minister of Interior and Justice, and prominent anti-Peronist businessmen as Ministers of Industry and Finance. Dell'Oro Maini's position as

Minister of Education was counterbalanced by the appointment of the country's leading socialist intellectual, José Luis Romero, to the Rectorship of Buenos Aires University. The liberal appointees spoke for a variety of groups demanding a purge and proscription of Peronism in opposition to the conciliatory line advocated by Lonardi. Socialist trade unionists demanded the expulsion of Peronist union leaders; liberal officers called for the dissolution of the Peronist Party and the public exposure of Peronist misdeeds in order to 'desanctify' the Perons in public eyes; capitalists sought new labour contracts in order to make up for lost profits; and militant liberals demanded the abolition of the 1949 Constitution and a return to that of 1853, with its strong emphasis on individual property rights, as well as the dissolution of the gamut of arbitration and other corporations established by the Peronist syndicalist state.

Lonardi's administration therefore began amidst tensions between the conciliatory line advocated by Catholics and the punitive, proscriptive strategy advocated by liberals. The difference in view was rapidly exposed in the matter of unions. The CGT was pleased with the appointment of Cerruti Costa, and promised to hold internal elections within six weeks. The assumption that there was widespread disaffection with Perón in the CGT, and that demonstrating respect for social justice and union autonomy would lead to his 'demythification', was lent credence both by the unions' acceptance of the justification for the coup and by their declaration of support for the provisional government. Despite isolated threats to the contrary, the unions had made no attempt to defend Perón in September 1955, and soon after declared the 17th of October a normal working day.[9] Lonardi appeared to offer a union relationship with the state which had initially been sought in the 1940s, one in which the state would protect labour and guarantee its independence, in return for which the CGT would act to co-ordinate and discipline labour demands. This was more a civic and structural than a political programme: it was important to the unions that Perón's deposition did not spark off liberal and capitalist revenge; it was a priority of the Lonardi government that the unions retained their civic importance while becoming both internally democratic and autonomous from the state.[10]

Among liberals this 'conciliatory' policy was greeted with disbelief. With the exception of young left-wing intellectuals in the magazine *Contorno*, who were anxious to understand Peronism in order to be 'at one' with the working class, liberals and socialists, many of whom had been exiled in the régime's last years, had made few adjustments to the categories with which they had viewed Perón in 1946. Their anger and scorn was supplemented by a triumphalism and sense of vindication. They were in no mood to talk of incorporation and *superación*, and continued to see Peronism as 'irrational', 'barbaric' and 'fascist', and the CGT as an instrument of totalitarianism. Hence, even if (as expected) the promised union elections would confirm the predominance of Peronists – especially those who had been displaced by *verticalidad* – liberals and the left, in spite of their own democratic principles, were unable to respect such an adhesion as a legitimate choice. They demanded a 'consciousness-raising' programme, to be conducted before elections could take place, that would lead workers to recognise the 'rationality' of their representation by the left. In the months following the coup, armed militants in 'civil commandos' composed of Radical, socialist and syndicalist competitors for working-class allegiance, with the backing of hardline liberal militias from the Navy, forcibly occupied union headquarters and expelled Peronists. Kangaroo trials of 'fascist' trade unionists were held, and lectures on Marxism given to disorientated workers. The liberal and socialist press backed the view that the Peronist unions had to be purged prior to any elections, and they advocated handing over all unions to 'democratic' trade unionists.[11]

Lonardi's continued commitment to allowing free elections within the CGT eventually convinced the liberal wing of the government that only the removal of both him and his conciliationist colleagues would allow for the defence of the principles of liberty that had inspired the coup against Perón. Lonardi's attempts to incorporate liberals' demands (such as a committee to investigate graft, and the appointment of a Consultative Committee of representatives of the political parties) were insufficient to satisfy them, and they pressed for resignations and replacements of conciliationists. Seeing the original aims of the Revolution increasingly compromised by militant anti-Peronism, the nationalists sought and received from Lonardi the appointment of a second Minister of the Interior, Luis María de Pablo Pardo, who had been close to the antimodernist scholasticism of Julio Meinvielle in the 1940s. This brought matters to a head: Busso resigned, and was followed out by all the parties in the Consultative Committee, save the Unión Federal. A junta of liberal officers confronted Lonardi, and demanded his resignation at gunpoint. His administration had lasted just sixty days.

Lonardi was overthrown not because he imposed 'an ideological taint that, given [the Revolution's] mixed origins, it could not endure',[12] but because the inclusive and conciliatory view of political society upheld by the Catholics was incompatible with the 'ideological community' sustained by liberalism. At the root of the divisions and contradictions in the Revolution was disagreement over its purpose. For the liberals and left, the coup represented the restoration of liberal democracy from tyranny. Yet their definitions of democracy were selective: they could not ignore the continued adhesion to Peronist ideals among workers; therefore there could be no democratic elections in the CGT, for an option for Peronism was not an exercise in democracy. This argument bears remarkable similarities to those used by liberals after Caseros, when it was argued that right reason (as defined in liberal ideology) overrode if necessary popular choice. Hence in 1955, the liberal left opposed elections on the grounds that voters would vote incorrectly, thus subverting the ideological aims of the Revolution. Democracy was subordinate to the liberal project; the political community was not an arena within which many different views could be expressed within a framework of law, but an ideological community which excluded certain views and ideologies as incompatible with it. The Lonardi view of the Revolution, by contrast, was that of a transitional government that could establish the civic and political framework within which democracy could be exercised: one that would permit prompt, free elections allowing all interests and views to be represented, and which would exclude only Perón and the leadership of the Peronist Party in 1955. The liberal call to purge Peronism in the name of the absolute values of freedom and democracy ignored the heteronomy of those values. Lonardi, following his rude ousting, criticised the puritanical view of political society espoused by liberals of both right and left, protesting that, 'at gunpoint they will achieve nothing more than exasperating the workers and reinforcing Peronism'. This remarkably accurate prediction was followed by another: that from this would come Perón's return or a civil war or both.[13]

Catholics had once again proved unable to maintain control of a transition; once again control of the state was seized by the upholders of the liberal project. In one sense, of course, this was inevitable: as Bonifacio del Carril subsequently reflected, to have imposed only one view of the Revolution, while the other view had been represented in the coup against Perón, would have been impossible to sustain. Yet equally, it was an impossible task to attempt to reconcile the two views of the Revolution when there had been virtually no discussion prior to the coup between liberals and Catholics.[14] The suspicions and mutual distrust between them was considerable. Liberals blamed Catholics and nationalists for Perón's rise, accusing them of collaborationism and sympathy for fascism, of holding medieval and authoritarian conceptions that rendered them unfit to restore democracy. Some feared that there was a conspiracy afoot to take over the acephalous Peronist movement by mobilising the unions. Suspicions would only be allayed by satisfactory democratic credentials – demonstrated, in 1955, by an advocacy of forced deperonisation.

7.2 THE 'LIBERAL' LIBERTADORA, 1955–1958

The assumption of Aramburu unleashed the full fury of *gorilismo*, or militant antiPeronism. Of Lonardi's followers, only the Air Force Minister and Dell'Oro Maini survived his deposition (Dell'Oro Maini would resign a few months later). The Aramburu cabinet was otherwise liberal–conservative in composition: appointees were close to the large landed interests, committed to free enterprise and constitutional government, and anxious to restrict political participation to the 'correct' groupings, which included neither the Peronist Party nor the Unión Federal, nor the Communist Party. The cabinet also included the editor of *La Prensa* at the time of Perón's expropriation, as well as the core of liberal officers who had masterminded Lonardi's deposition. In its character and composition, therefore, the Aramburu government resembled those of his general–president predecessors, Roca and Justo, seeing itself as the safeguard of a restricted democracy ruled by enlightened interests, and defender of the 'rational' interests of capital and industry. The administration was not however autonomous from the liberal political parties, who supported the *gorila* desire for a thorough purge of Peronism, lasting years if necessary, to prepare the country for elections. The liberal parties were seen by Aramburu as legitimate spokesmen, as opposed to the CGT, tainted by fascism, which was to be broken up into separate entities under political parties, while being simultaneously subordinated to the state.

Combining these various ambitions, Aramburu's strategy towards Peronism was fivefold. First, the Peronist Party, along with printed names and pictures of Perón and Evita, was made illegal, and Jacobin laws demanded that Perón could only be referred to in the press by the opprobrious sobriquets of 'deposed tyrant' or 'former dictator'. Second, elections in the CGT were suspended and Peronist unions were purged: hundreds of labour leaders were arrested and sixty thousand holders of union offices in the period 1952–1955 were disqualified and expelled. Third, socialists and communists, who were generally not workers but middle-class ideologues, were appointed to replace them, thus ironically reviving Perón's policy of politicizing unions from the state. Fourth, strikes by Peronists were declared to be 'political', therefore illegal, and were suppressed by mass incarcerations. Fifth, a concerted government and employer campaign of 'shopfloor rationalisation' was implemented, which attempted to redress the imbalance of capital–labour relations of the later years of the *peronato*. Enforced deperonisation was dramatically symbolised in a bloody put-down of a minor rebellion by Peronist officers in Corrientes. For the first time in twentieth-century Argentina, in an act that would set a precedent for subsequent military policies, the state in June 1956 ordered eighteen soldiers and nine civilians to be shot.

The initial, shocked response of the unionised working class to *gorilismo* rapidly hardened into one of determined resistance, manifest first in the strike figures for 1956, by far the highest thus far in Argentine history; and second, in spite of hasty concessions on wages in 1957, continued low productivity. The effect of *gorilismo* on workers' political alignments was varied, but the overall shift was as Lonardi had foreseen. Workers were confused, angry and bewildered, and took up a variety of stances. Those trade unionists who had favoured a Peronism without Perón were countered by young, militant cadres, different in culture and ethos from labour leaders of the mid-1940s, expressing a modern, intransigent, violent culture of struggle and martyrdom that became known as *La Resistencia*. Perón, the sanity, wisdom and integrity of whom had been called into question by even his loyal supporters in 1955, was transformed by these cadres into a symbol of dignity, social justice and defence from oppression. Although they were as yet distinct from the left, they mirrored communist discourse, and laid the groundwork for what would subsequently become known as the 'Peronist left'. The seeds of this encounter were also sown by the revival of communism in the mid-1950s. Just as originally workers abandoned communism in the face of a state willing to balance their needs against capital, so the restoration of the liberal state caused communism again to flourish. The unions split into two principal groups: the largest, *las 62*, remained Peronist; the others divided between communist, socialist and 'independent'. The Peronist and communist unions reverted to the pre-1943 union stance of obdurate resistance to state and capital. Not only was political society again now divided between Peronists and anti-Peronists, as in

1945, but as Amadeo had warned the predominantly labour component of the former gave the division an unmistakable class characteristic. Aramburu's policies would cast a long shadow over Argentine politics.[15]

Catholics responded vehemently. In *Criterio*, Del Carril defended the Suarezian conception of the coup as a legitimate defence against oppression, never to be deployed for political objectives:

> No revolution – an act of force – which is legitimate, that is, which has been an authentic act of resistance to oppression, should allow another act of force tending to deviate it from its original purpose. But every Revolution should stop there, at the point indicated by its own revolutionary objectives. Any attempt to deploy force in order to impose political objectives, however noble those objectives may be, inevitably produces another act of force which will inevitably destroy those political objectives, however much they may apparently have been reached.[16]

Jocistas, with support from bishops, insisted that the belief that the CGT was a political instrument flew in the face of evidence that workers sought to move on from Perón's last years. The persecutions, they noted, turned such accusations into self-fulfilling prophecies. The worker desire was for a united labour movement independent both of parties and the state; repression quashed that ambition and forced unions to revive their old political role.[17] *Criterio* criticised the liberals' exaltation of liberty at the same time as they denied workers the right to elect their own leaders. Civic liberty, the review noted, 'is not merely the freedom of elections, but the right of citizens to organise themselves as they think fit'.[18] Christian-Democratic trade unionists called for immediate union elections and an end to the persecution. As *obrerista* Catholics had feared, in spite of episcopal condemnations of Aramburu's policies, many workers made the connection between the Church's contribution to Perón's overthrow and the present political persecution.[19] The JOC assessors glumly registered a confirmation of workers' latent anticlericalism.[20]

Politically, however, the division among Catholics precluded a united and unambiguous opposition to the persecution of Peronism. The resurgence of the old liberal/nationalist dichotomy, which had so strongly affected the Catholic movement in the 1930s–1940s, rapidly dissolved the tentative union of political Catholics that had been attempted in 1954–1955. The divisions had surfaced in the Junta Consultiva under Lonardi. The Unión Federal, the architect of conciliation, had remained in the Junta Consultiva when the other parties had withdrawn, in order to defend Lonardi against liberal efforts to unseat him. Under Aramburu they were excluded from the Junta Consultativa, resentful that their conciliatory policy had been subverted.[21] The PDC, conversely, dominated by Ordóñez, considered itself part of the liberal project, and so left the Junta Consultativa under Lonardi along with the Radical and Socialist parties.[22] Following the Junta's reconstitution under General Aramburu, the PDC returned as party adviser to government, and was therefore initially compromised with *gorilismo*.

Because the success of any future multi-class party of Christian–Democratic inspiration depended on mass support, it was necessary for Peronist workers to surrender their loyalty to Perón and join up to an 'authentically' Christian party. With the deperonisation strategy, and the defensive stance adopted by workers, the chances of the UF or the PDC developing into dominant political forces, as their coevals were to do in Chile and Venezuela, were increasingly remote. To the exasperation of the Avanzada wing, the PDC was clearly identified in the eyes of Peronist workers with the liberal project; Ordóñez' references to Peronism as fascism were indistinguishable from those of Aramburu.[23] In spite of the party's declaration, in its Second National Convention, that 'authentic democratic cohabitation does not admit distinctions between reprobates and elect', a gap rapidly opened up between the *ordóñistas* and Christian Democrats close to workers.[24] Although they shared liberal perceptions of Peronism, both the Avanzada and Comunidad groups naturally identified with labour anger generally, and they condemned Ordóñez' unwillingness to distance himself from Aramburu.[25] By the time the PDC eventually withdrew from the Junta Consultiva, the damage had been done. The only leader standing in express opposition to the military government was Frondizi, who, with support from the *federales*, was elaborating a 'national and popular' platform which would revive the Lonardi banners.

7.3 THE UNIVERSITY AUTONOMY ISSUE

Liberal and Catholic divisions over definitions of the political community rapidly reappeared in the debates over religion in education. More than any other in Argentine political history, this issue lay at the heart of the secular–liberal project of the 1880s. During the Lonardi interregnum, most Peronist laws abolishing basic religious liberties were annulled, but the emotive issue of religious education in secondary schools was left over for congressional debate. The liberals were not prepared to wait until after future elections. The Religious Education Decree of 1943, subsequently ratified in 1947, was considered part of the Peronist legislation that was to be annulled. Following Aramburu's assumption, therefore, the UCRP and the left pressured him into restoring by decree the 1884 law forbidding religious instruction in school hours, while leaving open the possibility of provincial legislatures overriding the central government. (A number did, although in the teeth of federal pressure). In mid-1956, Aramburu imposed a programme of 'democratic education' of Positivist pedigree, which included studies of demagogy and electoral procedures, and lessons in 'civic virtues' in place of Peronist political doctrine. But Aramburu himself was close to the liberal–conservatives, and therefore unwilling to make too many concessions to the left. On the day that Law 1420 was restored, he withdrew the state's right to dissolve matrimony and restored subsidies to private Catholic schools (which flourished). In this way, the *status quo ante* 1943 was restored.

In the course of 1956 the secularist–Catholic debates over education shifted to universities. Ironically, Dell'Oro Maini's appointment of liberals and socialists as university rectors had given rise to purges, similar to those carried out in the CGT. Seeking revenge for the 1943 purges, and accused of 'civic–ethical flaws' such as collaboration with the 1949 Constitution, hundreds of Catholics were expelled from university posts and replaced by liberals and socialists. In order to put a definitive end to the sectarian political manipulation of universities, whether by liberals or Peronists, Dell'Oro Maini issued a university autonomy law, similar to the English model, in which universities would have complete political independence from the state, while retaining state subsidies.[26] Article 28 of the law allowed universities to award their own degrees (although according to national standards), on the North-American model. The logical consequence of this clause was to permit the foundation of private universities. As the Church was likely to be the major founder of private universities, the debate rapidly took on the familiar contours.[27] *Reformista* students, inheritors of the radical and secular tradition of the 1918 Córdoba movement, in protest held public demonstrations, occupied faculties and boycotted classes with the support of rectors who favoured a state university monopoly. The Catholic *Humanistas*, the major university grouping after the Reformists, defended the education minister against demands for his resignation, and held counter-demonstrations. In the furore, both Atilio Dell'Oro Maini and José Luis Romero resigned.[28]

As in the 1880s, underlying the technical discussions was the old secularist–Catholic dispute over the role of the state. Secularists advocated a state monopoly of education; Catholics argued for a restricted, supervisory role for the state and the freedom of expression of differing views of education. Secularists, fearing *deux jeunesses*, called for a monopoly of conscience within education in the name of liberty; Catholics, rejecting monistic definitions of liberty, argued for Church universities in the name of pluralism. The education debate therefore paralleled the debate over the inclusion or otherwise of Peronists in political society. For secularists, neither Catholics nor Peronists could be permitted the freedom to organise independently of the state on the grounds that the views to which they were purported to subscribe violated certain basic rules. Personal liberty was subordinate to the revived liberal project; only the state could teach, because only the state could instil the uniform moral virtues underlying 'democracy'. As a communist caustically observed, 'the very same people who demanded independent universities under Perón, appeared now favouring . . . a state monopoly'.[29]

In the liberal view, a Peronist state monopoly of education had been inadmissible; a liberal state monopoly of education was now indispensable. The apparent contradiction was resolved in the liberal paradigm because Peronism was fascism and liberalism was freedom of conscience. Yet this affirmation was no less ideological than the Peronist notion that the state should control education because it represented justice and equality. Both contradicted the Catholic argument that the very notion of an 'ideological' state was erroneous. The state was not concerned with the moral purpose of education. The state facilitated others to teach, without interfering in the dogmatic basis people might choose for their education; just as, if Peronists chose to be Peronist, as long as they operated within the framework of law, they were at liberty to participate in the democratic process.[30]

7.4 CATHOLICISM AND FRONDIZI

In 1957, Argentine politics was again in an unconstitutional vacuum. The democratic parties, right and left, were linked to an unelected military government determinedly suppressing the country's labour-based political movement. With the Peronist Party proscribed, the only party capable of substantial electoral support was the UCR. Faithful to a longstanding schismatic tradition, the Radicals had divided into two wings: the UCR 'Intransigente', led by Arturo Frondizi; and the UCR 'del Pueblo' under Ricardo Balbín. The schism reflected historical divisions within the party. Frondizi belonged to the Yrigoyenist nationalist tradition, Balbín to the liberal–conservative tendencies in the party stretching back to Alvear via the AntiPersonalist faction in the Concordancia. The two Radical wings were divided over the polarization of 1955–1956: Balbín's UCRP supported the liberal policy of deperonization; Frondizi's UCRI spoke out forcefully against *gorilismo* and made itself the defender of the legalization of the Peronist Party as well as the integrity of the CGT.

Support for the UCRI, as demonstrated in the 1957 Constituent Assembly poll, was about half of the traditional Radical constituency. By reaching out to the homeless Peronist vote, Frondizi hoped to create an irresistible electoral vehicle. This was more than electoral pragmatism. With their teleological faith in the industrial panacea, Frondizi and his adviser Rogelio Frigerio recognised that the Peronist unions were a force which could be harnessed to a 'developmentalist' strategy of planned industrialisation, within the Peronist and nationalist tradition of state corporatism. Frondizi had already established a reputation in 1955 as a critic of Perón's 'sell-out' to foreign oil companies; by being more Peronist than Perón on the issue of foreign capital, he resurrected the potency of the Yrigoyenist legacy which had proved so beneficial to Perón in 1946. At this stage, however, his discourse derived from a technocratic, positivist and Hegelian outlook, similar to that of Nehru and Bloomsbury, without roots in a wider framework of values. The crucial next step in his acquisition of a 'national and popular' discourse was his recognition of the importance of Catholic assumptions. Like Perón, to whom he had a Macchiavellian affinity, Frondizi was able to 'read' an electorate and to identify with its priorities. He was assisted in his abandonment of secularism by a number of *federales*, who saw in Frondizi an able politician willing to embrace the Lonardi banners. Mario Amadeo placed Frondizi in contact with bishops, and tutored him in Catholic priorities. By early 1957, the vehicle of *frondizismo*, the magazine *Qué*, had succeeded in linking the left, the 'oligarchy' and 'imperialism' with *irreligiosidad*. On the eve of the Constituent Convention Elections, Frondizi publicly identified himself as a Catholic, lauding the family as 'the basic cell of our society', and pronouncing himself against divorce, Church–state separation and state monopoly of education, and in favour of the 1949 constitution.[31]

In adopting a Catholic platform, Frondizi took a step that caused shock and disbelief among Radical intellectuals who shared his left-wing and Reformist background.[32] It was nevertheless both logical and astute. The two previous presidents elected on a popular vote in the twentieth century had been Yrigoyen and Perón. Both had been careful to identify with Catholic sentiment, and both had spurned the rationalist discourse of liberalism and socialism. As with Perón in 1946, implicit in Frondizi's turnaround was more than a strategic bid for Catholic votes by siding with canonical issues; it included a recognition that secularism was the cult of limited sectors of the urban middle class. Audaciously Frondizi noted that 'the Argentine liberals who have made the most effort to deny the particular characteristics, personality and autonomy of our community, are also those who have made most effort to circumscribe religion and the Church'.[33]

The 1957 Constituent Assembly Elections represented the first major test of political feeling since Perón's deposition two years before. Although the Peronist Party was prevented from participating, Perón-in-exile commanded his supporters to deliver blank ballots, which reached just under 25 per cent of the vote. Balbín's UCRP gained around 24 per cent, and Frondizi's UCRI around 21 per cent. The 1957 elections also showed that Christian Democracy, although it reached five per cent of the vote nationwide, putting it in fourth place just behind the Socialist Party, had far to go in terms of capturing popular imagination. The social composition of the PDC vote seemed to prove what its Catholic critics had maintained in 1954: that the party's language and discourse was identified with the liberal project, and was therefore alien from the substantial electorate. The PDC's greatest success (14–16 per cent) was in the wealthier areas of the Capital – the home of *Orden Cristiano*.[34] The Unión Federal, achieving less than 2 per cent, was largely spent in the electoral arena. Many *federales* had forged an alliance with Frondizi; the remainder, suspicious of Frondizi, continued to uphold the possibility of a separate party, but one that was pragmatic and scholastic. A number of them would go over to the PDC once that party abandoned Ordóñez in 1960 and began its *apertura al peronismo* or 'opening' to possible collaboration with Peronism.[35] The remaining parties – the Conservatives (Partido Demócrata), the PDP and the Communists all achieved between two and four per cent. In the event, the Constituent Assembly did not produce a Constitution. The absence of the Peronists anyway made the exercise dubious. Frondizi and the *federales* abandoned the assembly in protest.

The Constituent Assembly election results demonstrated that a quarter of the nation – approximately the size of organised labour – continued to support Perón: the guarantor, in worker eyes, against the recurrence of persecution. The failure of deperonization was further reinforced by the results of the CGT Congress in August 1957, which showed that the Peronists still dominated, even where as a result of interventions they did not lead, the majority of the industrial trade unions. The objective of the Aramburu administration had been the time-honoured model of a controlled democracy; yet with the UCR schism, it was not clear that the UCRP could win cleanly. If Frondizi were to win by means of a pact with Perón, the liberal objectives of the Liberating Revolution would have failed altogether. In spite of these premonitions, and against the advice of military hardliners who demanded an intensification of deperonisation, Aramburu honoured his commitment to move to elections, which were set for February 1958. He placated the hardliners by committing the army never to permit the legalization of the Peronist Party.

In the pre-election period Frondizi intensified his identification with Catholic feeling. References were made to the Catholic traditions of his family and to the value of the Church in society. He also clarified his stand on the education issue by promising to support ratification of the University Autonomy Law. Frondizi already had the endorsement of the Unión Federal. He countered the remaining threat from the PDC by creating a series of pseudo-organisations with Catholic-sounding names in support of his candidacy. Because of the PDC's novelty in the electoral arena, fictional entities such as the '*Rerum Novarum* Social Action Centre' and 'Christian–Democratic Community Action Centre' possibly succeeded in confusing voters.[36] Although he did not commit the UCRI to a restoration of religious education in secondary schools – which would have entailed too great a *volte-face* for the Radicals – the proliferation of state-subsidised Catholic private schools, which were preferred by Catholics for the 'integral' Christian education they offered, meant that the issue had ceased to be so pressing.[37] On the union issue, however, Frondizi ignored the bishops' call for pluralist syndicalism (as many unions per profession as were desired) within a single labour central, autonomous from the state.[38] The choice for unions, as in 1945, was again between, on the one hand, a privileged relationship to the state with the consequent loss of union autonomy, and on the other, vulnerability to a hostile state and political parties. As in 1945, therefore, the pattern was repeated: Frondizi's identification with Catholic culture and values undoubtedly assisted him in his electoral victory, while his attempt to harness the unions to the state resulted in legislation which was inadmissible to the Church.

There were other, deeper similarities between Perón and Frondizi. Identification with Catholic culture and an identification with ecclesiastical prerogatives disguised a secularist outlook. Frondizi's exposure to Catholic influences brought him no closer to the Catholic conception of politics. As his campaign speeches show, underlying his view of the Church was a time-honoured absolutism:

... for the effective climate of tranquillity, peace and unity, the Church must play a central role given its character of spiritual force rooted in the country's tradition. Because the majority of Argentines are attached in some way to the Catholic faith ... the Church constitutes an efficient agent of social cohesion ... In countries such as our own, which have not registered a complete development of forms of sociability as a consequence of the underdevelopment of economic relations and the dependence of our economy on other countries, religion occupies an important place as the stimulus of society. For example, the Church's opposition to divorce is not an indication of the retardation of our legislation, but is an essential stimulus to promote the family institution in a country which contains large areas where the statistics have time and again registered an astonishing number of illlegitimate births. That is to say, the opposition to divorce has an opportune objective of social progress.[39]

These lines bear familiar traits: the Church is laudable in so far as it conforms to the *a priori* ends of the state; it is to be deployed as a factor of social cohesion, and is thus subordinate to a political project which sees no authority higher than that of the state. As in the Alberdian formula, the Church is necessary because Argentina is underdeveloped (from which it would follow, as with Alberdi, that religion is a stage in development, eventually to be superseded): this made *desarrollistas* no more Catholic than Marxists who advocated capitalism as a stage towards communism were capitalist. Equally, divorce is here opposed because the indissolubility of marriage suits the state project of populating the country, and not, as in the Catholic view, because the state is not empowered to make or dissolve marriages. The state begins with certain political objectives – order and tranquillity, as well as a 'social stimulus' – and is grateful to find in the Church what it sees as a ready-made agent of such objectives. Theologically, there is no difference between Frondizi's view and that of Juárez Celman; both regarded the state as above the Church, and the latter as subject to the former. Where Juárez Celman saw the Church as opposed to his political project, Frondizi saw the Church as congenial to his: in the first case, in a tightly-restricted democracy, there was little need to defer to wider values; in the second case, appealing to popular sentiment in a mass democracy, it was essential. In the case of the liberal project, the Church is put outside political society; in the nationalist scheme, it is incorporated. But the limits of political society are always defined by the state, and not the obverse.

Logically, therefore, once in power Frondizi exposed himself as faithful to the traditions of Argentine absolutism. *Desarrollistas* sought to subordinate society to an overriding ideology – technocratic and determinist – to replace political society as an arena of debate and consensus.[40] Politics was his religion.[41] Developmentalists sought 'an ideological conformism, encouraged with a systematic spirit without precedent in the country'.[42]

Yet the basis of his policy, the unions, were not in Frondizi's control. The Peronist votes cast in his favour, which enabled him to secure a massive 40 per cent victory, had been granted on express, if secret, conditions, negotiated with Perón. The commitments included the holding of elections in the CGT and legalization of the Peronist Party, and directly contradicted the army's determination to prevent them occurring. Frondizi's administration therefore began with a near-impossible task. He secured the implementation of a Law of Professional Associations modelled on the Peronist labour code. He reiterated the Peronist vision of a harmonious collaboration of differing vital forces under the aegis of the state. Yet faced with union opposition to wage freezes in 1958, Frondizi opted for harsh repression, and the 'class alliance' soon collapsed. The government was forced to accept an increasing involvement of liberal officers; and economic policy came to reflect the priorities of the Aramburu administration. In 1960, the Plan Conintes gave the army full power in rooting out subversion and internal disturbances: the beginnings of a novel doctrine of national security which put teeth into the traditional liberal conception of the army as the guardian of the ideological project of the state. Some workers began to take up arms. Frondizi would eventually be removed in 1962; a controlled democracy was restored, interspersed with long periods of outright military rule.[43]

7.5 EPILOGUE

Although politics after Perón continued to conform to familiar patterns – patterns established in the nineteenth century – the Frondizi government brought to a close a cycle of Catholic influence in public life. If the late nineteenth and early twentieth centuries had been the high noon of Argentine liberalism, the Catholic movement of the 1930s–1940s had by the 1960s succeeded in reversing the laicist trend. Frondizi's appointment of a Catholic, Luis Mackay, as Minister of Education, over the veteran secularist Gabriel del Mazo, demonstrated his determination to see through the University Autonomy Law. In addition to the Ministry of Education and Worship, prominent Catholics – many of whom were *federales* – also occupied the Foreign Ministry, ambassadorships and a host of lesser posts in the Frondizi administration.[44] The ecclesiastical budget was doubled; the Argentine embassy sheltered victims of religious persecution in Cuba; and Argentina's representative, Mario Amadeo, fought UN attempts to encourage artificial birth control in developing countries. Divorce and abortion were excluded from congressional debates. Concrete moves were made towards the dissolution of the regalist *patronato* clauses of the Constitution. The constitutional impasse brought about by the Supreme Court's refusal under Aramburu to approve two bishops appointed by Rome, was resolved by Frondizi in Rome's favour. In contrast to previous delays and negotiations, the Vatican's appointment of Archbishop was immediately approved, and the wording of the nomination changed to accord with canon law. There were moves towards abolishing the state's self-appointed right to inspect papal bulls; and progress was made towards a Concordat, the signing of which was postponed by the 1962 coup until 1966. The Concordat continued to enshrine the principle of Argentina's Catholicity, and the duty of the state to protect the Church as the spiritual authority of the vast majority of Argentines; it also continued to enshrine the principle of freedom of religion. The substantial difference lay in the abolition of state control of the Church.[45]

The education issue was resolved amidst high tensions. *Reformistas* intensified their opposition to a pluralist university system in August 1958, parading the slogans of 1918 – 'Secular, Yes; Free, No' – and had pitched battles with *Humanistas* in the faculties. *Humanistas*, who had expanded within higher education, representing one in three students in the early 1960s (eventually gaining control of the University of Buenos Aires in 1962) in September 1958 organised a march of around 150,000, which was saluted by Frondizi from the balcony of the Casa Rosada. The University Autonomy Law was eventually ratified, to the disgust of Frondizi's former colleagues. *Reformistas* attempted to set Congress alight, had gun battles with the police in Tucumán, and in 1959 placed a bomb in the newly-founded Catholic University of Buenos Aires.[46] By 1967, there were nine state universities with 204,952 students, eight Catholic universities with 11,474 students, and five non-Catholic private universities, with 2,817 students.[47] The question of religion in secondary schools, meanwhile, was devolved to provincial governments. Significantly, those parties and groupings which had come of age since the 1940s favoured it, while those with roots in the liberal project of 1880–1930 opposed it. The UCRI, PDC, Peronist and Popular Conservative parties all favoured optional religious education in schools; the UCRP, PS, and PDP favoured retaining the ban. By 1972, five provinces, which together made up half of the total Argentine school population, included optional religious instruction in state secondary schools.[48]

As with Perón, Catholics rapidly abandoned the Frondizi administration. The 'eminent men' of the nationalist tradition, including the *federales*, would continue to weave in and out of administrations, opposing the hardline liberal preference for suppression and exclusion of Peronism, and usually abandoning them to the liberals whenever the hardline resurged. In 1962 the 'nationalist' Catholics formed the Ateneo de la República, a lobby which stood aloof from the liberal–Peronist divide, and which contributed leaders to Onganía's failed attempt at transcending it.[49] Other, less politically active members occupied teaching posts and taught at the new universities.

Much of this generation, with its origins in Catholic Action and the discourse of integral Catholicism, continued to uphold the ambitions of the 1930s–1940s. The attempt at uniting Catholics, which had begun in 1954 in the review *Polémica*, continued in the *Encuentro Nacional de Dirigentes Católicos* from 1959, as a meeting-place for a divided generation with common objectives. The *Encuentro* was a lobby, designed 'not to form a national project but to bring Christianity to bear on the national project'[50] – a scholastic, neo-Christendom theme familiar from the 1930s–1940s, which acknowledged the continued divorce between the ideologies of the political classes and the 'scholastic framework' of Argentine society. The Christian Democrats, meanwhile, continued on the party-political route, but with limited success. After the elections of 1958, the party engaged in a period of introspection which culminated in an *abertura al peronismo* in the early 1960s and a definitive abandonment of the *ordóñista* line. Behind this turnaround was a recognition that it had misread Peronism as fascism. But it was in many ways too late. The Aramburu years marked the beginnings of a longlasting strategy of suppression and exclusion of Peronism which succeeded only in reinforcing Perón's popularity. The ongoing polarisation between an army willing either to rule itself or supervise a controlled democracy, and the resolute Peronist resistance to the state, was not an atmosphere conducive to the formation of the sort of multiclass, broadly-based alliance which characterized Christian Democracy in Chile. Such an alliance would depend on 'converting' Peronism, when Peronism, faced with state suppression, had turned in on itself. A number of Christian Democrats in the late 1950s accepted the inevitability of this pattern, and actually became Peronists.[51]

The Second Vatican Council, and the specifically Latin-American interpretation of the Council at Medellín in 1968, nurtured a new generation of Catholic activism. Where the generation of the 1930s–1940s had been drawn to nationalism, that of the 1960s–1970s was attracted to a left-wing and anti-imperialist 'third-worldist' discourse, which placed particular emphasis on the Christ-like qualities of the poor.[52] Liberation Theology caused a further revision of Peronism; if the poor were Peronist, and the Church was with the poor, then the Church must reach out to Peronism. As with integral Catholic debates on nationalism, however, the relationship between Catholicism and a left-wing Peronism remained fraught with difficulties, just as, in the 1930s–1940s, it had been with nationalism. The political alliances had changed but the tensions remained the same: between withdrawal and engagement, orthodoxy and realism, and between a democracy that was a democracy only in name, and alternatives which threatened absolutism or even tyranny. Although the Catholic movement had had a profound impact on Argentine society, it had failed, overall, to wrest Argentine politics from its historical addiction to absolutism. Politics, therefore, continued to swing: between popular movements which carried absolutist impulses, and an enlightened absolutism which, in the name of reason, excluded popular participation: the dialectic of the Enlightenment.

Conclusion

In the introductory pages it was shown that the relationship of Catholics to the modern state depended on its political character. Catholics opposed states professing secularist ideologies – ideologies which might underlie either monarchies or democracies, or indeed any variety of political arrangements. The political *form* was less important than the conception of the state. The secularist premiss we defined as a view of the state as the origin and arbiter of law, above which there was no higher law. If the state sought to claim the totality of political society, or if the state regarded itself as autonomous from popular consensus, it aroused Catholic opinion against it. It was also noted that political movements might defer outwardly to the Catholic conception of politics while in practice adhering to a secularist conception; equally, movements could change.

The Argentine case presents a dramatic example of Catholic alienation from the state, and of a tension between scholasticism and secularism. Late-colonial Argentina was scholastic in outlook: in part because of the colony's insulation from the European Enlightenment and the predominance of the religious orders, and partly (until the 1770s) due to the relative ineffectiveness of Spanish colonial rule. The violation of scholastic tenets by the Bourbon Reforms was therefore all the greater, fostering an impulse to independence according to Suarezian contract theory. Yet the thinking of the liberal faction which triumphed in Buenos Aires after Independence did not share those scholastic suppositions. Whatever the differences between strains of the political Enlightenment expressed in the Bourbon Reforms on the one hand, and in Rivadavia's thinking on the other, the liberal project was in the absolutist tradition: the state sought to act on society, conditioning society according to the tenets of 'reason' autonomously defined. The spiritual community of the Church, which in scholastic thinking precedes the temporal community, was undermined by the state, which deferred to no authority outside itself. The tenets of liberalism, drawn from enlightened absolutism, were in opposition to those which subsisted in wider society and could only begin to be implemented after the state had achieved a monopoly of power. The outrage provoked by Rivadavia's reforms led quickly to his ousting and the dictatorship of Rosas. The statesmen of the 1860–1880 period recognised the need to defer to wider values, and so tempered their own radicalism with outward respect for the Church and a relatively moderate view of state power.

The liberal project, as it reached its apogee under Roca in the 1880s, was nourished by a radical, secularist ideal: that of creating new forms of communal and national allegiance. Its central political characteristic was its autonomous, self-justifying conception of sovereignty, as well as its detachment from wider social values. Liberals saw the project as that of countering Barbarism. The state had a civilizing mission: to that mission, and to the state, all else was subservient. Unlike Rosas, who was absolutist but demagogic, and personalistic in his methods of achieving and retaining power, the liberal project was both absolutist and detached. In both cases, political society is seen as unfettered. The major difference was that where Rosas needed to appeal to wider values, as Rivadavia had failed to do to his cost, the state of Roca and Juárez Celman had no need to do so. By the 1880s, the state was sufficiently powerful to achieve autonomy from wider society, and was able to carry forward its secularizing project.

Yet there were still many examples of popular reactions. The pattern throughout the nineteenth century was one of a liberal state attempting to secularize society in order to achieve a more thorough control; and in attempting to do so, encountering popular resistance. From Carlos III's expulsion of the Jesuits, through to Rivadavia's takeover of the monasteries, the Oroño laws in the 1860s and the education and marriage laws of the 1880s, popular reaction and indignation were never far behind. The state could never insulate itself entirely from wider values, and was forced constantly to compromise with those values for the sake of stability. Rivadavia failed, and was ousted; Sarmiento and Avellaneda compromised and maintained stability; Juárez Celman failed and was ousted; Roca, having failed to compromise in his first term, did so in his second. Even where this tension between the liberal project and wider values did not have a uniquely religious character, the pattern points to secularization (the creation of a new system of political allegiance which violated scholastic notions of community and authority) always encountering resistance in wider society. The liberal project eventually succeeded in the nineteenth century in creating an autonomous state, but it could only be sustained by a strong degree of compulsion: the dominance of institutions, the insulation of government from democratic majorities, a monopoly of violence and the aggrandizement of the state financed by economic expansion.

The three 'popular' presidencies of the period 1880–1960 – that is, those which rested on authentic democratic majorities and a strong degree of consensus – were those of Yrigoyen, Perón and Frondizi. All three were 'nationalists', in as much as they deferred, unlike the leaders of the liberal project, to wider values. The contrast between their political discourse and that of the liberal project was remarkable; they spoke not of right reason but of *pueblo*, tradition and justice. All three valued the institution of the Church, as part of their deference to wider values. Yet, as we have shown, from a theological perspective all three remained within a liberal–secularist continuum established in the nineteenth century. The essential political difference between liberalism and nationalism in Argentine politics is the difference between the enlightened absolutism of Carlos III and the collectivist democracy of Rousseau. Both are rooted in the Enlightenment in as much as they define sovereignty as limitless, and place state above Church. In both the liberal and the nationalist case, political society is defined by the state. This (from a Catholic perspective) shared identity aside, however, liberalism and nationalism speak for discrete political traditions, and in power have differed strongly. Liberalism has tended to define the state as autonomous from and above democratic majorities, defending the liberal project (the project of 'right reason') if necessary through restricted democracy and controlled elections. Yet it has been individualist and generally non-interventionist in economics, and generally circumspect in its use of coercion. Nationalism, on the other hand, has rested on strong electoral majorities, has been interventionist economically (especially with regard to unions), and has been more prone to the use of coercion over society.

If Argentine nationalism has drawn on Rousseaunian tenets, why did it hold an attraction for Catholics? This question cannot be answered without distinguishing between the many strains in nationalism. In its broadest sense, nationalism has been a movement seeking to overcome the divorce between state and society. Because the Catholic conception of politics defended sovereignty as delegated by the community and rooted in consensus, Catholics necessarily opposed the liberal project (with its absolutist and autonomous assumptions) and were therefore sympathetic to nationalism. As we observed in Chapter Three, Catholic anti-liberalism was based on two principal assumptions: the first, that liberal democracy was little more than a mechanistic means of defending the autonomous liberal project, and which was antithetical to democracy as defined in scholastic theory; the second, that liberal democracy was founded on individualist economic assumptions that resisted the Catholic view of the state's obligation to intervene in virtue of the common social good. In so far as nationalism appeared to uphold opposing tenets, therefore, it proved attractive to Catholics. Yet in so far as nationalism upheld absolute definitions of state sovereignty, it was opposed by Catholics. As in Europe, the philosophical underpinnings of nationalism were often obscure, or mixed. In Argentina in the 1930s–1940s, the strength of the anti-liberal reaction among Catholics was so strong that they tended to overlook those features of nationalism which, as Maritain had indicated in 1934, carried with them secularist heterodoxies.

Thus, between Catholics and nationalists in the 1930s–1940s there was a dialogue over desirable alternatives to liberal democracy as practised in Argentina. The common lament was for 'new forms of popular government' without these ever being concretely defined. Yet the boundaries were always clear: dictatorship and state corporatism were inadmissible, the state was delegated by the community and was of a separate realm to that of the Church, while nationalism could not transfer the Kantian moral autonomy of the individual onto either nation or state.

Unlike Christian Democrats in Europe, integral Catholics in the 1930s–1940s did not see much possibility of working within the liberal–democratic system as it stood. There were two main reasons for this. First, the liberal–democratic system in the 1930s depended on systems of patronage and electoral manipulation which guaranteed the perpetuation of the Radical and Conservative parties. Liberal democracy was not therefore a system open to newcomers: the 'insularity' of Congress was a point frequently stressed. Secondly, Catholics in the 1930s–1940s placed relatively less emphasis on institutional liberties when compared with the overriding importance of the social question. Individual political liberties were seen as coterminous with the excessive liberties of capital. The common good was therefore counterposed in Catholic thinking to individual freedoms. This emphasis was reinforced by the identification of Catholicism with the new classes, for whom 'liberal freedoms' were seen either as hypocrisy or irrelevant to a large section of society without basic standards of living.

The Catholic revival was coterminous with the arrival of the new social classes seeking political and socioeconomic integration. It was shown how the tension inherent between the liberal project and wider society was increasingly threatened by these social and demographic changes. The 1930s and 1940s saw the emergence of an *Argentina de masas*, and the new kind of society and government to which this pointed. The secularized political society envisaged by liberals, which conceived of a middle-class nation of producers and consumers, stood in uncomfortable juxtaposition to this new society, shaped by the Catholic revival. The phenomenal expansion of organisations such as Catholic Action offered a substitute for the sort of political organisation and mobilisation common in Europe in the late nineteenth and early twentieth centuries. Although communism was to recruit large numbers of workers in the late 1930s, the discourse of the new classes was strongly imbued with the language of the Catholic revival and of nationalism.

There also was evidence of the renaissance of the scholastic outlook in the changing self-conception of the military role in Argentine society. Refuting the assumptions of the liberal project, which viewed the army as enclosed within it, and subordinate to the state, the 'Professionalist' strain identified with wider values and refuted the role into which the liberal project had cast it. Behind the coup of 1943 (and to a less defined extent, that of 1930) was a resentment at the state's attempt to compromise the army in ballot rigging or the defence of the socioeconomic framework as it stood. Viewed from the perspective of the liberal project, the army in 1930 and in 1943 became 'political', just as the Church began to 'involve itself in politics'. Yet as the Professionalists saw it, they were defending apoliticism, which was coterminous with integrity. There was much in common between the army's resistance to its imposed role as defender of the liberal project, and that of the Church. From the 1920s–1930s, both Army and Church sought to recover their roles as guardians of the fundamental legal and moral framework of society. Not coincidentally, this common quest was coterminous with both the Catholic revival and the integration of immigrants.

These various strands came together in 1943. As both the Professionalist officers and the Catholic nationalists saw it, the purpose of the coup was of fundamental significance in closing the breach between state and society. The coup's character was to some extent exemplified by the decrees it issued: on the one hand, suppressing the liberal–democratic system in order to prevent an immediate restoration of the liberal project; on the other, freezing rents and easing the harsh effects of the wartime economy on the poor. In as much as it was a *de facto* administration, its purpose fundamentally that of restoring institutions abused by the outgoing government, the June Revolution was a holding operation. Yet the religious education decree pointed to a larger purpose: an opening of the state to wider values. From the perspective of the liberal project, this act was authoritarian; from the Catholic and nationalist perspective, it was a reversal of the absolutist doctrine of the state. Secular education was a cornerstone of the liberal project: a fundamental plank in the attempt to redefine political society. Yet as the nationalists saw it, the religious education decree was a victory for the silent majority that had never spoken in 1884. It was the first step in the liberation of society from an autonomous absolutist project that had always feared electoral majorities. A balanced perspective is that the decree did no more than take away from the state the right to determine the moral education of the nation's children. The nationalist thesis certainly appeared to be proved by the popularity of the measure.

In the event, the Catholic version of the June Revolution was ambiguous. In both the scholastic and the Professionalist perspective, the army could not rule autonomously. It could only effect a transition. The legitimacy of military rule depended first on its duty to act as the agent by which sovereignty was restored to the community, and second, on the need to defend the Argentine state from global pressures, especially from the US. The revocation of neutrality, however necessary in practice, was regarded as a betrayal of apoliticism and caused Catholics and Professionalists to leave the administration. There is little evidence to suggest what might have happened if they had remained. In the event, their departure paved the way for Perón. Unlike the Catholics in the June Revolution, Perón saw the army's possession of the state as an opportunity to build a political alliance. For that, they never forgave him.

Yet Peronism did appeal to wider, Catholic-informed values. It was shown how Perón acted as a conduit for the pent-up resistance to the liberal project of vast sectors of Argentine society. It has often been observed that Perón revived the Yrigoyenist legacy, just as Frondizi was to revive the legacy of Perón. There is a continuity between all three leaders – a continuity which lies in their shared refutation of all the assumptions of the liberal project. In as much as Perón appealed to a society shaped by 'other', non-liberal and Catholic assumptions, he appealed to Catholicism. Like Yrigoyen and subsequently Frondizi, however, Perón was Janus-faced: superficially Catholic, but essentially Rousseaunian. Church leaders and those who had been close to Perón recognised this trait earlier than others. An inspection of Perón's speeches and early documents, as well as an observation of the extent to which early laws – most especially the trade union legislation –

Conclusion

violated Catholic tenets, can easily lead the historian to the conclusion that Catholicism and Peronism were opposed from the start. Yet such a view is excessively abstracted from the context: when faced with a choice between the liberal project on the one hand and Perón on the other, there could be little initial doubt as to which way Catholic sympathy would go. Perón, after all, identified with virtually all Catholic priorities, offering a government rooted in popular consensus, that would actively intervene for the common social good, which would defend trade unions, defer to the Church in moral and spiritual matters, that valued the important elements in Argentine culture, and which would restore to women an important civic role. There was much evidence that Peronism was all these things, and it was less important at the time that it placed less emphasis on individual liberties or liberal–democratic institutions. As Peronism revealed its secularist, collectivist assumptions, however, Catholics began turning against the government. It was noted how this occurred at different times and among different groups, until it was universal by 1953–54. Peronism violated a host of fundamental tenets of the Catholic conception of state and society. The most important one of these, and the one which impelled the Church to act against Perón, was his attempt to create a civil religion and thus to demand an allegiance that, like the pagan Roman states or the French Revolution, was simultaneously spiritual and temporal.

The failure of Catholics to organise alternatives to Peronism has a variety of causes. The ambiguity of integral Catholicism in relation to political forms (should they form a party? Should that party work within the liberal–democratic system?), and the historical divisions between the Catholic wing of the liberal project (the 'democratic' Catholics) on the one hand, and those who looked to nationalism on the other. The central issue was Peronism itself: its meaning and character. For liberals (including the democratic Catholics), Peronism was an abomination which only served to remind them of the distance the liberal project still had to travel in overcoming the 'barbarous' and irrational tenets of wider society. For nationalist Catholics, who identified with the values of wider society, the decadence of Peronism lay not in those values but rather in the secularist and tyrannical assumptions of Perón himself and of those groups which, together, had distorted and twisted the original ideals for which vast sectors of the electorate had voted in 1946. These two views of Peronism were essentially incompatible. The nationalist Catholics continued to refute the liberal project and the liberal–democratic system which had emanated from it; their notion of a Christian Democracy was therefore one in which Peronism could develop: a multiclass movement which could be restored to its rightful place as a 'nationalist Christian Democracy'. For the 'democratic' Catholics, conversely, Peronism violated the tenets of the liberal project and therefore had to be expunged, rather than cooperated with.

In the Revolución Libertadora were concentrated all the divisions and contradictions in Argentine political society: the differences between the nationalist Catholic and liberal view of Peronism, the contradiction between the Professionalist and liberal conception of the army, as well as contrasting definitions of political society itself. For the nationalist Catholics, Peronism was a valid expression of the political sentiments and values of the organised working class and vast sectors of Argentine society. Whatever its abominations when in power, the exclusion of Perón and his cabinet was sufficient to allow Peronism to participate in political society. The concern of the nationalist Catholics was to restore the autonomy of institutions which the state had illegitimately attempted to harness to itself: the most pertinent examples in the late 1950s were the CGT and the universities. For the liberals, conversely, Peronism itself stood in direct contradiction to the liberal project, and had to be expunged from political society. Far from granting the CGT the freedom to organise as it wished, the liberals sought to purge the trade unions of Peronists and shape it according to the 'rational' demands of the liberal project. Just as the autonomy of the unions would lead to the predominance of Peronism, so university autonomy would lead to the proliferation of Catholic universities: neither could therefore be permitted. If the absolutism of the liberal project was ever so clearly manifested, it was in the Revolución Libertadora. The period 1955–1958 also showed up the difference between the Professionalist and the liberal conception of the army: the first regarded the coup as rescuing society's institutions; the army was therefore adopting its correct apolitical role. The second saw the army as coterminous with the liberal project; therefore, it could be deployed for three years in the service of 'democracy'. This meant in practice a return to the nineteenth-century struggle of the state against Barbarism: autonomous from society, and acting upon it.

The disastrous effects of the liberal version of the Revolución Libertadora were to be seen in the ensuing decades in Argentina. The liberal project was coterminous with liberal capitalism, and safeguarded its autonomy through a return to controlled elections. Peronism represented organised labour, was persecuted and deprived of a means of participating in political society. As the nationalist Catholics had predicted, Argentina by the late 1960s and early 1970s was in a state of latent civil war.

The Catholic conception of politics in Argentina opposed both the autonomous liberal project and the despotic tendencies in nationalism. It was closer to nationalism in political culture, but always showed strong differences with nationalism in power. The main bones of contention were the ways in which both Perón and Frondizi tied unions to the state and mobilised society, giving rise to an abominable combination of powers, an excessive interventionism and a totalitarian conception of state and society. Underlying the differences between nationalism in power and Catholicism was the contrast between the Suarezian concept of contract democratic theory and that of Rousseau.

The Catholic conception of politics was also opposed throughout to the liberal project. The main bones of contention derived from the liberal attempt to create new frameworks of political allegiance through secularization, claiming for the state areas which in the Catholic view should remain independent from the state. Catholics refuted the liberal notion that the state was outside and above the community, as well as its justification of controlled elections. In the 1880s as well as in the 1930s and 1950s, Catholics also strongly refuted the state's defence of a minimalist role for the state in the economy, and its refusal to grant legal recognition to unions. Underlying the differences between liberalism in power and Catholicism was the contrast between the role for the state specified by *Rerum Novarum* and that of the laissez-faire, minimalist conception, as well as the contrast between enlightened absolutism and the Thomist-Suarezian view of the state as delegated by the community, rooted in popular consensus.

The instability of Argentine politics in the nineteenth and twentieth centuries had as its underlying cause the intractable opposition of these two secularist conceptions of state and society. Enlightened absolutism, manifest in liberal democracy, encountered collectivist democracy, manifest in nationalism. Neither deferred to a realm outside themselves which might have acted as a curb. The self-arrogated right to rule independently of the community, for the sake of the community, encountered the self-arrogated right to claim the totality of political society because the community, in electing its leader, had handed over all rights to him. The clash of monistic definitions of liberty and democracy conspired against the creation of a political space within which a variety of groups could compete. An authentic democracy would have offered a political space in which the state's power was curbed, while at the same time ensuring that no group could rule without the broad consent of the governed. Such a democracy would have first required the abandonment of secularist assumptions.

That Catholics failed, overall, to wrest Argentine politics from its endemic clash of irreconcilable absolutes, points to the weakness of the institutional Church in the nineteenth and early twentieth centuries, which the Catholic revival was not entirely able to counteract. On the other hand, the scholastic framework, persistent in Argentine society in spite of its political classes, remained more or less intact in the period 1810–1960. Both enlightened absolutism (autonomous from society) and collectivist democracy (claiming the whole of political society) were checked by the Church's opposition at specific junctures and the rumble of tanks. Sovereignty was taken away from absolutists, tyrants and despots and handed back to the community. The liberal project could not prolong itself indefinitely in contradiction to wider society. Nor could nationalism descend fully into totalitarianism. Argentine politics remained, ultimately, within a framework. Although ideologically both liberalism and nationalism sought to realise the absolute in the relative, they were never permitted to do so beyond certain bounds. Politics remained a Hispanic family affair.

Appendix I

Argentine Catholicity in Figures

Table I.1 Number and size of diocese in relation to population growth

Year	No. of dioceses	Average km²	Overall population	Average population per diocese
1859	5	555,000		
1869			1,737,076	347,400
1895			3,954,911	791,000
1897	8	347,000		
1910	11	252,000		
1914			7,885,237	716,840
1934			12,729,000	1,157,180

Source: E. Amato, *La Iglesia en Argentina*, Buenos Aires, 1969, pp. 140–5

Table I.2 Population in 1910 classified by religious belief and nationality

Religion	Argentines	per cent	Foreigners	per cent	Total	per cent
Catholic	654,411	94.8	498,667	88.9	1,133,078	92.0
Protestant	11,855	1.7	18,936	3.4	30,791	2.5
Jewish	3,295	0.5	13,294	2.4	16,589	1.3
Other religions	1,358	0.2	4,717	0.8	6,055	0.5
No religion	19,614	2.8	25,571	4.6	45,185	3.7
Total	690,533	(100)	561,185	(100)	1,231,698	(100)

Source: H. Recalde, *Matrimonio Civil y Divorcio*, Buenos Aires, 1986, p. 12

Table I.3 Showing growth in membership of Catholic Action, 1933–1950

	Year	Centres	Members	Growth
Men (HAC)	1933	216	4,048	100
	1938	370	6,220	153
	1943	445	8,161	201
	1950	470	9,242	227
Women (AMAC)	1933	236	5,177	100
	1938	476	10,791	208
	1943	582	15,061	290
	1950	730	17,686	340
Young Men* (JAC)	1933	207	3,381	100
	1938	438	5,593	146
	1943	509	12,407	323
	1950	790	21,000	548
Young Women* (AJAC)	1933	297	7,150	100
	1938	628	12,707	177
	1943	931	22,871	319
	1950	1,117	24,635	344

Totals (all branches)

	Year	Centres	Members	Growth
	1933	956	19,756	100
	1938	1,912	35,311	179
	1943	2,467	58,500	344
	1950	3,107	72,563	468

(* Usually between fifteen and thirty years of age)

Source: Junta Central de la A.C.A., *Treinta años de la Acción Católica Argentina*, Buenos Aires, 1961, pp. 168–70

Appendix I

Table I.4 Relation of population to number and size of diocese, 1933–1961

Year	No. of dioceses	Surface area of diocese (Km^2)	Overall Population	Population per diocese
1933	11	252,000	12,729,000	1,157,180
1936	21	130,000		
1940	22		14,055,000	639,000
1947			15,800,000	717,500
1955			18,000,000	820,000
1957	35	80,000	20,000,000	570,000
1961	46	56,000		430,000

Source: E. Amato, *La Iglesia en Argentina*, Buenos Aires, 1969, pp. 42–3

Table I.5 Religious self-identification of Argentines, 1895–1947

	1895		1947	
Religion	No.	per cent	No.	per cent
Catholic	3,921,136	99.1	14,880,246	93.6
Protestant (*)	26,750	0.7	310,633	2.0
Jewish	6,065	0.2	249,330	1.6
No religion	(#)	(#)	239,949	1.5
Unknown	–	–	114,589	0.7
Orthodox	(@)	–	66,217	0.4
Other religions	940	–	30,738	0.2
Other Christians ($)	–	–	2,125	–
Total	3,954,911	(100)	15,893,827	(100)

(*) all denominations: e.g. Baptist, Lutheran, Anglican etc.
(#) unknowable
(@) included in 'other religions'
($) e.g. Coptic.

Source: Presidencia de la Nación, *IV Censo General de la Nación*, Buenos Aires, 1947, pp. lxxxiii–lxxxiv

Table I.6 Comparison of the number of pupils in postprimary and secondary education whose parents opted in 1944 for non-Catholic morality classes; by province, in order of state school population

	Pupils	Per cent religion	Per cent morality
(Provinces)			
Federal Capital	31,721	85.47	14.53
Buenos Aires	19,769	92.69	7.31
Santa Fe	9,361	91.12	8.88
Córdoba	6,122	94.89	5.11
Entre Ríos	5,928	90.81	9.19
Mendoza	4,012	93.64	6.36
Corrientes	3,845	96.20	3.80
Tucumán	2,674	92.37	7.63
Santiago del Estero	2,280	96.36	3.64
San Juan	1,988	98.05	1.95
Catamarca	1,922	99.01	0.99
La Rioja	1,806	98.72	1.27
San Luis	1,782	96.41	3.59
Salta	1,752	98.23	1.77
(*Gobernaciones*)			
Chaco y Formosa	698	92.12	7.88
Misiones	650	96.62	3.38
La Pampa	406	90.62	9.38
Río Negro	339	96.76	3.24
Chubut	132	81.06	18.94
Neuquén	102	81.37	18.63
Santa Cruz	20	50.00	50.00
Total	98,675	91.1	8.9

Source: Ministerio de Justicia e Instrucción Pública, Dirección General de la Enseñanza Religiosa, *Cuadro Estadístico de la Enseñanza Religiosa en los establecimientos de enseñanza post-primaria, secundaria y especial*, Buenos Aires, November 1944, p. 5

Table I.7 Numbers opting for sacramental marriage subsequent to obligatory civil ceremony in Buenos Aires, 1926–1946

Year	1926	1932	1940	1942	1944	1946
(1) Civil	18,029	17,355	21,952	24,516	26,163	27,279
(2) Church	9,479	10,767	16,133	18,538	19,893	20,138
(2) as per cent of (1)	52.6%	62%	73.5%	75.6%	71.9%	74%

Source: R. Nolasco, 'Geografía religiosa y sociología pastoral', *Notas de Pastoral Jocista* (March–April 1954) pp. 23–4

Appendix II

Text of Catholic Action's first flyer of leaflet campaign, 1936

LET'S THINK ABOUT IT!

What is the source of the profound social ills which surround us?

The ignorance of morality, the lack of justice, and the rejection of Christian brotherhood.
   Both rich and poor have grown away from the Gospel. They have lived together without caring for each other, helping each other, nor understanding each other.

How has this come about?

■ THE BOSSES – even those who claimed to be Christians – were generally deaf to *the principles of social justice* contained in the repeated declarations of the Popes, and placed workers and their dependents in *an unjust situation*, without possibilities of self-improvement...
   Equally, the 'liberal régime' tore down the *Christian elements* of the social order, precisely at the point when the big industries came into being.
   'Liberalism' liberated the most able and the strongest, enabling them to increase their profits immoderately, at the expense of others... In this way, *some fortunes* were made and *much misery* was created.

■ THE WORKERS, in their harsh struggle for survival, deprived of hope, *put their faith in the social reformers*, who called themselves 'socialists' and 'communists'.
   These promised, and continue to promise, *a justice that is no more than the suppression of all rights*, and the reduction of all men to the same condition, that of *slaves of the state*.
   So that nobody can take advantage of anybody, communists want *nobody to have a right to anything*, not even a small property, not even look after his home and educate his children.

Now is the time...

■ NOW IS THE TIME FOR WORKERS to realise that the supposed Communist solution will only make their lives worse, depriving them of any individual freedom, any hope of improvement, or any chance for well-being.
   The *true solution* lies not in hatred and class struggle but in a return to Christian principles of *love* and *fraternity*.
   Jesus Christ, who was Himself a worker, proclaimed these truths, and the workers of today should turn towards *Catholic Social Doctrine*, which enobles

the family, encourages the moral and material elevation of the popular classes, affirms the dignity of labour, calls for the worker's *just remuneration* and his easy access to ownership of property, proclaims the rights of the weak and the poor, within a framework of harmony, justice, and social peace.

■ NOW IS THE TIME FOR BOSSES to realise that 'they cannot have slaves for workers, and must respect in them the dignity of the human person ...' (Leo XIII).

The bosses are to procure the *well-being* of their employees, and to *satisfy their just aspirations*, sincerely applying *Catholic Social Doctrine*.

If the bosses do not hear the admonishing voice of the great Popes who have concerned themselves with the Social Question (Leo XIII and the present Pius XII), *the masses will be swept up* by the deceit of the false social reformers ...

And then will come a time when no-one, neither rich nor poor, will have even the right to his own house and family!

Will the bosses have deserved this punishment for not having in time what each of us have to do for the good of all?

THE CENTRAL SOCIO-ECONOMIC SECRETARIAT
OF ARGENTINE CATHOLIC ACTION

[*Source*: *Boletín de la Acción Católica Argentina* no. 135 (1 December 1936) pp. 730–1].

Notes and References

Introduction

1. Rock, *Authoritarian Argentina* p. xiv; similarly McGee, Deutsch and Dolkart (eds.) *The Argentine Right*.
2. Cit. in McIlwain, *Growth of Political Thought* p. 188.
3. Ullmann, *The Growth of Papal Government* chs. 2–5.
4. E. Fortin, 'St. Thomas Aquinas' in Strauss and Corpsey (eds) *History of Political Philosophy* p. 258.
5. *Summa Theologicae*, Pts. I–II, Questions 90–97, summarised in Bigongiari (ed.) *The Political Ideas of St. Thomas Aquinas* pp. 3–80. On Thomism: Copleston, *Aquinas* pp. 238–9.
6. McIlwain, *Growth of Political Thought* pp. 326–30.
7. L. Dupré, 'The Common Good and the Open Society' in Douglass and Hollenbach (eds) *Catholicism and Liberalism* pp. 174–6; Maritain, *The Person and the Common Good*; Gilby, *Principality and Polity* p. 244.
8. *Recopilación de Leyes de los Reinos de las Indias*, cit. in Elliot, *The Old World and the New* p. 81.
9. Véliz, *The Centralist Tradition of Latin America* pp. 21–5; Elliot, *Imperial Spain* p. 108.
10. Cragg, *Church and the Age of Reason* pp. 209–33.
11. G. Franceschi, 'Francisco Suárez y el origen del poder civil', in Dell'Oro Maini *et al.*, *Francisco Suárez* pp. 53–74; Hamilton, *Political Thought in Sixteenth-Century Spain* ch. 2; Plamenatz, *Man and Society* vol. I p. 226.
12. McDonald, *Rousseau and the French Revolution* pp. 27–29.
13. Distinctions made by Friedrich (ed.) *Totalitarianism* p. 274; Arendt, *Origins of Totalitarianism* pp. 464–7; and Marejko, *Rousseau et la dérive totalitaire* pp. 23–25.
14. Talmon, *Origins of Totalitarian Democracy* ch. 2.
15. McBrien, *Catholicism* p. 1108.
16. Micklem and Morgan, *Christ and Caesar* p. 112.
17. Micklem, *Theology of Politics* pp. 41–4. On Catholic clash with Revolution: Maier, *Revolution and Church* pp. 122–6; Tallett, 'Dechristianizing France: the Year II and the Revolutionary Experience' in Tallett and Atkin (eds) *Religion, Society and Politics in France* pp. 1–22.
18. Simon, 'The doctrinal issue between the Church and democracy', in Gurian and Fitzsimons (eds) *The Catholic Church in World Affairs* pp. 87–114; Rousseau, *The Social Contract* Bk. IV, ch viii, 'Civil Religion' pp. 176–87; Maier, *Revolution and Church* pp. 128–35. Theory of general will expressly deplored in encyclicals *Diuturnum* (1881), *Inmortale Dei* (1885) and the papal letter on the *Sillon* (1910).
19. The terms 'ecumenical' and 'sectarian' liberalism are those of Carlton J.H. Hayes. The American neoscholastic John Courtenay Murray

distinguished between 'Anglo-Saxon' and 'Continental' liberalism. For a discussion, see P. Gleason, 'American Catholics and liberalism, 1789–1960' in Douglass and Hollenbach, *Catholicism and Liberalism* p. 45.
20. On liberal Catholicism: Steinfels, 'The failed encounter: the Catholic Church and liberalism in the nineteenth century' in Douglass and Hollenbach (eds) *Catholicism and Liberalism* pp. 27–37; Gibson, 'Why Republicans and Catholics couldn't stand each other in the nineteenth century' in Tallett and Atkin (eds) *Religion, Society and Politics in France* pp. 107–118; Haag, 'The Political Ideas of Belgian Catholics, 1789–1914' in Moody (ed) *Church and Society* pp. 281–98; Reardon, *Liberalism and Tradition* ch. 2; Vidler, *Church in an Age of Revolution* ch. 6; Vidler, *Prophecy and Papacy* pp. 161–6 and 203.
21. For a discussion on 'Augustinian' vs. 'Thomist' models: Komonchak, 'Vatican II and the encounter between Catholicism and liberalism' in Douglass and Hollenbach (eds) *Catholicism and Liberalism* ch. 3.
22. A term borrowed from Poulat, *Eglise contre Bourgeoisie*.
23. Maier, *Revolution and Church* pp. 203–17.
24. Poulat, *Eglise contre Bourgeoisie* p. 121; Misner, *Social Catholicism in Europe* pp. 133–44, 152–62 and 171–81.
25. Equidistance advocated by Keller, *L'encyclique du 8 décembre 1864* and Donoso Cortés, *Ensayo sobre el catolicismo*.
26. Evans, *German Center Party* p. 404.
27. Whyte, *Catholics in western democracies* pp. 8–94; Mayeur, *Des partis catholiques à la démocratie chrétienne* p. 52; Lannon, *Catholic Church in Spain* ch. 5; Webster, *Christian Democracy in Italy* pp. 3–8.
28. Stock-Morton, *Development of 'morale laïque' in nineteenth-century France* pp. 27–44.
29. Chadwick, *Secularization of the European Mind* p. 237.
30. Stock-Morton, *Development of morale laïque* pp. 112–18 and 123; Poulat, *Liberté, laïcité* p. 38.
31. Micklem and Morgan, *Christ and Caesar* p. 107; Anderson, 'The Conflict in Education. Catholic Secondary Schools, 1850–70: A Reappraisal' in Zeldin (ed.) *Conflicts in French Society* pp. 51–93; McManners, *Church and State in France* pp. 46–63; Fogarty, *Christian Democracy in Western Europe* pp. 173–4; Vidler, *Church in an Age of Revolution* ch. 13.
32. Papal letter *Au Milieu des Solicitudes* (1892) and Encyclical *Inmortale Dei* (1885).
33. *Inmortale Dei* (1885) and *Sapientiae Christianae* (1890) summarised in Hughes, *Popes' New Order* pp. 65–70 and 85–93.
34. Molony, *The Worker Question* pp. 15–129; summary of *Rerum Novarum* in Encyclicals *Centesimus Annus* (1991) secs. 5–10; *Quadragesimo Anno*, 1931, paras. 46–52.
35. Later elaborated in Pius XI Encyclical *Quadragesimo Anno*, 1931, sec. 79.
36. Misner, *Social Catholicism* pp. 258–74; Ponson, *Les catholiques lyonnais* pp. 127–41; McManners, *Church and State in France* pp. 89–92; Fogarty, *Christian Democracy* pp. 208–210; Brenan, *Spanish Labyrinth* pp. 227–8; Carr, *Spain* pp. 456–8; Mayeur, *Catholicisme social* pp. 121–2.
37. Dawson, *Religion and the modern state* pp. 44–7.

38. Webster, *Christian Democracy in Italy* pp. 12–13 and 91–102; Molony, *Political Catholicism in Italy* pp. 75–78; Irving, *Christian Democratic Parties* pp. 26–28; Alzaga, *Democracia cristiana en España* pp. 127–35 and 177–327; Mayeur, *Des partis catholiques* pp. 110–13; Droulers, *Politique sociale* vol. II pp. 163–4; Irving, *Christian Democracy in France* pp. 41–7.
39. On Salazar's political background: Noguiera, *Salazar*, vol. 1 pp. 90–154.
40. Weber, *Action Française* pp. 65–6; Nolte, *Three Faces of Fascism* chs. 2–6.
41. Sutton, *Nationalism, Positivism and Catholicism* pp. 16–75, 84–89 and 252.
42. Bernanos, *Edouard Drumont* pp. 127–152.
43. Brenan, *Spanish Labyrinth* pp. 38–53; Martin, *General Theory of Secularization* pp. 248–51; Lannon, *Catholic Church in Spain* pp. 16–20.
44. Lannon, *Catholic Church in Spain* pp. 174–181 and 186–213; Montero, *La persecución religiosa*.
45. Rhodes, *Vatican in the Age of Dictators* pp. 12–13.
46. Church condemnation of Italian fascism: Encyclicals *Rappresentanti in Terra* (1930), *Quadragessimo Anno* (1931) paras. 29–38, 78–80 and 83–7, and *Non abbiamo bisogno* (1934). On the Church–state conflict in Italy: Pollard, *Vatican and Italian Fascism* pp. 103–62; Webster, *Christian Democracy in Italy* pp. 102–12; Pollard, *Vatican and Italian Fascism* pp. 8–101. Distinctions between Italian fascism and totalitarianism: Arendt, *Origins of Totalitarianism* pp. 258–60; Rhodes, *Vatican in an Age of Dictators* pp. 174–204. Condemnation of Nazism in encyclical *Mit Brennender Sorge* (1937).
47. Maritain, *Scholasticism and Politics* p. 222. Statements on Spanish Civil War published as 'Con el pueblo', *Sur* no. 31 (Buenos Aires, April 1937) pp. 22–40; considered by Doering, *Jacques Maritain* pp. 85–124. View of history: Maritain, *Christianity and Democracy* p. 48; Mounier, 'Christianity and the idea of progress' in Mounier, *Be Not Afraid* pp. 65–108; essays by Flynn, Hellman, Mancini and Sigmund, in Hudson and Mancini (eds) *Understanding Maritain*.
48. Condemnation of Maurras: Maritain, *Primauté du Spirituel*. Types of political engagement summarised in Maritain, *Du régime temporel*. Political vision outlined in *Humanisme Intégrale*. On tenets of Christian democracy: Mancini, 'Maritain's democratic vision', and Sigmund, 'Maritain on Politics', in Hudson and Mancini (eds) *Understanding Maritain* pp. 157–61 and 146–7; Maritain, *Scholasticism and Politics* p. 114. Indwelling rights: Maritain, *Les droits de l'homme et la loi naturelle*. Church–state relations: Maritain, *Man and the State* pp. 163–4.
49. The terms 'open' and 'closed' are those of Whyte, *Catholics in western democracies* pp. 7–8.

1 Scholasticism and Secularism, 1810–1920

1. On Jesuits: Furlong, 'las misiones jesuíticas' in Levene (ed.) *Historia de la nación argentina* pp. 595–622; Mörner, *Jesuits in the La Plata Region*; C. Eguía Ruíz, 'A staggering blow to éducation' in Mörner (ed.) *Expulsion*

of the Jesuits pp. 173–87. Diocese figures from Amato, *La Iglesia en Argentina* p. 119.
2. Stoetzer, *Scholastic Roots* pp. 2–4.
3. Furlong, *Filosofía en el Río de la Plata*; Romero, *ideas políticas en Argentina* pp. 58–9; Furlong, 'Francisco Suárez fué el filósofo de la Revolución Argentina de 1810', in Dell'Oro Maini *et al, Suárez* pp. 76–112; Levene, *Historia filosófica* p. 11.
4. Gandía, *Historia de las ideas políticas* vol. 1 p. 103.
5. Lynch, *Spanish–American Revolutions* p. 28; Furlong, *Nacimiento* p. 527.
6. J. Gorriti, *Reflexiones sobre las causas morales de las convulsiones internas en los nuevos estados americanos y examen de los medios eficaces para reprimirlas* [1836]; on Gorriti: Kennedy, *Catholicism, nationalism and democracy* pp. 51–55.
7. Cit. in Estrada, *Lecciones* vol. 2 p. 63.
8. Moreno, *Memorias y Autobiografías* vol. 2 pp. 16–22; Moreno, 'Sobre la libertad de escribir' in *Escritos* vol. 2 p. 287; 'Prólogo de la reedición de la obra "El Contrato Social"' [1810] in Moreno', *ibid* vol. 2 pp. 303 and 305.
9. Lynch, *Spanish Colonial Administration* pp. 84–9; and Furlong, *Santa Sede y la emancipación hispanoamericana* pp. 26–7.
10. Véliz, *Centralist Tradition* p. 86.
11. Lynch, *Spanish–American Revolutions* p. 15.
12. Stoetzer, *Scholastic Roots* p. 121.
13. Giménez Fernández, *Doctrinas Populistas* p. 57.
14. Stoetzer, *Scholastic Roots* pp. 146–56.
15. Both cit. in Lynch, *Spanish–American Revolutions* pp. 53–4.
16. On the influence of scholasticism in the Mayo pronouncements: Gandía, *Historia del 25 de mayo* p. 426; González, *Revolución de Mayo* p. 8; Carbia, *Revolución de Mayo* pp. 16–17.
17. Véliz, *The Centralist Tradition of Latin America* ch. 9.
18. Paz, *Memorias Póstumas* vol. 1 p. 60.
19. Piaggio, *Influencia del clero* pp. 23–7; Furlong, 'La revolución de mayo' in Furlong *et al, Etapas del catolicismo argentino* pp. 17–18; Furlong, *San Martín* pp. 37–39; and Gallardo, *La política religiosa* pp. 30–2.
20. Discussion in Estrada, *Iglesia y Estado* pp. 14–34 and 26–7, Zuretti, *Nueva Historia Eclesiástica* pp. 183–7; Sanguinetti, *La representación diplomática del Vaticano;* Furlong, *Santa Sede* pp. 125–7; and Carbia, *Revolución de Mayo* pp. 52–3.
21. Lynch, *Spanish–American Revolutions* pp. 59–64.
22. Gallardo, *Política Religiosa de Rivadavia* pp. 225–9; Gallardo, 'La venta de los bienes eclesiásticos en Buenos Aires', *Revista Eclesiástica* no. 678 (Sept. 1956) pp. 456–87; Carbia, *Revolución de Mayo y la Iglesia* pp. 90–1 and 109–14; Franceschi, '. . .Y al César lo que es del César', *Criterio* no. 844 (4 May 1944) p. 415; Véliz, *The Centralist Tradition* pp. 193–4.
23. Leturia, *Relaciones* vol. 3: 'Carta del Canónigo Mastai al Cardenal Carlo Odescalchi' pp. 353–5.
24. Paz, *Memorias Póstumas* vol. II p. 189.
25. Forbes, *Once años* p. 312; Levene, *History of Argentina* pp. 367–8; Shumway, *Invention of Argentina* pp. 103–5; Leturia, *Relaciones* vol. 103 [1493–1835] p. 110.

Notes and References

26. Areces and Ossana, *Rivadavia y su tiempo* p. 78.
27. Gallardo, *política religiosa de Rivadavia* p. 263.
28. Ferns, *Britain and Argentina* p. 85.
29. On Rosas: Halperín Donghi, *De la Revolución* p. 311; Mansilla, *Rozas* p. 106; and Lynch, *Argentine Dictator* p. 293. Also Ingenieros, *Evolución de las ideas argentinas* vol. 3 pp. 53–9; and Burgin, *Argentine federalism* pp. 109–110 and 154.
30. Gore to Palmerston, cit. in Lynch, *Argentine Dictator* pp. 185–6.
31. On Church under Rosas: Mansilla, *Rozas* pp. 112–13; Ramos Mejía, *Rosas y su tiempo* vol. 1 p. 265 and vol. 2 pp. 18–21, 75 and 34–9; Ingenieros, *Evolución de las ideas* vol. 3 pp. 53, 284–8 and 367; Lynch, *Argentine Dictator* pp. 183–5; Levene, *History of Argentina* p. 411; and King, *Veinticuatro años* p. 146. On Jesuits: Castagnino, *Rosas y los jesuítas* pp. 31–6; letter from Padre Berdugo, Jesuit Superior, recording interview with Pedro de Angelis, repr. in Rev. *Estudios* no. 302 (Buenos Aires, Aug. 1936) pp. 91–101.
32. Jesuit reports in Castagnino, *Rosas y los jesuítas* p. 36; and Ramos Mejía, *Rosas y su tiempo*, vol. 2 p. 26. Impressions of an American visitor in King, *Veinticuatro años* pp. 68, 83 and 177. On state of Church: Amato, *Iglesia en Argentina* pp. 120–1; and Soneira and Lumerman, *Iglesia y Nación* p. 19.
33. Furlong, 'El catolicismo argentino entre 1860 y 1930', in *Academia Nacional de Historia* vol. 2 pp. 251–2. Assessment by Goyena in Aúza, *Católicos y liberales* vol. I p. 1/5. Zuretti, *Nueva Historia Eclesiástica* pp. 287–356.
34. On Fahy: Ussher, *Padre Fahy*, and Keogh, 'Argentina and the Falklands (Malvinas): the Irish connection' in Hennessy and King (eds) *The Land that England Lost* pp. 134–6.
35. De Imaz, *Los que mandan* ch. IX.
36. Calculated from figures in Farrell, *Iglesia y pueblo en Argentina* pp. 60–1.
37. Rock, *Argentina* p. 129.
38. Botana, *El Orden Conservador* chs. 1 and 2. Also Sánchez Sorondo, *La Argentina por dentro* ch. XII.
39. Kennedy, *Catholicism, nationalism and democracy* pp. 76–97; Estrada, *La Política Liberal* pp. 50–7 and 124; Frías, 'Necesidad de la unión y del orden de la República Argentina' [1853] repr. in Halperín Donghi (comp.) *Proyecto y construcción de una nación* pp. 40–3.
40. Botana, *El Orden Conservador* p. 49; Echevarría, 'Organización de la patria sobre la base democrática' in *Dogma Socialista* [1846] para 10, no. 12 pp. 101–13; Ingenieros, *Evolución de las ideas* vol. 3 pp. 473–7.
41. Halperín Donghi, *Proyecto y Construcción* p. xvii.
42. Ingenieros, *Evolución* vol. 3 pp. 424–550; Shumway, *Invention of Argentina* p. 148; Echevarría, 'Fusión de todas las doctrinas progresivas en un centro unitario', *Dogma Socialista* para XII, no. 14 pp. 29–34.
43. Alberdi cit. in Shumway, *Invention of Argentina* p. 148.
44. Alberdi, 'De la inmigración como medio de progreso y de cultura para la América del Sud', *Bases* no. 15 pp. 67–93.
45. Alberdi, 'La religión católica es el medio de educar esas poblaciones', *Bases* p. 93; also Halperín Donghi, *Echevarría* pp. 85–6.
46. Shumway, *Invention of Argentina* p. 148.

47. Lloyd Mecham, *Church and state* p. 235; Estrada, *Iglesia y Estado*; Kennedy, *Catholicism, nationalism and democracy* pp. 91–2; Farrell, *Iglesia y pueblo* p. 57.
48. Furlong, 'El catolicismo argentino' in *Academia Nacional de la Historia* vol. 2 pp. 259–64; Furlong, *Colegio del Salvador* vol. 2 pp. 116–25; Zuretti, *Nueva Historia Eclesiástica* pp. 317–18.
49. Amato, 'Buenos Aires: su evolución demográfica y religiosa', *Notas de Pastoral Jocista* Año XI (September–October 1957) p. 26.
50. Taylor, *Rural Life* p. 320.
51. Zuviría cit. in Furlong, 'El catolicismo argentino...' p. 251.
52. Birschoff, *Historia de Córdoba* pp. 281–338.
53. On freemasonry: Zuretti, *Nueva Historia Eclesiástica* pp. 315–16; and Lazcano, *Las sociedades secretas*. On Córdoba warning: Recalde, *Matrimonio Civil* p. 78. On burning of Jesuit College: Furlong, *Colegio del Salvador* vol. 2 pp. 71–125.
54. cit. in Recalde, *Matrimonio Civil* 39–40.
55. Examples from Recalde, *La Iglesia y la cuestión social* p. 43 and Recalde, *Matrimonio Civil* pp. 16–88. On prostitution see Guy, *Sex and Danger* p. 13.
56. Recalde, *Matrimonio Civil* pp. 88–98.
57. Franceschi, 'El Congreso Católico Argentino de 1884', *Criterio* no. 1217 (12 August 1954) pp. 563–7.
58. Browning, *The River Plate* pp. 36–9.
59. Taylor, *Rural Life* pp. 320–2.
60. Aúza, *Católicos y liberales* vol. I p. 10/22.
61. e.g. Browning, *The River Plate* p. 135; Winter, *Argentina* p. 293; Hirst, *Argentina* p. 160; and Fraser, *The Amazing Argentine* p. 77. All were visiting Argentina prior to the 1930s.
62. Alvarez cit. in Terán, *Positivismo y nación* pp. 29–30.
63. Botana, *El Orden Conservador* p. 36.
64. For the remarkable statistics, see Cortés Conde, *El Progreso Argentino*.
65. On the political spirit of the 1880s: Halperín Donghi, '1880: un nuevo clima de ideas', in *Espejo de la Historia* pp. 241–76; Cornblit *et al*, 'La generación del '80 y su proyecto: antecedentes y consecuencias', in Di Tella *et al*, *Argentina, sociedad de masas* pp. 29–46; Gallo, 'Argentina: society and politics, 1880–1916', *Cambridge History of Latin America*, vol. V pp. 378–9. On elections: Cayró, 'El fraude patriótico' in Gorostegui de Torres (ed) *Historia Integral* vol. 7 pp. 173–96.
66. De Imaz, *Identidad Iberoamericana* ch. 5.
67. Estrada, *Discursos* pp. 107–19, 164–77 and 208; Furlong, 'El catolicismo argentino' p. 265; Aúza, *Católicos y liberales* vol. 1 pp. 2/5–8/9.
68. Secularist arguments from *La Nación*, and speeches by Gallo, Lago García and Wilde, in Weinberg (comp.) *Ley 1420*, vol. I pp. xxvi–xxviii, 48–64 and 136–7; vol. 2 pp. 197–207 and 229.
69. Rock, *Authoritarian* p. 34.
70. Speeches by Achával Rodríguez and Lugones in Weinberg (comp.) *Ley 1420* vol. 1 pp. 68–74 and 292; vol. 2 pp. 241 and 262–6. See also Pesce Battilana, *Los Diputados Católicos* pp. 65–89.
71. Cit. in Rock, *Authoritarian* pp. 32–3.

72. Jefferson, *Peopling the Argentine Pampa* pp. 100–1.
73. Recalde, *Matrimonio Civil* p. 23.
74. Cit. in Aúza, *Católicos y liberales* vol. 1 pp. 13/2–3.
75. Campo Wilson, 'El origen de las escuelas laicas argentinas', *Criterio* no. 1256 (22 Mar 1956) p. 567.
76. cit. in Aúza, *Católicos y liberales* vol. 2 p. 12/23.
77. Aúza, *Católicos y liberales* vol. 1 pp. 11/12–17.
78. As is maintained by e.g. Rock, *Argentina* pp. 159–60, and McGee Deutsch, *Counterrevolution* p. 53.
79. Recalde, *Matrimonio Civil* pp. 124–5.
80. Barroataveña, 'Origen de la Unión Cívica de la Juventud', in Alem *et al.*, *La Revolución del 90* pp. 19–49.
81. On role of Catholics *vis à vis* other opposition groups in 1890 uprising: recollections of Pizarro in *Diario de Sesiones*, Sesión Ordinaria del 6 de junio de 1891 pp. 88 *et seq.*; Mignone, 'Los católicos y la revolución de 1890', *Revista de Historia*, no. 1 (primer trimestre de 1957): 56–60; Ancarola, 'Los católicos y el noventa' in *Historia* (Año X-N°40, December 1990–February 1991) pp. 65–75, and Germán Herz, *La Revolución del 90* p. 115.
82. Groussac, *Los que Pasaban* p. 115.
83. *La Nación* 14 julio 1903, cit. in Recalde, *Matrimonio Civil* p. 152.
84. On social conditions and worker agitation at the turn of the century: Blackwelder and Johnson, 'Changing Criminal Patterns in Buenos Aires, 1890–1914' in *Journal of Latin-American Studies* vol. 14, no. 2 (1982): pp. 359–80; Bialet-Massé, *El estado de las clases obreras*; Gutiérrez and Suriano, 'Workers' Housing and Living Conditions in Buenos Aires, 1880–1930' in Adelman (ed.) *Argentine Labour History* pp. 35–51.
85. Adelman, 'The political economy of labour in Argentina, 1870–1930' in Adelman (ed.) *Argentine Labour History* pp. 5–6.
86. On Argentine socialism: Moreau de Justo, *Juan B. Justo* p. 60; Adelman, 'The Political Economy of Labour in Argentina', in Adelman (ed.) *Argentine labour history* p. 24.
87. On Argentine social Catholicism: Niklison, 'Acción Católica Obrera' in *Boletín del Departamento Nacional de Trabajo* no. 46 (May 1920) p. 154; Aúza, *Corrientes sociales* pp. 51–80; Pagés, 'Los ensayos sindicales de inspiración católica en la República Argentina' in *Anales de. . . . Ingenieros Católicos*, 1944 pp. 73–118; Aúza, *Aciertos y fracasos* vol. 1, pp. 137 and 155–217; Lamarca, 'Discurso sobre fundación de la Liga Social Argentina' in Recalde, *Iglesia y cuestión social* pp. 101–7; Ussher, 'Cien años de acción católica en la Argentina (1831–1931)' *Criterio* nos. 1272/3 (Dec 1956); Spalding, *Clase Trabajadora* pp. 504–48.
88. Zimmerman, 'Intellectuals, Universities and the Social Question: Argentina, 1989–1916' in Adelman (ed.) *Argentine Labour History* pp. 200 and 207; Aúza, *Aciertos y Fracasos* vol. 2 pp. 302–16; García Costa, *Alfredo L. Palacios* pp. 109–10; Walter, *The Socialist Party* p. 75; Luchía Puig, *Medio Siglo* pp. 16–35.
89. For example, speeches by Mgr. De Andrea at centenary celebrations of 1910, especially 'Oración Patriótica', in Romero Carranza, *Monseñor De Andrea* pp. 124–8.

90. Smith, 'The breakdown of democracy in Argentina, 1916–30' in Linz and Stepan (eds) *The Breakdown* p. 15.
91. See comments by *La Vanguardia* in Rock, *Politics in Argentina* p. 96.
92. On UCR Krausism: Rock, 'Intellectual precursors of conservative nationalism in Argentina, 1900–1927', *Hispanic American Historical Review* vol. 67, no. 2 (May 1987) pp. 294–6; and Guerrero, 'Krausismo y radicalismo' in Biagini (comp.) *Orígenes de la democracia* pp. 175–82.
93. Cit. in del Mazo, *Yrigoyen* p. 39.
94. Walter, *Student Politics* chs. 1 and 2.
95. Ballent, 'La Iglesia y la vivienda popular: la Gran Colecta Nacional de 1919' in Armus (ed.) *Mundo urbano* p. 208; McGee Deutsch, *Counterrevolution* pp. 36–37; Aúza, *Aciertos y Fracasos* vol. 2 pp. 20–1; De Andrea, 'Oración Patriótica' in Romero Carranza, *De Andrea* pp. 124–8.
96. On absorption of female unions, cf. de Arenza, *Sin memoria* pp. 24–5; and of Social League: Aúza, *Aciertos y fracasos*, vol. 2 pp. 254–5 and vol. 3 p. 77; and in general: Zuretti, *Nueva Historia Eclesiástica* p. 393. On failure of early Christian Democracy: Ghirardi, *La Democracia Cristiana* pp. 57–8; and Parera, *Los Demócrata Cristianos Argentinos* vol. 1 pp. 62–3.
97. Quijada, *Manuel Gálvez* pp. 79–83; Rock, 'Intellectual precursors...' pp. 271–300; Rojas, *Restauración Nacionalista* pp. 116–21; Barbero and Devoto, *Los nacionalistas* pp. 22–8.
98. Cit. in Escudé, *Fracaso del Proyecto Argentino* p. 44.
99. McGee Deutsch, *Counterrevolution* pp. 44–50; Guy, *Sex and Danger* pp. 5–10 and 17–20.
100. See Lugones' polemic with Tomás Casares in Irazusta, *Genio y figura* pp. 112–13.
101. Rock, *Authoritarian* pp. 66–8.

2 The Catholic Revival, 1920s–1950s

1. Lloyd Mecham, *Church and State* p. 242 and Zuretti, *Nueva Historia Eclesiástica* pp. 396–7.
2. Dell'Oro Maini speech in *Tercera Asamblea de la Juventud Católica Argentina* pp. 11–16. On CCC: Ordóñez interview, Instituto Di Tella no. C. 11–5 pp. 92–6; 'Libros y lecturas recomendadas...' in *Circular...de los Cursos de la Cultura Católica* no. 3 (Dec 1923); Olazábal, *Por una cultura católica*; and 'Homenaje al Dr. Tomás D. Casares, *Universitas* Año 9, No. 38 (July–September 1975) pp. 23–58.
3. 'El administrador apostólico...' in *Circular...de los CCC* no. 7 (Mar 1925); also Dell'Oro Archive.
4. Dell'Oro Maini to Rómulo Ayerza (6 February 1925) [Dell'Oro Archive].
5. 'Apuntes...', Dell'Oro Maini to Ayerza (28 May 1925) [Dell'Oro Archive]; editorial, *Criterio* no. 1 (8 March 1928).
6. 'Nota elevada al Excmo......Arzobispo de Buenos Aires' signed by Ayerza, Pereyra Iraola, Casares, and Dell'Oro Maini (23 March 1927) [Dell'Oro Archive].
7. On *Criterio*'s early history: Mallimaci, 'Catholicisme et état militaire...'; Gálvez, *Entre la Novela*, vol. 5 pp. 11–16 and Franceschi, 'Alberto Molas Terán', *Criterio* no. 742 (21 May 1942).

8. *XXXII Congreso Eucarístico Internacional [CEI]* vol. I pp. 7 and 54.
9. *CEI* vol. I p. 7.; Carranza, 'Martín Jacobé', in *ACA: Cincuenta años* pp. 41–6; 'El CEI según el Cardenal Verdier'; *Boletín de la ACA*. [*Bol. ACA*] no. 90 (15 January 1935) pp. 37–9.
10. Recollections of P. Moledo in De Imaz, *Escuchando a Moledo* p. 62.
11. Franceschi, 'El Congreso de las Jóvenes Católicas'; *Criterio* no. 755 (20 August 1942) pp. 405–8.
12. Figures from *Sursum* nos. 168–169 (September–October 1943) and 190 (July–August 1945); Fasolino, 'Los Congresos de la Juventud' in ACA, *20 años* pp. 59–63.
13. Martínez, 'La segunda asamblea de la Acción Católica Argentina', *Criterio* no. 796 (3 June 1943) p. 245.
14. For an excellent discussion of ACA's *método propio*: Mallimaci, 'Catholicisme et état militaire...' pp. 86–90.
15. Farrell, *Iglesia y Pueblo* pp. 60–61; Amato, *Iglesia en Argentina* pp. 158–99 and 209; Franceschi, 'Catolicismo rioplatense', *Criterio* no. 569 (5 January 1939) p. 345; Amato, 'Buenos Aires: su evolución demográfica y religiosa', *Notas de Pastoral Jocista* [*NPJ*] (September–October 1957) pp. 21–2; 'Inquietud pastoral frente a descristianización', *NPJ* (July–August 1953) pp. 231–2.
16. E. Rau, 'La propaganda protestante...' *Bol ACA* no. 280 (August 1945) p. 54; also J. White, *Argentina* ch. XIV: 'Why Americans are disliked'. On rural apostolate: Serafini, 'Problemas del Apostolado Rural', in ACA, *20 años* pp. 52–54; Jacob, 'la Acción Católica en las parroquias rurales', *Bol ACA* no. 77 (29 June 1934) pp. 386–8.
17. *CEI*, vol. I pp. 101–4; Mallimaci, *Catolicismo integral* pp. 10–11; Zuretti, *Nueva Historia Eclesiástica* pp. 443–4; Serrano, 'La Acción Católica...en los años 30', in ACA, *50 años* p. 156.
18. 'El ejército argentino recibe la sagrada comunión junto a la cruz de Palermo', *CEI* vol. 1 pp. 281–95. For a discussion: Mallimaci, 'Catholicisme et état militaire' pp. 244–65, and Potash, *The Army and Politics* pp. 177–8.
19. De Imaz, *Los que mandan* pp. 164–83.
20. For example, Leonard, *Politicians, Pupils and Priests* p. 75: 'the bishops came primarily from the upper class'.
21. Potash, *Army and Politics* pp. 22–3.
22. Leonard, *Politicians, Pupils and Priests* pp. 46–7 and 174.
23. Discussed by Forni, 'Reflexión sociológica sobre el tema de la religiosidad popular' in *Sociedad y Religión* no. 3 (1986) pp. 212–64 and Mallimaci, 'Catholicisme et état militaire' pp. 78–79.
24. By Franceschi, 'La posición católica en la Argentina', *Criterio* no. 884 (8 February 1945) p. 133, in reply to an article published in the United States alleging only 13 per cent 'regular' and 7 per cent 'occasional' attendance: G. Doherty, 'The Cross and the Sword: a Catholic view of Argentine nationalism', *Harpers* (Jan 1945) reproduced in *Criterio* no. 884 (8 February 1945) p. 142. Franceschi used current curial statistics.
25. Bunge, *Nueva Argentina* pp. 174–5 and 177–8.
26. On declining birth rate and illegitimacy: Belaúnde, 'La familia argentina y los problemas demográficos', *Bol. ACA*, no. 333 (January 1950):

pp. 30–40 and Figuerola, 'La realidad social argentina', in ACA, *IIIa Semana de Estudios Sociales* [1941] pp. 203–15.
27. Justo speech and new openness recorded by *Criterio* nos. 345 (11 October 1934) and 347 (25 October 1934). On 1934 agreeements: Papal Bull, *Nobiles Argentinae Nationis Ecclesia* (11 June 1934), details of which in Casiello, 'Hacia soluciones definitivas...' in ACA, *Treinta años* pp. 48–9. On growing Church presence in public sphere: Palacio, *Historia* vol. 2 p. 387 and Mallimaci, *Catolicismo Integral* p. 25. On spread of RE: Escudé, *Fracaso del Proyecto Nacional* pp. 111–14.
28. On De Andrea's vision of social Catholicism: Carranza, *De Andrea* pp. 227–56 and prologue to De Andrea, *El Catolicismo Social* pp. 24–50. Concept of 'corporative democracy' outlined in De Andrea sermons and speeches, reproduced in De Andrea, *Obras Completas* vol. 4 pp. 145–78.
29. Falcoff, 'Intellectual developments', in Falcoff and Dolkart (eds) *Prologue to Perón* pp. 110–35.
30. 'Hacia los nuevos años', *Criterio* no. 253 (5 January 1933).
31. 'La inquietud de esta hora', *Criterio* no. 335 (2 August 1934).
32. 'Carta autógrafa de SS Pío XI...' *Bol. ACA* no. 2 (1 June 1931) p. 27.
33. 'La Acción Católica y la Política', *Bol. ACA* no. 11 (15 October 1931); and '*Criterio*', *Criterio* no. 523 (10 March 1938).
34. Velazco Blanco, 'El apostolado intelectual de la mujer...' in ACA, *20 años* pp. 93–95; and AJAC, *Clases sobre la 'misión femenina'* pp. 23–7.
35. *Sursum* 146 (February 1937) p. 26.
36. Vanini, 'La unidad...' *Bol. ACA* no. 235 (November 1941).
37. 'Discurso...' *CEI* vol. I pp. 247–65 and 277.
38. 'Discurso...'; *CEI* vol. II pp. 37–43.
39. 'La Acción Católica y la Jerarquía', *Bol. ACA* no. 47 (1 April 1933) pp. 169–75; Di Pasquo, 'Los Métodos...', *Bol. ACA* no. 246 (October 1942) pp. 193–204; and interviews with former ACA militants: Basilio Serrano, José Luis De Imaz, Emilio Mignone.
40. A profile of ACA in retrospectives: e.g. *20 años* pp. 36–44 pp. 55–8 and *50 años* pp. 59–63, 83–7 and 155–6. Also JAC, *Manual del Socio*; articles from *Bol. ACA* and *Sursum*; plus interviews with former ACA militants: Emilio Mignone, Sara Mackintach and Basilio Serrano.
41. 'La Acción Católica y la Jerarquía', *Bol. ACA* no. 48 (15 April 1933); interview, José Luis De Imaz.
42. Among his many books, the most influential was *Concepción Católica de la Política*, first published in 1932 and frequently re-edited. There are many criticisms of Meinvielle's antisemitism in *Criterio* in the 1930s.
43. For example, Amadeo, 'La primera condición', *Bol. ACA* no. 12 (1 November 1931); and 'Córdoba docet', *Bol. ACA* no. 13 (15 November 1931).
44. *Criterio* (23 August 1944), cit. in Mallimaci, *El Catolicismo Integral* p. 4. Also, 'Nacionalismo y catolicismo', *Bol. ACA* no. 100 (15 June 1935); and 'Derecha, Izquierda', *Criterio* no. 424 (16 April 1936).
45. On Franceschi's influence: De Imaz, *Escuchando a Moledo* p. 63; Ponsati, 'Maritain in Argentina' in Papini (ed) *Jacques Maritain* p. 359; Parera, *Los Demócrata Cristianos*, vol. 1 pp. 77–9. Part of Franceschi's vast output is collected in his *Obras Completas*; biographical details in various

Criterio tributes and in Avellá Chafer, *Diccionario Biográfico* vol. 2 pp. 88–100. *Criterio* was not the 'organ of Catholic Action', as Navarro Gerassi, *Los nacionalistas* p. 37, maintains, but a semi-official independent weekly.
46. 'Carta Pastoral...' *Criterio* no. 431 (4 June 1936); '¿Comunista o católico?' *Criterio* no. 426 (30 April 1936); Valsecchi, 'El pensamiento...', *Bol. ACA* no. 77 (29 June 1934) pp. 380–5.
47. 'Sobre verdadera y falsa caridad', *Criterio* no. 505 (4 November 1937); 'Liberalismo y realismo', *Criterio* no. 612 (23 November 1939) pp. 277–9; '¿Para qué hablé?', *Criterio* no. 624 (15 February 1940).
48. 'Estado totalitario, estado cristiano', *Criterio* no. 278 (29 June 1933) p. 234.
49. 'Ante el problema del trabajo', *Criterio* no. 322 (3 May 1934).
50. Discussions of corporativism in *Criterio*: 'moral y política' no. 311 (15 February 1934); 'La inquietud de esta hora' no. 335 (2 August 1934); 'Ante la guía telefónica' no. 778 (28 January 1943); 'Las Fuerzas Vivas', no. 788 (8 May 1943); 'socialismo, capitalismo, catolicismo' no. 225 (23 June 1932); 'Hacia los nuevos años' no. 253 (5 January 1933).
51. From *Criterio*: 'el capital y el trabajo y un paso adelante' no. 197 (10 December 1931); 'Gobernar' no. 227 (7 July 1932); 'el liberalismo y el socialismo', no. 280 (13 June 1933); 'ante el problema del trabajo' no. 322 (3 May 1934); 'Anticomunismo' no. 337 (16 August 1934); 'Carta pastoral...la Iglesia frente a los problemas actuales' no. 431 (4 June 1936).
52. Palau's *La AC: cómo debe entenderse* was widely read. On Palau and ASP, Lannon, *Privilege* pp. 157–9.
53. Valsecchi's *Silabario Social* was the standard manual for the Catholic social activist. Family wage schemes: *Bol. ACA* no. 198 (15 July 1939) pp. 457–63, no. 220 (August 1940) and no. 231 (July 1941). First social week in 1937: *Bol. ACA* no. 155 (1 October 1937) pp. 581–87. Leaflet campaign: 'Campaña...', *Bol. ACA* no. 132 (15 October 1936) pp. 637–8; and 'Plan de acción', *Bol. ACA* no. 75 (1 June 1934).
54. For example, *Bol. ACA* no. 175 (1 August 1938) pp. 469–70, no. 203 (1 October 1939) p. 620; no. 237 (January 1942) pp. 33–4.
55. 'Nota presentada al senado...', *Bol. ACA* no. 136 (15 December 1936) pp. 766–8.
56. A. Caggiano, 'La Acción Católica y las obras económico-sociales', *Bol. ACA* no. 218 (June 1940) p. 342.
57. Arana Díaz, 'En torno a la sindicación cristiana'; *Bol. ACA* no. 144 (15 April 1937) pp. 249–52; Interview, Marta Ezcurra.
58. Interview, Marta Ezcurra.
59. 'Los apóstoles obreros', *Bol. ACA* no. 125 (29 July 1936) p. 64.
60. Valsecchi, 'Los apóstoles obreros', *Bol. ACA* no. 125 (29 July 1936). Reports of working-class suspicion of Church: Salas, 'Experiencias....', *Bol. ACA* no. 151 (1 August 1937). List of services provided by Junta de Gobierno de los CCO, 'Los Círculos Católicos de Obreros', and J. Saraco, 'Vanguardias Obreras Católicas' in ACA, *20 años* pp. 113–20.
61. Interview, Mario Seijó.
62. Interview, Francisco Guido.

63. Segunda, 'La JOC en marcha', *Bol. ACA* no. 273 (January 1945) p. 17. On the JOC method: Fievez and Meert, *Cardijn* pp. 84–170; *Manuel de la JOC*; interviews, Francisco Guido and Mario Seijó. On JOC in Argentina: 'Principios de un núcleo jocista', *Bol. ACA* no. 238 (February 1942) pp. 67–8; 'Cómo comenzar una sección jocista', *NPJ* Año V (May–June 1949) pp. 23–7; and Soneira, 'La Juventud Obrera Católica. . ..' in *Justicia Social* (Revista del CEDEL) Año 5, no. 8 (June 1989) pp. 76–88.
64. 'Argentinizar la política', *Criterio* no. 585 (18 May 1939).
65. Falcoff, 'Argentina', in Falcoff and Pike, *The Spanish Civil War* pp. 321–2. Fresco discussed by Walter, *The Province* pp. 160–1.
66. Examples from: Parera, *Los Demócrata Cristianos* vol. 1 p. 74; Gaudio and Pilone, 'Estado y relaciones laborales. . .' in Torre (ed.) *La formación* pp. 57–98; 'Amanece', *Bol. ACA* no. 173 (29 June 1938) pp. 405–8; and Potash, *Army and Politics* p. 97.

3 Catholicism and Nationalism, 1930–1939

1. Rock, *Argentina* p. 212; Potter, 'The failure of democracy in Argentina' pp. 101–2; Walter, *Province of Buenos Aires* pp. 85–9.
2. Smith, 'The Breakdown of Democracy: Argentina'; and Potash, *The Army and Politics* pp. 9–12.
3. Castellani, 'Libros Políticos' [1943], reproduced in *Deciamos Ayer* p. 40.
4. Irazusta, *Testimonios* pp. 19–22; Carulla, *Medio Siglo* pp. 145–7.
5. On *LNR*: Buchrucker, *Nacionalismo y Peronismo* pp. 45–77; McGee Deutsch, *Counterrevolution* pp. 194–5. Indictment of Maurras and Mussolini in early *Criterio*: 'El estado corporativo', no. 45 (10 January 1929); '"Action Française" y fascismo ante la santa sede', no. 58 (11 April 1929); 'Católicos y fascistas en Italia', no. 119 (12 June 1930); 'el fascismo como hecho y como cultura', no. 123 (10 June 1930); 'el nacionalismo y la Iglesia', no. 109 (3 April 1930); and 'Las naciones y la catolicidad', no. 97 (9 January 1930). On Catholic view of *LNR*: Amadeo, 'El grupo Baluarte y los CCC', *Universitas*, Año 9, no. 38 (July–September 1975) pp. 23–6; and Ordóñez, interview in *Todo es Historia* no. 211, Año XVII (October 1984) pp. 9–64.
6. Carulla, *Medio Siglo* pp. 206–14; Uriburu's addresses in Verbitsky (ed.) *Proclamas Militares* pp. 43–6; and 'Discurso. . .' in Uriburu, *La Palabra* pp. 91–2; Ibarguren, *El significado*.
7. Floria and García Belsunce, *Historia política* p. 124.
8. Whitaker, *Argentina* p. 78.
9. Weil, *Argentine Riddle* p. 6. On UCR in 1930s: Rock, 'Argentina, 1930–1946 pp. 16–17; Luna, *El 45* p. 19; Ciria, *Partidos y Poder* pp. 149–55; Floria and Belsunce, *Historia política* pp. 128–9; Walter, *Province* pp. 153–81.
10. For a favourable view of economic policy in the 1930s, see the revisionist study by Aguinaga and Azaretto, *Ni Década Ni Infame*.
11. D. Kelly, *The Ruling Few*, London, 1952 p. 291.

12. On the triangular relationship, early critique by Bunge, *La Economía Argentina*, vol. I, ch. 7; also Phelps, *The International Economic Position* p.225. Political implications considered by Escudé, *Declinación Argentina* pp. 28–33; Di Tella and Platt, *Political Economy* pp. 142–3; and Di Tella and Cameron Watt, *Argentina between the Great Powers* pp. 142–3. On public cynicism: Falcoff, 'Intellectual currents' in Falcoff and Dolkart, *Prologue to Perón* pp. 100–135; Botana, *Tras los dientes del perro* p. 171; and the widely-read classic by Martínez Estrada, *Radiografía de la Pampa* pp. 240–2.
13. On the rural crisis: Adelman, 'The Harvest Hand...' in Adelman (ed.) *Argentine Labour History* pp. 92–108; Halperín Donghi, 'Canción de otoño...' in *Espejo de la Historia* pp. 253–76; Rock, 'Argentina, 1930–1946', in Bethell (ed.) *CHLA* vol. 8 pp. 29–30; Solberg, 'Land tenure...'in Di Tella and Platt (eds) *Argentina, Australia and Canada* p. 56. On the Depression: O'Connell, 'Argentina...' R. Thorp (ed.) *Latin America in the 1930s* ch. 2.
14. On social conditions: Alhadeff, 'Social welfare...' in Platt (ed.) *Social Welfare* pp. 169–76; Bergquist, *Labor* p. 121; Peter, *Crónicas proletarias* pp. 55–7; Figuerola, 'La realidad social...' in ACA, *IIIa Semana* pp. 203–15; Tibaudin, 'El problema' *Bol. ACA* no. 238 (February 1942): 142–50.
15. Matsushita, *Movimiento obrero* pp. 23–43 and 68–185; Alexander, *Communism* pp. 73–9; Poppino, *International Communism* pp. 111–13, 124 and 153.
16. Catholic voting obligations outlined in 'Pastoral del Episcopado Argentino', *Criterio* no. 188 (8 October 1931).
17. 'Carta pastoral colectiva del Episcopado Argentino sobre la Acción Católica', *Bol. ACA* no. 1 (15 May 1931) pp. 5–10; 'La Acción Católica y la Política', *Bol. ACA* no. 11 (15 October 1931) pp. 265–70; E. Cárdenas, 'Disciplina necesaria', *Bol. ACA* no. 231 (July 1941) pp. 72–3.
18. Social reforms advocated in 'Carta Pastoral...' in *Criterio* no. 431 (4 June 1936).
19. On UCR's adoption of secularism: 'Un gesto inoportuno', *Criterio* no. 509 (2 December 1937); '*Hechos e Ideas*' no. 541 (14 July 1938).
20. Cf. *La Prensa* editorial, 'De religión y política' (15 June 1937) and critique in *Criterio* no. 486 (24 June 1937) pp. 176–7.
21. Interview, Emilio Mignone.
22. On PS and PDP dogmatic anticlericalism, from *Criterio*: 'Las elecciones' no. 316 (22 March 1934); 'La Iglesia y los partidos', no. 465 (28 January 1937); 'La política en *Criterio*' no. 490 (22 July 1937); and 'No pueden ser candidatos' no. 486 (24 June 1937). On PDP's laicist platform, Molinas and Barberis, *El Partido Demócrata Progresista* pp. 52–7. On differences between Catholics and the PDP, see the famous polemic between Franceschi and Senator Lisandro De La Torre, waged in a number of national newspapers in 1937: De La Torre, 'La cuestión social y los cristianos sociales' repr. in De la Torre, *Intermedio Filosófico* vol. 4, and response in *Criterio* articles: 'Ante una diatriba' no. 495 (26 August 1937); 'Hombre, no te enojes' no. 497 (9 September 1937); '¿Enemigo que

huye?' no. 499 (23 September 1937); and 'Los procedimientos de un polemista' no. 501 (7 October 1937). Summary of the polemic in: *Criterio* nos. 503 (21 October 37), 505 (4 November 1937) and 513 (30 December 1937).
23. See below pp. 148–9.
24. 'Las elecciones', *Criterio* no. 316 (22 March 1934).
25. 'La política en *Criterio*', *Criterio* no. 490 (22 July 1937).
26. 'El llamado a la fuerza', *Criterio* no. 256 (26 January 1933).
27. On fate of the diminutive Partido Popular: Parera, *Los Demócrata Cristianos*, vol. 1 p. 63 and Pagés, *Orígenes y desarrollo*...Objections of ACA to a Catholic political party, cf. discussion between Pagés and Ferreyra, 'La Acción Católica y la Política', *Criterio* no. 151 (22 January 1931) and 'Los católicos y la política', *Criterio* no. 189 (15 October 1931).
28. On futility of a coup: 'Una cuestión mal planteada', *Criterio* no. 245 (10 November 1932).
29. 'Estado totalitario, estado cristiano', *Criterio* no. 278 (29 June 1933).
30. 'Política y Acción Católica', *Criterio* no. 545 (11 August 1938).
31. From *Criterio*: 'Los católicos y la dictadura', no. 275 (8 June 1933).'¿Totalitarismo o liberalismo?', no. 582 (27 April 1939); 'Iglesia y estado', no. 357 (3 January 1935). Distinctions between the 'inadmissible' state corporatism of Mussolini, and the 'natural' corporativism espoused by Catholic social doctrine, 'Estado totalitario, estado Cristiano', *Criterio* no. 278 (29 June 1933) and 'Ante el problema del trabajo', *Criterio* no. 322 (3 May 1934). Condemnation of Nazism by the antimodernist Meinvielle in *La Iglesia y el Tercer Reich*.
32. Among the most important revisionist histories of Rosas were Gálvez, *Vida de Don Juan Manuel*, Irazusta, *Ensayo sobre Rosas* and Font Ezcurra, *San Martín y Rosas*. Revisionism is discussed by Gandía, *La revisión* and Halperín Donghi, *El revisionismo histórico*.
33. Comisión de Estudios..., *Nacionalismo* p. 54.
34. Cit. in Ibarguren, *La Historia* p. 627.
35. 'Nacionalismo y catolicismo', *Bol. ACA* no. 100 (15 June 1935) p. 364.
36. 'El despertar nacionalista', *Criterio* 242 (14 October 1932).
37. 'Los católicos y la dictadura', *Criterio* no. 275 (8 June 1933); 'Nacionalismo', *Criterio* no. 290 (21 September 1933); 'La inquietud de esta hora', *Criterio* no. 335 (2 August 1934); 'Jacobinismo y despotismo', *Criterio* no. 243 (27 October 1932).
38. 'Nacionalismo y catolicismo', *Bol. ACA* no. 100 (15 June 1935) pp. 356–64.
39. 'La inquietud de esta hora', *Criterio* no. 335 (2 August 1934).
40. 'El problema constitucional argentino', *Criterio* no. 698 (17 July 1941).
41. On Maritain's reputation in Argentina prior to 1936: Martínez Paz, *Maritain* ch. IV and Castellani, *Conversación* pp 82–4. Speeches in Buenos Aires recorded in Olazábal, *Por Una Cultura Católica* pp. 88–94; and *Criterio* no. 446 (17 September 1936). They are collected in Maritain, *Filosofía de la Persona Humana*. Address to PEN Congress reported by *La Nación* (11 September 1936); visit to Córdoba can be traced in the Catholic daily *Los Principios*, (1–4 October 1936) and *La Voz del Interior* (1–2 October 1936). Link with *Sur* considered by King, *'Sur'* pp. 61–8. Antimodernist refutations of Maritain by Maldonado and Meinvielle,

and defences by Ordóñez and Pividal, in *Criterio* nos. 484 (10 June 1937) and 486 (24 June 1937). Meinvielle's refutation of Maritain's 'modernism' is summarised in *De Lammenais a Maritain*, and followed by *Críticas* and *Cartas al P. Garrigou–Lagrange*, both of which were deployed by conservatives in the Vatican against Maritain in the 1940s. See discussion by Doering, *Jacques Maritain* p. 209.
42. The ambiguity of Maritain's classification is discussed by Franceschi in his open letter to the philosopher in 'Posiciones', *Criterio* no. 493 (12 August 1937) p. 351, and by C. Pico, *Carta a Jacques Maritain*.
43. See, by Maritain: 'Por el bien común', *Criterio* no. 325 (24 April 1934); 'De un nuevo humanismo', *Sur* no. 31 (April 1937) pp. 22–49; 'Carta sobre la independencia', *Sur* no. 22 (July 1936) pp. 54–86.
44. J. Maritain, 'A propósito de la 'Carta sobre la Independencia"', *Sur* no. 27 (December 1936) pp. 25–36.
45. King, *'Sur'* p. 62.
46. Castellani, 'Maritain, hombre de acción', *Criterio* no. 489 (15 July 1937) pp. 257–9.
47. On the clutch of *maritenianos*: Parera, *Los Demócrata Cristianos* vol. 1 pp. 73–75. There were three works of Maritain's on the 1939 ACA booklist, all of which were solidly scholastic: *Acción Católica y Acción Política*, *Para una filosofía* and *León Bloy*. Absent were *Humanismo Integral* and the *Esprit* articles, published in *Sur*. In the 'collaboration with nationalism' school were the following: Ezcurra Medrano, *Catolicismo y nacionalismo*; Llambías, *Dialéctica Comunista*; Meinvielle, *Un juicio católico* and Pico, *Carta a Jacques Maritain*.
48. Quijada, *Aires de República*; and Falcoff, *The Spanish Civil War* pp. 291–347. Among many memoirs are those of the Spanish Republic's Ambassador: Ossorio y Gallardo, *Mis memorias* chs. 3 and 4; the son of the editor of the mass pro-Republican tabloid *Crítica*: Botana, in *Tras los dientes del perro* pp. 182–4; a communist: Real, *Treinta años* pp. 52–3; and two Catholics: Amadeo, *Ayer, Hoy, Mañana* pp. 34–5, and De Imaz, *Promediados los cuarenta* pp. 18–25.
49. On Maritain's reasons for detachment, see Introduction.
50. It is untrue that Franceschi 'took over a large collection of church plate to help the Franco cause', as is maintained by King, *'Sur'* p. 67. He did, on the other hand, deliver both crates of sacramental paraphernalia (chalices, vestments) as well as funds to assist in the rehabilitation of churches – an altogether different proposition. See 'Cruzada pro-Iglesias Devastadas de España', *Criterio* no. 456 (26 November 1936); and Falcoff, *Spanish Civil War* p. 324.
51. 'Mártires, rehenes y verdugos', *Criterio* no. 461 (31 December 1936) and 'Demencia', *Criterio* no. 451 (22 October 1937).
52. On liberal–conservative, socialist and Catholic analyses, Falcoff, 'Argentina', in Falcoff and Pike (eds) *The Spanish Civil War. American Hemispheric Perspectives* pp. 313–31.
53. Maritain, 'Con el pueblo', *Sur* no. 31 (April 1937).
54. 'El movimiento español y el criterio católico', *Criterio* no. 489 (15 July 1937). A similar analysis by Meinvielle, *¿Qué saldrá de la España que sangra?* p. 3.

55. Pividal, 'Católicos fascistas y católicos personalistas', *Sur* no. 35 (August 1937) pp. 7–9; and Durelli, letter to Ocampo in *Sur* no. 47 (August 1938).
56. *Criterio* analysis: 'El eclipse de la moral', no. 486 (27 May 1937); 'Vida burguesa, vida heroica', no. 484 (10 June 1937); 'El Jefe', no. 485 (17 June 1937); 'El movimiento español y el criterio católico', no. 489 (15 July 1937). See also polemic between Maritain ['Sobre la guerra santa', *Sur* no. 35 (August 1937) pp. 98–117; and letter to Franceschi in 'Posiciones' *Criterio* no. 493 (12 August 1937) p. 349] and Meinvielle ['Los desvaríos de Maritain', *Criterio* no. 488 (8 July 1937); 'Contestación a Jacques Maritain', *Criterio* no. 493 (12 August 1937) pp. 356–60; and 'De la guerra santa', *Criterio* no. 494 (19 August 1937)]. Arguments summarised in 'Puntualizaciones', *Criterio* no. 498 (16 September 1937) p.55.
57. From *Criterio*, on Guernica: 'El eclipse de la moral', no. 482 (27 May 1937); and on Lorca, J. Assaf, 'Pemán y García Lorca', no. 477 (22 April 1937) and 'sobre la muerte de García Lorca', no. 509 (2 December 1937).
58. 'Posición de *Sur*', *Sur* no. 35 (August 1937) pp. 7–9. On *Sur*'s philosophical pedigree and intellectual disdain for Catholicism: King, '*Sur*' pp. 60–68, 71 and 97, who follows the dispute.
59. '*Sur* y *Criterio*', *Criterio* no. 499 (23 September 1937) p. 78 and 79.

4 War, Crisis and Military Intervention, 1939–1944

1. Kelly, *The Ruling Few* p. 302. On origins of Argentine isolationism: McGann, *Argentina* ch. 14. Argentina in the war is considered by Di Tella and Cameron Watt (eds), *Great Powers* pp. x–xiv and 58–9; and Humphreys, *Latin America* vol. 1 pp. 148–9.
2. On military reasons for neutrality: Potash, *The Army and Politics* p. 117; and Rouquié, *Pouvoir militaire* p. 301. On nationalists: Ibarguren, *La historia* pp. 463–7; and Buchrucker, *Nacionalismo y Peronismo* pp. 221–230. On UCR neutrality: Tcach, *Sabattinismo y Peronismo* p. 47. On left: Matsushita, *Movimiento obrero* pp. 219–34. General: Rapoport, *Clases Dirigentes Argentinas* chs. 1–4.
3. Rouquié, *Politique et état militaire* p. 301. The appropriation of the communist matrix by liberals is acknowledged by Abelardo Ramos, *El partido comunista* p. 156.
4. Attacks on *El Pueblo* neutralism in *Orden Cristiano*: e.g. 'Lo que dice *El Pueblo*', no. 36 (1 March 1943) p. 13 and '*El Pueblo* encumbra a masones y perseguidores de la Iglesia', no. 37 (15 March 1943) pp. 14–15. An example of the disapproval of these attacks is evident from the ban on Catholic Action members reading *Orden Cristiano* in Río Cuarto: cf. no. 46 (1 August 1943) p. 5.
5. Silveyra de Oyuela, '¿Es usted Nazi?', *OC* no. 25 (15 September 1942) pp. 10–11. Other examples from *OC*: 'La Iglesia y la libertad', no. 1 (15 September 1941) p. 3; Duhau, 'En torno al liberalismo', no. 33 (15 January 1943) pp. 3–5; Luchía Puig, 'Porque recelamos...', no. 7 (15 December 1941) pp. 6–12.
6. Olazábal, *Por Una Cultura* pp. 166–9, lists the publications emanating from the CCC in this period. *Hispanidad* is defined by Amadeo, *Ayer, Hoy, Mañana* pp. 34–5; and Pico, 'Hacia la hispanidad', in *Sol y Luna* no.

9 (July 1942) pp. 78–85. See also Goyeneche, 'Discurso. . .' repr. in Goyeneche, *Ensayos* pp. 21–5.
7. *Sur* quoted by King, *'Sur'* p. 127; *Sol y Luna* no. 5 (February 1940) p. 20.
8. Nationalist attacks on Franceschi: *'Crisol'*, *Criterio* no. 605 (5 October 1939) and Pico, 'Democracia y catolicismo', *La Fronda* (11 April 1942). Integral Catholic position on war outlined in various articles in *Criterio*: 'La absurda guerra' no. 580 (13 April 1939); 'Totalitarismo o liberalismo', no. 582 (27 April 1939); 'Hacia la catástrofe' no. 599 (24 August 1939); 'El comunismo y la democracia', no. 835 (2 March 1944); and P. Carner in letter criticising *Orden Cristiano*: 'Tribuna' no. 18 (1 June 1942). Critique of Acción Argentina in *Criterio*: 'Totalitarismo, liberalismo, catolicismo' no. 662 (7 November 1940); 'Corporativismo, catolicismo, democracia' no. 666 (5 December 1940); 'Esto no puede seguir así' no. 671 (9 January 1941); and 'El problema constitucional argentino II' no. 698 (17 July 1941). Critique of Hispanism in *Criterio*: 'Latinismo, hispanismo, cristianismo' no. 749 (9 July 1942); and 'Otra vez la hispanidad' no. 764 (22 October 1942). Concern about direction of Franco régime in '¿Totalitarismo o liberalismo?' no. 582 (27 April 1939) and 'Argentinizar la política' no. 585 (18–05–39).
9. Various strictures: 'Pastoral conjunta del Episcopado alemán. . .', *Bol. ACA* no. 238 (February 1942) pp. 67–70; Caggiano, 'El Pontificado y los totalitarismos', *Bol. ACA* no. 278 (June 1945) pp. 253–61. My understanding of Catholic attitudes to the war was assisted by interviews with Mario Seijó, José Luis De Imaz, and Emilio Mignone.
10. B. Serrano, 'Crisis', *Sursum* no. 142 (July 1941) pp. 2–3.
11. White, *Argentina* ch. XXV: 'Why Americans are disliked'.
12. For examples of these classifications, see the influential work of J. Mackay, *The Other Spanish Christ: A Study in the Spiritual History of Spain and Spanish America*, New York–London, 1932, espec. p. 22.
13. Discussed by Stack, 'Avoiding the Greater Evil. . .' pp. 140–9, and Rhodes, *The Vatican in the age of the Cold War* pp. 215–16. Catholic warnings: Santos Gaynor, 'El proselitismo protestante. . .' *OC* no. 75 (15 October 1944) pp. 585–6; Rau, 'La propaganda protestante y nuestra defensa católica', *Bol. ACA* no. 280 (August 1945); and Vanini, 'La unidad de la Iglesia como defensa de la nación', *Bol. ACA* no. 235 (November 1941) pp. 262–8.
14. Rapoport, *Clases dirigentes argentinas* pp. 78–145; Fodor and O'Connell, 'La Argentina y la economía atlántica. . .' in *Desarrollo Económico* vol. 13 no. 49 (April–June 1973) pp. 1–67. On Pinedo Plan: Pinedo, *Argentina* pp. 71–4; and Llach, 'El Plan Pinedo. . .' *Desarrollo Económico* vol. 23, no. 92 (January–March 1984) pp. 516–24.
15. Josephs, *Argentine Diary*.
16. Research into the war papers has produced a number of startling conclusions about the fanaticism and irrationality of the US campaign against Argentina. The best remains that of Escudé, *Declinación Argentina* especially pp. 223–45 and 253–68. Revisionist conclusions are gathered in Di Tella and Cameron Watt (eds) *Argentina between the Great Powers*. British exasperation at US policy is made clear in Kelly,

The Ruling Few, ch. XIV. Anti-Argentine pathology of State Department is evident from Welles, *Where are we heading?* especially p. 186.
17. Díaz Araujo, *Conspiración* p. 17. On UCR plots: Potash, *Army and Politics* p. 190.
18. Rapoport, 'Foreign and Domestic Policy in Argentina' in Di Tella and Cameron Watt (eds) *Great Powers* pp. 78–84.
19. On Bunge's connections with Church, see obituary, 'Fue un católico', *Criterio* no. 796 (2 June 1943) and many references to Franceschi in *Una Nueva Argentina*, Buenos Aires, 1940 pp. 22–3 and 176–8. Influence on Figuerola and Perón: J. L. De Imaz, 'Alejandro E. Bunge, economista y sociólogo, 1880–1943', *Desarrollo Económico* vol. 14 (October–December 1984) pp. 566–7.
20. Bunge, *Nueva Argentina* espec. pp. 21–5, 93–110, 158–66, 321–2, 470–5.
21. *Tercera Semana Nacional* pp. 61–9, 70–101, 203–16 and 219–31; Avila, 'Pío XII. . .' *Bol. ACA* no. 239 (March 1942); 'El problema de la vivienda propia', *Criterio* no. 762 (8 October 1942); 'El alza de los precios. . .' *Bol. ACA* no. 243 (July 1942).
22. 'Informe', *Bol. ACA* no. 237 (January 1942); 'En torno a la esperada Ley de Salario Mínimo', *Bol. ACA* no. 244 (August 1942); 'Régimen Legal de Asociaciones Profesionales. Proyecto de Ley del Diputado Nacional Francisco Casiello', *Bol. ACA* no. 254 (June 1943) pp. 371–85; 'Pastoral colectiva sobre las condiciones actuales y los salarios de los obreros', *Revista Eclesiástica* (April 1941) pp. 234–9; and Cantini, 'Directivas prácticas para el establecimiento en nuestra Patria de un nuevo orden social', *Bol. ACA* no. 250 (February 1943) pp. 78–88.
23. Bonamino, 'Los cristianos y la restauración social', *Criterio* no. 774 (31 December 1942) pp. 422–26.
24. Del Carril, *Memorias Dispersas* pp. 16–17.
25. Renovación discussed by Parera, *Demócrata Cristianos* vol. 1 p. 75. On connections with hierarchy: Bonamino interview. Positions gleaned from *Renovación* no. 1 (October 1941) pp. 1–4; Renovación, *Tres discursos*; and del Carril, *Crónica Interna* pp. 21–2.
26. From *Criterio*: 'Liberalismo y realismo' no. 612 (23 November 1939); 'Las declaraciones del Dr. Pinedo' no. 707 (18 September 1941); 'El Plan Pinedo y la doctrina católica' no. 667 (12 December 1940); 'Esto no puede seguir así' no. 671 (9 January 1941); '¿Conservadores o reformistas?' no. 690 (22 May 1941); 'Despotismo, dictadura, tiranía', *Criterio* no. 750 (16 July 1942). A fascinating exchange took place in *Criterio* between a reluctant advocate of a coup – Anon., 'De un tío estanciero a un sobrino diputado' no. 675 (6 February 1941) – and a defender of the *status quo*: Anon., 'De sobrino a tío' no. 677 (20 February 1941).
27. From *Criterio*: 'El soldado' no. 710 (9 October 1941); N. Lotus, 'En el día del soldado' no. 727 (5 February 1942); R. Wilkinson, 'el carácter y la milicia' no. 752 (30 July 1942).
28. From *Criterio*: 'Despotismo, dictadura, tiranía' no. 750 (16 July 1942); 'El problema constitucional argentino' nos. 697 (10 July 1941) and 698 (17 July 1941); 'El liberalismo y las encíclicas pontificias' no. 781 (18 February 1943).

Notes and References

29. Potash, *Army and Politics* p. 202.
30. On the coup's preparation and early days: Rodríguez Lamas, *Rawson/Ramírez/Farrell* pp. 24–7; Potash, *Army and Politics* pp. 179–97; Rouquié, *Pouvoir militaire* pp. 313–14 and 324; Díaz Araujo, *Conspiración* pp. 47–73; Kelly, *The Ruling Few* p. 295; Galetti, 'Ambigüedades e incongruencias. . .' in *Todo es Historia* no. 193 (June 1983) pp. 19–21.
31. Mallimaci, 'Catholicisme et état militaire en Argentine' pp. 259–62.
32. Ramírez' address in Verbitsky, *Proclamas Militares* pp. 47–9.
33. 'Carta del Excmo. Sr. Presidente de la Nación al Director de *Criterio*', *Criterio* no. 800 (1 July 1943) p. 197.
34. 'Consideraciones sobre la revolución', *Criterio* no. 798 (17 June 1943) pp. 149–53.
35. 'Nuevas consideraciones sobre la revolución', *Criterio* no. 800 (1 July 1943) p. 200.
36. Decree repr. in Mallimaci, *El Catolicismo Integral* pp. 82–3.
37. In an interview with Leonard, *Politicians, Pupils and Priests* p. 53.
38. 'Las recientes medidas económico-sociales', *Bol. ACA* no. 255 (July 1943); 'El significado de la ley de alquileres', *Criterio* no. 803 (22 June 1943); 'Régimen legal de las Asociaciones Profesionales', *Bol. ACA* no. 256 (August 1943). See quote from DNT president, Col. Giani, in del Campo, *Sindicalismo y Peronismo* pp. 122–3.
39. On the Storni affair: Kelly, *Ruling Few* p. 298; Potash, *Army and Politics* p. 222; Escudé, *Declinación Argentina* p. 117. List of civilian appointments in Buchrucker, *Nacionalismo y Peronismo* p. 281. On Renovación participation: del Carril, *Crónica interna* pp. 22–31; interview, Basilio Serrano. Lamas, *Rawson. . .* p. 73.
40. This view has passed into much historiography: e.g. Alexander, *Perón Era* p. 126; and Goldwert, *Democracy* p. 82.
41. For example, Rock, *Argentina* p. 250.
42. 'Un grave problema argentino imaginario', *Criterio* no. 830 (27–01–44).
43. On take-up, see Table 6, Appendix I. On trends towards implementation: Leonard, *Politicians* p. 59. Church unpreparedness argued by Stack, 'Avoiding the Lesser Evil' pp. 164–9, and Kennedy, *Catholicism* p. 197. Guarded response of Catholic press: Echevarría, 'Gratitud. . .' *OC* no. 56 (1 January 1944); and in *Criterio*: 'El decreto. . .' no. 829 (20 January 1944); 'Los puntos. . .' no. 834 (24 February 1944).
44. Discussion of this recovery of the public sphere in Mallimaci, 'Catholicisme et état militaire' pp. 303–7. On growing significance of 'national' and 'Christian' discourse in worker movement: Matsushita, *Movimiento obrero* pp. 240–8.
45. Amadeo, *Ayer, Hoy, Mañana* pp. 21–2.
46. del Carril, *Memorias Dispersas* pp. 30–1.

5 Catholicism and Peronism, 1945–1954

1. Floria and García Belsunce, *Historia política* pp. 139–42. Significance of Figuerola–Ortiz policies considered by Gaudio and Pilone, 'Estado y relaciones. . .' in Torre (comp.) *La Formación* pp. 57–98.

2. Migrant thesis revised by: Halperín Donghi, 'Algunas observaciones...' in Mora y Araujo and Llorente (comps.) *Voto Peronista*. pp. 221–50; Little, 'The popular origins...' in Rock (ed.) *Argentina in the twentieth century* pp. 164–5; and Kenworthy, 'The function...' *Comparative Politics* 6:1 (October 1973) p. 33. Instrumentalist thesis reviewed in Roxborough, 'Unity and diversity...' *JLAS* 16:1 (1984) pp. 1–26; contested by Little, 'La organización obrera...' in Torre (comp.) *La formación* pp. 121–81.
3. Matsushita, *Movimiento* pp. 240–8.
4. On ideological shifts within unions: Horowitz, *Argentine Unions* pp. 182–3; Del Campo, *Sindicalismo y Peronismo* pp. 216–19; Matsushita, *Movimiento* pp. 262–7 and 272–6; James, *Resistance and Integration* pp. 12–40; and Doyon, 'La organización...' in Torre (comp.) *La Formación* pp. 185–219.
5. Kelly, *The Ruling Few* p. 311.
6. Especially Del Campo, *Sindicalismo y Peronismo* pp. 195–105; Torre, 'Interpretando (una vez más) los orígenes del peronismo', *Desarrollo Económico* vol. 28, no. 112 (January–March 1989) p. 545; and Matsushita, *Movimiento* p. 288.
7. Rapoport, 'Foreign and Domestic Policy...' in Di Tella and Cameron Watt (eds) *Great Powers* pp. 95–99; Real, *Treinta años* p.77; Torre, 'Interpretando...' pp. 539 and 545; Potash, *Army and Politics* pp. 262–3; Del Campo, *Sindicalismo y Peronismo* pp. 195–205 and 214–15; Horowitz, *Argentine Unions* pp. 187–8; and Doyon, 'La Organización...' in Torre (comp.) *La Formación* pp. 189–91.
8. Pont, *Partido Laborista* pp. 20–3.
9. MacDonald, 'The Braden Campaign...' in Di Tella and Cameron Watt, *Great Powers* pp. 137–53; Buchrucker, *Nacionalismo y Peronismo* pp. 296–7; Miguens, 'Actualización....' in E. Miguens and Turner (eds) *Racionalidad del Peronismo* pp. 24–5.
10. Smith, 'The Social Base of Peronism', *HAHR LII*: 1 (February 1972) pp. 55–71; González Esteves, 'La Argentina Electoral...' in Del Barco *et al.*, *Historia Política* pp. 230–2; Llorente, 'Alianzas políticas...' in Mora y Araujo y Llorente (eds) *Voto Peronista* p. 303; and Mora y Araujo, 'Populismo, laborismo y clases medias...' *Criterio* nos. 1755–1756 (27 January 1977) p. 16. Erroneous categorisation of Peronism as 'populist': e.g. Rock, *Argentina* ch. VI.
11. Interpretations of Peronism as fascism: e.g. Sebreli, *Los deseos imaginarios*; and Calello, *Peronismo y bonapartismo*. Contested by: Buchrucker, *Nacionalismo y Peronismo* pp. 392–9; Miguens, 'Actualización...' in Turner and Miguens (eds) *Racionalidad del Peronismo* pp. 29–39; and Ciria, *Política y cultura popular* pp. 41–7. On labour participation in government and early relations with unions: Pont, *Partido laborista* pp. 21 and 49; Little, 'La organización obrera...' in Torre (ed) *La formación* pp. 286–7; Munck, *Argentina* pp. 130–1; Del Campo, *Sindicalismo y Peronismo* pp. 241–4; and Torre, 'Interpretando...' pp. 546–8.
12. Potash, *Army and Politics* p. 46.
13. Variety of nationalist responses to Perón considered by Buchrucker, *Nacionalismo y Peronismo* pp. 309–10, and Rock, *Authoritarian*

Argentina pp. 153–6. ALN reactions to Perón: De Imaz, *Promediados* p. 44. For a summary of the main lines of division in 1946 see Fayt, *Naturaleza del Peronismo* pp. 332–3.
14. Blanksten, *Perón's Argentina* p. 236.
15. For example, Alexander, *The Perón Era* pp. 125–32.
16. Importance of religious factor suggested e.g. Llorente, 'La composición social...' in Mora y Araujo y Llorente, *Voto Peronista* p. 371; Luna, *El 45* p. 146; and Fayt, *Naturaleza* pp. 356–391. 'Collusion' argument sustained by e.g. Alexander, *The Perón Era* p. 125; Blanksten, *Perón's Argentina* pp. 63–4 and 188–9; and Frigerio, *El Síndrome* vol. 1 pp. 43–6. Ecclesiastical independence sustained by McGeagh, *Relaciones* ch. 3; Kennedy, *Catholicism* ch. 5; and Whitaker, *The United States* pp. 143–4. For a summary of the various interpretations: Forni, review in *Desarrollo Económico* vol. 29, no. 114 (July–September 1989) pp. 283–4.
17. Rock, *Authoritarian Argentina* p. 176.
18. His only recorded comment, guardedly supporting ratification, was made to the diminutive Rosario paper *Tribuna*; Canclini, *Los evangélicos* pp. 280–1. No mention of RE in Perón's collected speeches, *El Pueblo Quiere Saber*.
19. On Catholic component of UCR–JR: Tcach, *Sabbatinismo y Peronismo* p. 84.
20. 'Manifiesto de los demócrata cristianos...' *OC* no. 104 (February 1946) pp. 412–15; Río, '¿Prohibe la Pastoral votar por Tamborini–Mosca?'; and 'El Dr. Manuel V. Ordóñez fija posiciones', radio speech, 24 February 1946, both in *OC* no. 105 (March 1946) pp. 457–9 and 463.
21. From *Criterio*: 'Las posibilidades del totalitarismo', no. 901 (21 June 1945); 'Una medalla' nos. 931–2 (24 January 1946); '"Oligarcas" y "descamisados"' no. 933 (31 January 1946); and 'La Cola del totalitarismo' no. 934 (7 February 1946). On responses of *El Pueblo*: Stack, 'Avoiding the Greater Evil' p. 182. Opposition to trade union decree: 'Un decreto inaceptable', *Criterio* no. 925 (13 December 1945); and De Andrea, 'Discurso...' *OC* no. 69 (15 July 1944) pp. 409–13. Opposition of *Los Principios* in Córdoba: Tcach, *Sabattinismo y Peronismo* p. 175. See discussion between Catholics who voted differently in 1946 in Flores, *Operación Rosa Negra* p. 26.
22. Duhau to Braden and Spellman, 5 December 1946, State Department Archives, 835.00/12–546. On attitude of domestic hierarchy: Forni, 'Catolicismo y peronismo (1)', *Unidos* no. 14 (September 1987) p. 223. On attitude of Vatican: Stack, 'Avoiding the Greater Evil' pp. 252–4 and Rhodes, *Cold War* pp. 192–3.
23. Perón's first references in *El Pueblo Quiere Saber* pp. 99–101, 157–68 and 228. Figuerola, *Organización Social y La Colaboración Social*. Aspiazu, *Estado Católico*. Discussion of these influences in Chávez, *Perón y el peronismo* vol. 2 pp. 110–11; and De Imaz, 'Alejandro E. Bunge, economista y sociólogo' p. 567. Perón acknowledges Figuerola's influence in *Yo, Juan Domingo Perón* p. 38. Filippo justifies support for Perón as Christian justice in Filippo, *El Plan Quinquenal* pp. 270–2; and Benítez in *La Aristocracia* pp. 369 and 409.
24. Interviews, Roberto Bonamino and José Luis De Imaz.

25. 'Nuestras ideas se abren camino', *Bol. ACA* no. 258 (October 1943).
26. On Catholic Action reactions from *Bol. ACA*: 'Nuevos eslabones...' no. 257 (September 1943); 'Legislación social', no. 264 (April 1944); 'Guía de la Campaña...' nos. 269–270 (Sep-October 1944); and 'Diez años...' no. 265 (May 1944).
27. On social composition of Peronist vote in Córdoba and elsewhere: Mora y Araujo y Llorente, *Voto Peronista* pp. 336 and 371; Tcach, *Sabattinismo y Peronismo* pp. 50, 83–86, 92 and 170.
28. Torre, 'Interpretando...' p. 541.
29. Cf. memoirs of Gálvez, *Entre la Novela* vol. 4 p. 290, on neighbours' reactions to his wife's article: Delfina Bunge de Gálvez, 'Una emoción nueva en Buenos Aires', *El Pueblo* (25 October 1945). Also memoirs of De Imaz, *Promediados los cuarenta* p. 46.
30. Bustamante, 'La gran experiencia', *OC* no. 107 (April 1946) p. 575.
31. On AASF: Hörne de Burmeister, *Cómo se organizó...* Divisions within women's movement: Bianchi and Sanchis, *Partido Peronista Femenino*, vol. I pp. 34–42; and Navarro, 'Evita...' in Miguens y Turner (eds), *Racionalidad del Peronismo* p. 111.
32. Castellani, 'La Argentina de 1943 y de hoy...' in *Seis Ensayos* p. 174.
33. Examples of language: Sábato, *Sobre héroes y tumbas* p. 31; Munck, *Argentina* pp. 129–130; Del Campo, *Sindicalismo y Peronismo* pp. 207–8; Ranis, *Argentine workers* p. 24.
34. Perelman, *Cómo hicimos* p. 65. Emphasis mine.
35. cit. in Del Campo, *Sindicalismo y Peronismo* p. 241.
36. Presidencia de la Nación, *Memoria del Ministerio de Relaciones Exteriores y Culto*, Buenos Aires, 1947–87 pp. 545–6 and 979; 'El Justicialismo y la Doctrina Social Cristiana', in Perón, *Comunidad Organizada* pp. 109–31.
37. 'Discurso del Presidente... Cervantes' (12 October 1947).
38. 'Principios doctrinarios de la política social...' (24 February 1947).
39. On constitution in Córdoba: Tcach, *Sabattinismo y Peronismo* p. 174; on 1949 constitution: Forni, 'Catolicismo y Peronismo (2)' p. 211; Martínez, *Nueva Argentina* vol. 1 p. 124; Buchrucker, *Nacionalismo y Peronismo* p. 308; Del Barco, *Régimen Peronista* pp. 119–20. Thinking behind consitution in Sampay, *Crisis del Estado de Derecho Liberal-Burgués y Constitución Argentina de 1949*.
40. Bianchi y Sanchis, *Partido Peronista Femenino* vol. 1 pp. 44–51; Taylor, *Evita Perón* p. 76.
41. *El Buen Amigo*, no. 137 (19 May 1946), cit. in *OC* no. 112 (June 1946) p. 846.
42. Doyon, 'La organización...' in Torre (comp.) *La Formación* pp. 188–191. On Salas application: *Criterio* no. 1162 (24 May 1944), *El Pueblo* (5 August 1944 and 15 September 1944) discussed by Stack, 'Avoiding the Greater Evil' pp. 184–7. Perón's advocacy of 'neutrality': 'En respuesta...' (4 August 1944) in *El Pueblo Quiere Saber* pp. 130–3. *Criterio* critique: 'El deber de sindicarse, *Criterio* no. 856 (27 April 1944) and 'Un decreto inaceptable', *Criterio* no. 926 (13 December 1945).
43. Interviews: Alfredo Di Pace, José Luis De Imaz, Mario Seijo. 'La ACA formula reparos sobre organización y funcionamiento de las asociaciones profesionales obreras', *OC* no. 121 (November 1946) pp. 23–5.

44. Ramella, 'Proyecto de Ley de Modificación del Régimen Legal de las Asociaciones Profesionales', *Bol. ACA* no. 315 (July 1948).
45. As observed by Miles, '¿Tercera posición o socialismo?', *Criterio* no. 1115 (11 April 1950); and Meinvielle, 'Hacia un nacionalismo marxista', *Presencia* (23 December 1949) in *Política Argentina* pp. 113–21.
46. Freyre's speech to CGT, commented in *Criterio* No. 985 (30 January 1947); review of these tendencies in Meinvielle, 'El fenómeno peronista y la masa trabajadora' *NPJ* (March–April 1956) p. 86.
47. RE ratification studied by Leonard, *Politicians, Pupils and Priests* pp. 80–1. On Reyes plot: *El Pueblo* (25 September 1948) and comment in 'Justicia', *Criterio* no. 1071 (07 October 1948). Other examples from Martínez, *Nueva Argentina* vol. 2 pp. 169–75.
48. 'Los derechos del trabajador (1)' *Criterio* no. 990 (13 March 1947).
49. Speech to De Carlo repr. in *Comunidad Organizada* pp. 109–120.
50. Speech closing V Congreso Eucarístico Nacional (29 October 1950) repr. in *Comunidad Organizada* pp. 121–4.
51. Martínez, *Nueva Argentina* vol. I pp. 99–100.
52. Tcach, *Sabattinismo y Peronismo* p. 175.
53. Perón, *Razón de Mi Vida* p. 181.
54. Cit. in Buchrucker, *Nacionalismo y Peronismo* p. 331. My emphasis.
55. E. Perón, *La Razón de Mi Vida* p. 257.
56. 'Predicar la doctrina' (29 March 1951); 'Sentido espiritual' (21 March 1948); 'La Verdad y la Libertad' (11 October 1948), 'Los valores morales' (9 April 1949), in *Doctrina Peronista* pp. 93, 348, 72–3, 126–7.
57. Discussion in Stack, 'Avoiding the Greater Evil' pp. 330–45. Examples from E. Perón, *La Razón de Mi Vida* pp. 38, 218, 225–7, 251, 255 and 257.
58. Cit. in Buchrucker, *Nacionalismo y Peronismo* p. 325.
59. These examples from: *Doctrina Peronista* pp. 20, 47, 53, 68–9, 83, 108, and 119; E. Perón, *La Palabra* p. 70 and *Razón de Mi Vida* pp. 185–93.
60. 'Valor de los principios' (27 January 1949), *Doctrina Peronista* p. 77.
61. Presidencia de la Nación, *Segundo Plan Quinquenal* pp. 431–2.
62. Waldmann, *El Peronismo* p. 71.
63. 'Estatuto del Partido Peronista', *Doctrina Peronista* p. 33.
64. Cit. in Martínez, *La Nueva Argentina* vol. 2 pp. 189–90.
65. 'Las doctrinas' (1 March 1951), *Doctrina Peronista* p. 89.
66. 'Armonía Colectiva' (25 July 1949) and 'Escuela Superior Peronista' (1 May 1953); *Doctrina Peronista* pp. 86–87 and 161–2.
67. Little, 'Party and State...' *HAHR* vol. 53: no. 54 (November 1973) pp. 644–62; Waldmann, *El Peronismo* pp. 68–72; and Martínez, *Nueva Argentina* vol. 2 pp. 227–32.
68. 'Verdad absoluta' (25 July 1949), *Doctrina Peronista* pp. 161–2.
69. Interviews, José Luis De Imaz, Juan Gatti and Emilio Mignone.
70. Interviews: Emilio Mignone, José Luis De Imaz, Juan Gatti and Basilio Serrano.
71. From *Criterio* : 'Nacionalización' no. 942 (4 April 1946); 'Angustia de la clase media' no. 950 (30 March 1946); and 'El problema de las nacionalizaciones' no. 971 (24 October 1946).
72. 'Justicia social', *Criterio* no. 985 (20 January 1947).
73. 'Los derechos del trabajador II' *Criterio* no. 991 (20 March 1947).

74. 'El discurso del señor Truman', *Criterio* no. 391 (20 March 1947).
75. From *Presencia*: 'El Pacto de Rio' (14 July 1950); Política del Kominform' (9 March 1951); and 'Reunión de cancilleres' (13 April 1951); in Meinvielle, *Política Argentina* pp. 179–86, 247–54 and 259–65.
76. On which, see above p. 124.
77. 'Posición', *Criterio* no. 925 (6 December 1945); and 'Comentarios', nos. 928 and 929 (17/24 January 1946).
78. 'Preparación política de los católicos', *Criterio* no. 900 (14 June 1945).
79. *Criterio* on Maritain and Christian Democracy: 'Jacques Maritain. . .' pts. I, II, and III, nos. 885 (1 March 1945), 886 (8 March 1945) and 887 (15 March 1945); 'Democracia real y democracia verbal' no. 997 (1 May 1947) and 998 (8 May 1947); 'En torno a Maritain' no. 1092 (26 May 1949); L. Lattanzi, 'La democracia cristiana. . .' no. 1086 (10 February 1949); De Gasperi, 'José Toniolo. . .' no. 1102 (27 October 1949); Baliña, 'Los europeos piensan y trabajan; ¿y nosotros?' no. 1140 (24 May 1951). Criticism of Peronism: 'Evoluciones y revoluciones' no. 1185 (9 April 1953); 'Atraso retórico' no. 1143 (12 July 1951); and 'Pornografía encubierta' no. 1085 (27 January 1949). Meinvielle, *Política Argentina* pp. 266–7, 255–6, and 257–8.
80. Gambini, *Perón y la Iglesia* p. 41.
81. 'El ausentismo, las huelgas ilegales, y el trabajo a desgano', *Criterio* no. 1080 (9 December 1948). Articles from *Presencia* in Meinvielle, *Política Argentina* pp. 9–14, 15–19, 35–40, 41–8, 130–1, 152–9, 160–8, 227–35 and 280–8.
82. Interview, Basilio Serrano.
83. Amadeo, *Ayer, Hoy, Mañana* pp. 25–36.
84. C. Belaúnde, 'La familia argentina y los problemas demográficos' and F. Sarría, 'Relaciones de la familia y el estado en la Argentina', in *Bol. ACA* no. 333 (January 1950) pp. 30–40 and 55–64; J.B. Terán, 'Defensa de la familia contra los proyectos de divorcio y de equiparación de los hijos legítimos e ilegítimos', *Bol. ACA* no. 334 (February 1950) pp. 83–93. Discussion in McGeagh, *Relaciones entre el poder eclesiástico y el poder político* pp. 88–90.
85. On Spiritist affair: Rhodes, *Cold War* pp. 194–5 and Stack, 'Avoiding the Greater Evil' pp. 274–5. Detailed report in *Criterio* : '*A quien me confesare ante los hombres*' no. 1126 (26–10–50) pp. 871–2.
86. AUDAC, *Primera Concentración..*
87. *Bases y Principios del Movimiento Universitario Humanista* pp. 30–1; manifesto reproduced in De Imaz, *Promediados los cuarenta* pp. 65–73. On Humanists after 1955: Mayol *et al*, *Los católicos postconciliares* pp. 103–5; and Forni, 'Catolicismo y Peronismo (2)' pp. 197–8.
88. Doyon, 'El crecimiento sindical. . .' and 'La organización. . .' in Torre (ed.) *La formación* pp. 175–7, 194–9 and 223–6.
89. On JOC in Peronist years: Soneira, 'La Juventud Obrera Católica. . .' in *Justicia Social* (Rev. del CEDEL), Año 5, no. 8 (June 1989) pp. 82–3.
90. On 'loyal opposition' in Córdoba, see Tcach, *Sabattinismo y Peronismo* pp. 175–9 and 223–7.
91. Interview, Basilio Serrano; also Amadeo, *Ayer, Hoy, Mañana* pp. 105–20.

Notes and References

92. From *Orden Cristiano*: McGinnis, '¿Qué es la democracia cristiana?' no. 113 (July 1946); 'Fijáronse las bases para un movimiento demócrata cristiano' no. 134 (May 1947) pp. 692–4; Potenze, 'Democracia cristiana y partidos políticos' no. 137 (July 1947) pp. 794–5. Ordóñez interview.
93. On the 'new generation': Parera, *Demócrata Cristianos* vol. 1 pp. 81–8; and Busacca, *Camino a la democracia cristiana* pp. 26–7. Interview, Floreal Forni.
94. From *Polémica*: Busacca and Pece, 'El nacionalismo y la democracia cristiana' nos. 2–3 (November–December 1953) pp. 2–7; Herrero *et al*, 'Controversias y diálogos' nos. 4–5 (January–February 1954) pp. 3–12; and De Imaz, 'La oportunidad política de la democracia cristiana en la Argentina'; Barberán, 'Acerca del nacionalismo' nos. 6–8 (March–May 1954) pp. 1–7. On *Polémica*: De Imaz, *Promediados* pp. 112–13; and Parera, *Demócrata Cristianos* vol. 1 pp. 93–4.
95. Amadeo, *Ayer, Hoy, Mañana* p. 44.
96. *Criterio* no. 1187 (8 April 1954).
97. As is suggested by, for example, Rock, *Authoritarian* p. 179: 'the Church intended to create a Christian Democratic Party'; and Farrell, *Iglesia y pueblo* pp. 106–8, who talks of a Rome-led project to plant PDCs around the world.
98. Interview, Ricardo Parera. This is borne out by episcopal documents.
99. Martínez, *Nueva Argentina* vol. 2 p. 185.
100. Potash, *The Army and Politics* p. 177.
101. Caggiano, 'Posibilidades de apostolado en la juventud obrera', *NPJ* (March–April 1954); Tcach, *Sabattinismo y Peronismo* pp. 230–2; Martínez, *Nueva Argentina* vol. 2 pp. 184–5; Marsal, *Perón y la Iglesia* p. 17.
102. *La Prensa* (11 November 1954).
103. Interview, Mario Seijó.
104. For example, Whitaker, *Argentina* pp. 141–3.
105. 'Nuestra contribución a la paz de la patria. Declaración Episcopal denunciando la persecución religiosa en la Argentina'; *Criterio* no. 1240 (28 July 1955) pp. 523–643. See mock-advertisement for the Argentine National Church in 'Fides Intrepida', in Lafiandra (ed.), *Los Panfletos* no. 9 pp. 45–7.

6 Ecclesia contra Peronum, 1954–1955

1. The best among many summaries of the conflict are: de Hoyos, 'The Role of the Catholic Church. . . .' ; Martínez, *Nueva Argentina* vol. 2 pp. 184–238; Frigerio, *El Síndrome*, 3 vols.; and Rhodes, *Cold War* ch. 15. An excellent novelistic account by one of the main participants is Flores, *Operación Rosa Negra*, which complements Lafiandra, *Los Panfletos*.
2. Interviews: Jorge A. Ramos and J. Gobello, in Frigerio, *El Síndrome* vol. 3 pp. 271–84.
3. Flores, *Operación Rosa Negra* p. 43.
4. Pamphlets nos. 3, 6, 8, 11, 12, 21, 22, 34 and 38 in Lafiandra, *Los Panfletos* pp. 36–7, 41–5, 51–3, 72–90, 108, 114–15 and 120–1.

5. Leonard, *Politicians, Pupils and Priests* pp. 148–50.
6. Martínez, *La Nueva Argentina* vol. II p. 197.
7. Cit. in Crassweller, *Perón* p. 302.
8. Rhodes, *Cold War* pp. 197–8; pamphlets nos. 17 and 18 in Lafiandra, *Los Panfletos* pp. 57–68. On divorce law of 1954: 'La estabilidad del matrominio'; *Criterio* no. 1972 (11 September 1986) p. 463.
9. Flores, *Operación Rosa Negra* p. 78. Pamphlets collated in Lafiandra, *Los Panfletos* pp. 15–27. Campaign methods descrived in Martínez, *Nueva Argentina* vol. 2 pp. 198–9.
10. Amadeo, *Ayer, Hoy, Mañana* p. 44; Flores, *Operación Rosa Negra* pp. 97–8.
11. See De Hoyos, 'The role of the Catholic Church' pp. 144–66.
12. For example, 'Carta al excelentísimo señor presidente' and 'A su excelencia el señor ministro de educación' nos. 21 and 22 in Lafiandra, *Los Panfletos* pp. 72–90.
13. 'Carta abierta de los católicos argentinos al Cardenal Copello'; reproduced in Marsal S., *Perón y la Iglesia* pp. 81–4; 'Carta abierta del pueblo argentino al general Perón' in Lafiandra, *Los Panfletos* no. 172 pp. 372–4.
14. Flores, *Operación Rosa Negra* pp. 152–172; 'Texto de la excomunicación' (no. 76), 'Perón cumple' (no. 77), 'La verdad total sobre la quema de la bandera' (no. 88), '¿Quién es el culpable de todo?' (no. 101), in Lafiandra (comp.) *Los Panfletos* pp. 200–2, 218–22 and 236–7.
15. M. Amadeo, 'Carta abierta al General Embrioni' (no. 111), 'Carta al Dr. Amadeo y al General Embrioni' (no. 112) and 'Carta a su excelencia el señor Ministro de Ejército, General de División Franklin Lucero' (no. 114) in Lafiandra (comp.) *Los Panfletos* pp. 256–65.
16. Potash, *Army and Politics* pp. 195–201.
17. Real, *Treinta años* p. 169.
18. N. Balbini, *Frondizi: de la oposición al gobierno*, Buenos Aires, 1984 pp. 123–7.
19. 'Al cuidadano Arturo Frondizi. . .' (no. 133) and 'Carta abierta de un grupo de católicos argentinos al doctor Arturo Frondizi' (no. 134) in Lafiandra, *Los Panfletos* pp. 297–301.
20. Amadeo, 'Al día siguiente' (no. 193) in Lafiandra, *Los Panfletos* pp. 485–504.

7 Secularism Revisited, 1955–1960

1. From *Criterio* : Betanzos, *'Criterio y. . .Sur'* no. 1252 (26 January 1956); 'Reaparición de *La Prensa*' no. 1253 (10 February 1956).
2. *Jocista* interview in Soneira, 'La Juventud Obrera. . .' in *Justicia Social* (Rev. del CEDEL) Año 5, no. 8 (June 1989) p. 84. Document by '300 sacerdotes cordobeses' in *Criterio* nos. 1249–50 (November 1955) p. 964. 'Carta Pastoral Colectiva del Episcopado Argentino sobre la promoción de los trabajadores', *Revista Eclesiástica* (May–June 1956) pp. 120–5.
3. Ganchegui, 'Momento obrero', *NPJ* (Sep-October 1955); Christian Democrats: *Avanzada* no. 1 (4 November 1955); PDC manifesto, 'La

Democracia Cristiana al pueblo y al gobierno' (11 July 1955) in Parera, *Demócrata Cristianos* vol. 1 pp. 98–103.
4. 'La Restauración', *Criterio* no. 1247 (10 November 1955); and 'La Iglesia y la Revolución', *Criterio* no. 1248 (24 November 1955).
5. del Carril, 'Democracia y autenticidad', *Criterio* no. 1254 (23 February 1956).
6. 'Revolución libertadora y justicia social', *Criterio* no. 1251 (12 January 1956).
7. Lonardi's assumption speech: 'Al pueblo argentino...', in Verbitsky, *Proclamas Militares* pp. 60–2.
8. On Lonardi's cabinet appointments, see Lewis, 'The Right and Military Rule' in McGee Deutsch and Dolkart (eds.) *The Argentine Right* pp. 151–2.
9. On unions' disaffection with Perón in 1955, see Makin, 'Political Crises...' ch. 5.
10. On unions' response to Lonardi: Torre y Senén González, *Ejército y sindicatos* pp. 12–17; Cavarozzi, *Sindicatos y Política* pp. 18–21; James, *Resistance and Integration* pp. 43–8.
11. James, *Resistance and Integration* pp. 44–46 and 66; and Cavarozzi, *Sindicatos y Política* pp. 20–3.
12. Szusterman, ' "Revolución Libertadora"...' in Di Tella and Dornbusch (eds) *The Political Economy* p. 92.
13. Speech repr. in Frigerio, *Síndrome* vol. 2 pp. 235–7. Catholic critique of liberal view of Revolution: Palumbo, '¡Libertad!'; *NPJ* (Sep-October 1955); and Del Carril, 'Democracia y autenticidad', *Criterio* no. 1254 (23 February 1956).
14. Del Carril, 'Democracia y autenticidad'; also, *Crónica Interna...* pp. 132–3.
15. On Aramburu labour policies and their effects: O'Donnell, 'Permanent Crisis...' in Linz and Stepan, *The Breakdown* pp. 147–8; James, *Resistance and Integration* pp. 54–70 and ch. 8; Cavarozzi, *Sindicatos y Política* pp. 25–32; and Amadeo, *Ayer, Hoy, Mañana* pp. 90–100.
16. 'La Política y la Fuerza', *Criterio* no. 1261 (14 June 1956).
17. From *NPJ*: 'Tercera semana nacional...' (March–April 1956) pp. 47–89; 'Nuestro instante' (May–June 1956); 'Nota enviada por el Obispo de San Luis Mons. Dr. Emilio Di Pasquo, al Ministro Interino de Trabajo y Previsión...sobre procedimientos de represión' (November–December 1956).
18. 'El problema obrero argentino', *Criterio* no. 1260 (24 May 1956) pp. 363–5.
19. From *Avanzada*: M. Seijó, 'Se pretende aplastar la clase obrera' no. 3 (2 December 1955); 'Medite el gobierno' no. 5 (6 January 1955); 'El revanchismo debe eliminarse' no. 7 (May 1956).
20. 'Cuarta Semana Nacional de los Asesores de la JOC', *NPJ* (July–December 1958) pp. 45–56.
21. On Unión Federal position: B. Serrano in *Encuentro Nacional* p. 86.
22. On PDC view of nationalists: Parera, *Democracia Cristiana* pp. 95–7.
23. Interview with Ordóñez in *Avanzada* no. 2 (18 November 1955).
24. Cit. in Parera, *Los Demócrata Cristianos Argentinos* vol. 1 p. 113.

25. 'Hay revancha en la Revolución: desastrosas consecuencias...' *Avanzada* no. 3 (2 December 1955); 'El zorro libre en el gallinero libre', *Comunidad* no. 2 (January 1956).
26. 'Organización y autonomía: decreto-ley no. 6403' (Buenos Aires, 23 de diciembre de 1955) in *La Revolución Libertadora y la Universidad, 1955–1957* pp. 61–70.
27. Junta Consultiva Nacional, *8 Reunión Extraordinaria* (29 February 1956) pp. 1–38.
28. An account of the dispute in: Leonard, *Politicians* pp. 167–79; and Walter, *Student Politics* pp. 159–63.
29. J. Real, *Treinta años de historia argentina*, Buenos Aires, 1976 p. 212.
30. From *Criterio*: 'Enseñanza libre', no. 1253 (9 February 1956) pp. 83–5; 'Universidades libres', no. 1254 (23 February 1956) pp. 123–5; Olivera Lahore, 'Los términos...'; Baliña, 'Las universidades libres...' no. 1254 (23 February 1956) pp. 131–2; Visovich, 'Libertad de enseñanza...' no. 1255 (8 March 1956); Derisi, 'Enseñanza libre...' no. 1257 (12 April 1956) pp. 246–7.
31. On Amadeo's links with Frondizi: Forni, 'Catolicismo y Peronismo (3)' p. 128; and Rouquié, *Radicales y Desarrollistas* pp. 87–8. On Frondizi's intellectual background and sudden adoption of Catholic values: Szusterman, 'Developmentalism...' ch. 4 and pp. 119–21.
32. Balbini, *Frondizi* pp. 178–80; *Contorno* critique: Katra, '*Contorno*' ch. 4.
33. cit. in *Encuentro Nacional de Dirigentes Católicos* p. 81.
34. On PDC performance in 1957: Zalduendo, *Geografía electoral* pp. 31, 47 and 57.
35. Parera, *Demócrata Cristianos* vol. 1 p. 116.
36. Reproved in 'Religión y electoralismo', *Criterio* no. 1302 (27 February 1958).
37. Leonard, *Politicians* p. 200.
38. 'Declaración del Episcopado Argentino sobre el momento político nacional', *Criterio* no. 1286 (27 June 1957) pp. 427–30 and 'La situación actual de la clase trabajadora', *Criterio* no. 1295 (14 November 1957) pp. 793–4.
39. Cit. in *Encuentro Nacional* p. 81.
40. Szusterman, 'Developmentalism and Political Change' p. 314.
41. Crawley, *Una Casa Dividida* pp. 195–8.
42. Halperín Donghi, *Argentina* p. 101.
43. James, *Resistance and Integration* ch. 5.
44. On appointments: Szusterman, 'Developmentalism...' p. 123.
45. Details of religious policy in: Centeno, *Cuatro años*; history of negotiations with Rome in Centeno, 'El Acuerdo con la Santa Sede', *Criterio* no. 2080 (24 October 1991) pp. 588–90; and Zuretti, *Nueva Historia* pp. 453–9.
46. On university disputes: Walter, *Student Politics* pp. 164–73; Soneira y Lumerman, *Iglesia y Nación* pp. 49–51; and Luna, *Argentina* pp. 129–30.
47. Snow, *Political Forces* ch. 5.
48. Leonard, *Politicians* pp. 203–22.

49. For details of the Ateneo's contribution to the Onganía administration, see Lewis, 'The Right and Military Rule, 1955–1983' in McGee Deutsch and Dolkart, *Argentine Right* pp. 163–6.
50. *Tercer Encuentro Nacional* p. 178.
51. Useful biographies of Christian Democrats can be found in Parera, *Demócrata Cristianos* vol. 2. A history of the PDC post-1960 is that of Ghirardi, *Democracia Cristiana*.
52. For a summary of the complexities of postconciliar Argentine Catholicism, see Mayol, Habegger and Armada, *Los católicos postconciliares*.

Bibliography

The bibliography is divided as follows:
1. Periodicals
2. General Works
3. Argentine Catholicism
4. Argentine Politics

1. PERIODICALS (DATES REFER TO PERIODS CONSULTED)

Avanzada, 1955–1957
Boletín de la Acción Católica Argentina, 1931–1956
Comunidad, 1955–1960
Criterio, 1928–1960
El Pueblo, 1944–46
Notas de Pastoral Jocista, 1953–1958
Orden Cristiano, 1941–1948
Polémica, 1953–1954
Presencia, 1949–1951
Renovación, 1942–1944
Revista Eclesiástica del Arzobispado de Buenos Aires, 1931–1960
Siglo Cero, 1960–1961
Sol y Luna, 1938–1943
Sur, 1934–1937
Sursum, 1938–1942

2. GENERAL WORKS

Alzaga, O., *La primera democracia cristiana en España*, Barcelona, 1973
Arendt, Hannah, *The Origins of Totalitarianism*, 5th ed., London, 1973
Bernanos, Georges, *La grande peur des bien-pensants: Edouard Drumont*, Paris, 1931
Bigongiari, D. (ed.), *The Political Ideas of St. Thomas Aquinas. Representative Selections*, New York, 1953
Brenan, Gerald, *The Spanish Labyrinth. An account of the social and political background of the Spanish Civil War*, 17th ed., Cambridge, 1988
Carr, Raymond, *Spain, 1808–1975*, 2nd ed., Oxford, 1982
Chadwick, Owen, *The Secularization of the European Mind in the Nineteenth Century*, 4th ed., Cambridge, 1990
Copleston, F.C., *Aquinas. An introduction to the life and work of the great medieval thinker*, 13th ed., London, 1988
Cragg, Gerald, *The Church and the Age of Reason 1648–1789*, Penguin History of the Church, vol. 4, 3rd. ed., London, 1970

Dawson, Christopher, *Religion and the modern state*, 3rd. ed., London, 1936
Doering, Bernard E., *Jacques Maritain and the French Catholic Intellectuals*, Notre Dame, 1983
Donoso Cortés, Juan, *Ensayo sobre el catolicismo, el liberalismo y el socialismo*, Madrid, 1851
Douglas, R. Bruce, and Hollenbach, D. (eds.), *Catholicism and Liberalism. Contributions to American Public Philosophy*, Cambridge, 1994
Droulers, Paul, *Politique Sociale et christianisme. Le père Desbuquois et l'Action Populaire*, vol. 1, *Débuts, syndicalisme et intégristes, 1903–1918*, Paris, 1969
— *Politique Sociale et christianisme. Le père Desbuquois et l'Action Populaire*, vol. 2, *Dans la gestation d'un monde nouveau, 1919–1946*, Paris, 1981
Elliot, John H., *Imperial Spain, 1469–1716*, 7th. ed., London, 1981
— *The Old World and the New, 1492–1650*, 10th ed., Cambridge, 1992
Evans, Ellen L., *The German Center Party, 1870–1933: a study in political Catholicism*, Illinois, 1981
Fievez, Marguerite, and Meert, Jacques, *Cardijn. The Life and Times of Cardinal Joseph Cardijn, founder of the International Movement of Young Christian Workers, Pioneer of the Lay Apostolate*, trans. Edward Mitchinson, YCW England, 1974
Fogarty, Michael, *Christian Democracy in Western Europe, 1820–1953*, London, 1957
Friedrich, C.-J., *Totalitarianism*, New York, 1964
Gilby O.P., Thomas, *Principality and Polity. Aquinas and the rise of state theory in the West*, London, 1958
Gurian, Waldemar, and Fitzsimons, M.A. (eds), *The Catholic Church in World Affairs*, Notre Dame, 1954
Hamilton, Bernice, *Political thought in sixteenth-century Spain: a study of the political ideas of Vitoria, De Soto, Suárez & Molina*, Oxford, 1963
Hudson, Deal W. and Matthew J. Mancini, (eds) *Understanding Maritain. Philosopher and Friend*, Mercer, 1987
Hughes, Philip, *The Pope's New Order. A systematic summary of the social encyclicals and addresses, from Leo XIII to Pius XII*, London, 1943
Irving, R.E.M., *Christian Democracy in France*, London, 1973
— *The Christian Democratic Parties of Western Europe*, London, 1979
Jeunesse Ouvrière Catholique (JOC), *Manuel de la JOC*, Editions Jocistes, Brussels, 1925
Keller, Emile, *L'encyclique du 8 décembre 1864 et les principles de 1789, ou l'Eglise, l'état et la liberté*, Paris, 1865
Lannon, Frances, *Privilege, Persecution and Prophecy. The Catholic Church in Spain, 1875– 1975*, Oxford, 1987
Lloyd Mecham, John, *Church and State in Latin America*, 2nd ed., N. Carolina, 1966
Madariaga, Salvador de, *Spain. A modern history*, London, 1961
Maier, Hans, *Revolution and Church. The early history of Christian Democracy 1789–1901*, Notre Dame, 1969
Marejko, Jan, *Jean–Jacques Rousseau et la dérive totalitaire*, Lausanne, 1984
Maritain, Jacques, *Antimoderne*, Paris, 1922
— *Trois Réformateurs: Luther, Desartes, Rousseau*, Paris, 1925

— *Primauté du spirituel*, Paris, 1927 (trans. as *The things that are not Caesar's*, London, 1930
— *Du régime temporel et de la liberté*, Paris, 1933
— *Humanisme intégral: problèmes temporels et spirituels d'une nouvelle chrétienté*, Paris, 1936
— *Scholasticism and Politics*, London, 1940
— *Les droits de l'homme et la loi naturelle*, New York, 1942
— *Christianisme et démocratie*, [Ed. Maison Française, New York, 1943]: *Christianity and Democracy*, trans. D. Anson, San Francisco, 1986
— *Man and the State*, Chicago, 1956
— *The Person and the Common Good*, Notre Dame, 1966
Martin, David, *The Religious and the Secular: studies in secularization*, London, 1969
— *A General Theory of Secularization*, Oxford, 1978
Mayeur, Jean-Marie, *Des partis catholiques à la démocratie chrétienne, xixe–xxe siècles*, Paris, 1980
— *Catholicisme social et démocratie chrétienne: principes romains, expériences françaises*, Paris, 1986
McBrien, Richard, *Catholicism*, Study edition, San Francisco, 1981
McDonald, J., *Rousseau and the French Revolution 1762–1791*, London, 1963
McIlwain, Charles H., *The Growth of Political Thought in the West*, New York, 1932
McManners, John, *Church and State in France, 1870–1914*, London, 1972
Micklem, Nathaniel, *The Theology of Politics*, Oxford, 1941
— and Morgan, Herbert, *Christ and Caesar*, London, 1921
Misner, Paul, *Social Catholicism in Europe from the onset of industrialisation to the First World War*, London, 1991
Molony, John, *The Worker Question. A new historical perspective on 'Rerum Novarum'*, Dublin, 1991
— *The emergence of political Catholicism in Italy: Partito Popolare, 1919–1926*, London, 1977
Montero Moreno, Antonio, *Historia de la persecución religiosa en España, 1936–1939*, Madrid, 1961
Moody, Joseph N. (ed) *Church and Society. Catholic social and political thought and movements, 1789–1950*, New York, 1950
Mounier, Emmanuel, *Be Not Afraid. Studies in Personalist Sociology*, trans. C. Rowland, London, 1951
Noguiera, Franco, *Salazar*, vol. 1, *A Mocidade e os Princípios*, Coimbra, 1977
Nolte, Ernst, *Three Faces of Fascism: Action Française, Italian Fascism, National Socialism*, trans. L. Vennewitz, London, 1965
Plamenatz, John, *Man and Society. A Critical Examination of some important social and political theories from Macchiavelli to Marx*, [1963], 2 vols, 14th ed., London 1986
— *Man and Society. Political and social theories from Macchiavelli to Marx*, revised by M. E. Plamenatz and R. Wokler, vol. 1, *From the Middle Ages to Locke*, London, 1992
Pollard, John F., *The Vatican and Italian Fascism, 1929–1932*, Cambridge 1985
Ponson, Christian, *Les catholiques lyonnais et la Chronique Sociale, 1892–1914*, Lyons, 1980

Poulat, Emile, *Eglise contre bourgeoisie. Introduction au devenir du catholicisme actuel*, Paris, 1977
— *Liberté, laïcité: la guerre des deux France et le principe de la modernité*, Paris, 1987
Reardon, Bernard, *Liberalism and Tradition. Aspects of Catholic thought in nineteenth century France*, Cambridge, 1975
Rhodes, Anthony, *The Vatican in the age of the dictators 1922–1945*, London, 1973
— *The Vatican in the age of the Cold War, 1945–1980*, Norwich, 1992
Rousseau, Jean–Jacques, *The Social Contract*, trans. M. Cranston [1968], London, 1986
Stock-Morton, Phyllis, *Moral Education for a secular society: the development of 'morale laïque' in nineteenth-century France*, New York, 1988
Strauss, Leo, and Joseph Cropsey, (eds) *History of Political Philosophy*, 3rd. ed., Chicago, 1987
Sturzo, Luigi, *Il Partito Popolare*, Rome, 1956
Sutton, Michael, *Nationalism, Positivism and Catholicism. The politics of Charles Maurras and French Catholics, 1890–1914*, Cambridge, 1982
Tallet, Frank, and Nicholas Atkin, (eds) *Religion, society and politics in France since 1789*, London, 1991
Talmon, Jacob, *The Origins of Totalitarian Democracy*, London, 1961
Ullmann, Walter, *The growth of papal government in the Middle Ages. A Study in the ideological relation of clerical to lay power*, [1955], 2nd. ed., London, 1962
Vidler, Alec, *The Church in an age of Revolution: 1789 to the present day*, Penguin History of the Church, vol. 5, 3rd. ed., London, 1990
— *Prophecy and Papacy. A study of Lammenais, the Church and the Revolution*, London, 1954
Weber, Eugene, *Action Française*, Stanford, 1962
Webster, Richard, *Christian Democracy in Italy, 1860–1960*, London, 1960
Winston, C.M., *Workers and the Right in Spain, 1900–1936*, Princeton, 1985
Whyte, John H., *Catholics in western democracies: a study in political behaviour*, New York, 1981
Zeldin, Theodore, 'Religion and anticlericalism', in Zeldin, *France 1848–1945*, vol. 2, *Intellect, Taste and Anxiety*, Oxford, 1973
— (ed) *Conflicts in French Society*, London, 1970

3. ARGENTINE CATHOLICISM

Acción Católica Argentina (ACA), *Cincuenta años de apostolado en la Argentina*, Junta Central, Buenos Aires, 1981
— *Veinte años de Acción Católica, 1931–1951*, Junta Central, Buenos Aires, 1951
— *Treinta años de Acción Católica, 1931–1961*, Buenos Aires, 1961
— *Tercera Semana Nacional de Estudios Sociales Organizada por la Acción Católica, Buenos Aires 1941, del 21 al 36 de octubre: El Nuevo Orden Social Cristiano según las encíclicas 'Rerum Novarum' y 'Quadragesimo Anno'*, Buenos Aires, 1945

Bibliography

— JAC, *Manual del Socio Efectivo Provisorio*, 2nd ed., Buenos Aires, 1946
— Consejo Superior de la AUDAC, *Primera Concentración de Dirigentes de la Agrupación de Universitarias de la Acción Católica Argentina*, Buenos Aires, 1953
— AJAC, *Clases sobre la misión femenina: 3 parte: responsabilidades cívicas*, Buenos Aires, 1949
Amadeo, Mario, *Ayer, Hoy, Mañana*, Buenos Aires, 1956
— 'El grupo Baluarte y los CCC', *Universitas*, no. 38 (July–September 1975): 23–58
Amato, Enrique, 'Buenos Aires: su evolución demográfica y religiosa', *Notas de Pastoral Jocista* Año XI (Buenos Aires, September–October 1957): 14–34
— *La Iglesia en Argentina*, Buenos Aires, 1969
Ancarola, Gerardo, 'Los católicos y el noventa', *Historia*, Buenos Aires, Año X, no. 40 (December 1990–February 1991): 65–75
Arenza, Celia de, *Sin Memoria*, Buenos Aires, 1980
Aspiazu S.J., José, *El estado católico*, Madrid, 1939
Aúza, Néstor T., *Aciertos y Fracasos sociales del catolicismo argentino*, 3 vols, Buenos Aires, 1987–1988
— *Católicos y liberales en la generación del ochenta*, Sondeos no. 6, 2 vols., Cuernavaca-Mexico, 1966
— *Corrientes sociales del catolicismo argentino*, Buenos Aires, 1984
Avellá Chafer, A., *Diccionario biográfico del clero secular de Buenos Aires*, 2 vols., Buenos Aires, 1985
Ballent, A., 'La Iglesia y la vivienda popular: la Gran Colecta Nacional de 1919' in D. Armus (ed), *Mundo urbano y cultura popular. Estudios de historia social*, Buenos Aires, 1990
Benítez, Hernán, *La Aristocracia frente a la Revolución y la verdad justicialista en lo social, político, económico y espiritual*, Buenos Aires, 1953
Busacca, Salvador, *Camino a la Democracia Cristiana*, Buenos Aires, 1951
Buschiazzo, Mario J., *Estancias Jesuíticas de Córdoba*, Buenos Aires, 1969
Canclini, A., *Los evangélicos en el tiempo de Perón. Memorias de un pastor bautista sobre la libertad religiosa en la Argentina*, Buenos Aires, 1972
Carbia, Rómulo D., *La Revolución de Mayo y la Iglesia. Contribución histórica al estudio de la cuestión del patronato nacional, con anotaciones póstumas del autor*, Buenos Aires, 1945
— *Historia eclesiástica del Río de la Plata*, Buenos Aires, 1924
Carranza, Ambrosio R., *Itinerario de Monseñor de Andrea*, Buenos Aires, 1957
Carrizo, Juan, *Frorilegio. El cristianismo en los cantares populares*, Buenos Aires, 1934
— *Cancionero Popular de Tucumán*, Buenos Aires, 1937
— *Cuadernos de navidad tradicionales en nuestro país*, Buenos Aires, 1945
Casiello, Juan, *Iglesia y estado en la Argentina*, Buenos Aires, 1948
Castagnino, Raúl H., *Rosas y los jesuitas*, Buenos Aires, 1970
Castellani, Leonardo, *Seis ensayos y tres cartas*, Biblioteca Dictio vol. 20, Buenos Aires, 1978
— *Decíamos Ayer*, Buenos Aires, 1968
— *Las ideas de mi tío el cura*, Buenos Aires, 1984
— *Conversación y Crítica Filosófica*, Buenos Aires, 1941
Centeno, Angel, *Cuatro años de una política religiosa*, Buenos Aires, 1964

Congreso Eucarístic Internacional, *XXXII Congreso Eucarístico Internacional, Buenos Aires 10–14 de octubre de 1934*, 2 vols., Buenos Aires, 1935

Cursos de Cultura Católica, *Circular Informativa y Bibliográfica de los Cursos de la Cultura Católica*, (Buenos Aires, 1923–1925)

— *Plan de estudios y programas de los Cursos de Cultura Católica*, Buenos Aires, 1945

De Andrea, Mons. Miguel, *El catolicismo social y su aplicación*, Buenos Aires, 1941

— *Obras Completas*, vol. IV, Buenos Aires, 1956

Dell'Oro Maini, Atilio, et al, *Presencia y sugestión del filósofo Francisco Suárez: su influencia en la Revolución de Mayo*, Buenos Aires, 1959

De Hoyos, Rubén J., 'The role of the Catholic Church in the Revolution against President Juan D. Perón. Argentina, 1954–1955' (Phd Thesis, University of New York, 1970)

Dussel, Enrique D., *A History of the Church in Latin America: colonialism to liberation, 1492–1979*, trans. and rev. A. Neely, Michigan, 1981

Encuentro, *Versión Taquigráfica del Encuentro Nacional de Dirigentes Católicos: Buenos Aires, 24 al 26 de julio de 1959*, Buenos Aires, 1959

— *Tercer Encuentro Nacional. Informe y Versión Taquigráfica*, Buenos Aires, 1971

Estrada, José Manuel de, *La política liberal bajo la tiranía de Rosas*, Buenos Aires, 1955

— *Iglesia y Estado y otros ensayos políticos*, Buenos Aires, 1929

— *Lecciones sobre la historia de la República Argentina*, 3rd ed., 2 vols., Buenos Aires, 1925

— *Discursos*, prol. Tomás D. Casares, 2 vols., Buenos Aires, 1946

Ezcurra Medrano, Alberto, *Catolicismo y nacionalismo*, Buenos Aires, 1939

Farrell, Gerardo T., *Iglesia y Pueblo en Argentina. Cien años de pastoral*, 3rd ed., Buenos Aires, 1988

Figuerola, José, *La Colaboración Social en Hispanoamérica*, Buenos Aires, 1943

— *Organización Social*, Buenos Aires, 1938

Filippo, Virgilio, *El Plan Quinquenal de Perón y los comunistas*, 5th ed., Buenos Aires, 1948

Flores, José, *Operación Rosa Negra*, Buenos Aires, 1956

Forni, Floreal, 'Catolicismo y peronismo', series of three, *Unidos* Año V, no. 14 (September 1987): 212–226; Año V, no. 17 (December 1987): 196–216; Año V, no. 18 (April 1988): 120–144

— Review of McGeagh, *Desarrollo Económico*, vol. 29, no. 114 (July–September 1989): 283–4

Franceschi, Mons. Gustavo J., *Obras Completas*, 6 vols., Buenos Aires, 1944–1946

— 'Argentina', in Richard Pattee (ed) *El catolicismo contemporáneo en Hispanoamérica*, Buenos Aires, 1951

Frigerio, José O., 'Perón contra la Iglesia', *Todo es Historia*, no. 210 (October 1984): 20–65

— *El Síndrome de la Revolución Libertadora: la Iglesia contra el justicialismo*, Biblioteca Política Argentina nos. 285–7, 3 vols., Buenos Aires, 1990

Furlong Cardiff, Guillermo, 'El catolicismo argentino entre 1860 y 1930', in *Academia Nacional de Historia*, vol. 2., *Historia argentina contemporánea 1862–1930*, Buenos Aires, 1964
— *La Santa Sede y la emancipación hispanoamericana*, Buenos Aires, 1957
— 'Las misiones jesuíticas', in R. Levene (ed) *Historia de la Nación Argentina*, vol. 3, Buenos Aires, 1937, pp. 595–622
— *Historia del Colegio del Salvador*, 2 vols., Buenos Aires, 1944
— *El General San Martín: ¿masón–católico–deísta?*, Buenos Aires, 1963
— *Nacimiento y desarrollo de la filosofía en el Río de la Plata, 1536–1810*, Buenos Aires, 1952
— et al, *Etapas del catolicismo argentino*, Buenos Aires, 1952
Gallardo, Guillermo, *La Política Religiosa de Rivadavia*, Buenos Aires, 1962
— 'La venta de los bienes eclesiásticos en Buenos Aires', *Revista Eclesiástica de Buenos Aires*, no. 678 (Sept. 1956): 456–87
Gambini, Hugo, *Perón y la Iglesia*, Buenos Aires, 1956
Gálvez, Manuel, *La noche toca su fin*, Buenos Aires, 1934
— *Entre la Novela y la Historia. Recuerdos de una vida literaria*, vol. 5 Buenos Aires, 1962
Ghirardi, Enrique, *La Democracia Cristiana*, Buenos Aires, 1983
González O.P., Rubén C., *Las Ordenes Religiosas y la Revolución de Mayo*, Buenos Aires, 1960
Gorriti, Juan Ignacio, *Reflexiones sobre las causas morales de las convulsiones internas en los nuevos estados americanos y examen de los medios eficaces para reprimirlas* [Valparaíso 1836], Buenos Aires, 1916
Goyeneche, Juan C., *Ensayos, artículos, discursos*, Buenos Aires, 1976
Horne de Bürmeister, C. *Cómo se organizó en la Argentina el movimiento femenino a favor de los derechos políticos de la mujer*, Buenos Aires, 1933
Imaz, José Luis de, *Los que mandan*, Buenos Aires, 1964
— *Sobre la identidad iberoamericana*, Buenos Aires, 1984
— *Promediados los cuarenta (no pesa la mochila)*, Buenos Aires, 1977
— *Escuchando a Moledo*, Buenos Aires, 1987
— 'Alejandro E. Bunge, economista y sociólogo, 1880–1943', *Desarrollo Económico* no. 14 (October–December 1974) pp. 545–67
Kennedy, John J., *Catholicism, Nationalism and Democracy in Argentina*, Notre Dame, 1958
Lafiandra, Félix (recop. y com.), *Los Panfletos: su aporte a la Revolución Libertadora*, Buenos Aires, 1956
Legón, Faustino J., *Doctrina y ejercicio del patronato nacional*, Buenos Aires, 1920
Leonard, Virginia W., *Politicians, Pupils and Priests: Argentine education since 1943*, New York, 1989
Leturia y Mendía, Pedro de, *Relaciones entre la Santa Sede e Hispanoamérica, 1493–1835*, 3 vols., Caracas, 1959–1960
Liga de Estudiantes Humanistas, *Bases y Principios del Movimiento Universitario Humanista*, Buenos Aires, 1956
Llambías, Héctor, *La Dialéctica Comunista y el concepto de la libertad*, Buenos Aires, 1936
Lubertino Beltrán, María J., *Perón y la Iglesia*, 2 vols., Buenos Aires, 1987

Luchía Puig, Agustín, *Medio siglo, y con sotana*, Buenos Aires, 1959
Mackay, John A., *The Other Spanish Christ: a study in the spiritual history of Spain and South America*, London, 1932
Makin, Guillermo, 'Political Crises in Argentina: 1955 and 1975–6' (Phd Thesis, Cambridge University 1984)
Mallimaci, Fortunato, 'Catholicisme et état militaire en Argentine, 1930–1946' (Thèse du dotorat, Ecole des Hautes Etudes Sociales en Sciences Sociales, Paris, 1986)
— *El Catolicismo Integral en la Argentina, 1930–1946*, Monograph, Fundación Simón Rodríguez, Buenos Aires, 1988
Marsal, Pedro S., *Perón y la Iglesia*, Buenos Aires, 1955
Martínez Paz, Fernando, *Maritain: política, ideología: revolución cristiana en la Argentina*, Buenos Aires, 1966
Martínez Paz, Enrique, *El Deán Funes*, Córdoba, 1950
Mayol, Alejandro et al, *Los católicos posconciliares en la Argentina, 1963–1969*, Buenos Aires, 1970
McGeagh, Robert, *Relaciones entre el poder político y el poder eclesiástico en la Argentina*, Buenos Aires, 1987
Meinvielle, Julio, *Concepción Católica de la Política*, [1932], 4th ed., Buenos Aires, 1961
— *Qué saldrá de la España que sangra*, Buenos Aires, 1937
— *La Iglesia y el Tercer Reich*, Buenos Aires, 1937
— *Un juicio católico sobre los problemas nuevos de la política*, Buenos Aires, 1938
— *De Lammenais a Maritain*, Buenos Aires, 1945
— *Cartas al P. Garrigou-Lagrange a propósito de la crítica a Maritain*, Buenos Aires, 1947
— *Críticas a la Concepción de la Persona Humana de Jacques Maritain*, Buenos Aires, 1948
— *Política Argentina, 1949–1956*, Buenos Aires, 1956
Methol Ferré, A., 'La Iglesia en el Cono Sur', *Actualidad Pastoral*, Año XV, no. 144, (Buenos Aires, September–December 1982): 252–298
Mignone, Emilio, 'Los católicos y la revolución de 1890', *Revista de Historia*, Buenos Aires, no. 1 (primer trimestre de 1957): 56–60
Mörner, Magnus, *The political and economic activities of the Jesuits in the La Plata Region*, Stockholm, 1953
— (ed) *The Expulsion of the Jesuits from Latin America*, New York, 1965
Movimiento de la Renovación, *Tres Discursos. Una Nueva Posición*, Buenos Aires, 1941
Niklison, José E., 'Acción Social Católica Obrera', *Boletín del Dpto. Nacional del Trabajo*, no. 46 (Mar. 1920): 15–386
Olazábal, Raúl Rivero de, *Por Una Cultura Católica. El Compromiso de una Generación Argentina*, Buenos Aires, 1986
Pagés, José, 'Los ensayos sindicales de inspiración católica en la República Argentina', *Anales de la Comisión de Estudios y Conferencias de la Corporación de Ingenieros Católicos*, Buenos Aires (1944): 73–118
— *Orígenes y desarrollo de las ideas demócrata-cristianas en nuestro país*, Buenos Aires, 1945
Palau, Gabriel, *La Acción Católica: cómo debe entenderse*, Buenos Aires, 1931

Parera, Ricardo G., *Los Demócrata Cristianos Argentinos. Testimonio de una experiencia política*, 2 vols., Buenos Aires, 1986
— *Democracia Cristiana en la Argentina. Los hechos y las ideas*, Buenos Aires, 1967
Pesce Battilana, C., *Los Diputados Católicos ante la Ley 1420*, Buenos Aires, 1933
Piaggio, Agustín, *La influencia del clero en la Revolución de Mayo*, Buenos Aires, 1910
Pico, César, 'Hacia la hispanidad', *Separata del no. 18 de la Revista de Estudios Políticos*, Madrid, 1944
— 'Carta a Jacques Maritain sobre la colaboración de los católicos con los regímenes de tipo fascista', Buenos Aires, 1937
Ponsati, Arturo, 'Maritain in Argentina' in Papini, Roberto (ed) *Jacques Maritain e la società contemporanea*, Milan, 1978, pp. 351–71
Recalde, Héctor, *Matrimonio civil y divorcio*, Buenos Aires, 1986
— *La Iglesia y la cuestión social, 1874–1910*, Biblioteca Política Argentina no. 110, Buenos Aires, 1985
Ruiz–Guiñazú, Enrique, *La Política argentina y el futuro de América*, Buenos Aires, 1944
Sampay, Arturo, *La Constitución Argentina de 1949*, Buenos Aires, 1963
— *La Crisis del Estado de Derecho Liberal-Burgués*, Buenos Aires, 1942
Sanguinetti, J., *La representación diplomática del Vaticano en los países del Plata*, Buenos Aires, 1943
Soneira, Abelardo J., 'La Juventud Obrera Católica en la Argentina: de la secularización a la justicia social', CEDEL, *Justicia Social*, Año 5, no. 8 (June 1989): 76–88
— *Las estrategias institucionales de la Iglesia Católica, 1880–1976*, Biblioteca Política Argentina nos. 269–270, 2 vols., Buenos Aires, 1989
Soneira, Abelardo J. and Lumerman, Juan P., *Iglesia y Nación. Aporte para un estudio de la historia contemporánea de la Iglesia en la Comunidad Nacional*, Buenos Aires, 1986
Stack, Noreen F., 'Avoiding the Greater Evil. The Response of the Argentine Catholic Church to Juan Perón, 1943–1955' (Phd Thesis, Rutgers University, New Jersey, 1976)
Stoetzer, Carlos O., *The Scholastic Roots of the Spanish-American Revolution*, New York, 1979
Ussher, Santiago M., *Padre Fahy. Biografía de Antonio Domingo Fahy*, Buenos Aires, 1952
Valsecchi, Francisco, *Silabario Social*, Buenos Aires, 2nd ed., 1943
Zuretti, Juan C., *Nueva Historia Eclesiástica Argentina. Del Concilio de Trento al Vaticano Segundo*, Buenos Aires, 1972

4. ARGENTINE POLITICS

Adelman, Jeremy (ed) *Essays in Argentine Labour History, 1870–1930*, Oxford, 1992
Aguinaga, Carlos, and Roberto, Azaretto, *Ni Década Ni Infame: del '30 al '43*, Buenos Aires, 1991

Alberdi, Juan Bautista, *Bases y punto de partida para la organización política de la República Argentina*, [1858], Buenos Aires, 1966
Alem, Leandro, et al, *La Revolución del noventa*, Buenos Aires, 1940
Alexander, Robert J., *The Perón Era*, 2nd ed., New York, 1965
— *Communism in Latin America*, New Jersey, 1957
Alhadeff, Peter, 'Dependency, historiography and objections to the Roca pact', in Christopher Abel and Colin Lewis (eds) *Latin America: economic imperialism and the state* (London, 1985): 369–76
— 'Social welfare and the slump: Argentina in the 1930s' in D.C.M. Platt (ed) *Social Welfare, 1850–1950: Australia, Argentina and Canada compared*, Oxford, 1989
Areces, Nidia and Edgardo, Ossana, *Rivadavia y su tiempo*, Buenos Aires, 1984
Baily, Samuel L., *Labor, nationalism and politics in Argentina*, New Brunswick, 1967
Balbini, Nicolás, *Frondizi: de la oposición al gobierno*, Buenos Aires, 1984
Balestra, Juan, *El Noventa*, 3rd ed., Buenos Aires, 1959
Barbero, María I. and Fernando, Devoto, *Los nacionalistas*, Biblioteca Política Argentina no. 9, Buenos Aires, 1983
Belloni, Alberto, *Del anarquismo al peronismo*, Buenos Aires, 1960
Bergquist, Charles, *Labor in Latin America*, Stanford, 1986
Biagini, Hugo (comp.) *Orígenes de la democracia argentina. El trasfondo krausista*, Buenos Aires, 1989
Bialet-Massé, Juan, *El estado de las clases obreras argentinas a comienzos del siglo*, 2nd ed, Córdoba, 1968
Bianchi, Susana, and Sanchis, Norma, *El partido peronista femenino*, 2 vols., Buenos Aires, 1988
Birschoff, E., *Historia de Córdoba*, Buenos Aires, 1979
Blackwelder, J.K. and Johnson, L.L., 'Changing Criminal Patterns in Buenos Aires, 1890–1914', *Journal of Latin American Studies*, vol. 14, no. 2 (1982): 259–380
Blanksten, George, *Perón's Argentina*, Chicago, 1953
Botana, Natalio, *El Orden Conservador: la política argentina entre 1880 y 1916*, 2nd ed., Buenos Aires, 1979
Botana, Helvio, *Memorias: tras los dientes del perro*, Buenos Aires, 1977
Browning, Webster, *The River Plate Republics. A survey of religious, economic and social conditions of Argentina, Paraguay, Uruguay*, London, 1938
Buchrucker, Cristián, *Nacionalismo y Peronismo. La Argentina en la Crisis Ideológica Mundial, 1927–1955*, Buenos Aires, 1987
Bunge, Alejandro, *Una Nueva Argentina*, Buenos Aires, 1940
— *La Economía Argentina*, vol. I: *La conciencia nacional y el problema económico*, Buenos Aires, 1928
Burgin, Miron, *The economic aspects of Argentine federalism, 1820–1852*, Harvard, 1946
Calello, Oswaldo, *Peronismo y Bonapartismo 1843–1945*, Buenos Aires, 1986
Cantón, Dario, *Los partidos políticos argentinos entre 1912 y 1955*, Doc. de Trabajo no. 31. Inst. T. Di Tella, Buenos Aires, 1967
Carulla, Juan E., *Al filo de medio siglo*, Buenos Aires, 1964
Cavarozzi, Marcelo, *Sindicatos y Política en Argentina*, Buenos Aires, 1984

Cayró, Antonio, 'El fraude patriótico' in H. Gorostegui de Torres (ed) *Historia Integral Argentina*, vol. 7, Buenos Aires, 1970, pp. 173-96
Chávez, Fermín, *Perón y el peronismo en la historia contemporánea*, 2 vols., Buenos Aires, 1984
Ciria, Alberto, *Política y cultura popular: la Argentina peronista, 1946-1955*, Buenos Aires, 1983
— *Partidos y Poder en la Argentina Moderna, 1930-1946*, Buenos Aires, 1969
Comisión de Estudios de la Sociedad Argentina en Defensa de la Tradición, Familia y Propiedad, *El Nacionalismo. Una incógnita en constante evolución*, Buenos Aires, 1970
Conil Paz, Alberto, and Gustavo, Ferrari, *Argentina's Foreign Policy, 1930-1962*, trans. J. Kennedy, Notre Dame, 1966
Cornblit, Oscar, *et al*, 'La generación del 80 y su proyecto: antecedentes y consecuencias', in Di Tella, Torcuato, *et al*, *Argentina, sociedad de masas*, Buenos Aires, 1965
Crassweller, R., *Perón y los enigmas de la Argentina*, Buenos Aires, 1988
Cortés Conde, Roberto, *El Progreso Argentino, 1880-1914*, Buenos Aires, 1979
Crawley, Eduardo, *Una Casa Dividida. Argentina, 1880-1980*, Buenos Aires, 1987
De la Torre, Lisandro, *Intermedio Filosófico*, vol. 4, Buenos Aires, 1961
Del Barco, Ricardo, *El Régimen Peronista, 1946-1955*, Buenos Aires, 1983
— *et al, Historia Política Argentina, 1943-1982*, Buenos Aires, 1983
Del Carril, Bonifacio, *Crónica Interna de la Revolución Libertadora*, Buenos Aires, 1959
— *Memorias Dispersas. El Colonel Perón*, Buenos Aires, 1984
Del Campo, Hugo, *Sindicalismo y Peronismo: los comienzos de un vínculo perdurable*, Buenos Aires, 1983
Del Mazo, Gabriel, *La Primera Presidencia de Yrigoyen*, Buenos Aires, 1984
Di Tella, Guido, and Dornbusch, Rudiger, *The Political Economy of Argentina, 1946-1983*, Oxford, 1989
Di Tella, Guido and Platt, D.C.M. (eds), *Argentina, Australia and Canada. Studies in comparative development, 1870-1965*, Oxford, 1985
— and D.C.M. Platt, (eds) *The Political Economy of Argentina, 1880-1946*, Oxford, 1986
— and Cameron Watt, Donald, *Argentina between the Great Powers, 1939-1946*, Oxford, 1989
Díaz Araujo, Enrique, *La Conspiración del '43. El GOU: una experiencia militarista en la Argentina*, Buenos Aires, 1971
Díaz-Alejandro, Carlos, *Essays on the economic history of the Argentine Republic*, Yale, 1970
Doll, Ramón, *Acerca de una política nacional*, Buenos Aires, 1939
Domingorena, H.O. *Universidades Privadas en la Argentina: sus antecedentes*, Buenos Aires, 1959
Echevarría, J. Esteban, *Dogma Socialista de la Asociación de Mayo*, [1846], Buenos Aires, 1947
Escudé, Carlos, *El Fracaso del Proyecto Argentino. Educación e ideología*, Buenos Aires, 1990
— *Gran Bretaña, Estados Unidos y la Declinación Argentina, 1942-1949*, Buenos Aires, 1983

Etchepareborda, Roberto, *La revolución argentina del 90*, 2nd ed., Buenos Aires, 1966
Falcoff, Mark, and Frederick B. Pike (eds) *The Spanish Civil War, 1936–1939. American Hemispheric Perspectives*, Nebraska 1982
Falcoff, Mark, and R.H. Dolkart (eds) *Prologue to Perón. Argentina in Depression and War, 1930–1945*, Berkeley, 1975
Fayt, Carlos F., *La naturaleza del peronismo*, Buenos Aires, 1967
Ferns, H.S., *Britain and Argentina in the nineteenth century*, Oxford, 1960
— *Argentina*, London, 1969
Floria, Carlos A., and Belsunce, García César A., *Historia Política de la Argentina Contemporánea, 1880–1983*, 2nd ed., Buenos Aires, 1988
Fodor, Jorge, and Arturo, O'Connell, 'La Argentina y la economía atlántica en la primera mitad del siglo veinte', *Desarrollo Económico* vol. 13, no. 49 (April–June 1973) pp. 1–67.
Font Ezcurra, Ricardo, *San Martín y Rosas*, Buenos Aires, 1943
Forbes, John M., *Once años en Buenos Aires, 1820–1831. Las Crónicas Diplomáticas de John Murray Forbes*, translated Felipe A. Espil, Buenos Aires, 1956
Francis, Michael J., *The Limits of Hegemony: U.S. Relations with Argentina and Chile during World War II*, Notre Dame, 1977
Fraser, John F., *The Amazing Argentine*, London, 1914
Frondizi, Silvio, *La realidad argentina. Ensayo de interpretación sociológica*, vol. 1, *El sistema capitalista*, 2nd ed., Buenos Aires, 1957
Galasso, Norberto, *Ramón Doll: ¿socialismo o fascismo?*, Buenos Aires, 1989
Galetti, Alfredo, 'Ambigüedades e incongruencias de la Revolución de los coroneles', *Todo es Historia* no. 193 (June 1983): 19–32
— *La Política y los Partidos*, Buenos Aires, 1961
Gandía, Enrique de, *Historia de las ideas políticas en la Argentina*, 10 vols., Buenos Aires, 1960
— *Historia del 25 de mayo. Nacimiento de la libertad y de la independencia argentinas*, Buenos Aires, 1960
— *La revisión de la historia argentina*, Buenos Aires, 1952
Germán Herz, Enrique, *La Revolución del 90*, Buenos Aires, 1991
Germani, Gino, 'Mass immigration and modernization in Argentina' in Irving L. Horowitz (ed) *Masses in Latin America*, New York, 1970
— *Política y sociedad en una época de transición*, Buenos Aires, 1967
Giménez Fernández, Manuel, *Las Doctrinas Populistas en la independencia de Hispanoamérica*, Seville, 1947
Gálvez, Manuel, *Vida de don Manuel de Rosas*, Buenos Aires, 1946
García Costa, Víctor O., *Alfredo L. Palacios. Un socialismo argentino y para la Argentina*, Buenos Aires, 1986
Gillespie, Richard, *Soldados de Perón: los Montoneros*, trans. A. Pigrau, 3rd ed., Buenos Aires, 1987
Goldwert, Marvin, *Democracy, Militarism and Nationalism in Argentina, 1930–1966*, Texas, 1972
Gorraíz Beloqui, R., *Tandil a través de un siglo*, Buenos Aires, 1958
Groussac, Pablo, *Los que pasaban*, Buenos Aires, 1939
Guy, Donna, *Sex and Danger in Buenos Aires: prostitution, family and nation in Argentina*, Lincoln–London, 1991

Halperín Donghi, Tulio, *De la revolución de independencia a la confederación rosista*, Buenos Aires, 1972
— *El Espejo de la Historia. Problemas argentinos y perspectivas hispanoamericanas*, Buenos Aires, 1987
— *Proyecto y Construcción de una Nación*, Sucre, 1980
— 'El revisionismo histórico argentino como visión decadentista de la historia nacional', *Alternativas*, Buenos Aires (June 1984): 72–93
— (comp.) *El pensamiento de Echevarría*, Buenos Aires, 1951
— *El revisionismo histórico argentino*, Buenos Aires, 1970
— *Argentina en el callejón*, Montevideo, 1964
Hennessy, Alistair and King, John, *The Land that England Lost: Argentina and Britain, a special relationship*, London, 1992
Hernández Arregui, Juan José, *La Formación de la Conciencia Nacional*, Buenos Aires, 1956
Hirst, W.A., *Argentina*, London, 1911
Horowitz, Joel, *Argentine Unions, the state and the rise of Perón, 1930–1945*, Berkeley, 1990
Humphreys, Robert A., *Latin America and the Second World War*, 2 vols., London, 1981–1982
Ibarguren, Carlos, *La historia que he vivido*, 2nd ed., Buenos Aires, 1969
Ingenieros, José, *La evolución de las ideas argentinas*, 3 vols., Buenos Aires, 1951
Irazusta, Julio, *Genio y figura de Leopoldo Lugones*, Buenos Aires, 1961
— *Tomás de Anchorena. Prócer de la Revolución, la Independencia y la Federación, 1784–1847*, Buenos Aires, 1950
— *El pensamiento político nacionalista*, Buenos Aires, 1975
— *Ensayo sobre Rosas en el centenario*, Buenos Aires, 1935
James, Daniel, *Resistance and Integration. Peronism and the Argentine Working Class, 1946–1976*, Cambridge, 1988
Jefferson, Mark, *Peopling the Argentine Pampa*, [1926], 2nd ed., New York–London, 1971
Josephs, Ray, *Argentine Diary. The Inside Story of the coming of fascism*, New York, 1944
Katra, William H., *'Contorno': Literary enagagement in post-Peronist Argentina*, London, 1988
Kelly, Sir David, *The Ruling Few, or the Human Background to Diplomacy*, London, 1952
Kenworthy, Eldon, 'The Function of a Little-Known Case in Theory Formation: or what Peronism wasn't', *Comparative Politics* vol. 6, no. 1 (Oct. 1973): 1–35
King, John A., *Veinticuatro años en la República Argentina*, trans. J. Heller, Buenos Aires, 1921
King, John, *'Sur': a study of the Argentine literary journal and its role in the development of a culture, 1931–1970*, Cambridge, 1986
Kirkpatrick, Jean, *Leader and Vanguard in Mass Society: a study of Peronist Argentina*, Cambridge Mass., 1971
Kroeber, Clifton B., *Rosas y la revisión de la historia argentina*, Buenos Aires, 1964
Lamas, Daniel R., *La Revolución Libertadora*, Biblioteca Política Argentina no. 117, Buenos Aires, 1985

— *Rawson-Ramírez-Farrell*, Biblioteca Política Argentina no. 41, Buenos Aires, 1983
Lazcano, Martín V., *Las sociedades secretas políticas y masónicas en Buenos Aires*, Buenos Aires, 1927
Levene, Ricardo, *A History of Argentina*, [1937], 2nd ed., trans. William S. Robertson, New York, 1963
— *Historia filosófica de la Revolución de Mayo*, La Plata, 1941
— (ed) *Historia de la Nación Argentina*, vol. III, Buenos Aires, 1938
Liga Republicana, *Bases y programa de acción de la Liga Republicana*, Buenos Aires, 1929
Little, Walter, 'Party and State in Peronist Argentina, 1946–1955', *Hispanic American Historical Review* vol. 53, no. 54 (November 1973): 644–62
Luna, Félix, *Argentina de Perón a Lanusse*, Barcelona, 1972
— *Alvear*, Buenos Aires, 1958
— *El 45. Crónica de un año decisivo*, Buenos Aires, 1969
— *Diálogos con Frondizi*, 2nd ed., Buenos Aires, 1963
Lynch, John, *The Spanish American Revolutions, 1808–1826*, 2nd ed., New York–London, 1973
— *Argentine Dictator. Juan Manuel de Rosas, 1829–1852*, Oxford, 1981
— *Spanish Colonial Administration, 1782–1810. The Intendant System in the Viceroyalty of the Río de la Plata*, London, 1958
MacDonald, Calum, 'The politics of intervention: the United States and Argentina, 1941–1946', *Journal of Latin American Studies* vol. 12, pt. 2 (November 1980): 365–95
Mansilla, Lucio V., *Rozas. Ensayo histórico psicológico*, Buenos Aires, 1933
Martínez Estrada, Ezequiel, *Radiografía de la Pampa*, [1933], 11th ed., Buenos Aires, 1985
Martínez S., Pedro, *La Nueva Argentina*, 2 vols, Buenos Aires, 1976
Matsushita, Hiroschi, *Movimiento obrero argentino 1930–1945. Sus proyecciones en los orígenes del peronismo*, Buenos Aires, 1983
Mayo, Carlos A., *La masonería en crisis, 1902–1922*, Centro Editor de América Latin no. 5, Buenos Aires, 1988
Mayo, Carlos A. and Fernando, García Molina, *El positivismo en la política argentina, 1880–1906*, Centro Editor de América Latina no. 19, Buenos Aires, 1988
McGann, Thomas F., *Argentina, the United States and the inter-American system, 1880–1914*, Cambridge Mass., 1957
McGee Deutsch, Sandra, *Counterrevolution in Argentina, 1900–1932. The Argentine Patriotic League*, Nebraska, 1986
McGee Deutsch, Sandra and Ronald H. Dolkart, (eds.) *The Argentine Right. Its History and Intellectual Origins, 1910 to the present*, Wilmington Del., 1993
Miguens, José E. and Frederick C. Turner, *Racionalidad del peronismo. Perspectivas internas y externas que replantean un debate inconcluso*, Buenos Aires, 1988
Mirelman, Victor A., *Jewish Buenos Aires, 1890–1930*, Detroit, 1990
Mitre, Bartolomé, *Obras Completas*, Buenos Aires, 1938
Molinas, R. and Barberis, S., *El Partido Demócrata Progresista*, Buenos Aires, 1983

Mora y Araujo, Manuel, and Ignacio Llorente, (eds) *El Voto Peronista: ensayos de sociología electoral argentina*, Buenos Aires, 1980
Moreau de Justo, Alicia, *Juan B. Justo y el socialismo*, Buenos Aires, 1984
Moreno, Manuel, *Memorias y Autobiografías*, 2 vols., Buenos Aires, 1910
— *Escritos*, Prol. de R. Levene, 2 vols., Buenos Aires, 1956
Munck, Ronaldo, *Argentina from Anarchism to Peronism: Workers, Unions and Politics, 1855–1985*, London, 1987
Nario, Hugo, *Los crímenes de Tandil, 1872*, Centro Editor de América Latina no. 5, Buenos Aires, 1983
Navarro Gerassi, Marysa, *Los nacionalistas*, trans. Alberto Ciria, Buenos Aires, 1968
Newton, Ronald C., *The 'Nazi Menace' in Argentina, 1931–1947*, Stanford, 1992
Oddone, Jacinto, *La burguesía terrateniente argentina*, [1930], 2nd ed., Buenos Aires, 1975
O'Donnell, Guillermo, 'Permanent crisis and the failure to create a democratic régime: Argentina, 1955–66' in Juan L. Linz and Alfred Stepan (eds) *The Breakdown of Democratic Régimes: Latin America*, Johns Hopkins, 1978
Oliver, María Rosa, *Mi fe en el hombre*, Buenos Aires, 1978
Palacio, Ernesto, *Historia de la Argentina*, vol. II, Buenos Aires, 1960
Pandolfi, R., *Frondizi por él mismo*, Buenos Aires, 1986
Paz, José María, *Memorias Póstumas*, 4 vols., Buenos Aires, 1957
Pereira, Enrique, 'La guerra civil española en la Argentina', *Todo es Historia*, no. 110 (July 1976): 6–34.
Perelman, Angel, *Cómo hicimos el 17 de octubre*, Buenos Aires, 1961
Perón, Eva, *La Razón de Mi Vida*, Buenos Aires, 1952
— *La Palabra, el pensamiento y la acción de Eva Perón*, Buenos Aires, 1951
Perón, Juan D., 'Principios doctrinarios de la política social del...Presidente de la Nación General Juan D. Perón: discurso pronunciado en el acto organizado por la CGT y realizado en el Teatro Colón el 24 de febrero de 1947', Buenos Aires, 1947
— 'Discurso del Presidente de la Nación General Juan D. Perón con motivo del día de la raza, y como homenaje en memoria de don Miguel de Cervantes', Buenos Aires, 12 Oct. 1947
— 'Perón conversa con los escritores argentinos', Buenos Aires, 11 Dec. 1947
— *La Comunidad Organizada y otros discursos académicos*, Prol. de E. Pavón Pereyra, Buenos Aires, 1983
— *El Pueblo Quiere Saber de Qué Se Trata*, Buenos Aires, 1944
— *Doctrina Peronista*, Buenos Aires, 1952
— *Yo, Juan Domingo Perón. Relato Autobiográfico*, Barcelona, 1976
Peter, José, *Crónicas Proletarias*, Buenos Aires, 1986
Phelps, Vernon L., *The International Economic Position of Argentina*, London, 1938
Piccirilli, Ricardo, *Rivadavia y su tiempo*, 2nd ed., 3 vols., Buenos Aires, 1960
Pike, Frederick B., *'Hispanismo', 1898–1936. Spanish conservatives and liberals and their relations with Spanish America*, Notre Dame, 1971
Pinedo, Federico, *Argentina en la Vorágine*, Buenos Aires, 1943
Pont, Elena S., *Partido Laborista. Estado y sindicatos*, Buenos Aires, 1987
Poppino, Rollie E., *International Communism in Latin America. A history of the movement, 1917–1963*, New York, 1964

Potash, Robert, *The Army and Politics in Argentina, 1928–1945. Yrigoyen to Perón*, Stanford, 1969
— *The Army and Politics in Argentina, 1945–1962. Perón to Frondizi*, London, 1980
Potter, Anne L., 'The failure of democracy in Argentina, 1916–1930: an institutional perspective', *Journal of Latin American Studies* vol. 13, no. 1 (1981): 83–109
Presidencia de la Nación, *IV Censo General de la Nación*, Buenos Aires, 1947
— *Junta Consultiva Nacional: 8 Reunión Extraordinaria, 29 de febrero de 1956*, Buenos Aires, 1956
— *La Revolución Libertadora y la Universidad, 1955–1957*, Buenos Aires, 1957
— *Memoria del Ministerio de Relaciones Exteriores y Culto*, Buenos Aires, 1947–48
— *Segundo Plan Quinquenal*, Buenos Aires, 1953
— Ministerio de Justicia e Instrucción Pública, Dirección General de la Enseñanza Religiosa, *Cuadro Estadístico de la Enseñanza Religiosa en los establecimientos de enseñanza post-primaria, secundaria y especial*, Buenos Aires, 1944
Quijada, Mónica, *Aires de República, Aires de Cruzada: la guerra civil española en Buenos Aires*, Barcelona, 1991
— *Manuel Gálvez: 60 años de pensamiento nacionalista*, Buenos Aires, 1985
Ramos Mejía, J.M., *Rosas y su tiempo*, 3 vols., 3rd ed., Buenos Aires, 1927
Ramos, Jorge Abelardo, *El partido comunista en la política argentina. Su historia y su crítica*, Buenos Aires, 1962
Ranis, Peter, *Argentine workers. Peronism and contemporary class consciousness*, Pittsburgh, 1992
Rapoport, Mario, *Los partidos de izquierda, el movimiento obrero y la política internacional, 1930–1946*, Centro Editor no. 15, Buenos Aires, 1988
— *Gran Bretaña, Estados Unidos y las Clases Dirigentes Argentinas, 1940–1945*, Buenos Aires, 1981
— 'Patrón Costas y la Revolución del '43', *Todo es historia*, no. 150 (November 1979): 8–21
— 'La política británica en la Argentina a comienzos de la década de 1940', *Desarrollo Económico* vol. 16 no. 62 (July–September 1976) pp. 203–228
Ravignani, Emilio, *Inferencias sobre Juan Manuel de Rosas y otros ensayos*, Buenos Aires, 1945
Real, Juan José, *Treinta años de historia argentina*, Buenos Aires, 1962
Reyes, Cipriano, *Yo hice el 17 de octubre*, Buenos Aires, 1973
Rock, David, *Argentina 1516–1987: from Spanish Colonization to the Falklands War and Alfonsín*, 2nd ed., London 1987
— (ed), *Argentina in the twentieth century*, London, 1975
— 'Intellectual Precursors of Conservative Nationalism in Argentina, 1900–1927', *Hispanic American Historical Review* vol. 67, no. 2 (May 1987): 271–300
— *Politics in Argentina, 1890–1930: the rise and fall of Radicalism*, Cambridge, 1975
— 'Argentina, 1930–1946', *Cambridge History of Latin America* (ed. L. Bethell), vol. VIII (1991): 3–72

— *Authoritarian Argentina. The nationalist movement, its history and its impact*, California, 1993
Rojas, Ricardo, *La Restauración Nacionalista*, 2nd ed., Buenos Aires, 1922
Romero, José Luis, *Las ideas políticas en la Argentina*, 2nd ed., Buenos Aires, 1956
Rouquié, Alain, *Pouvoir Militaire et société politique en République Argentine*, Paris, 1978
— *Poder Militar y sociedad política en la Argentina*, trans. A.I. Echegaray, 2 vols., Buenos Aires, 1981
— *Radicales y desarrollistas en la Argentina*, Buenos Aires, 1975
Roxborough, Ian, 'Unity and diversity in Latin American history', *Journal of Latin American Studies*, vol. 16, no. 1 (1984): 1–26
Sábato, Ernesto, *Sobre héroes y tumbas*, Buenos Aires, 1956
Sánchez Sorondo, Marcelo, *La Argentina por dentro*, Buenos Aires, 1988
Sarmiento, Domingo F., *Facundo*, Buenos Aires, 1957
Scenna, Miguel, 'El largo malentendido. Historia de las relaciones argentino–yanquis', pt. 3: 'El tiempo del enfrentamiento, 1917–1945', in *Todo es Historia* Año III, No. 28 (August 1969): 76–91
Scobie, James R., *Buenos Aires. Plaza to Suburb, 1870–1910*, New York, 1974
— *Argentina: A City and a Nation*, New York, 1967
Sebreli, J., *Los deseos imaginarios del peronismo*, Buenos Aires, 1983
Shumway, Nicholas, *The Invention of Argentina*, California–Oxford, 1991
Smith, Peter H., *Argentina and the failure of democracy*, Wisconsin, 1974
— 'The social base of Peronism', *Hispanic–American Historical Review*, vol. LII, no. 1 (February 1972): 55–71
— *Politics and Beef in Argentina*, Columbia, 1969
— 'The Breakdown of Democracy in Argentina, 1916–30' in Juan J. Linz and Alfred Stepan (eds) *The Breakdown of Democratic Regimes: Latin America*, Baltimore, 1978, pp. 3–27
Snow, Peter, *Argentine Radicalism: the history and doctrine of the Radical Civic Union*, Iowa, 1965
— *Political Forces in Argentina*, New York, 1979
Soler, Ricuarte, *El positivismo argentino*, Buenos Aires, 1968
Sommi, Luis, *La Revolución del 90*, 2nd ed., Buenos Aires, 1957
Spalding, Hobart, *La Clase Trabajadora Argentina. Documentos para su Historia, 1890–1912*, Buenos Aires, 1970
Szusterman, Celia, 'Developmentalism and Political Change in Argentina, 1955–1962' (D.Phil. Thesis, Oxford University, 1986) published as *Frondizi and the Politics of Developmentalism in Argentina, 1955–62*, Oxford, 1993
Taylor, Julie M., *Evita Perón. The myths of a woman*, Oxford, 1979
Taylor, Carl C., *Rural Life in Argentina*, Baton Rouge, 1948
Tcach, César, *Sabattinismo y Peronismo: partidos políticos en Córdoba, 1943–1955*, Buenos Aires, 1991
Terán, Oscar, *Positivismo y nación en la Argentina. Con una selección de textos de J.M. Ramos Mejía, A. Alvarez, C.O. Bunge y J. Ingenieros*, Buenos Aires, 1987
Thorp, Rosemary (ed) *Latin America in the 1930s: the role of the periphery in world crisis*, Oxford, 1984

Tissenbaum, M., *La codificación del derecho del trabajo ante la evolución legislativa argentina*, Santa Fe, 1947
Torre, Juan Carlos, 'Interpretando (una vez más) los orígenes del peronismo', *Desarrollo Económico* vol. 28, no. 112 (January–March 1989): 525–48
— (ed) *La Formación del sindicalismo peronista*, Buenos Aires, 1988)
Torre, Juan Carlos, and S. Senén González, *Ejército y sindicatos: los 60 días de Lonardi*, Buenos Aires, 1969
Troncoso, Oscar, *Los nacionalistas argentinos*, Buenos Aires, 1957
Turner, Frederick C., and José Enrique, Miguens, *Juan Perón and the reshaping of Argentina*, Pittsburgh, 1983
Uriburu, José, *La palabra del General Uriburu*, Buenos Aires, 1933
Véliz, Claudio, *The Centralist Tradition of Latin America*, Princeton, 1980
Verbitsky, Horacio, *Proclamas Militares*, Buenos Aires, 1983
Waisman, Carlos H., *Reversal of Development in Argentina. Postwar Counterrevolutionary Policies and their Structural Consequences*, Princeton, 1987
Waldmann, Peter, *El Peronismo, 1943–1955*, [1973], trans. Nélida M. de Machain, Buenos Aires, 1981
Walter, Richard J., *Student Politics in Argentina: the University Reform and its effects, 1918–1964*, New York, 1968
— *The Socialist Party of Argentina, 1890–1930*, Texas, 1977
— *The Province of Buenos Aires and Argentine Politics, 1912–1943*, Cambridge, 1988
Weil, Felix J., *Argentine Riddle*, New York, 1944
Weinberg, Gregorio (estudio preliminar, selección y notas), *Ley 1420, 1883–1884: debate parlamentario*, Biblioteca Política Argentina no. 57, 2 vols., Buenos Aires, 1984
Welles, Sumner, *Where are we heading?*, New York, 1946
Whitaker, Arthur P., *La Argentina y los Estados Unidos*, Buenos Aires, 1956
— *Argentine Upheaval. Perón's Fall and the New Régime*, New York, 1956
— *Argentina*, New Jersey, 1964
White, John J., *Argentina. The Life Story of a Nation*, New York, 1942
Winter, Nevin O., *Argentina And Her People of Today*, Boston, 1911
Zalduendo, Eduardo, *Geografía electoral de la Argentina*, Buenos Aires, 1958

Index

absolutism, *see* enlightened absolutism
Acción Católica, *see* Catholic Action
Action Française, *see* Maurras
Alberdi, Juan Bautista, 51, 52, 72, 198
Amadeo, Mario, 126, 139, 165, **181–2**, 184, 185, 200
Anglicanism, 44, 46, 53, 69, 70, 129, 215
antisemitism, 90
Aquinas, St. Thomas, *see* Thomism
Aramburu, Gen. Pedro E., 180, 189–91, 197, 199, 202
Argentine Patriotic League, *see* Liga Patriótica
Army
  scholasticism in, 73–4, 98, 104, 136–7, 141
  religious observance of, 80
  social characteristics of, 80–1
  and WW2, 137–8
  see also coups; Roca; Justo; Ramírez; Lonardi; Aramburu
Ateneo de la República, 201
Augustine, St., 17
Avellaneda, Nicolás, 53, 204

Belgrano, Gen. Manuel, 40, 43
Benítez, Fr. Hernán, 150
Bourbon Reforms, 39–40, 203
Braden, Spruille, 145–6, 150
Buenos Aires, Province of, 44, 56, 79
Buenos Aires, Federal Capital, 49–50, 57, 58, 83
Buenos Aires, Archbishopric, 179
Bunge, Alejandro, 83, **132–3**, 136, 150, 161

cabildo, 39, 41, 45
Carlos III, King, 39, 40, 43, 50, 204, 205

Castellani SJ, Fr. Leonardo, 118–19
Castillo, President Ramón, 108, 123–4, 125, 130, 131, 134
Catamarca, Province of, 82, 216
Catholic Action
  formation of, 30, 77–8
  growth and character of, 86, 87, **88–90**, 93–6, **214**, 219–20
  in 1930s, 98, 113, 116, 119
  in 1940s, 127, 128, 129, 133–6, 139, 151–2, 156–7
  and Peronism, 151–2, 156–7, 166, 168, 171, 175, 177–9
  in 1950s, 166–7, 168, 171, 175, 177–9
  in Church–state conflict (1954–55), 177–9
  see also Catholic Church; Juventud Católica Obrera
Catholic Church in Argentina, the
  expansion in C19, 53–5, **213**
  expansion in C20, 76–82, **213**, **215**
  eucharistic congresses, 76–80, 84, 86, 87, 166
  and education, *see* education
  and the state, *see* Church and State
  and Independence (1810), 42–3
  under Rivadavia, 44–5
  under Rosas, 46–9
  C19 liberal view of, 51
  and Yrigoyen, 68
  Gallican tendencies of, 68–72
  scholastic revival in, 73–6
  social characteristics of, 80–2
  pastoral letters of, 113, 134, 148–9, 172, 173–4, 177, 184
  publications of, *see* Criterio; Editorial Difusión; El Pueblo
  and World War II, 128–9
  and the US, 129
  and June Revolution (1943), 136–42

269

Catholic Church in Argentina (*cont.*)
  and Perón (1945–55), 148–50,
    153–4, 167, 171–4, 175–80,
    183–4
  and Christian Democracy, 171
  and Revolución Libertadora
    (1955–58), 183–4
  and Frondizi, 195–6, 197–202
  see also Catholic Action;
    Catholicism and Politics;
    Church and State;
    Gallicanism; *patronato*;
    religious affiliation; religious
    orders; religious observance;
    scholasticism; social
    Catholicism
Catholicism and politics
  demarcation of, 17–18
  'closed' vs. 'open' models, 18–19
  independence of, 18, 31, 112
  and the Right, 28–31
  and liberalism, 29, 50–1, 92, 187–9
  and fascism, 30–1, 93, 115–17
  and nationalism, *see* nationalism
  and socialism, 93, 95, 97
  and political parties in
    1930s, 112–13
  and Spanish Civil War, 119–22
  'democratic' vs. 'nationalist',
    125–7, 140–2, 155, 168–9
  in Argentine history, 203–12
  see also Catholic Action; Catholic
    Church; Christian
    Democracy; scholasticism;
    social Catholicism
Catholic Kings, 9
Catholic Union, *see* Unión Católica
Catholic Worker Youth, *see*
  Juventud Católica Obrera
Christian Democracy
  origins of, 16, 24, 32
  in early C20, 65–6, 69–70, 73, 93,
    114
  influence of Maritain on, 117–19,
    168
  in 1940s–50s, 164, 167, **168–71**,
    184, 191, 192, 196, 197, 201–2,
    209–10

see also Partido Demócrata
  Cristiano; Ordóñez
Church, *see* Catholic Church
Church and State
  in Middle Ages, 4–6
  in France, 28
  according to Maritain, 33
  in C19, 53–4
  in C20, 73, 84, 112, 148–9, 171–80
  conflict (1954–55), 171–80
  after Perón, 196
  see also concordats; constitutions;
    patronato; Catholic Church;
    Catholicism and politics;
    education
churches, burning of (1955), 179–80
Círculos Católicos de Obreros, *see*
  Workers' Circles
civil marriage, *see* marriage
communism, **110–11**, 124, 143, 196
Comte, Auguste, 20, 28, 158
  see also Positivism
concordats, 8, 75, 200
Conservatives, 103, 104, 113, 125,
  136, 196, 206
  see also PAN, PDN, PDP
Constituent Assembly (1957), 196–7
Constitutions
  (of 1819), 43
  (of 1853), 51, 53, 103, 186
  (of 1949), 154, 160, 186, 193
Copello, Archbishop (later Cardinal)
  Santiago Luis, 150, 158
Córdoba, City and Province of
  in C19, 39, 45, 48, 54, 55, 60
  in C20, 82, 124, 145, 151, 154, 159,
    167, 172, 185, 216
  Bishop of, 61
Corrientes, Province of, 56, 216
coups, military
  (of 1890), 62, 104
  (of 1930), 80, 104,
  (of 1943), 80, **136–42**
  (of 1955), 165, 180, **181–2**, 185
Criterio, 80, 86, 91, 92, 127–8, 135,
  155, 162, 171, 176, 183, 184
  articles cited, *see* 'Notes and
    References'

Index

foundation of, 75–6
early period of, 104–6
see also Franceschi
Cursos de Cultura Católica (CCC), 74–6, 104, 117, 139, 164

De Andrea, Mgr. Miguel, 69–70, 73, 85, 125, 152, 169, 176
del Carril, Bonifacio, 141–2, 184, 188, 191
Dell'Oro Maini, Atilio, 74–5, 139, 185, 189, 193–4
divine right of kings, heresy of, 4–5, 11, 114–5, 176
divorce, civil, 166, 177, 193, 196, 198, 200
Dominicans, 39, 48

ecumenical liberalism, 15–16
Editorial Difusión, 80, 176
education
 conflicts in, 19–21, 56, 58–61, 71, 140–2, 157, 192–4, 193–4, 197, 200–1
 Catholic universities, 74, 80, 97, 166, **201**
 Catholic schools, 81–2, 175–6, 193, 197
 popularity of RE, 83–4, 140–2, **216**
 RE decreed (1943), 140–2, 207–8
 RE ratified (1947), 153, 157
 RE teachers vs. Perón (1954), 172
 RE banned (1955–56), 175–6, 192–4
 RE devolved to provinces, 193, 197, **201**
 see also universities; Dell'Oro Maini
El Pueblo, 80, 126, 162, 176
Encuentro Nacional de Dirigentes Católicos, 201
enlightened absolutism, 10, 41, 42, 50, 115, 189–91, 198–9, 203, 210
Entre Ríos, Province of, 53, 216
Espinoza, Archbishop Mariano Antonio, 85
Estrada, José Manuel de, 50–1, 58–62
 see also Unión Católica; education

Eucharistic Congress, International (1934), 76–80, 84, 86, 87
Eucharistic Congress, National (1950), 166

Federación de Asociaciones Católicas de Empleadas (FACE), 85, 95, 159
Figuerola, José, 132, 143, 150, 154
Filippo, Fr. Virgilio, 150, 164, 176
Franceschi, Mgr. Gustavo J.
 as editor of *Criterio*, 76, 91
 as orator and broadcaster, 79, 88
 as social activist, 96, 94
 and Spanish Civil War, 120, 121, 128
 and critique of liberalism, 113–14
 view of nationalism, 115, 164
 and Maritain, 121, 164
 and Renovación, 135
 and coup (of 1943), 136, 138–9
 gaoled by Perón, 176, 183
 view of Peronism, 184
 see also Criterio
Franciscans, 39, 41
Franco, Francisco, 120–2, 126, 128, 154
freemasonry, 53, 54, 55, 171
French Revolution, 10, 14, 16, 19, 27
Fresco, Manuel, 98
Frías, Félix, 50–1
Frondizi, Arturo, 181, 192, **194–201**, 205, 211
Fuerza de Orientación Radical de la Juventud Argentina (FORJA), 72, 124, 138, 150

Gallicanism
 vs. papalism, 6, 8, 16
 in Argentina, 53, 65, 66, 70, 73, 125
Gálvez, Manuel, 70
Gorriti, Juan Ignacio, 40
Goyena, Pedro, 58
 see also Unión Católica
Grote, Fr., 69
 see also Workers' Circles (CCO)

Hispanism/Hispanidad, 90, 126, 154, 169
Hitler, *see* Nazism
Humanist League, *see* Movimiento Universitario Humanista
Ibarguren, Federico, 70, 139
Irazusta, Julio, 105

Jesuits
  in colony/early C19, 39, 41, 44, 204
  under Rosas, 46–7
  in late C19, 48, 53, 55
  in C20, 69, 70, 73, 80, 94, 150
  see also Salvador
Juárez Celman, Miguel, 58, 61, 199, 204
Junta de Historia Eclesiástica, 80
Justo, Gen Agustín P., 84, 104, **106–11**, 125, 130–1, 180
Juventud Católica Obrera (JOC), **97–8**, 151, 156, 167, **171–2**, 184, 191

Kant, Immanuel, 15, 52, 117, 206
Krausism, *see* Unión Cívica Radical

Lacordairists, 48
Lamarca, Emilio, 60, 74
Lammenais, *see* liberal Catholicism
La Plata, Province of, 79, 216
La Rioja, Province of, 82, 216
Leo XIII, Pope (1878–1903), 17, 21–3, 24
liberal Catholicism, 16–18, 51
Liga de Estudiantes Humanistas, 166–7, 193, 200–1
Liga Patriótica Argentina (LPA), 71
Liga Social, *see* social Catholicism
Liga Demócrata Cristiana, *see* Christian Democracy
Lonardi, Gen. Eduardo, 165, 171, 180, **183–9**, 193
Lugones, Leopoldo, 71, 72, 104

Maritain, Jacques
  political thought of, 31–8
  visit to Argentina (1934), 117–19

and *Sur*, 117, 121–2, 125
and refutation by integral Catholics, 119–22
in 1940s–50s, 150, 164
see also Spanish Civil War; Christian Democracy
marriage, civil vs. canonical, 56, 61, 83–4, 166, **217**
Martínez Zuviría, Gustavo, 139, 141
Maurras, Charles, 27–28, 31, 33
  and Argentine nationalism, 71, 104, 115
Meinvielle, Fr. Julio, 90, 163, 187
Middle Ages, political theory of, 4–9
  influence of, 105
Moreno, Manuel, 40, 42
Movimiento Universitario Humanista, 166–7, 193, 200–1
Mussolini, 25, 27, 30, 105, 114

nationalism
  in early C20, 70–2
  Church view of, 90
  and Uriburu, 104–6
  critique of economic dependence, 108–9
  and neutrality in WW2, 124
  and Catholicism, 114–23, 205–6
  and June Revolution, 138–42
  and Perón, 148, 175
  and Frondizi, 195
Nazism, 30, 114, 124, 126, 146
neoscholasticism
  generally, 22, 24, 31
  in Argentina, 73–6
  see also scholasticism

Orden Cristiano, 125–6, 149–50, 152, 162, 169, 196
Ordóñez, Manuel, 169–71, 192, 196
Ortiz, Roberto, 98, 107, 113, 123–4, 130, 136, 143

Paraná
  Province of, 54, 216
  Bishop of, 55
Partido Autonomista Nacional (PAN), 58, 63, 66

Index

Partido Demócrata Cristiano (PDC), 170–1, 178, 192, 196, 197, 201–2
  see also Christian Democracy
Partido Demócrata Nacional (PDN), 106
Partido Demócrata Progresista (PDP), 106, 113, 196, 201
Partido Socialista (PS), 64, 106, 113, 145, 192, 196, 201
Partido Socialista Independiente (PSI), 103, 106–7
Partito Popolare Italiano (PPI), 25–6, 114
patronato
  origins of, 9
  in C19, 39, 42, 46, 53, 54, 66
  critique of, 75–6
  in C20, 84, 200
Paul VI, Pope (1963–78), 150
Paz, Gen. José María, 45
Perón, Eva, 154, 160, 168, 171
Perón, Juan Domingo, 80, 94, 99, 132, 138, 142, 143, 205
  labour support for, 143–8
  discourse of, 145, 150–1, 160–1
  analysis of vote for, 146–8, 151–2
  Catholic support for, 148–53, 156–7, 163, 208–9
  and the Vatican, 150, 179
  endorsement of Catholic priorities, 153–5
  Five Year Plan, 154, 161
  Catholic opposition to, 155–7, 162–8, 171–4, 208–9
  view of Church, 157–9, 172–4
  totalitarian impulse of, 161–2, 211
  persecution of Church, 175–80
Peronism
  and unions, 95, 155–8, 167–8, 186–7, 190–1, 199
  political character of, 146–51, 153, 157–9, 160–2, 164–5, 181–2
  and scholasticism, 148–53
  Third Position, 150, 160, 163, 167
  and women, 154
  liberal repudiation of, 152–3, 186–7
  secular-theocratic impulse in, 155–62
  justicialismo, 158
  persecution of by Aramburu, 189–91
  and Frondizi, 195, 199
Pinedo Plan, 108, 130–1, 136
Pius XI, Pope (1922–39), 30, 86
Pius XII, Pope (1939–58), 150, 179
Polémica, 170–1, 201
Positivism, 28, 29, 54, 55, 56, **57–8**, 86, 158, 193, 195
  and nationalism, 70–72, 104, 116, 195
  see also Comte
Protestantism
  in early C19, 44, 46
  in late C19, 50, 52, 53, 56, 57, 60
  in C20, 75, 79, 82, 83, 129, 166, 172, 215

Quadragesimo Anno (encyclical of 1931), 92, 93, 98, 133, 156

Radical Party, see Unión Cívica Radical
Ramírez, Gen. Pedro, 138–9, 141
Redemptorists, 48
regalism, 41, 43, 44, 54
religious affiliation in Argentina, 82–3, **213**, **215**
religious education, see education
religious observance in Argentina, 213–17
  under Rosas, 47–8
  in late C19, 55–7
  in C20, 76–7, **82–4**
religious orders, 39, 41, 44, 46, **48**, 54
  see also Dominicans; Franciscans; Jesuits; Lacordairists; Redemptorists; Salesians
Rerum Novarum (encyclical of 1891), **22–3**, 64, 92, 98, 133, 151
revisionism, of Argentine history, 40, 47–8, 80, 115
Rivadavia, Benardino, 40, 47–8, 203, 204
Roca, Gen. Julio A., 48, 57, 62, 180, 204
Rojas, Ricardo, 70, 72
Romero, José Luis, 186, 194
Rosas, Juan Manuel de, 45–7, 203, 204

Rosas (cont.)
  Catholic vs. liberal view of, 50–1
  Catholic vs. nationalist view of, 115
Rousseau, Jean-Jacques
    vs. Suárez, 11–15, 114
  political thought of, 19, 127
  and Argentine Independence, 40
  and Argentine liberals, 52, 126
  influence on UCR, 68, 72
  influence on Perón, 153, 158, 160, 164
  influence on Argentine nationalism, 205–6

Sabbatini, Amadeo, 124, 145, 151
Salazar, Oliveira, 27, 117
Salesians, 48
Salvador, Colegio del, 48, 53, 55
  see also Jesuits
Salvador, Universidad del, see universities, Catholic
San Juan, Province of, 45, 216
Santa Fe
  Province of, 45, 53, 56, 60, 79, 98, 216
  Bishop of, 73
Sarmiento, Domingo F., 53, 57, 204
scholasticism
  political theory of, 5–8
  vs. secularism, 10–15, 31, 187–8, 194, 197–9, 203
  and Independence, 40–1
  in late C19, 57, 59
  revival of, 73–6
  and political engagement, 122
  and working class, 144
  and Peronism, 145–53, 164, 168
  and Frondizi, 179–9
  see also neoscholasticism; Suárez; Thomism
Social League, see social Catholicism
social Catholicism
  in Europe, 18, 23–4
  in Argentina, 63–7, 91–9, 132–5
Socialist Party, see Partido Socialista
Society of Jesus, see Jesuits
Sol y Luna, 126–7, 185
Soviet Union, 124, 126, 154

Spanish Civil War, 29, 31, 32
  and Argentina, 111, 119–21
Sturzo, Luigi, see Partito Popolare
Suárez SJ, Francisco
  political thought of, 11–13, 16
  influence in Argentina, 40–4, 203
  see also scholasticism
Syllabus (papal letter of 1862), 17, 69

Thomism, 6–8, 22, 93, 105
  vs. secular messianism, 14
  vs. St. Augustine, 17
  vs. Positivism, 28
  revival of, 31
  in RE, 140
  and Peronism, 154, 158
  see also Maritain; scholasticism; Suárez
totalitarianism
  definitions, 12–15, 29–31, 115
  in Argentina, 156, 158, 171, 172–3, 181–2

Unión Católica (Argentina), 58, 61–2, 84
  see also Estrada; Goyena
Unión Cívica Radical (UCR/Radical Party)
  origins, 61–2
  in government (1916–28), 66–8, 103, 206
  in 1930s, 105, 106–8, 111, 112–13, 119
  and Catholic revival, 112–13
  and neutrality, 124–5
  in 1940s, 130, 132, 146, 151,
  and Church–state conflict, 177, 180–1
  and Revolución Libertadora, 186–7, 192
  del Pueblo (UCRP), 193, 195–6, 201
  Independiente (UCRI), 195–201
  in government (1958–62), 199–201
  see also Yrigoyen; Sabbatini; Frondizi
Unión Demócrata Cristiana, see Christian Democracy

Unión Federal (UF) 170–1, 178, 185, 187, 192, 196–7, 201
Unión Popular Católica Argentina (UPCA), 69–70, 88
  see also De Andrea
United States
  trade with, 108, 130
  policy towards Argentina of, 123–5, 130–1, 141–2, 144
  see also Braden
University Reform Movement, 68, 80, 113, 181, 193, 200
universities
  Catholic, 74, 80, 97, **201**
  Catholic organisations in, 166
  conflicts in, 192–4, 197, **200–1**
  see also Movimiento Universitario Humanista
Uriburu, General José F., 104–6

Vatican I (First Vatican Council), 54
Vatican II (Second Vatican Council), 17, 24, 33, 202

Wilde, Eduardo, 60–1, 176
women
  and Catholicism, 87, 89, 98, 154, 157, 166
  and Perón, 152, 154
Workers' Circles (CCO/VOC), **64–5**, 69, 97, 134, 151, 155
  see also social Catholicism
World War II, 108, 123–31
  Catholic positions on, 125–9

Yrigoyen, Hipólito, 67–8, 103–4, 106, 123, 205
  see also Unión Cívica Radical